THE RED BADGE
OF COURAGE

AN ADAPTED CLASSIC

THE RED BADGE OF COURAGE

STEPHEN CRANE

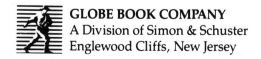

GLOBE BOOK COMPANY
A Division of Simon & Schuster
Englewood Cliffs, New Jersey

Cover design: Marek Antoniak
Cover illustration: William Giese
Interior illustrations: George Ulrich

ISBN: 0-83590-032-0

Printed in the United States of America
1 2 3 4 5 6 7 8 9 0

 **GLOBE BOOK COMPANY**
A Division of Simon & Schuster
Englewood Cliffs, New Jersey

ABOUT THE AUTHOR

Stephen Crane was born in Newark, New Jersey, in 1871. He attended Lafayette College and Syracuse University, but did not graduate from either. At Syracuse he spent most of his time playing baseball and at one point was urged by friends to make baseball a career. However, he decided instead to be a writer.

Crane's first novel attracted few readers. But his second novel, *The Red Badge of Courage,* made him famous in both America and Europe. The book was written when Crane was only 23. He had never been in the army nor seen a battle. Yet his book pictured the confusion and bloodshed of a Civil War battle more vividly than any other novel about the war.

In 1895 Crane began a series of journeys that continued through the rest of his short life. At one point he headed for Cuba to report on a war there. But his ship sank, and Crane spent days in a lifeboat with three other men. He used this experience as the basis for a masterful short story, "The Open Boat." Later Crane went to Greece and after that to England, where he spent his last two years. In addition to his several novels and many short stories, Crane published two volumes of poetry. He died in 1900 at the age of 28.

PREFACE

This is the story of a few days in the life of Henry Fleming, a teen-aged soldier in the American Civil War. As Henry faces his first battle, he worries about how well he will do. When the battle comes, he does badly at some times, well at other times. By the end of the battle, he has learned many things—about war, about death, about himself.

The Red Badge of Courage is one of the great novels about war. It is not a story of generals and their strategies. Rather, it shows the individual soldier in war—dirty, sweaty, often exhausted, sometimes frightened and confused, and at other times courageous.

ADAPTER'S NOTE

In preparing this edition of *The Red Badge of Courage,* we have kept closely to what Stephen Crane wrote. We have modified some of Crane's vocabulary and shortened and simplified many of his sentences and paragraphs. None of the story, however, has been omitted.

CONTENTS

1

The cold passed gradually from the earth, and the fogs lifted to show an army stretched out on the hills, resting. As the landscape changed from brown to green, the army awakened, and began to tremble eagerly at the noise of rumors. It looked at the roads, which were changing from long ruts of liquid mud to proper roads. A river, brownish in the shadow of its banks, flowed past the army. At night, when the stream had turned black, one could see across it the red gleam of enemy camp-fires set in the distant hills.

Once a certain tall soldier went to wash a shirt. He came flying back from a brook waving the shirt like a flag. He was full of a story he had heard from a reliable friend, who had heard it from a truthful cavalryman, who had heard it from his trustworthy brother, one of the orderlies at division headquarters. He had the air of a person with important news.

"We're going to move tomorrow—sure," he announced to a group in the company street. "We're going way up the river, cut across, and come around in behind them."

He drew a loud and complicated plan of a very brilliant campaign. When he had finished, the soldiers scattered into small groups between the rows of squat brown huts. A wagon driver who had been dancing on a wooden box with the laughing encouragement of forty soldiers was left alone. He sat sadly down. Smoke drifted lazily from a large number of chimneys.

"It's a lie! That's all it is—a thundering lie!" said another private loudly. His smooth face was flushed, and his hands were thrust into his trousers pockets. He took the subject as an insult to himself. "I don't believe the darned old army is ever going to move. We're set. I've got ready to move eight times in the last two weeks, and we ain't moved yet."

The tall soldier felt called upon to defend the truth of a rumor that he himself had introduced. He and the loud one came near to fighting over it.

A corporal began to swear before the group. He had just put an expensive board floor in his house, he said. During the early spring, he had decided not to improve his house because he had felt that the army might start on the march at any moment. Lately, however, he had felt that they were in a sort of never-ending camp.

Many of the men joined in a lively debate. One of them outlined, in a peculiarly clear manner, all the plans of the commanding general. He was argued with by men who were sure that there were other plans of campaign. They shouted at each other, trying unsuccessfully to get each other's attention. Meanwhile, the soldier who had brought the rumor bustled about importantly. He was continually attacked by questions.

"What's up, Jim?"

"The army is going to move."

"Ah, what are you talking about? How do you know it is?"

"Well, you can believe me or not, just as you like. I don't care a hang. I tell you what I know, and you can take it or leave it. Suit yourselves. It don't make no difference to me."

The way that he replied gave them something to think about. By not bothering to produce proofs, he almost convinced them. They grew very excited over it.

There was a youthful private who listened eagerly to the words of the tall soldier and to the comments of his comrades. After hearing as much about marches and attacks as he cared to hear, he went to his hut and crawled through an intricate hole that served as its door. He wished to be alone with some new thoughts that had recently come to him.

He lay down on a wide bunk that stretched across the end of the room. In the other end, cracker boxes were made to serve as furniture. They were grouped about the fireplace. A picture from an illustrated weekly was on one of the log walls, and three rifles hung on pegs. Equipment hung on other pegs, and some tin dishes lay upon a small pile of firewood. A folded tent served as a roof. The sunlight, beating upon it, made it glow a light yellow shade. A small window shot a square of whiter light on the cluttered floor. The smoke from the fire at times came into the room instead of going up the clay chimney. This flimsy chimney of clay and sticks made endless threats to set fire to the whole house.

The youth was in a trance of astonishment. So

they were at last going to fight. Tomorrow, perhaps, there would be a battle, and he would be in it. For a while he had to work to make himself believe. He could not easily accept that he was about to take part in one of the great affairs of the earth.

He had, of course, dreamed of battles all his life—of vague and bloody conflicts that had thrilled him with their sweep and fire. He had seen himself in many struggles. He had imagined people safe under his protection. But when he was awake, he thought of battles as bright red stains on the pages of the past. In his mind, he had put them with things of the past, like kings' crowns and high castles. There was a portion of the world's history which he had thought of as the time of wars. But, he thought, that time had been long gone over the horizon and had disappeared forever.

At home, he had looked on the war in his own country with distrust. He thought that it must be some sort of a play affair. He had long since given up hope of seeing a struggle like those of ancient Greece. There would be no more like that, he had said. Men were better, or else they were more timid. Education had removed the killer instinct, or else the love of money kept their emotions under control.

He had wanted several times to enlist. Tales of great battles shook the land. They might not be exactly like the battles in Homer, but there seemed to be much glory in them. He had read of marches, sieges, conflicts, and he had longed to see it all. His busy mind had imagined large, brightly-colored pictures, glowing with acts of heroism.

But his mother had discouraged him. She had pretended to have a low opinion of his eagerness and patriotism. She could calmly seat herself and, with no apparent difficulty, give him many hundreds of reasons why he was vastly more important on the farm than on the battlefield. The way she talked had convinced him that her statements came from a deeply held belief.

In the end, however, he had overcome her arguments. The newspapers, the gossip of the village, and his own imagination had aroused him. They were, in truth, fighting well down there. Almost every day the newspapers printed accounts of an important victory.

One night, as he lay in bed, the winds had carried to him the clanging of the church bell. Someone was pulling the rope frantically to tell the confused news of a great battle. This rejoicing in the night had made him shiver with excitement. Later, he had gone down to his mother's room and had said, "Ma, I'm going to enlist."

"Henry, don't be a fool," his mother had replied. She had then covered her face with the quilt. There was an end to the matter for that night.

Nevertheless, the next morning he had gone to a town that was near his mother's farm, and he had enlisted in a company that was forming there. When he had returned home, his mother was milking a cow. Four other cows stood waiting. "Ma, I've enlisted," he had said to her timidly. There was a short silence. "The Lord's will be done, Henry," she had finally replied, and had continued to milk the cow.

Later he had stood in the doorway with his soldier's clothes on his back. He had seen two tears leaving their trails on his mother's scarred cheeks.

Still, she had disappointed him by saying nothing whatever about returning with his shield or on it. He had prepared himself for a beautiful scene. He had prepared certain sentences which he thought would be very moving. But her words destroyed his plans. She had doggedly peeled potatoes and addressed him as follows: "You watch out, Henry, and take good care of yourself in this here fighting business. Don't go thinking you can lick the whole rebel army at the start, because you can't. You're just one little fellow amongst a whole lot of others, and you've got to keep quiet and do what they tell you. I know how you are, Henry.

"I've knit you eight pair of socks, Henry, and I've put in all your best shirts, because I want my boy to be just as warm and comfortable as anybody in the army. Whenever they get holes in them, I want you to send them right-away back to me, so I can darn them.

"And always be careful and choose your company. There's lots of bad men in the army, Henry. The army makes them wild. They like nothing better than leading off a young feller like you, who ain't never been away from home much and has always had a mother, and learning them to drink and swear. Keep clear of them folks, Henry. I don't want you to ever do anything, Henry, that you would be ashamed to let me know about. Just think as if I was watching you. If you keep that in your mind always, I guess you'll come out about right.

"You must always remember your father, too, child, and remember he never drunk a drop of liquor in his life, and seldom swore a cross oath.

"I don't know what else to tell you, Henry, excepting that you must never worry, child, on my account. If a time comes when you have to be killed or do a mean thing, why, Henry, don't think of anything except what's right. There's many a woman has to bear up against such things these times, and the Lord will take care of us all. Don't forget about the socks and the shirts, child. And I've put a cup of blackberry jam with your bundle, because I know you like it above all things. Goodbye, Henry. Watch out, and be a good boy."

Of course, this speech had made him impatient. It had not been quite what he expected, and he had listened with an air of irritation. When he left, he had felt vaguely relieved.

Still, when he had looked back from the gate, he had seen his mother kneeling among the potato parings. Her brown face, upraised, was stained with tears, and her thin body was trembling. He bowed his head and went on, feeling suddenly ashamed of his purposes.

From his home he had gone to the school to say goodbye to many schoolmates. They had crowded around him with surprise and respect. He had felt the gulf that was now between them, and he had swelled with calm pride. He and some of his friends who had put on the blue uniform were quite showered with privileges for all of one afternoon, and it had been a very delicious thing. They had strutted.

A certain light-haired girl had made playful

fun of his military spirit. But there was another and darker girl whom he had gazed at steadfastly, and he thought she grew quiet and sad at sight of his blue and brass. As he had walked down the path between the rows of oaks, he had turned his head and noticed her at a window watching him leave. When he perceived her, she had immediately begun to stare up through the high tree branches at the sky. He had seen a good deal of flurry and haste in her movement. He often thought of it.

On the way to Washington, his spirit had soared. The regiment was fed and hugged at station after station until the youth had believed that he must be a hero. There was a huge amount of bread and cold meats, coffee, and pickles and cheese. As he enjoyed the smiles of the girls and was patted and complimented by the old men, he had felt growing within him the strength to do mighty deeds of arms.

After complicated travels with many pauses, there had come months of monotonous life in a camp. He had believed that real war was a series of death struggles, with small time in between for sleep and meals. But since his regiment had come to the field, the army had done little but sit still and try to keep warm.

He was brought gradually back to his old ideas about war. Greek-like struggles would be no more. Men were better now, or more timid. Education had erased the killer instinct, or else the feeling was held down by concern for money.

He had come to think of himself merely as a part of a huge blue parade. His assignment was to look out, as far as he could, for his personal comfort. For recreation he could twiddle his thumbs and try to guess what the generals were thinking about. Also, he was drilled and drilled and reviewed, and drilled and drilled and reviewed.

The only foes he had seen were some pickets along the river bank. They were a suntanned, casual lot, who sometimes shot casually at the blue pickets. When criticized for this afterwards, they usually expressed sorrow, and swore by their gods that the guns had exploded without their permission. The youth, on guard duty one night, talked across the stream with one of them. He was a slightly ragged man, who spat skillfully between his shoes. The youth liked him personally.

"Yank," the other had informed him, "you're a right good fellow." This sentiment, floating to him on the still air, had made him for a moment regret war.

Veterans had told him tales. Some talked of gray, bearded hordes who were advancing with fierce curses, and chewing tobacco with incredible bravery. Others spoke of tattered and hungry men who fought to get food. "They'll charge through hell's fire and brimstone to get hold of a haversack, and such stomachs ain't lasting long," he was told. From the stories, the youth imagined the red, live bones sticking out through slits in the faded uniforms.

Still, he could not entirely trust the veterans' tales, for recruits were their prey. They talked much of smoke, fire, and blood, but he could not tell how much might be lies.

However, he realized now that it did not greatly matter what kind of soldiers he was going to fight, so long as they fought. There was a more serious problem. He lay in his bunk thinking about it. He tried to mathematically prove to himself that he would not run from a battle.

Previously he had never felt the need to wrestle too seriously with this question. In his life he had taken certain things for granted, never challenging his belief in final success, and bothering little about means and roads. But here he was facing something important. It had suddenly occurred to him that perhaps in a battle he might run. He was forced to admit that as far as war was concerned, he knew nothing of himself.

Earlier he would have put the problem out of his mind, but now he felt compelled to give serious attention to it.

A little panic grew in his mind. As he imagined going forward to fight, he saw hideous possibilities. He thought about the menaces of the future, and was unable to see himself standing stoutly in the middle of them. He remembered his visions of glory. But in the shadow of the coming battle, he suspected them to be impossible pictures.

He jumped from the bunk and began to pace nervously back and forth. "Good Lord, what's the matter with me?" he said aloud.

He felt that in this crisis, his laws of life were useless. Whatever he had learned about himself was of no use here. He was an unknown quantity. He saw that he would again have to learn about himself, as he had when he was younger. Meanwhile he resolved to be careful to keep those qualities of which he knew nothing from disgracing him. "Good Lord!" he repeated in dismay.

After a time the tall soldier slid through the hole. The loud private followed. They were arguing.

"That's all right," said the tall soldier as he entered. He waved his hand meaningfully. "You can believe me or not, just as you like. All you got to do is to sit down and wait as quiet as you can. Then pretty soon you'll find out I was right."

His comrade grunted stubbornly. For a moment he seemed to be searching for a clever reply. Finally he said, "Well, you don't know everything in the world, do you?"

"Didn't say I knew everything in the world," answered the other sharply. He began to stow various articles snugly into his knapsack.

The youth, pausing in his nervous walk, looked down at the busy figure. "Going to be a battle, sure, is there, Jim?" he asked.

"Of course there is," replied the tall soldier. "Of course there is. You just wait until tomorrow, and you'll see one of the biggest battles that ever was. You just wait."

"Thunder!" said the youth.

"Oh, you'll see fighting this time, my boy, regular out-and-out fighting," added the tall soldier, with the air of a man who is about to put a battle on exhibit for the benefit of his friends.

"Huh!" said the loud one from a corner.

"Well," remarked the youth, "like as not this story will turn out just like them others did."

"Not much it won't," replied the tall soldier, annoyed. "Not much it won't. Didn't the cavalry all start this morning?" he glared about him. No one denied his statement. "The cavalry started this morning," he continued. "They say there ain't hardly any cavalry left in camp. They're going to Richmond, or someplace, while we fight all the Johnnies. It's some dodge like that. The regiment's got orders, too. A fellow what seen them go to headquarters told me a little while ago. And they're raising blazes all over camp—anybody can see that."

"Shucks!" said the loud one.

The youth remained silent for a time. At last he spoke to the tall soldier. "Jim!"

"What?"

"How do you think the regiment will do?"

"Oh, they'll fight all right, I guess, after they once get into it," said the other, with cold judgment. "There's been heaps of fun poked at them because they're new, of course, and all that; but they'll fight all right, I guess."

"Think any of the boys will run?" persisted the youth.

"Oh, there may be a few of them run, but there's them kind in every regiment, especially when they first goes under fire," said the other in a tolerant way. "Of course, it might happen that the whole kit-and-boodle might start and run, if some big fighting came right at the start. Then again, they might stay and fight like fun. But you can't bet on nothing. Of course, they ain't never been under fire yet, and it ain't likely they'll lick the whole rebel army all at once the first time. But I think they'll fight better than some, if worse than others. That's the way I figure. They call the regiment 'fresh fish' and everything. But the boys come of good stock, and most of them will fight like sin after they once get shooting," he added, with a mighty emphasis on the last four words.

"Oh, you think you know——" began the loud soldier with scorn.

The other turned savagely upon him. They had a rapid and heated argument, in which they called each other various strange names.

The youth at last interrupted them. "Did you ever think you might run yourself, Jim?" he asked. On concluding the sentence, he laughed as if he had meant to aim a joke. The loud soldier also giggled.

The tall private waved his hand. "Well," he said profoundly, "I've thought it might get too hot for Jim Conklin in some of them scrimmages, and if a whole lot of the boys started and run, why, I suppose I'd start and run. And if I once started to run, I'd run like the devil, and no mistake. But if everybody was standing and fighting, why, I'd stand and fight. By jiminey, I would. I'll bet on it."

"Huh!" said the loud one.

The youth was grateful for these words of his comrade. He had feared that all of the other untried men had the proper confidence. He now was somewhat reassured.

2

The next morning the youth discovered that his tall comrade's information had been mistaken. There was much scoffing at the tall soldier by those who yesterday had agreed with him. There was even a little sneering by men who had never believed the rumor. The tall one fought with a man from Chatfield Corners and beat him severely.

The youth felt, however, that his problem was in no way lifted from him. The story had made him very concerned about himself. Now, with the newborn question in his mind, he was required to sink back into his old place as part of a blue parade.

For days he made endless calculations, but they were all unsatisfactory. He finally concluded that the only way to prove himself was to go into the blaze, and then see what happened. He reluctantly admitted that he could not sit still and figure out an answer. To do that, he must have blaze, blood, and danger, even as a chemist requires this, that, and the other. So he worried about having the opportunity.

Meanwhile he continually tried to measure himself by his comrades. The tall soldier, for one, gave him some confidence, for he had known him since childhood. The youth did not see how the tall soldier could be capable of anything that was beyond him, the youth. Still, he thought that his comrade might be mistaken about himself. Or, on the other hand, he might be a man made to shine in war.

The youth would have liked to have discovered another soldier who was not sure of himself. A comparison of mental notes would have been a joy to him.

He occasionally tried to sound out a comrade. He looked about to find men in the proper mood. All attempts failed to bring forth any statement which looked in any way like a confession to doubts like his own. He was afraid to state his concern openly, because he did not wish to put himself in a position to be made fun of.

In regard to the other soldiers, his mind wavered between two opinions, according to his mood. Sometimes he was inclined to believe that they were all heroes. In fact, he usually admitted to himself that others had higher qualities than he did. He could imagine men who seemed insignificant, yet who went about the world bearing a load of unseen courage. Although he had known many of his comrades since boyhood, he began to fear that his judgment of them had been blind. Then, in other moments, he assured himself that his fellows were all privately wondering and shaky.

His emotions made him feel strange around men who talked excitedly of a coming battle as if it were a drama they were about to witness. Their faces showed nothing but eagerness and curiosity. Often he suspected them to be liars.

He did not pass such thoughts without

condemning himself severely. He was convicted by himself of many shameful crimes.

In his great anxiety, his heart was continually blaming what he saw as the intolerable slowness of the generals. They seemed content to sit calmly on the river bank, and leave him bowed down by the weight of a great problem. He wanted it settled at once. He could no longer bear such a load, he said. Sometimes his anger at the commanders reached an acute stage, and he grumbled about the camp like a veteran.

One morning, however, he found himself in the ranks of his regiment. The men were guessing in whispers and retelling the old rumors. In the gloom before the break of the day, their uniforms glowed a deep purple hue. From across the river the red eyes were still peering. In the eastern sky, there was a yellow patch like a rug laid for the feet of the coming sun. Against it, black and patternlike, loomed the gigantic figure of the colonel on a gigantic horse.

From off in the darkness came the trampling of feet. The youth could occasionally see dark shadows that moved like monsters. The regiment stood at rest for what seemed a long time. The youth grew impatient. It was disgraceful the way these affairs were managed. He wondered how long they were to be kept waiting.

As he looked all about him, he began to believe that at any moment the ominous distance might be lit up, and the rolling crashes of a battle come to his ears. Staring once at the red eyes across the river, he conceived them to be growing larger, like the eyes of a row of advancing dragons. He turned toward the colonel and saw him lift his gigantic arm and calmly stroke his mustache.

At last he heard from along the road and the foot of the hill the clatter of a horse's galloping hoofs. It must be the coming of orders. He bent forward, scarcely breathing. The exciting clickety-click, as it grew louder and louder, seemed to be beating upon his soul. Soon a horseman with jangling equipment drew rein before the colonel of the regiment. The two held a short, sharp-worded conversation. The men in the foremost ranks stretched their necks.

As the horseman wheeled his animal and galloped away, he turned to shout over his shoulder. "Don't forget that box of cigars!" The colonel mumbled in reply. The youth wondered what a box of cigars had to do with war.

A moment later the regiment went swinging off into the darkness. It was now like one of those moving monsters with many feet. The air was heavy, and cold with dew. A mass of wet grass, marched upon, rustled like silk.

There was an occasional flash and glimmer of steel from the backs of all these huge crawling reptiles. From the road came creakings and grumblings as some guns were dragged away.

The men stumbled along, still muttering guesses. There was a subdued debate. Once a man fell down, and as he reached for his rifle a comrade, unseeing, stepped on his hand. The man with the injured fingers swore bitterly and aloud. A low, tittering laugh went among his fellows.

Soon they passed into a roadway and marched forward with easy strides. A dark regiment moved before them, and from behind also came the tinkle of equipment on the bodies of marching men.

The rushing yellow of the coming day went on behind their backs. When the sunrays at last struck full upon the earth, the youth saw that the landscape was streaked with two long, thin, black columns which disappeared on the brow of a hill in front, and rearward vanished in a wood. They were like two snakes crawling from the cavern of the night.

The river was not in view. The tall soldier burst into praises of what he thought to be his powers of observation.

Some of the tall one's companions cried that they, too, had reached the same conclusion, and they congratulated themselves. But there were others who said that the tall one's plan was not the true one at all. They persisted with other theories. There was a vigorous discussion.

The youth took no part in them. As he walked along in line, he was engaged with his own eternal debate. He could not keep himself from dwelling on it. He was depressed and sullen, and threw shifting glances about him. He looked ahead, often expecting to hear from ahead the rattle of firing.

But the long snakes crawled slowly from hill to hill without gusts of smoke. A grayish brown cloud of dust floated away to the right. The sky overhead was of a fairy blue.

The youth studied the faces of his companions, looking for evidence of emotions like his own. He was disappointed. Something was in the air which was causing the veteran regiments to move with glee—almost with song—and it had infected the

new regiment. The men began to speak of victory as of a thing they were familiar with. Also, the tall soldier proved to be right. They were certainly going to come around in behind the enemy. They expressed pity for that part of the army which had been left on the river bank, congratulating themselves upon being a part of a blasting host.

The youth, seeing himself as different from the others, was saddened by the cheerful and merry speeches that went from rank to rank. The company jokers all made their best efforts. The regiment tramped to the tune of laughter.

And it was not long before all the men seemed to forget where they were going. Whole brigades grinned in unison, and regiments laughed.

A rather fat soldier attempted to steal a horse from a yard. He planned to load his knapsack on it. He was escaping with his prize when a young girl rushed from the house and grabbed the animal's mane. There followed an argument. The young girl, with pink cheeks and shining eyes, stood like a fearless statue.

The watching regiment, standing at rest in the roadway, whooped at once, and entered entirely on the side of the girl. The men became so absorbed in this affair that they entirely forgot their own large war. They jeered the stealing private, and called attention to various flaws in his personal appearance. They were wildly enthusiastic in support of the young girl.

To her, from some distance, came bold advice: "Hit him with a stick."

There were jeers and ridicule showered upon him when he retreated without the horse. The regiment cheered his downfall. Loud congratulations were showered on the girl, who stood panting and watching the troops with defiance.

At nightfall the column broke into regiments, and the fragments went into the fields to camp. Tents sprang up like strange plants. Campfires, like peculiar red blossoms, dotted the night.

The youth kept from talk with his companions as much as he could. In the evening he wandered a few steps into the gloom. From this little distance, the many fires, with the black forms of men passing to and fro before the crimson rays, made weird and satanic effects.

He lay down in the grass. The blades pressed tenderly against his cheek. The moon had been lighted and was hung in a treetop. The liquid stillness of the night made him feel vast pity for himself. There was a caress in the soft winds; and the whole mood of the darkness, he thought, was one of sympathy for himself in his distress.

He wished, without reserve, that he were at home again, making the endless rounds from the house to the barn, from the barn to the fields, from the fields to the barn, from the barn to the house. He remembered he had often cursed the cow and her mates, and had sometimes flung milking stools. But, from his present point of view, there was a halo of happiness about each of their heads. He would have given up all the brass buttons in America to have been able to return to them. He told himself that he was not made for a soldier. And he thought about on the differences between himself and those men who were dodging around the fires.

As he mused, he heard the rustle of grass. On turning his head, he saw the loud soldier. He called out, "Oh, Wilson!"

The latter approached and looked down. "Why hello, Henry. Is it you? What you doing here?"

"Oh, thinking," said the youth.

The other sat down and carefully lighted his pipe. "You're getting blue, my boy. You're looking thundering pale. What the dickens is wrong with you?"

"Oh, nothing," said the youth.

The loud soldier launched into the subject of the coming fight. "Oh, we've got them now!" As he spoke, his boyish face had a gleeful smile, and his voice had a boastful ring. "We've got them now. At last, by the eternal thunders, we'll lick them good!"

"If the truth was known," he added more soberly, "they've licked us about every clip up to now. But this time—this time—we'll lick them good!"

"I thought you was objecting to this march a little while ago," said the youth coldly.

"Oh, it wasn't that," explained the other. "I don't mind marching, if there's going to be fighting at the end of it. What I hate is this getting moved here and moved there, with no good coming of it, as far as I can see, excepting sore feet and short rations."

"Well, Jim Conklin says we'll get plenty of fighting this time."

"He's right for once, I guess, though I can't see how it come. This time we're in for a big battle, and we've got the best end of it, certain sure. Gee rod! how we will thump them!"

He stood up and began to pace to and fro excitedly. The thrill of his enthusiasm made him walk with a bouncy step. He was vigorous, fiery in his belief in success. He looked into the future with clear, proud eye, and he swore with the air of an old soldier.

The youth watched him for a moment in silence. When he finally spoke, his voice was bitter. "Oh, you're going to do great things, I suppose!"

The loud soldier blew a thoughtful cloud of smoke from his pipe. "Oh, I don't know," he remarked with dignity. "I don't know. I suppose I'll do as well as the rest. I'm going to try like thunder." He seemed to be complimenting himself for the modesty of this statement.

"How do you know you won't run when the time comes?" asked the youth.

"Run?" said the loud one. "Run? Of course not!" He laughed.

"Well," continued the youth, "lots of good enough men have thought they was going to do great things before the fight, but when the time come, they skedaddled."

"Oh, that's all true, I suppose," replied the other. "But I'm not going to skedaddle. The man that bets on my running will lose his money, that's all." He nodded confidently.

"Oh, shucks!" said the youth. "You ain't the bravest man in the world, are you?"

"No, I ain't," exclaimed the loud soldier indignantly. "And I didn't say I was the bravest man in the world, neither. I said I was going to do my share of fighting—that's what I said. And I am, too. Who are you, anyhow? You talk as if you thought you was Napoleon Bonaparte." He glared at the youth for a moment, and then strode away.

The youth called in a savage voice after his comrade, "Well, you needn't get mad about it!" But the other continued on his way and made no reply.

He felt alone in space when his insulted comrade had disappeared. His failure to discover any resemblance in their viewpoints made him more miserable than before. No one seemed to be wrestling with such a terrific personal problem. He was a mental outcast.

He went slowly to his tent and stretched himself on a blanket by the side of the snoring tall soldier. In the darkness, he saw visions of a fear that would babble at his back and cause him to flee, while others were going coolly about their country's business. He admitted that he would not be able to cope with the monster. He felt that every nerve in his body would respond to the voices, while other men would remain stolid and deaf.

And as he sweated with the pain of these thoughts, he could hear low, relaxed sentences. "I'll bid five." "Make it six." "Seven." "Seven goes."

He stared at the red shivering reflection of a fire on the white wall of his tent until, exhausted and ill from his suffering, he fell asleep.

3

When another night came, the columns of soldiers, looking now like purple streaks, filed across two pontoon bridges. A glaring fire gave the waters of the river a wine-red tint. Its rays, shining on the moving troops, brought forth here and there sudden gleams of silver or gold. On the other shore, a dark and mysterious range of hills was outlined against the sky. The voices of insects sang solemnly in the night.

After this crossing, the youth was sure that at any moment they might be suddenly and fearfully attacked from the woods. He kept his eyes on the darkness.

But his regiment went safely to a camping place, and its soldiers slept the brave sleep of weary men. In the morning they were awakened early and hustled along a narrow road that led deep into the forest.

During this rapid march, the regiment lost many of the marks of a new command.

The men had begun to count the miles on their fingers, and they grew tired. "Sore feet and damned short rations, that's all," said the loud soldier. There was perspiration and grumbling. After a time, they began to shed their knapsacks. Some just tossed them down; others hid them carefully, saying they planned to return for them at some convenient time. Men freed themselves from thick shirts. Soon few carried anything but their necessary clothing, blankets, haversacks, canteens, and arms and ammunition. "You can now eat and shoot," said the tall soldier to the youth. "That's all you want to do."

There was sudden change from the clumsy infantry of theory to the light and speedy infantry of practice. The regiment felt that it was relieved of a burden. But there was much loss of valuable knapsacks, and, on the whole, very good shirts.

But the regiment did not yet look like veterans. Veteran regiments in the army were likely to be very small groups of men. Once, when the command had first come to the field, some veterans, noting the length of their column, had asked them, "Hey, fellows, what brigade is that?" And when the men had replied that they formed a regiment and not a brigade, the older soldiers had laughed, and said, "O God!"

Also, there was too great a similarity in the hats. The hats of a regiment should properly represent the history of headgear for a period of years. And, moreover, there were no streamers with faded gold letters attached to the flags. The flags were new and beautiful, and the color-bearer routinely oiled the pole.

Soon the army again sat down to think. The odor of the peaceful pines was in the men's nostrils. The sounds of axe blows rang through the forest, and the insects crooned like old women. The youth returned to his theory of a blue parade.

One gray dawn, however, he was kicked in the

leg by the tall soldier. Then, before he was entirely awake, he found himself running down a wood road in the midst of men who were panting from their running. His canteen banged rhythmically upon his thigh, and his haversack bounced softly. His musket also bounced slightly at each stride and made his cap feel uncertain upon his head.

He could hear the men whisper jerky sentences: "Say—what's all this about?" "What the thunder we skedaddling this way for?" "Billie, keep off my feet. You run like a cow." And the loud soldier's shrill voice could be heard: "What the devil they in such a hurry for?"

The youth thought the damp fog of early morning was moved by the rush of a great body of troops. From the distance came a sudden spatter of firing.

He was confused. As he ran with his comrades, he tried hard to think. But all he knew was that if he fell down, those behind would step on him. His entire mind seemed to be needed to guide him over and past obstacles. He felt carried along by a mob.

The sun came out, and, one by one, regiments burst into view like armed men just sprung from the earth. The youth felt that the time had come. He was about to be measured. For a moment, he felt like a baby as he faced his great trial. He took time to look about him cautiously.

But he saw at once that it would be impossible for him to escape from the regiment. It surrounded him. And there were iron laws of tradition and law on four sides. He was in a box.

As he noticed this fact, it occurred to him that he had never wanted to come to the war. He had not joined the army of his free will. He had been dragged in by the merciless government. And now they were taking him out to be killed.

The regiment slid down a bank and waded across a little stream. The mournful current moved slowly. From the black-shaded water, white bubbles like eyes looked at the men.

As they climbed the hill on the farther side, artillery began to boom. Here the youth suddenly felt curious. He scrambled up the bank with a speed that could not be exceeded by a bloodthirsty man.

He expected a battle scene.

There were some little fields surrounded and squeezed by a forest. Spread over the grass and in among the tree trunks, he could see knots and waving lines of skirmishers, who were running and firing at the landscape. A dark battle line lay on a sunnny clearing. A flag fluttered.

Other regiments stumbled up the bank. The brigade was formed in line of battle. After a pause, it started slowly through the woods in the rear of the skirmishers, who were continually melting into the scene to appear again farther on. They were always busy as bees, deeply absorbed in their little battles.

The youth tried to observe everything. He did not look out for trees and branches, and his feet were constantly knocking against stones or getting tangled up in briers. The battalions seemed red and startling against the soft greens and browns of the fields. It looked to be a wrong place for a battlefield.

Once the line encountered the body of a dead

soldier. He lay upon his back staring at the sky. He was dressed in an awkward suit of yellowish brown. The youth could see that the soles of his shoes had been worn to the thinness of writing paper. A dead foot projected from a great tear in one of the shoes. It was as if fate had betrayed the soldier. In death, it told his enemies about poverty which in life he had perhaps concealed from his friends.

The ranks opened to avoid the corpse. The youth looked keenly at the ashen face. The wind raised the tawny beard. It moved as if a hand were stroking it. He vaguely desired to walk around and around the body and stare.

During the march, the enthusiasm that the youth had acquired when away from the field rapidly faded to nothing. His curiosity was quite easily satisfied. If an intense scene had caught him as he came to the top of the bank, he might have gone roaring on. This advance was too calm. He had a chance to reflect. He had time in which to wonder about himself and to try to examine his feelings.

Absurd ideas took hold of him. He thought that he did not like the landscape. It threatened him. A coldness swept over his back, and his trousers felt that they were not fit for his legs at all.

A house standing peacefully in distant fields looked threatening to him. The shadows of the woods were frightening. He was certain that in this landscape there lurked fierce-eyed armies. The thought came to him that the generals did not know what they were doing. It was all a trap. Suddenly those close forests would bristle with rifle barrels. Enemy brigades would appear in the rear. They were all going to be sacrificed. The generals were stupid. The enemy would presently swallow the whole command. He glared about him, expecting to see the stealthy approach of his death. He thought that he must break from the ranks and deliver a speech to his comrades. They must not all be killed like pigs. He was sure it would happen unless they were informed of these dangers. The generals were idiots to send them marching into a regular pen. There was only one pair of eyes in the corps. He would step forth and make a speech. Shrill and passionate words came to his lips.

The line went calmly on through fields and woods. The youth looked at the men nearest him, and saw, for the most part, expressions of deep interest, as if they were looking into something that had fascinated them. One or two stepped as if they were already plunged into war. Others walked as if on thin ice. Most of the untested men appeared quiet and deep in thought. They were going to look at war, the red animal—at war, the blood-swollen god. And they were deeply wrapped up in this march.

As he looked, the youth held back his outcry. He saw that even if the men were about to collapse with fear, they would laugh at his warning. They would jeer at him, and, if possible, throw things at him. Admitting that he might be wrong, such a speech would turn him into a worm.

Instead, he tried to look like a person doomed to carry an invisible burden. He fell behind, with tragic glances at the sky. He was soon surprised by the young lieutenant of his company, who began to beat him with a sword, calling out in a loud and insolent voice, "Come, young man, get up into the ranks there. No skulking will do here." He caught up quickly. And he hated the lieutenant, who did not appreciate fine minds. He was a mere brute.

After a time the brigade was halted in the cathedral light of a forest. The busy skirmishers were still popping. Through the aisles of the wood could be seen the floating smoke from the rifles. Sometimes it went up in little balls, white and compact.

During this halt many men in the regiment began to build tiny hills in front of them. They used stones, sticks, earth, and anything they thought might turn a bullet. Some built rather large ones, while others seemed content with little ones.

This activity caused a discussion among the men. Some wanted to fight as if they were in a duel. They believed they should stand up straight and be a target from their feet to their foreheads. They said they had no respect for what the cautious ones did. But the others were scornful. They pointed to the veterans on the flanks, who were digging at the ground like terriers. In a short time, there was quite a barricade along the regimental front.

Soon, however, they were ordered to withdraw from that place. This astonished the youth. He forgot his stewing over the forward movement. "Well, then, what did they march us out here for?" he demanded of the tall soldier. The latter began a long explanation, although he had had to leave behind a little barrier of stones and dirt to which he had devoted much care and skill.

When the regiment was lined up in another position, each man's worries about his own safety caused another line of small defenses to be built. They ate their noon meal behind a third one. They were moved from this one also. They were marched from place to place with apparent aimlessness.

The youth had been taught that a man became another thing in a battle. He saw such a change as his salvation. Therefore, this waiting was an ordeal for him. He was in a fever of impatience. He believed that the generals were showing a lack of purpose. He began to complain to the tall soldier. "I can't stand this much longer," he cried. "I don't see what good it does to make us wear out our legs for nothing." He wished to return to camp, or else to go into a battle and discover that he was, in truth, a man of courage. He felt he could not put up with the strain of the present situation.

The tall soldier made a sandwich of crackers and pork and swallowed it in a nonchalant manner. "Oh, I suppose we must keep moving around the country just to keep them from getting too close, or to develop them, or something."

"Huh!" said the loud soldier.

"Well," cried the youth, still fidgeting, "I'd rather do almost anything than go tramping around the country all day doing no good to nobody and just tiring ourselves out."

"So would I," said the loud soldier. "It ain't right. I tell you, if anybody with any sense was running this army, it——"

"Oh, shut up!" roared the tall private. "You little fool. You little damn cuss. You ain't had that there coat and them pants on for six months, and yet you talk as if——"

"Well, I want to do some fighting, anyway," interrupted the other. "I didn't come here to walk. I could have walked at home, around and around the barn, if I just wanted to walk."

The tall one, red-faced, swallowed another sandwich as if taking poison in despair.

But gradually, as he chewed, his face again became quiet and contented. He could not argue angrily in the presence of such sandwiches. During his meals, he always had an air of thinking happily about the food he had swallowed. His spirit seemed to be communing with the food.

He accepted new situations with great coolness, eating from his haversack at every opportunity. On the march, he went along with the stride of a hunter, objecting to neither the speed nor the distance. And he had not raised his voice when he had been ordered away from three little protective piles of earth and stone, each of which had been an engineering feat.

In the afternoon, the regiment went out over the same ground it had taken in the morning. The landscape then ceased to threaten the youth. He had been close to it and become familiar with it.

When, however, they began to pass into a new region, his old fears of stupidity and lack of skill came back to him, but this time he doggedly let them babble. He was occupied with his problem, and he concluded that stupidity did not greatly matter.

For a time he thought that it would be better to get killed right away and end his troubles.

Looking at death this way, as if out of the corner of his eye, he imagined it to be nothing but rest. For a moment, he was astonished that he should have made such a commotion over the mere matter of getting killed. He would die; he would go to some place where he would be understood. It was useless to expect such men as the lieutenant to appreciate his profound and fine senses. To be understood, he must wait for the grave.

The skirmish fire increased to a long rattling sound. Faraway cheering was mixed with it. A cannon spoke.

Soon the youth would see the skirmishers running. They were pursued by the sound of musketry fire. After a time, the hot, dangerous flashes of the rifles were visible. Smoke clouds went slowly across the fields like watching ghosts. The din grew louder, like the roar of an oncoming train.

A brigade ahead of them and on the right went into action with a roar. It was as if it had exploded. And after that, it lay stretched in the distance behind a long gray wall of smoke.

The youth, forgetting his neat plan of getting killed, gazed spellbound. His eyes grew wide with the action of the scene. His mouth was a little ways open.

Suddenly he felt a heavy hand laid upon his shoulder. Awakening from his trance of observation, he turned and saw the loud soldier.

"It's my first and last battle, old boy," said the latter, with intense gloom. He was quite pale, and his lip was trembling.

"Eh?" murmured the youth in great surprise.

"It's my first and last battle, old boy," continued

the loud soldier. "Something tells me——"

"What?"

"I'm a gone coon this first time, and I want you to take these here things to my folks." He ended in a sob of pity for himself. He handed the youth a little packet done up in a yellow envelope.

"Why, what the devil——" began the youth again.

But the other gave him a glance as if from the depths of a tomb, raised his limp hand in a prophetic manner, and turned away.

The brigade was halted at the edge of a grove. The men crouched among the trees and pointed their guns out at the fields. They tried to look beyond the smoke.

Out of this haze they could see running men. Some shouted and gestured as they hurried.

The men of the new regiment watched and listened eagerly, passing along rumors that flew like birds.

"They say Perry has been driven in with a big loss."

"Yes, Carrott went to the hospital. He said he was sick. That smart lieutenant is commanding 'G' Company. The boys say they won't be under Carrott no more if they all have to desert. They always knew he was a——"

"Hannis's battery is took."

"It ain't either. I saw Hannis's battery off on the left not more than fifteen minutes ago."

"Well——"

"The general, he says he is going to take the whole command of the 304th when we go into action, and then he says we'll do such fighting as never another one regiment done."

"They say we're catching it over on the left. They say the enemy drove our line into a devil of a swamp and took Hannis's battery."

"No such thing. Hannis's battery was along here about a minute ago."

"That young Hasbrouck, he makes a good officer. He ain't afraid of nothing."

"I met one of the 148th Maine boys, and he says his brigade fought the whole rebel army for four hours over on the turnpike road and killed about five thousand of them. He says one more such fight as that, and the war will be over."

"Bill wasn't scared either. No, sir! It wasn't that. Bill ain't getting scared easy. He was just mad, that's what he was. When that fellow trod on his hand, he up and said that he was willing to give his hand to his country, but he be damned if he was going to have every damn bushwhacker in the country walking around on it. So he went to the hospital regardless of the fight. Three fingers was crunched. The darn doctor wanted to amputate them, and Bill, he raised a hell of a row, I hear. He's a funny fellow."

The noise in front swelled to a tremendous chorus. The youth and his fellows were frozen in silence. They could see a flag that tossed in the smoke angrily. Near it were the blurred forms of troops. A turbulent stream of men came across the fields. A battery, changing positions at a gallop, scattered the stragglers right and left.

A shell screamed over the huddled head of the reserves. It landed in the grove and exploded. There was a little shower of pine needles.

Bullets began to whistle among the branches and nip at the trees. Twigs and leaves came sailing down. It was as if a thousand axes, tiny and invisible, were being wielded. Many of the men were constantly ducking their heads.

The lieutenant of the youth's company was shot in the hand. He began to swear so wonderfully, that a nervous laugh went along the regimental line. The officer's swearing relieved the tension of the new men. It was as if he had hit his fingers with a tack hammer at home.

He held the wounded hand carefully away from his side so that the blood would not drip on his trousers.

The captain of the company, tucking his sword under his arm, produced a handkerchief and began to bind up the lieutenant's wound. They disputed as to how the binding should be done.

The battle flag in the distance jerked about madly. It seemed to be struggling to free itself from suffering. The billowing smoke was filled with flashes.

Running men swiftly emerged from the smoke. They grew in numbers until it was seen that the whole command was fleeing. The flag suddenly sank down as if dying. Its motion was a gesture of despair.

Wild yells came from behind the walls of smoke. The scene dissolved into a mob that galloped like wild horses.

The veteran regiments on the right and left of the 304th immediately began to jeer. Loud catcalls and advice about places of safety mingled with the singing of the bullets and the shrieks of the shells.

But the new regiment was breathless with horror. "God! Saunders's got crushed!" whispered

the man next to the youth. They shrank back and crouched as if awaiting a flood.

The youth shot a swift glance along the blue ranks of the regiment. The profiles were motionless. Afterward he remembered that the sergeant with the flag was standing with his legs apart, as if he expected to be pushed to the ground.

The fleeing soldiers went whirling around the flank. Here and there were officers carried along the stream like angry chips of wood. They were striking about them with their swords and with their left fists, punching every head they could reach. They cursed like bandits.

An officer on horseback displayed the furious anger of a spoiled child. He raged with his head, his arms, and his legs.

Another, the commander of the brigade, was galloping about yelling. His hat was gone and his clothes were crooked. He looked like a man who has gotten out of bed to go to a fire. The hoofs of his horse often threatened to kick the heads of the running men, but they managed to keep out of their way. In this rush they all seemed deaf and blind. They paid no attention to the oaths that were thrown at them from all directions.

Frequently the grim jokes of the sarcastic veterans could be heard over the noise. But the retreating men apparently were not even aware that they had an audience.

There was an appalling expression on these faces. The struggle in the smoke had left its mark on the bleached cheeks and in the wild eyes.

The stampede exerted a floodlike force that seemed able to drag sticks and stones and men from the ground. The reserves had to hold on. They grew pale and firm, and red and quaking. The youth had one little thought in the midst of this chaos. The monster which had caused the other troops to flee had not appeared to him. He resolved to get a view of it. Then, he thought, he might very likely run better than the best of them.

5

There were moments of waiting. The youth thought of the village street on a spring day at home before the arrival of the circus parade. He remembered how he had stood, an excited small boy, prepared to follow the lady on the white horse, or the band in its faded chariot. He saw the yellow road and the lines of expectant people. He particularly remembered an old fellow who used to sit on a cracker box in front of the store and pretend to despise the parade. A thousand details surged in his mind.

Someone cried, "Here they come!"

There was rustling and muttering among the men. They showed a strong desire to have every possible cartridge within reach. The cartridge boxes were pulled around into various positions, and adjusted with great care. It was as if seven hundred new hats were being tried on.

The tall soldier, having prepared his rifle, produced a red handkerchief of some kind. He was tying it around his neck with great care, when the cry was repeated up and down the line in a muffled roar of sound.

"Here they come! Here they come!" Gun locks clicked.

Across the smoke-infested fields came a brown

swarm of running men who were giving shrill yells. They came on, stooping and swinging their rifles at all angles. A flag, tilted forward, sped near the front.

As he caught sight of them, the youth was startled for a moment by a thought that perhaps his gun was not loaded. He stood trying to recollect the moment when he had loaded, but he could not. A hatless general pulled his dripping horse to a stand near the colonel of the 304th. He shook his fist in the other's face. "You've got to hold them back!" he shouted savagely. "You've got to hold them back!"

The colonel began to stammer. "A-a-all r-r-right, General, all right, by God! We-we'll do our—we-we'll d-d-do—do our best, General." The general made a gesture and galloped away. The colonel, perhaps to relieve his feelings, began to scold like a wet parrot. The youth, turning swiftly to make sure that the rear was safe, saw the commander regarding his men in a highly resentful manner, as if he regretted his association with them.

The man at the youth's elbow was mumbling, as if to himself, "Oh, we're in for it now! Oh, we're in for it now!"

The captain of the company had been pacing excitedly to and fro in the rear. He coaxed like a grade-school teacher, as if teaching boys how to read. He said the same thing over and over. "Reserve your fire, boys—don't shoot till I tell you— save your fire—wait till they get close up—don't be damned fools——"

Perspiration streamed down the youth's face, which was dirty like that of a weeping child. He often, with a nervous movement, wiped his eyes with his coat sleeve. His mouth was still a little way open.

He took one look at the field full of enemy soldiers in front of him, and instantly stopped worrying about his rifle being loaded. Before he was ready to begin, he threw the obedient, well-balanced rifle into position and fired a first wild shot. In a short while he was working his weapon automatically.

He suddenly stopped worrying about himself. He became not a man but a member of a group. He felt that something he belonged to—a regiment, an army, a cause, or a country—was in a crisis. He was welded into a common personality with a single desire. For some moments he could not flee, any more than a little finger can rebel against its hand.

If he had thought the regiment was about to be wiped out, perhaps he could have cut himself off from it. But its noise gave him assurance. The regiment was like a firework that, once lit, keeps going until it fades. It wheezed and banged with a mighty power. He imagined the ground in front of it as strewn with enemy dead.

He was always aware of his comrades about him. He felt that the subtle brotherhood of battle was stronger even than the cause for which they were fighting. It was a mysterious brotherhood born of the smoke and danger of death.

He was at work. He was like a carpenter who has made many boxes, making still another box, only there was a furious haste in his movements. His mind was wandering off to other places, just as the carpenter's mind does when he works.

Soon he began to feel the effects of the war atmosphere—a blistering sweat, a sensation that his eyeballs were about to crack like hot stones. A burning roar filled his ears.

Following this came a red rage. He developed the anger of a pestered animal, a well-meaning cow worried by dogs. He had a mad feeling against his rifle, which could only be used against one life at a time. He wished to rush forward and strangle with his fingers. He craved a power that would enable him to brush everything back with one world-sweeping gesture. His weakness made his rage into that of a driven animal.

Buried in the smoke of many rifles, he was angry not so much against the men rushing toward him as against the smoke. He fought frantically for air, as a babe being smothered attacks the deadly blankets.

There was a mixture of rage and concentration on all faces. Many of the men were making low-toned noises. These subdued cheers, snarls, curses, and prayers made a wild, barbaric song. It was like an undercurrent of sound, strange and chantlike, against the resounding chords of the war march. The man next to the youth was babbling. There was something soft and tender in it, like the babble of a baby. The tall soldier was swearing in a loud voice. From his lips came a string of curious oaths. All of a sudden, another broke out in a peevish way, like a man who has mislaid his hat: "Well, why don't they support us? Why don't they send supports? Do they think——"

The youth heard this as one hears when he is half asleep.

There were no heroic poses. The men, bending and surging in their haste and rage, were in every possible position. The steel ramrods clanked and clanged as the men pounded them furiously into the hot rifle barrels. The flaps of the cartridge boxes were all unfastened, and bounced with each movement. The rifles, once loaded, were jerked to the shoulder and fired without apparent aim into the smoke, or at one of the blurred and shifting forms which had been growing larger and larger.

The officers were bobbing to and fro, roaring directions and encouragements. Their howls were extraordinary. Often they nearly stood on their heads in their anxiety to observe the enemy on the other side of the smoke.

The lieutenant of the youth's company had caught a soldier who had fled screaming at the first volley of his comrades. Behind the lines, these two were acting a little isolated scene. The man was blubbering and staring with sheeplike eyes at the lieutenant, who had seized him by the collar and hit him repeatedly. The lieutenant drove him back into the ranks with many blows. The soldier went mechanically, with his dull eyes on the officer. He tried to reload his gun, but his shaking hands prevented it. The lieutenant had to help him.

Men dropped here and there.

The captain of the youth's company had been killed in an early part of the action. His body lay stretched out like a tired man resting. On his face was an astonished and sorrowful look, as if he thought some friend had done him an ill turn. The babbling man was grazed by a shot that made the blood stream down his face. He clasped both hands

to his head. "Oh!" he said, and ran. Another grunted suddenly as if he had been struck by a club in the stomach. He sat down and stared sorrowfully. Further up the line a man, standing behind a tree, had his knee joint splintered by a ball. Immediately he dropped his rifle and gripped the tree with both arms. And there he remained, holding on desperately and crying for help, so that he could let go of the tree.

At last a yell of victory went along the trembling line. The firing died down from an uproar to a last pop. As the smoke slowly drifted away, the youth saw that the charge had been driven back. The enemy were scattered. He saw a man climb to the top of the fence, straddle the rail, and fire a parting shot. The waves had receded, leaving bits of dark debris upon the ground.

Some in the regiment began to whoop wildly. Many were silent. Apparently they were thinking about themselves.

After the fever had left his veins, the youth thought that he was going to suffocate. He became aware of the foul atmosphere in which he had been struggling. He was grimy and dripping like a laborer in a foundry. He grasped his canteen and took a long swallow of the warm water.

A sentence with variations went up and down the line. "Well, we've held them back. We've held them back. Darned if we haven't." The men said it joyfully, smiling at each other with dirty smiles.

The youth turned to look behind him, and off to the right, and off to the left. He felt the joy of a man who at last has a chance to look around him.

Underfoot, a few ghastly forms lay motionless.

They lay twisted in grotesque positions. Arms were bent and heads were turned in incredible ways. It seemed that the dead men must have fallen from some great height to get into such positions. They looked to be dumped out upon the ground from the sky.

From a position in the rear of the grove, a battery was throwing shells over it. The flash of the guns startled the youth at first. He thought they were aimed directly at him. Through the tree he watched the black figures of the gunners as they worked swiftly and intently. Their labor seemed to be a complicated thing. He wondered how they could remember what to do in the midst of so much confusion.

The guns squatted in a row like savage chiefs. They spoke with sudden violence. It was a grim pow-wow. Their busy servants ran hither and thither.

A small procession of wounded men were going toward the rear. It was a flow of blood from the torn body of the brigade.

To the right and to the left were the dark lines of other troops. Far in front he thought he could see lighter masses poking out in places from the forest. They suggested many thousands of soldiers.

Once he saw a tiny battery go dashing along the lines of the horizon. The tiny riders were beating the tiny horses.

From a sloping hill came the sounds of cheering and clashes. Smoke welled slowly through the leaves.

Batteries were speaking with thunderous effort. Here and there were flags, the red in the stripes dominating. They splashed bits of warm color on the dark lines of troops.

The youth felt the old thrill at the sight of the flag. They were like beautiful birds who were strangely fearless in a storm.

As he listened to the din from the hillside, he noticed a deep thunder that came from far to the left, and lesser noises that came from many directions. It occurred to him that they were fighting, too, over there, and over there, and over there. Up to now he had supposed that all the battle was directly under his nose.

As he gazed around him, the youth felt a flash of astonishment at the blue, pure sky and the sun shining brightly on the trees and fields. It was surprising that Nature had gone on calmly in the midst of so much mischief.

The youth awakened slowly. He came gradually back to a position in which he could look at himself. For moments he had been studying his body in a dazed way, as if he had never seen himself before. Then he picked up his cap from the ground. He wriggled in his jacket to make it more comfortable. Kneeling, he replaced his shoe. He thoughtfully mopped his sweating face.

So it was all over at last! The supreme trial had been passed. The huge challenge of war had been defeated.

He went into an ecstasy of self-satisfaction. He had the most delightful feelings of his life. Standing as if apart from himself, he observed that last scene. He saw that the man who had fought like that was magnificent.

He felt that he was a fine fellow. He even saw himself as having ideals that he had once thought of as far beyond him. He smiled in deep satisfaction.

He beamed tenderness and good will upon his fellows. "Gee! Ain't it hot, hey?" he said in a friendly way to a man who was wiping his streaming face with his coat sleeves.

"You bet!" said the other, grinning sociably. "I never seen such dumb hotness." He sprawled out comfortably on the ground. "Gee, yes! And I hope we don't have no more fighting till a week from Monday."

There were some handshakings and deep speeches with men whose faces were familiar, but with whom the youth now felt new bonds. He helped a cursing comrade to bind up a wound of the shin.

But, all of a sudden, cries of amazement broke out along the ranks of the regiment. "Here they come again! Here they come again!" The man who had sprawled on the ground started up and said, "Gosh!"

The youth quickly turned his eyes to the field. He saw forms begin to swell in masses out of a distant wood. He again saw the tilted flag speeding forward.

The shells, which had ceased to trouble the regiment for a time, came swirling again, and exploded in the grass or among the leaves of the trees. They looked like strange war flowers bursting into fierce bloom.

The men groaned. The brightness faded from their eyes. Their smudged faces now showed a deep letdown. They moved their stiff bodies slowly, and sullenly watched the frantic approach of the enemy.

They fussed and complained to each other. "Oh, say, this is too much of a good thing! Why can't somebody send us supports? We ain't never going to stand this second banging. I didn't come here to fight the whole damn rebel army."

There was one who raised a cry of sadness. "I wish Bill Smithers had stepped on my hand, instead of me stepping on his." The sore joints of the regiment creaked as it stumbled into position. The youth stared. Surely, he thought, this impossible thing was not about to happen. He waited as if he expected the enemy to suddenly stop, apologize, and retire. It was all a mistake. But the firing began somewhere on the line and ripped along in both directions. The level sheets of flame developed great clouds of smoke that rolled through the ranks. In the sun, the clouds were dirt-colored yellow. In the shadows, they were a sorry blue. The flag was sometimes lost in this mass of vapor, but more often it stood out, sun-touched, shining brightly.

Into the youth's eyes there came a look that one can see in the eyes of a tired horse. His neck was trembling with nervous weakness, and the muscles of his arms felt numb and bloodless. His hands, too, seemed large and awkward, as if he was wearing invisible mittens. And there was a great unsteadiness in his knee joints.

The things that comrades had said before the firing came back to him. "Oh, say, this is too much of a good thing! What do they take us for—why don't they send supports? I didn't come here to fight the whole damned rebel army."

He began to exaggerate the strength, the skill, and the bravery of those who were coming. Exhausted as he was himself, he was astonished at such nerve. They must be machines of steel. It was very gloomy struggling against them, ready perhaps to fight until sundown.

He slowly lifted his rifle. Catching a glimpse of the thick-spread field, he blazed at a cluster of figures. He stopped then and began to peer as best he could through the smoke. He caught changing views of the ground covered with men who were all running like devils, and yelling.

To the youth, it was an attack of fearsome dragons. He seemed to shut his eyes and wait to be gobbled.

A man near him, who up to this time had been working feverishly at his rifle, suddenly stopped and ran with howls. A nearby lad whose face had expressed high courage was instantly made cowardly. He blanched like one who has come to the edge of a cliff at midnight and is suddenly made aware. There was a revelation. He, too, threw down his gun and fled. There was no shame in his face. He ran like a rabbit.

Others began to scamper away through the smoke. The youth turned his head, shaken from his trance by this movement, as if the regiment were leaving him behind.

He yelled with fright and swung about. For a moment, in the great confusion, he lost his sense of direction. Destruction threatened him from everywhere.

He began to speed toward the rear in great leaps. His rifle and cap were gone. His unbuttoned coat bulged in the wind. The flap of his cartridge box bobbed wildly, and his canteen, by its slender cord, swung out behind. On his face was all the horror of those things which he imagined.

The lieutenant sprang forward, shouting. The youth saw his angry red face and saw him do something with his sword. The youth thought that it was peculiar of the lieutenant to be interested in such things at a time like this.

He ran like a blind man. Two or three times he fell down. Once he knocked his shoulder so heavily against a tree that he went headlong.

Since he had turned his back on the fight, his fears had grown. Death from behind was more dreadful than death from in front. When he thought about it later, he had the idea that it is better to see what is frightening than to be merely within hearing of it. The noises of the battle were like stones. He believed himself liable to be crushed.

As he ran on, he mixed with others. He dimly saw men on his right and on his left, and he heard footsteps behind him. He thought that all the regiment was fleeing, pursued by these awful crashes.

In his flight, his one slight comfort was the sound of these following footsteps. He felt vaguely that death must strike the men who were nearest first. The first victims would be those behind him. So he displayed the zeal of an insane sprinter in effort to stay ahead. There was a race.

As he, leading, went across a little field, he found himself in a region of shells. They hurtled over his head with long, wild screams. As he listened, he imagined them to have rows of cruel teeth that grinned at him. Once one lit before him, and the explosion made him change directions. He clung to the ground. Then he sprang up and went rushing off through some bushes.

He was amazed when he came within view of a battery in action. The men there seemed to be in an ordinary mood, completely unaware of the coming destruction. The battery was disputing with a far-off enemy battery, and the gunners were admiring their shooting. They were continually bending over the guns. They seemed to be patting them on the back and encouraging them with words. The guns, stolid and fearless, spoke with dogged bravery.

The gunners were coolly enthusiastic. They looked at every chance to the smoke-wreathed hill where the hostile battery was shooting at them. The youth pitied them as he ran. Unhurried idiots! Machine-like fools! The pleasure of planting shells in the midst of the other battery would appear a little thing when the infantry came swooping out of the woods.

He was deeply impressed by the face of a young rider, who was jerking his frantic horse with an abandon of temper. He knew that he was looking at a man who would soon be dead.

He also felt sorry for the guns, six good comrades standing in a bold row.

He saw a brigade going to the relief of its pestered fellows. He scrambled up a small hill and watched it move, keeping formation in difficult places. The blue of the line was sprinkled with steel color, and the brilliant flags stood out. Officers were shouting.

This sight also filled him with wonder. The brigade was hurrying briskly to be gulped into the hellish mouths of the war god. What kind of men were they, anyhow? Ah, they were some wonderful new breed! Or else they didn't understand—the fools.

A furious order caused excitement in the

artillery. An officer on a bounding horse made crazy motions with his arms. The horses went swinging up from the rear, the guns were whirled about, and the battery hurried away. The cannon, their noses poked slantingly at the ground, grunted and grumbled like fat men, brave but not liking to hurry. The youth went on, slowing down since he had left the place of noises.

Later he came upon a general of division seated on a horse. The horse stuck up its ears in an interested way at the battle. There was a great gleaming of yellow and patent leather about the saddle and bridle. The quiet rider looked mouse-colored on such a splendid animal.

Officers of the general's staff were galloping back and forth. Sometimes the general was surrounded by horsemen. At other times he was quite alone. He looked to be much troubled. He had the appearance of a businessman whose market is swinging up and down.

The youth went slinking around this spot. He went as near as he dared, trying to overhear words. Perhaps the general, unable to understand the disaster, might call on him for information. And he could tell him. He knew everything about it. Unquestionably the force was in a fix, and any fool could see that if they did not retreat while they had opportunity—why——

He felt that he would like to beat the general up, or at least tell him in plain words exactly what he thought he was. It was criminal to stay calmly in one spot and make no effort to stop the destruction. He waited eagerly for the division commander to ask him.

As he moved cautiously about, he heard the general call out irritably: "Tompkins, go over and see Taylor, and tell him not to be in such an all-fired hurry. Tell him to halt his brigade at the edge of the woods. Tell him to detach a regiment. Say I think the center will break if we don't help it out some. Tell him to hurry up."

A slim youth on a fine chestnut horse caught these swift words from the mouth of his superior. In his haste to go on his mission, he made his horse bound into a gallop almost from a walk. There was a cloud of dust.

A moment later, the youth saw the general bounce excitedly in his saddle.

"Yes, by heavens, they have!" The officer leaned forward. His face was aflame with excitement. "Yes, by heavens, they've held them! They've held them!"

He began to roar cheerfully at his staff: "We'll wallop them now. We'll wallop them now. We've got them sure." He turned suddenly to an aide: "Here—you—Jones—quick—ride after Tompkins—see Taylor—tell him to go in—everlastingly—like blazes—anything."

As another officer sped his horse after the first one, the general smiled upon the earth like a sun. In his eyes was a desire to chant a song of joy. He kept repeating, "They've held them, by heavens!"

His excitement made his horse plunge, and he merrily kicked and swore at it. He held a little carnival of joy on horseback.

7

The youth cringed as if discovered in a crime. By heavens, they had won after all! The line had remained and had won. He could hear cheering.

He lifted himself up on his toes and looked toward the fight. A yellow fog lay on the treetops. From beneath it came the clatter of muskets. Hoarse cries told of an advance.

He turned away amazed and angry. He felt that he had been wronged.

He had fled, he told himself, because death approached. In saving himself, he had done a good thing. After all, he was a little piece of the army. He had believed, he said, that it was the duty of every little piece to rescue itself if possible. Later the officers could fit the little pieces together again, and make a battle front. If none of the little pieces were wise enough to save themselves from death, why, then, where would be the army? It was plain that he had proceeded according to very correct rules. His actions had been wise. They had been part of a plan. They were the work of a master.

He thought about his comrades. The fragile blue line had resisted the attack and won. He grew bitter over it. It seemed that the stupidity of those men had betrayed him. He had been crushed by their lack of sense in holding the position. If they were intelligent, they would have known that it was impossible. He, the wise man, had fled because of his superior insights and knowledge. He felt a great anger against his comrades. He knew it could be proved that they had been fools.

He wondered what they would say when he returned to camp. In his mind, he heard howls of scorn. Their stupidity would keep them from understanding his sharper point of view.

He began to feel great pity for himself. He was treated unfairly. He was trampled beneath the feet of injustice. He had acted wisely and for the most moral reasons under heaven, only to be let down.

A dull, animal-like rebellion grew within him. He shambled along with bowed head, weighed down with agony and despair. When he looked up, trembling at each sound, his eyes had the expression of a criminal.

He went from the fields into a thick wood, as if he intended to bury himself. He wished to get out of hearing of the crackling shots, which to him were like voices.

The ground was cluttered with vines and bushes. The trees grew close, and spread out like bunches of flowers. He had to make his way with much noise. The creepers, catching against his legs, cried out harshly as they were torn from the barks of trees. The swishing noise of the saplings followed after him. He was afraid that these noises and cries would bring men to look at him. So he kept going, seeking dark and mysterious places.

After a time, the sound of musketry grew faint, and the cannon boomed in the distance. The sun suddenly blazed among the trees. The insects seemed to be grinding their teeth in unison. A woodpecker stuck his sassy head around the side of a tree. A bird flew on lighthearted wing.

The rumble of death was far away. It seemed now that Nature had no ears.

This landscape gave him confidence. It was the religion of peace. It would die if its timid eyes were forced to see blood. He thought of Nature as a woman with a strong dislike of tragedy.

He threw a pine cone at a cheerful squirrel, and it ran noisily. High in a treetop it stopped, and poking his head cautiously from behind a branch, looked down anxiously.

The youth felt triumphant. Nature had given him a sign. The squirrel, as soon as it recognized danger, had taken to its legs. It did not bare its furry belly to the missile, and die with an upward glance at heaven. On the contrary, it had fled as fast as its legs could carry it. It was just an ordinary squirrel, too, not one of the great thinkers of its race. The youth walked on, feeling that Nature agreed with him.

Once he found himself almost in a swamp. He had to walk on clumps of grass and to watch his feet to keep them from the oily mud. Pausing to look about him, he saw, out at some black water, a small animal leap in and come out quickly with a gleaming fish.

The youth went again into the deep forest. The branches as he brushed against them made a noise that drowned the sounds of cannon. He walked on, going from darkness into promises of a greater darkness.

At length he reached a place where the high, arching boughs made a chapel. He softly pushed the green doors aside and entered. Pine needles were a gentle brown carpet. There was a religious half light.

Near the threshold he stopped, horror-stricken by what he saw.

He was being looked at by a dead man, who was seated with his back against a tree. The corpse was dressed in a uniform that once had been blue, but was now faded to a shade of green. The eyes, staring at the youth, had changed to the dull color seen in the eye of a dead fish. The mouth was open. Its red had changed to a horrible yellow. Over the gray skin of the face ran little ants. One ant was dragging some sort of bundle along the upper lip.

The youth gave a shriek as he faced the thing. He was for moments turned to stone before it. He remained staring into the liquid-looking eyes. The dead man and the living man exchanged a long look. Then the youth cautiously put one hand behind him and brought it against a tree. Leaning on this, he retreated, step by step, with his face still toward the thing. He feared that if he turned his back, the body might spring up and follow him.

The branches, pushing against him, threatened to throw him over on it. His feet, too, caught in brambles. With it all, he felt a faint suggestion that he touch the corpse. As he thought of his hand on it, he shuddered deeply.

At last he burst the bonds that held him to the spot and fled, paying no attention to the underbrush. He was pursued by a sight of the black ants swarming greedily on the gray face and coming horribly near to the eyes.

After a time he paused and listened. He imagined some strange voice would come from the dead throat and squawk after him in horrible threats.

The trees at the entrance to the chapel rustled in a soft wind. There was a sad silence over the little shrine.

8

The trees began to sing a soft hymn of twilight. The sun sank until slanted rays struck the forest. There was a lull in the noises of insects, as if they had bowed their heads and were praying. There was silence except for the chanted chorus of the trees.

Then, upon this stillness, there suddenly broke a tremendous crash of sounds. A roar came from the distance.

The youth stopped. He was made motionless by this terrific mixture of all noises. It was as if worlds were being torn apart. There was the ripping sound of muskets and the breaking crash of the artillery.

His mind flew in all directions. He imagined the two armies to have leaped at each other like panthers. He listened for a time. Then he began to run in the direction of the battle. He saw that it was odd for him to be running toward what he had tried so hard to avoid. But he said to himself that if the earth and the moon were about to crash, many persons would no doubt go up on the roofs to watch the collision.

As he ran, he became aware that the forest had stopped its music, as if finally hearing the foreign sounds. The trees stood quiet and motionless.

Everything seemed to be listening to the crackle and clatter and ear-shaking thunder.

It suddenly occurred to the youth that the fight in which he had been was not much of a battle. Listening to this present din, he was doubtful if he had seen real battle scenes.

He saw a sort of a humor in the point of view of himself and his fellows. They had taken themselves and the enemy very seriously. They had imagined that they were deciding the war. Individuals supposed that they were making their names sacred forever in the hearts of their countrymen. In fact, however, the affair would appear in printed reports under a modest title. But he saw that it was good. Otherwise, he said, in battle every one would surely run.

He went rapidly on. He wished to come to the edge of the forest so that he could look out.

As he hurried along, his mind formed pictures of mighty conflicts. His collected thoughts on such subjects were put together to form scenes.

Sometimes the brambles formed chains and tried to hold him back. Trees stretched out their arms and forbade him to pass. This new resistance of the forest filled him with bitterness. It seemed that Nature could not be quite ready to kill him.

But he stubbornly took roundabout ways. Soon he was where he could see long gray walls where the battle was. The voices of cannon shook him. The muskets sounded in long, irregular waves that were painful to his ears. He stood watching for a moment. His eyes had an expression of fear and wonder. He stared in the direction of the fight.

Soon he moved forward again. The battle was

like the grinding of an immense and terrible machine. Its grim processes fascinated him. He must go close and see it produce corpses.

He came to a fence and climbed over it. On the far side, the ground was littered with clothes and guns. A newspaper, folded up, lay in the dirt. A dead soldier was stretched with his face hidden in his arm. Farther off, there was a group of four or five corpses keeping mournful company. A hot sun had blazed upon the spot.

In this place the youth felt that he was an invader. This forgotten part of the battleground was owned by the dead men. He hurried on, in the vague fear that one of the swollen forms would rise and tell him to be gone.

He came finally to a road. In the distance he could see dark and rapidly moving bodies of troops, smoke-fringed. In the lane was a bloodstained crowd streaming to the rear. The wounded men were cursing, groaning, and wailing. In the air, always, was a mighty sound that seemed to sway the earth. And from this region of noises came the steady current of the wounded.

One of the wounded men had a shoeful of blood. He hopped like a schoolboy in a game. He was laughing hysterically.

One was swearing that he had been shot in the arm because of the commanding general's misman-agement of the army. One was marching, as if he were imitating some grand drum major. On his face was an unholy mixture of merriment and agony. As he marched, he sang a bit of doggerel in a high and quavering voice:

> "Sing a song of victory,
> A pocketful of bullets,
> Five and twenty dead men
> Baked in a—pie."

Parts of the procession limped and staggered to this tune.

Another had the gray seal of death already upon his face. His lips were curled in hard lines, and his teeth were clenched. His hands were bloody from where he had pressed them on his wound. He seemed to be awaiting the moment when he would fall. He walked stiffly like the ghost of a soldier. His eyes burned with the power of one who stares into the unknown.

There were some who moved sullenly, full of anger at their wounds. They were ready to blame anything.

An officer was carried along by two privates. He was in a bad humor. "Don't joggle so, Johnson, you fool," he cried. "Think my leg is made of iron? If you can't carry me decent, put me down and let someone else do it."

He bellowed at the staggering crowd who blocked the quick march of his bearers. "Say, make way there, can't you? Make way, dickens take it all."

They parted sullenly and went to the road-sides. As he was carried past, they made rude remarks to him. When he raged in reply and threatened them, they told him to be damned.

The shoulder of one of the officer's bearers knocked heavily against the ghostly soldier who was staring into the unknown.

The youth joined this crowd and marched

along with it. The torn bodies told of the awful machinery of war in which the men had been caught up.

Messengers on horseback occasionally broke through the throng in the roadway. They scattered wounded men right and left, then galloped on, followed by howls. The march was continually disturbed by these messengers, and sometimes also by batteries that came swinging and thumping down upon them, the officers shouting orders to clear the way.

There was a tattered man who trudged quietly at the youth's side. The man was dirty with dust, blood, and gunpowder stain from hair to shoes. He was listening eagerly to the gruesome stories of a bearded sergeant. His thin face had an expression of wonder and admiration. He was like a person in a country store listening to wondrous tales told among the sugar barrels. His mouth hung open as he listened.

The sergeant noticed the open mouth. He paused in his story to comment sarcastically, "Be careful, honey, you'll be catching flies," he said.

The tattered man shrank back, embarrassed.

After a time he began to edge up to the youth and try in a different way to make him a friend. His voice was gentle as a girl's voice, and his eyes were pleading. The youth saw with surprise that the soldier had two wounds. One was in the head and was bound with a blood-soaked rag. The other was in the arm, making it dangle like a broken bough.

After they had walked together for some time, the tattered man worked up enough courage to

speak. "Was a pretty good fight, wasn't it?" he timidly said. The youth, deep in thought, glanced at the
bloody and grim figure with its eyes like a lamb's.
"What?" he said.
"Was a pretty good fight, wasn't it?"
"Yes," said the youth shortly. He walked faster.
But the other limped stubbornly after him.
There was an air of apology in his manner. But he
seemed to think that he needed only to talk for a
while, and the youth would see that he was a good
fellow.
"Was a pretty good fight, wasn't it?" he began in
a small voice. Then he gained the strength to continue. "Darn me if I ever see fellows fight so. Laws,
how they did fight! I knowed the boys would do good
when they once got square at it. The boys ain't had
no fair chance up to now, but this time they showed
what they was. I knowed it would turn out this way.
You can't lick them boys. No, sir! They're fighters,
they be."
He drew a deep breath of respect. He had
looked at the youth several times for encouragement. He received none, but gradually he seemed
to get caught up in his subject.
"I was talking across pickets with a boy from
Georgia, once, and that boy, he says, 'Your fellows
will all run like hell when they once hear a gun,' he
says. 'Maybe they will,' I says, 'but I don't believe
none of it,' I says. 'And by jiminey,' I says back to
him, 'maybe your fellows will all run like hell when
they once hear a gun,' I says. He laughed. Well, they
didn't run today, did they, hey? No, sir! They fought,
and fought, and fought."
His homely face was filled with love for the

army, which was to him all things beautiful and powerful.

After a time he turned to the youth. "Where you hit, old boy?" he asked in a brotherly tone.

The youth felt instant panic at the question, although at first its full meaning did not occur to him.

"What?" he asked.

"Where you hit?" repeated the tattered man.

"Why," began the youth, "I—I—that is—why—I——"

He turned away suddenly and slid through the crowd. His face was flushed, and his fingers were picking nervously at one of his buttons. He bent his head and fastened his eyes on the button, as if it were a little problem.

The tattered man looked after him in astonishment.

The youth fell back until the tattered soldier was not in sight. Then he started to walk on with the others.

But he was amid the wounded. The mob of men was bleeding. Because of the tattered soldier's question, he now felt that his shame could be seen. He was continually looking sideways to see if the men were looking at the marks of guilt that he felt were burned into his forehead.

At times he envied the wounded soldiers. He thought that persons with torn bodies were particularly happy. He wished that he, too, had a wound, a little red badge of courage.

The ghostly soldier was at his side like a walking rebuke. The man's eyes were still fixed in a stare into the unknown. His gray, appalling face had drawn attention in the crowd, and men, slowing to his dreary pace, were walking with him. They were discussing his situation, asking him questions, and giving him advice. In a stubborn way, he rejected them, gesturing for them to go away and leave him alone. The shadows of his face were deepening, and his tight lips seemed to be holding back a moan of despair. His body moved stiffly, as if he were taking great care not to provoke his wounds. As he went on, he seemed to be always looking for a place, like one who goes to choose a grave.

Something in the gesture of the man as he waved the soldiers away made the youth start as if bitten. He yelled in horror. Tottering forward, he laid a shaking hand on the man's arm. As the latter slowly turned his wax-like features toward him, the youth screamed:

"God! Jim Conklin!"

The tall soldier made a little everyday smile. "Hello, Henry," he said.

The youth swayed on his legs and frowned strangely. He stuttered and stammered. "Oh, Jim—oh, Jim—oh, Jim——"

The tall soldier held out his bloody hand. There was a curious red and black combination of new blood and old blood on it. "Where you been, Henry?" he asked. He continued in a flat voice. "I thought maybe you got keeled over. There's been thunder to pay today. I was worrying about it a good deal."

The youth still lamented. "Oh, Jim—oh, Jim—oh, Jim——"

"You know," said the tall soldier, "I was out there." He made a careful gesture. "And, Lord, what a circus! And by jiminey, I got shot—I got shot. Yes, by jiminey, I got shot." He repeated this fact in a bewildered way, as if he did not know how it had happened.

The youth tried anxiously to help him, but the tall soldier went firmly on, as if being pushed. Since the youth's arrival as a guardian for his friend, the other wounded men no longer showed much interest. They occupied themselves again in dragging their own tragedies toward the rear.

Suddenly, as the two friends marched on, the tall soldier seemed to be overcome by terror. His face became like gray paste. He clutched the youth's arm and looked all about him, as if dreading to be overheard. Then he began to speak in a shaking whisper:

"I tell you what I'm afraid of, Henry—I'll tell you what I'm afraid of. I'm afraid I'll fall down—and then you know—them damned artillery wagons—they like as not will run over me. That's what I'm afraid of——"

The youth cried out, "I'll take care of you, Jim! I'll take care of you! I swear to God I will!"

"Sure—will you, Henry?" the tall soldier beseeched.

"Yes—yes—I tell you—I'll take care of you, Jim!" repeated the youth. He could not speak clearly because of the gulping in his throat.

But the tall soldier continued to beg. He now hung to the youth's arm like a small child. His eyes rolled in the wildness of his terror. "I was always a good friend to you, wasn't I, Henry? I've always been a pretty good fellow, ain't I? And it ain't much to ask, is it? Just to pull me along out of the road? I'd do it for you, wouldn't I, Henry?"

He paused anxiously to await his friend's reply.

The youth's sobs choked him. He tried to express his loyalty, but he could only make gestures.

However, the tall soldier seemed suddenly to forget all those fears. He became again the grim, stalking ghost of a soldier. He went stiffly forward. The youth wanted his friend to lean on him, but the other always shook his head. "No—no—no—leave me be—leave me be——"

His look was fixed again upon the unknown. He moved with mysterious purpose, and all of the youth's offers he brushed aside. "No—no—leave me be—leave me be——"

The youth had to follow.

Soon the youth heard a voice talking softly near his shoulder. Turning, he saw that it belonged to the tattered soldier. "You'd better take him out of the road, partner. There's a battery coming hellity-whoop down the road, and he'll get runned over. He's a goner anyhow in about five minutes—you can see that. You'd better take him out of the road. Where the blazes does he get his strength from?"

"Lord knows!" cried the youth. He was shaking his hands helplessly.

He ran forward and grasped the tall soldier by the arm. "Jim! Jim!" he coaxed. "Come with me."

The tall soldier weakly tried to wrench himself free. "Huh," he said vacantly. He stared at the youth for a moment. At last he spoke as if dimly understanding. "Oh! Into the fields? Oh!"

He started blindly through the grass.

The youth turned once to look at the riders and guns of the battery. He was startled from this view by a shrill outcry from the tattered man.

"God! He's running!"

Turning his head swiftly, the youth saw his friend running in a staggering and stumbling way toward a little clump of bushes. His heart seemed to wrench itself almost free from his body at the sight. He made a noise of pain. He and the tattered man began a pursuit. There was a singular race.

When he overtook the tall soldier, he began to plead with all the words he could find.

"Jim—Jim—what are you doing—what makes you do this way—you'll hurt yourself."

The same purpose as before was in the tall soldier's face. He protested in a weakened way, keeping his eyes fastened on the mystic place that he was going toward. "No—no—don't touch me—leave me be—leave me be——"

The youth, frightened and filled with wonder at the tall soldier, began with a shaking voice to question him. "Where you going, Jim? What you thinking about? Where you going? Tell me, won't you Jim?"

The tall soldier turned around as if they were chasing him. In his eyes there was a great appeal. "Leave me be, can't you? Leave me be for a minute."

The youth recoiled. "Why, Jim," he said, in a dazed way, "What's the matter with you?"

The tall soldier turned and, staggering dangerously, went on. The youth and the tattered soldier followed, sneaking as if they had been whipped. They felt unable to face the stricken man if he should again resist them. They began to have thoughts of a solemn ceremony. There was something like a ceremony in these movements of the doomed soldier. And there was a resemblance in him to a follower of a mad religion, blood-sucking, muscle-wrenching, bone-crushing. They were amazed and afraid. They hung back, as if he might have some dreadful weapon under his command.

At last, they saw him stop and stand motionless. Hurrying up, they could tell by his expression that he had at last found the place for which he had struggled. His gaunt figure was erect. His bloody hands were quietly at his side. He was waiting patiently for something that he had come to meet. They paused and stood, waiting.

There was a silence.

Finally, the chest of the doomed soldier began to heave with a strained motion. It increased in violence until it was as if an animal was within and was kicking and tumbling furiously to be free.

This sight made the youth twist in pain. Once, as his friend rolled his eyes, he saw something in them that made him sink wailing to the ground. He raised his voice in a last supreme call.

"Jim—Jim—Jim——"

The tall soldier opened his lips and spoke. He made a gesture. "Leave me be—don't touch me—leave me be——"

There was another silence while he waited.

Suddenly, his form stiffened and straightened. Then it was shaken by a long, drawn-out shiver. He stared into space. To the two watchers, there was a strange and profound dignity in the firm lines of his awful face.

A creeping strangeness slowly enclosed him. For a moment, the tremor of his legs caused him to dance a sort of hideous dance. His arms beat wildly about his head in an expression of mischievous enthusiasm.

His tall figure stretched itself to its full height. There was a slight tearing sound. Then he began to swing forward, slow and straight, like a falling tree. A sudden twist made the left shoulder strike the ground first.

The body seemed to bounce a little way from the earth. "God!" said the tattered soldier.

The youth had watched, spellbound, this ceremony at the place of meeting. His face had been twisted into an expression of every kind of suffering he had imagined for his friend.

He now sprang to his feet and, going closer, gazed upon the paste-like face. The mouth was open, and the teeth showed in a laugh.

As the flap of the blue jacket fell away from the body, he could see that the side looked as if it had been chewed by wolves.

The youth turned, with sudden, livid rage, toward the battlefield. He shook his fist. He seemed about to deliver a bitter speech.

"Hell——"

The red sun was pasted in the sky like a wafer.

10

The tattered man stood reflecting.

"Well, he was a regular jim-dandy for nerve, wasn't he," he finally said in a little, awestruck voice. "A regular jim-dandy." He thoughtfully poked one of the limp hands with his foot. "I wonder where he got his strength from? I never seen a man do like that before. It was a funny thing. Well, he was a regular jim-dandy."

The youth wanted to scream out his grief. He was stabbed, but his tongue lay dead in his mouth. He threw himself again to the ground and began to brood.

The tattered man stood reflecting.

"Look here, partner," he said after a time. He looked at the corpse as he spoke. "He's up and gone, ain't he, and we might was well begin to look out for old number one. This here thing is all over. He's up and gone, ain't he? And he's all right here. Nobody won't be bothering him. And I must say I ain't enjoying any great health myself these days."

The youth, awakened by the tattered soldier's tone, looked quickly up. He saw that he was swinging uncertainly on his legs and that his face had turned to a shade of blue.

"Good Lord!" he cried, "you ain't going to—not you, too."

The tattered man waved his hand. "Never die," he said. "All I want is some pea soup and a good bed. Some pea soup," he repeated dreamily.

The youth arose from the ground. "I wonder where he came from. I left him over there." He pointed. "And now I find him here. And he was coming from over there, too." He indicated a new direction. They both turned toward the body as if to ask of it a question.

"Well," at length spoke the tattered man, "there ain't no use in our staying here and trying to ask him anything."

The youth nodded wearily. They both turned to gaze for a moment at the corpse.

The youth said something softly.

"Well, he was a jim-dandy, wasn't he?" said the tattered man, as if in response.

They turned their backs on it and started away. For a time they stepped softly, walking on tiptoes. It remained laughing there in the grass.

"I'm commencing to feel pretty bad," said the tattered man, suddenly breaking one of his little silences. "I'm commencing to feel pretty damn bad."

The youth groaned. "O Lord!" He wondered if he was to be the witness of another grim encounter.

But his companion waved his hand reassuringly. "Oh, I'm not going to die yet! There's too much depending on me for me to die yet. No, sir! Never die! I can't! You ought to see the flock of children I've got, and all like that."

The youth, glancing at his companion, could see by the shadow of a smile that he was making some kind of fun.

As they plodded on, the tattered soldier continued to talk. "Besides, if I died, I wouldn't die the way that fellow did. That was the funniest thing. I'd just flop down, I would. I never seen a fellow die the way that fellow did.

"You know Tom Jamison, he lives next door to me up home. He's a nice fellow, he is, and we was always good friends. Smart, too. Smart as a steel trap. Well, when we was fighting this afternoon, all of a sudden he began to rip up and cuss and bellow at me. 'You're shot, you blamed infernal——.' He swore horrible. I put up my hand to my head, and when I looked at my fingers, I seen sure enough, I was shot. I gave a holler and begin to run, but before I could get away another one hit me in the arm and whirled me clean around. I got scared when they was all shooting behind me, and I run to beat all, but I caught it pretty bad. I have an idea I would have been fighting yet, if wasn't for Tom Jamison."

Then he made a calm announcement: "There's two of them—little ones—but they're beginning to have fun with me now. I don't believe I can walk much further."

They went slowly on in silence. "You look pretty weak yourself," said the tattered man at last. "I bet you've got a worse one than you think. You'd better take care of your hurt. It don't do to let such things go. It might be inside mostly, and them plays thunder. Where is it located?" But he kept on talking without waiting for a reply. "I saw a fellow get hit plum in the head when my regiment was standing at ease once. And everybody yelled out to him: 'Hurt, John? Are you hurt much?' 'No,' he says. He looked kind of surprised, and he went on telling them how he felt. He said he didn't feel nothing. But, by dad, the first thing that fellow knew he was dead. Yes, he was dead—stone dead. So, you want to watch out. You might have some queer kind of hurt yourself. You can't never tell. Where is yours located?"

The youth had been squirming since the introduction of this topic. He now gave a cry of annoyance and made an angry motion with his hand. "Oh, don't bother me!" he said. He was enraged against the tattered man, and could have strangled him. His companions always seemed to play unwelcome parts. By their curiosity, they were always raising the ghost of shame. He turned toward the tattered man as if he had been cornered. "Now, don't bother me," he repeated in the tone of a desperate threat.

"Well, Lord knows I don't want to bother anybody," said the other. There was a hint of despair in his voice as he replied, "Lord knows I've got enough of my own to tend to."

The youth had been holding a bitter debate with himself. From time to time he cast glances of hatred and contempt at the tattered man. Now he spoke in a hard voice. "Goodbye," he said.

The tattered man looked at him in amazement. "Why—why, partner, where you going?" he asked unsteadily. The youth, looking at him, could see that he, too, like that other one, was beginning to act dumb and animal-like. His thoughts seemed to be floundering about in his head. "Now—now— look—here, you Tom Jamison—now—I won't have this—this here won't do. Where—where you going?"

The youth pointed vaguely. "Over there," he replied.

"Well, now look—here—now," said the tattered man, rambling on dully. His head was hanging forward, and his words were slurred. "This thing won't do, now, Tom Jamison. It won't do. I know you, you pig-headed devil. You want to go tramping off with a bad hurt. It ain't right—now Tom Jamison—it ain't. You want to leave me take care of you, Tom Jamison. It ain't—right—it ain't—for you to go—tramping off—with a bad hurt—it ain't—ain't—ain't right—it ain't."

In reply, the youth climbed a fence and started away. He could hear the tattered man pleading.

Once he faced about angrily. "What?"

"Look—here, now, Tom Jamison—now—it ain't——"

The youth went on. Turning at a distance, he saw the tattered man wandering about helplessly in the field.

He wished he was dead. He believed that he envied those men whose bodies lay on the grass of the fields and on the fallen leaves of the forest.

The simple questions of the tattered man had been knife thrusts to him. They spoke for a society that digs pitilessly at secrets until everything is uncovered. He felt that he could not keep his crime hidden. It was sure to be brought out by one of those questions that constantly threaten to dig up what has been buried. He admitted that he could not defend himself against this process. It was not something that watchfulness could prevent.

11

He became aware that the roar of the battle was growing louder. Great brown clouds had floated to the air above him. The noise, too, was approaching. Men filtered out of the woods and dotted the fields.

As he rounded a hillock, he saw that the roadway was now a mass of wagons, teams, and men. Fear was sweeping them along. The cracking whips bit, and horses plunged and tugged. The white-topped wagons strained and stumbled like fat sheep.

The youth felt somewhat comforted by this sight. They were all retreating. Perhaps, then, he was not so bad after all. He seated himself and watched the terror-stricken wagons. They fled like soft, awkward animals. Watching this wild march, the youth felt a certain pleasure. It was as though the retreating army helped to justify what he himself had done.

Presently the calm head of a column of infantry appeared in the road. It came swiftly on, going in the opposite direction, toward the front. Avoiding the obstructions gave it the zigzagging movements of a snake. The men at the head butted mules with their musket stocks. They prodded teamsters, ignoring their howls. The men forced their way through parts of the dense mass by strength. The blunt head of the column pushed. The teamsters swore many strange oaths. The commands to make way had the ring of great importance. The men were going forward to the heart of the din. They were to face the eager rush of the enemy. They felt the pride of moving forward when the rest of the army seemed trying to dribble down this road going the other way. They tumbled mule teams about, feeling that it did not matter so long as their column got to the front in time. This importance made their faces grave and stern. And the backs of the officers were very rigid.

As the youth looked at them, the black weight of his misery returned to him. He felt that he was watching a procession of chosen beings. The difference between him and them was as great as if they had marched with weapons of flame and banners of sunlight. He could never be like them. He could have wept.

The haste of the column to reach the battle seemed to the forlorn young man to be something much finer than actual fighting. Heroes like these, he thought, had excuses for anything that might happen later. They could retreat with perfect self-respect.

He wondered what those men had eaten to make them in such a hurry to face the grim chances of death. As he watched, his envy grew until he thought that he wished to change lives with one of them. He pictured himself as one of them—a blue, desperate figure leading terrible charges with one knee forward and a broken sword held high—a blue, determined figure standing before a crimson and steel assault, getting calmly killed on a high place before the eyes of all. He thought of the magnificent pity and sorrow of his dead body.

These thoughts uplifted him. He felt the shiver of war desire. In his ears, he heard the ring of victory. He knew the frenzy of a rapid, successful charge. The music of the trampling feet, the sharp voices, the clanking arms of the column near him made him soar on the red wings of war. For a few moments, he felt noble.

He thought that he was about to start for the front. Indeed, he saw a picture of himself, dust-stained, weary, panting. In this vision, he was flying to the front at just the right moment to seize and choke the dark, leering witch of disaster.

Then the difficulties of the thing began to bother him. He paused, balancing awkwardly on one foot.

He had no rifle. He could not fight with his hands. Well, rifles could be had for the picking. They were lying everywhere.

Also, he continued, it would be a miracle if he found his regiment. Well, he could fight with any regiment.

He started forward slowly. He stepped as if he expected to step on some explosive thing. He was struggling with his doubts.

He would truly be a worm if any of his comrades should see him returning like this, with the marks of his flight on him. There was a reply that fighters did not care what happened rearward so long as the enemy did not appear there. In the battle his face would, in a way, be hidden.

But then he said, when the fighting lulled for a moment, someone would ask him for an explanation. He imagined himself being questioned by his companions as he painfully labored through some lies. Eventually, his courage was used up by these objections. The debates drained him of his fire.

He was not depressed by this defeat of his plan. On studying the affair carefully, he could only admit that the objections were very strong. Furthermore, he discovered that he had a scorching thirst. His face was so dry and grimy that he thought he could feel his skin crackle. Each bone of his body had an ache in it, and threatened to break with each movement. His feet were like two sores. Also, his body was calling for food. There was a dull, weight-like feeling in his stomach, and, when he tried to walk, his head swayed and he tottered. He could not see clearly. Small patches of green mist floated before his eyes.

While he had been tossed by many emotions, he had not been aware of these ailments of the body. Now he was at last forced to pay attention to them, and his capacity for self-hate grew. In despair, he declared that he was not like those others. He now admitted that it was impossible for him ever to become a hero. He was a cowardly clod. Those pictures of glory were pitiful things. He groaned from his heart and went staggering off.

A certain mothlike quality in him kept him near the battle. He had a great desire to see it, and to get news. He wanted to know who was winning.

He told himself that he had never lost his greed for a victory. Yet, he said, in a half-apologetic manner to his conscience, a defeat for the army this time might work out well for him. The battle would splinter regiments into fragments. Thus, many brave men, he reasoned, would be forced to desert the flag and scurry like chickens. He would join them. They would be sullen brothers in distress. He could then believe that he had not run any farther or faster than they. And if he himself could believe it, he figured that there would be small trouble in convincing others.

He said, as if to excuse this hope, that previously the army had encountered great defeats and in a few months had recovered from them. The people at home would complain for a time, but it was usually the generals who had to answer them. He of course did not object to offering a general as a sacrifice. It was quite probable that public opinion would hit the wrong man who, after he had recovered from his amazement, would spend the rest of his life defending his alleged failure. It would be very unfair, no doubt, but in this case a general was of no consequence to the youth.

In a defeat, there would be a sort of excusing of himself. He thought it would prove, in a way, that he had fled early because of his superior understanding. A prophet who predicts a flood should be the first person to climb a tree. When the flood came, it would demonstrate that he was indeed a prophet.

The youth regarded a moral justification as a very important thing. Without it he could not, he thought, wear the sore badge of his dishonor through life.

If the army had gone on gloriously, he would be

lost. If the din meant that now his army's flags were tilted forward, he was doomed. If the men were advancing, their feet were trampling on his chances for a successful life. As these thoughts went rapidly through his mind, he tried to push them away. He cursed himself as a villain. He said that he was the most selfish man in existence. In his mind, he saw the soldiers who would place their bodies defiantly in front of the yelling enemy. As he saw their dripping corpses on an imagined field, he said that he was their murderer.

Again he wished he were dead. He believed that he was jealous of a corpse. He developed a great contempt for some of the killed, as if they were guilty for having died in the way they did. They might have been killed by good luck, he said, before they had a chance to run away, before they had been really tested. Yet they would be praised as heroes. He cried out bitterly that their fame was stolen and their glorious memories were lies. However, he still said that it was a great pity that he was not one of them.

He had thought that a defeat of the army would be an escape from the consequences of his action. He thought now, however, that it was useless to think of such a possibility. He had been taught that success for that mighty blue machine was a sure thing; that it would make victories as a machine makes buttons. He soon gave up thinking that anything different might happen.

He tried to think up a good story that he could take back to his regiment, and so avoid the ridicule that he expected.

But, much as he feared ridicule, he could not invent a story that he felt he could trust. He tried many plots, but threw them aside one by one as flimsy. He was quick to see weak places in them all.

Furthermore, he was afraid that ridicule might lay him low before he could tell his protecting story.

He imagined the whole regiment saying, "Where's Henry Fleming? He run, didn't he? Oh, my!" He thought of several persons who would leave him no peace about it. They would question him with sneers, and laugh at his stammering answers. In the next battle, they would watch him to discover when he would run.

Wherever he went in camp, he would be met by rude and cruel stares. He imagined himself passing near a crowd of comrades and hearing someone say, "There he goes!" Then, as if the heads were moved by one muscle, all the faces would turn toward him with wide, sarcastic grins. He seemed to hear some one make a humorous remark in a low tone. At it, the others all crowed and cackled. He was a slang phrase.

12

The column that had butted stoutly at the obstacles in the roadway was barely out of the youth's sight before he saw dark waves of men come sweeping out of the woods and down through the fields. He knew at once that the steel fibers had been washed from their hearts. They were bursting out of their coats and their equipment as if they were traps. They charged down upon him like terrified buffaloes.

Behind them, blue smoke curled and clouded above the treetops. Through the thickets he could sometimes see a distant pink glare. The cannon were booming in an endless chorus.

The youth was struck with horror. He stared in agony and amazement. He forgot that he was engaged in fighting the universe. He lost concern for himself.

The fight was lost. The army, helpless in the matted thickets and blinded by the overhanging night, was going to be swallowed.

Within him, something wanted to cry out. He had the impulse to make a rallying speech, to sing a battle hymn. But he could only get his tongue to call into the air, "Why—why—what—what's the matter?"

Soon he was in the midst of them. They were

leaping and scampering all about him. Their blanched faces shone in the dusk. They seemed, for the most part, to be very burly men. The youth turned from one to another of them as they galloped along. His garbled questions were lost. They paid no attention to his appeals. They did not seem to see him.

They sometimes babbled insanely. One huge man was asking of the sky, "Say, where's the plank road? Where's the plank road?" It was as if he had lost a child. He wept in his pain and dismay.

Soon there were men running in every direction. The artillery booming on all sides made a muddle of ideas of direction. Landmarks had vanished into the falling night. The youth began to imagine that he had got into the center of the tremendous quarrel, and he could see no way out of it. From the fleeing men came a thousand wild questions, but no one answered.

The youth, after rushing about and throwing questions at the retreating infantry, finally clutched a man by the arm. They swung around face to face.

"Why—why——" stammered the youth, struggling with his own tongue.

The man screamed, "Let go me! Let go me!" His face was gray, and his eyes were rolling uncontrolled. He was heaving and panting. He still grasped his rifle, perhaps having forgotten to let go of it. He tugged frantically, and the youth was dragged several paces.

"Let go me! Let go me!"

"Why—Why——" stuttered the youth.

"Well, then!" bawled the man in a fury. He

skillfully and fiercely swung his rifle. It crashed into the youth's head. The man ran on.

The youth's fingers had turned to paste. The energy was gone from his muscles. He saw lightning flash before his vision. There was a deafening rumble of thunder inside his head.

Suddenly his legs seemed to die. He sank to the ground. He tried to arise. In his efforts against the numbing pain, he was like a man wrestling with a creature of the air.

There was a sinister struggle.

Sometimes he would reach a position half standing, battle with the air for a moment, and then fall again, grabbing at the grass. His face was pale and clammy. Deep groans were torn from him.

At last, with a twisting movement, he got up on his hands and knees. From there, like a baby trying to walk, he got to his feet. Pressing his hands to his temples, he went stumbling over the grass.

He fought an intense battle with his body. His dulled senses wanted him to faint, and he fought them stubbornly, imagining worse injuries if he should fall upon the field. He went as the tall soldier had. He imagined hidden spots where he could fall and be unharmed. To search for one, he struggled against the tide of his pain.

Once he put his hand to the top of his head and timidly touched the wound. The pain of the contact made him draw a long breath through his clenched teeth. His fingers were spotted with blood. He looked at them with a fixed stare.

Around him he could hear the grumble of cannon as the horses were lashed toward the front.

Once, a young officer on horseback nearly ran him down. He turned and watched the mass of guns, men, and horses sweeping in a wide curve toward a gap in a fence. The officer was making excited motions with his hand. The guns followed the horses with an air of being dragged by the heels.

Some officers of the scattered infantry were cursing and violently complaining. Their scolding voices could be heard above the din. Into the confusion in the roadway rode a squadron of cavalry. The faded yellow on their uniforms shone bravely. There was a mighty argument.

The artillery were assembling as if for a conference.

The blue haze of evening was on the field. The lines of the forest were long purple shadows. One cloud lay along the western sky, partly smothering the red.

As the youth left the scene behind him, he heard the guns suddenly roar out. He imagined them shaking in black rage. They belched and howled like devils guarding a gate. At the same time came the shattering sound of enemy infantry. Turning to look behind him, he could see sheets of orange light illumine the shadowy distance. There were sudden flashes in the distance. At times he thought he could see masses of men.

He hurried on in the dusk. The day had faded until he could barely see where he was stepping. The purple darkness was filled with men. Sometimes he could see them gesturing against the blue and somber sky. There seemed to be a great crowd of men and munitions spread about in the forest and in the fields.

The little narrow roadway now lay lifeless. There were overturned wagons like sun-dried boulders. The bed of the former stream was choked with the bodies of horses and splintered parts of war machines.

By now his wound pained him little. He was afraid to move rapidly, however, for fear of disturbing it. He held his head very still and took care not to stumble. He was filled with anxiety. His face was pinched and drawn in fear of the pain of any sudden mistake of his feet in the gloom.

His thoughts, as he walked, fixed intently on his hurt. There was a cool, liquid feeling about it, and he imagined blood moving slowly down under his hair. His head felt so swollen that his neck seemed unable to hold it.

He was worried that his wound did not hurt. The earlier, smaller pain seemed to have told him how much danger he was in. He believed that it told him how bad his wound was. But when the pain remained silent, he became frightened. He imagined that terrible fingers were clutching into his brain.

He began to think about various incidents and conditions of the past. He remembered certain meals his mother had cooked at home. He saw the spread table. The pine walls of the kitchen were glowing in the warm light from the stove. Too, he remembered how he and his friends used to go from school to a shaded pool. He saw his clothes piled up on the grass of the bank. He felt the swish of the water on his body. The leaves of the overhanging maple rustled in the wind of youthful summer.

He was soon overcome by a dragging weariness. His head hung forward, and his shoulders
were stooped, as if he were carrying a great burden. His feet shuffled along the ground.

He could not decide whether he should lie
down and sleep at some near spot, or force himself
on until he reached a safe shelter.

At last he heard a cheery voice near his shoulder: "You seem to be in a pretty bad way, boy?"

The youth did not look up, but he agreed with
thick tongue. "Uh!"

The owner of the cheery voice took him firmly
by the arm. "Well," he said, with a rough laugh,
"I'm going your way. The whole gang is going your
way. And I guess I can give you a lift." They began
to walk like a drunken man and his friend.

As they went along, the man questioned the
youth. He helped him answer like a person drawing answers out of a child. Sometimes he added
little stories to the conversation. "What regiment
do you belong to? Eh? What's that? The 304th New
York? Why, what corps is that in? Oh, it is? Why I
thought they wasn't engaged today. They're way
over in the center. Oh, they was, eh? Well, pretty
nearly everybody got their share of fighting today.
By dad, I give myself up for dead any number of
times. There was shooting here and shooting there,
and hollering here and hollering there, in the damn
darkness, until I couldn't tell to save my soul which
side I was on. Sometimes I thought I was sure
enough from Ohio, and other times I could of swore
I was from the bitter end of Florida. It was the
most mixed up darn thing I ever see. And these
here whole woods is a regular mess. It'll be a

miracle if we find our regiments tonight. Pretty soon, though, we'll meet plenty of guards and provost-guards, and one thing and another. Ho! There they go with an officer, I guess. Look at his hand dragging. He's got all the war he wants, I bet. He won't be talking so big about his reputation and all when they go to sawing off his leg. Poor fellow! My brother's got whiskers just like that. How did you get way over here, anyhow? Your regiment is a long way from here, ain't it? Well, I guess we can find it. You know, there was a boy killed in my company today that I thought the world and all of. Jack was a nice fellow. By ginger, it hurt like thunder to see old Jack just get knocked flat. We was standing pretty peaceable for a spell, though there was men running every way all around us, and while we was standing like that, along come a big fat fellow. He began to pick at Jack's elbow, and he says: 'Say, where's the road to the river?' And Jack was looking ahead all the time, trying to see the Johnnies coming through the woods, and he never paid no attention to this big fat fellow for a long time. But at last he turned around and he says: 'Ah, go to hell and find the road to the river!' And just then a shot slapped him bang on the side of the head. He was a sergeant, too. Them was his last words. Thunder, I wish we was sure of finding our regiments tonight. It's going to be long hunting. But I guess we can do it."

In the search that followed, the man of the cheery voice seemed to the youth to possess a magic wand. He threaded the mazes of the tangled forest with a strange good luck. In encounters with guards and patrols, he showed keenness and bravery. Obstacles fell before him. The youth, with his chin still on his breast, stood woodenly by. The forest seemed a vast hive of men buzzing about in frantic circles, but the cheery man conducted the youth without mistakes. At last he began to chuckle with glee and satisfaction.

"Ah, there you are! See that fire?"

The youth nodded stupidly.

"Well, there's where your regiment is. And now goodbye, old boy. Good luck to you."

A warm and strong hand clasped the youth's limp fingers for an instant. Then he heard a cheerful and irreverent whistling as the man strode away. As the man who had been such a friend to him was thus passing out of his life, it suddenly occurred to the youth that he had not once seen his face.

13

The youth went slowly toward the fire that his friend had indicated. As he reeled, he thought about the welcome his comrades would give him. He was sure that he would soon feel the barbs of ridicule. He had no strength to invent a story. He would be an easy target.

He made vague plans to go off into the darkness and hide, but the plans were destroyed by the exhaustion and pain of his body. He was forced to seek the place of food and rest, at whatever cost.

He swung unsteadily toward the fire. He could see the forms of men throwing black shadows in the red light. As he went nearer, he realized that the ground was covered with sleeping men.

Suddenly he was faced by a monstrous figure in the darkness. A rifle barrel reflected some beams from the fire. "Halt!" He was dismayed for a moment. But then he thought that he recognized the nervous voice. As he stood tottering before the rifle barrel, he called out, "Why, hello, Wilson, you—you here?"

The rifle was lowered to a position of caution, and the loud soldier came slowly forward. He peered into the youth's face.

"That's you, Henry?"

"Yes, it's—it's me."

"Well, well, old boy," said the other, "by ginger, I'm glad to see you! I gave you up for a goner. I thought you was dead sure enough." There was husky emotion in his voice.

The youth found that now he could barely stand on his feet. There was a sudden sinking of his strength. He thought he must hurry to produce his story. So, staggering before the loud soldier, he began: "Yes, yes. I've—I've had an awful time. I've been all over. Way over on the right. Terrible fighting over there. I had an awful time. I got separated from the regiment. Over on the right I got shot. In the head. I never seen such fighting. Awful time. I don't see how I could have got separated from the regiment. I got shot, too."

His friend had stepped forward quickly. "What? Got shot? Why didn't you say so first? Poor old boy, we must—hold on a minute. What am I doing? I'll call Simpson."

Another figure at that moment loomed in the gloom. They could see that it was the corporal. "Who you talking to, Wilson?" he demanded. His voice was angry. "Who you talking to? You're the darnedest sentinel—why—hello, Henry, you here? Why, I thought you was dead four hours ago! Great Jerusalem, they keep turning up every ten minutes or so! We thought we'd lost forty-two men by straight count, but if they keep on coming this way, we'll get the company all back by morning. Where was you?"

"Over on the right. I got separated——" began the youth.

But his friend had interrupted hastily. "Yes, and he got shot in the head, and he's in a fix, and we must see to him right away." He rested his rifle in the hollow of his left arm and his right around the youth's shoulder.

"Gee, it must hurt like thunder!" he said.

The youth leaned heavily upon his friend. "Yes, it hurts—hurts a good deal," he replied. There was a weakness in his voice.

"Oh," said the corporal. He linked is arm in the youth's and drew him forward. "Come on, Henry. I'll take care of you."

As they went on together, the loud private called out after them: "Put him to sleep in my blanket, Simpson. And—hold on a minute—here's my canteen. It's full of coffee. Look at his head by the fire and see how it looks. Maybe it's a pretty bad one. When I get relieved in a couple of minutes, I'll be over and see to him."

The youth's senses were so deadened that his friend's voice sounded far off, and he could scarcely feel the pressure of the corporal's arm. He let the corporal lead him. His head was hanging forward on his chest. His knees wobbled.

The corporal led him into the glare of the fire. "Now, Henry," he said, "let's have a look at your old head."

The youth sat down obediently and the corporal, laying aside his rifle, began to fumble in the youth's bushy hair. He turned the youth's head so that the full flush of the firelight would shine on it. He drew up his mouth with a critical air. He drew back his lips and whistled through his teeth when his fingers came in contact with the splashed blood and the raw wound.

"Ah, here we are!" he said. "Just as I thought,"

he added shortly. "You've been grazed by a ball. It's raised a queer lump, just as if some fellow had lammed you on the head with a club. It stopped bleeding a long time ago. The most about it is that in the morning, you'll feel that a number ten hat wouldn't fit you. And your head will be all hot and feel as dry as burnt pork. And you may get a lot of other sicknesses, too, by morning. You can't never tell. Still, I don't much think so. It's just a damn good belt on the head, and nothing more. Now, you just sit here and don't move, while I go rout out the relief. Then I'll send Wilson to take care care of you."

The corporal went away. The youth remained on the ground. He stared with a vacant look into the fire.

After a time he began to notice the things around him. He saw that the ground in the deep shadows was cluttered with men, sprawling in every possible position. Glancing into the more distant darkness, he caught occasional glimpses of faces that loomed pale and ghostly, lit with an unearthly glow. These faces expressed the exhaustion of the soldiers. They made them appear like men drunk with wine. This bit of forest might have appeared to a stranger as the scene of some frightful binge.

On the other side of the fire, the youth observed an officer asleep. He was seated bolt upright, with his back against a tree. There was something unsafe in his position. Bothered by dreams, perhaps, he swayed with little bounces, like an old grandfather dozing in a corner. There were dust and stains on his face. His lower jaw hung down as if it was too weak to hold its normal position. He was the picture of an exhausted soldier after a feast of war. He had evidently gone to sleep with his sword in his arms. In time, the weapon had fallen unnoticed to the ground. The brass-mounted hilt lay in contact with some parts of the fire. Within the gleam of the fires were other soldiers, snoring and tossing, or lying deathlike in slumber. The shoes displayed the mud or dust of marches. Bits of trousers, sticking out from the blankets, showed tears from hurried running through the dense brambles.

The fire crackled musically. From it swelled light smoke. Overhead the foliage moved softly. The leaves, with their faces turned toward the blaze, were colored shifting shades of silver, often edged with red. Far off to the right, through a window in the forest, could be seen a handful of stars.

Occasionally a soldier would turn his body to a new position. Or perhaps he would lift himself to a sitting position and blink at the fire for an unintelligent moment. Then, after throwing a swift glance at his sleeping companions, he would cuddle down again with a grunt of sleepy content.

The youth sat in a forlorn heap until his friend the loud young soldier came, swinging two canteens by their light strings. "Well, now, Henry, old boy," said the latter, "we'll have you fixed up in just about a minute."

He had the bustling ways of an amateur nurse. He fussed around the fire. He made his patient drink from the canteen of coffee. It was delicious to the youth, who tilted his head back and held the canteen to his lips for a long time. Having finished, he sighed comfortably.

The loud young soldier watched his comrade with an air of satisfaction. He later produced a large handkerchief from his pocket. He folded it like a bandage and wet it with water from the other canteen. He tied this crude arrangement around the youth's head, tying the ends in an odd knot at the back of the neck.

"There," he said, moving off and examining his work. "You look like the devil, but I bet you feel better."

The youth looked gratefully at his friend. The cold cloth was like a tender woman's hand on his aching and swelling head.

"You don't holler nor say nothing," remarked his friend approvingly. "I know I'm a blacksmith at taking care of sick folks, and you never squeaked. You're a good one, Henry. Most men would have been in the hospital long ago. A shot in the head ain't fooling business."

The youth made no reply, but began to fumble with the buttons of his jacket.

"Well, come, now," continued his friend, "come on. I must put you to bed and see that you get a good night's rest."

The other got carefully to his feet, and the loud young soldier led him among the sleeping forms lying in groups in rows. Presently he stooped and picked up his blankets. He spread the rubber one on the ground and placed the woollen one around the youth's shoulders.

"There now," he said, "lie down and get some sleep."

The youth, with his manner of doglike obedience, got carefully down. He stretched out with a murmur of relief and comfort. The ground felt like the softest couch.

But suddenly he exclaimed, "Hold on a minute! Where you going to sleep?" His friend waved his hand impatiently. "Right down there by you."

"Well, but hold on a minute," continued the youth. "What are you going to sleep in? I've got your——"

The loud young soldier snarled, "Shut up and go on to sleep. Don't be making a damn fool of yourself," he said severely.

After the scolding, the youth said no more. A delicious drowsiness had spread through him. He was surrounded by the warm comfort of the blanket. His head fell forward on his crooked arm, and his heavy lids went softly down over his eyes. Hearing a splatter of musketry from the distance, he wondered indifferently if those men ever slept. He gave a long sigh, snuggled down into his blanket, and in a moment was like his comrades.

14

When the youth awoke, it seemed to him that he had been asleep for a thousand years and that he would open his eyes on a different world. Gray mists were slowly shifting before the first rays of the sun. A coming splendor could be seen in the eastern sky. An icy dew had chilled his face, and as soon as he awoke, he curled farther down into his blanket. He stared for a while at the leaves overhead.

The distance was cracking and roaring with the noise of fighting. There was a kind of deadly stubbornness in the sound, as if it had always existed and would never end.

Around him were the rows and groups of men that he had dimly seen the night before. They were getting a last bit of sleep before awakening. The gaunt, careworn features and dusty figures were made plain by the dawn light, but it made the men's skin look as though they were dead. The youth started up with a little cry when his eyes first swept over this pale, motionless mass of men. His confused mind interpreted the forest as a collecting place for corpses. He believed for an instant that he was in the house of the dead, and he did not dare to move lest these corpses start up, squalling and squawking. In a second, however, his mind returned to normal, and he swore at himself. He saw that the corpses were not a present fact, but a prophecy.

He heard then the noise of a fire crackling briskly in the cold air, and, turning his head, he saw his friend pottering busily about a small blaze. A few other figures moved in the fog, and he heard the hard cracking of axe blows.

Suddenly there was a hollow rumble of drums. A distant bugle sang faintly. Similar sounds, varying in strength, came from near and far over the forest. The bugles called to each other like sassy roosters. The thunder of the regimental drums rolled nearby.

The body of men in the woods rustled. There was a general raising of heads. A murmur of voices broke upon the air. In it there was much grumbling of oaths. An officer's bossy voice rang out and quickened the stiff movements of the men. The corpse-colored faces were hidden behind fists that twisted slowly in the eye sockets.

The youth sat up and let out an enormous yawn. "Thunder!" he remarked peevishly. He rubbed his eyes. Then, raising his head, he felt carefully for the bandage over his wound. His friend, perceiving him to be awake, came from the fire. "Well, Henry, old man, how do you feel this morning?" he demanded.

The youth yawned again. His head, in truth, felt exactly like a melon, and there was an unpleasant sensation in his stomach.

"Oh, Lord, I feel pretty bad," he said.

"Thunder!" exclaimed the other. "I hoped you would feel all right this morning. Let's see the bandage—I guess it's slipped." He began to tinker at the wound in rather a clumsy way until the youth exploded.

"Gosh-darn it!" he said in sharp irritation. "You're the hangdest man I ever saw! You wear muffs on your hands. Why in good thunderation can't you be more easy? I'd rather you'd stand off and throw guns at it. Now, go slow, and don't act as if you was nailing down carpet."

He glared with arrogant command at his friend, but the latter answered soothingly. "Well, well, come now, and get some grub," he said. "Then maybe you'll feel better."

At the fireside, the loud young soldier watched over his comrade's wants with tenderness and care. He was very busy arranging the little black tin cups and pouring into them the steaming, iron-colored mixture from a small and sooty tin pail. He had some fresh meat, which he roasted hurriedly on a stick. He sat down then and happily watched the youth eat.

The youth noticed a remarkable change in his comrade since those days of camp life on the river bank. He seemed no more to be continually thinking about his own abilities. He did not get angry at small words that poked fun at his attitudes. He was no longer a loud young soldier. He now showed a quiet belief in his purposes and his abilities. And this inward confidence seemed to make him not care about little words that others aimed at him.

The youth had been used to thinking of his comrade as childish. He saw him as thoughtless, reckless, jealous, and with a boldness that grew only from his lack of experience. The youth wondered when his comrade had made the great discovery that there were many men who would refuse to be managed by him. Apparently, the other had now climbed a peak of wisdom from which he could see himself as a very small thing. And the youth saw that ever after, it would be easier to live in his friend's neighborhood.

His comrade balanced his black coffee cup on his knee. "Well, Henry," he said, "what do you think the chances are? Do you think we'll wallop them?"

The youth thought for a moment. "Day before yesterday," he finally replied, with boldness, "you would have bet you'd lick the whole kit and caboodle all by yourself."

His friend looked slightly amazed. "Would I?" he asked. He thought about it. "Well, perhaps I would," he decided at last. He stared humbly at the fire.

The youth was quite taken aback at this surprising reaction to his remarks. "Oh, no, you wouldn't either," he said hastily.

But the other made a disapproving gesture. "Oh, you needn't mind, Henry," he said. "I believe I was a pretty big fool in those days." He spoke as if years had gone by.

There was a little pause.

"All the officers say we've got the rebs in a pretty tight box," said the friend, clearing his throat. "They all seem to think we've got them just where we want them."

"I don't know about that," the youth replied. "What I saw over on the right makes me think it was the other way about. From where I was, it looked as if we was getting a good pounding yesterday."

"Do you think so?" inquired the friend. "I thought we handled them pretty rough yesterday."

"Not a bit," said the youth. "Why, lord, man, you didn't see nothing of the fight. Why!" Then a sudden thought came to him. "Oh! Jim Conklin's dead."

His friend started. "What? Is he? Jim Conklin?"

The youth spoke slowly. "Yes. He's dead. Shot in the side."

"You don't say so. Jim Conklin . . . poor cuss!"

All about them were other small fires surrounded by men with their little black utensils. From one of these nearby came sudden sharp voices. It appeared that two soldiers had been teasing a huge, bearded man, causing him to spill coffee on his leg. The man had gone into a rage. Stung by his language, his tormentors had made a great show of resenting his oaths. Possibly there was going to be a fight.

The friend arose and went over to them, making pacific motions with his arms. "Oh, here now, boys, what's the use?" he said. "We'll be at the rebs in less than an hour. What's the good fighting among ourselves?"

One of the soldiers turned on him, red-faced and violent. "You needn't come around here with your preaching. I suppose you don't approve of fighting since Charley Morgan licked you; but I don't see what business this here is of yours or anybody else."

"Well, it ain't," said the friend mildly. "Still I hate to see——"

There was a tangled argument.

"Well, he——" said the two, pointing at their opponent.

The huge soldier was quite purple with rage. He

pointed at the two soldiers with his great hand, extending clawlike. "Well, they——"

But while they were arguing, the desire to fight seemed to pass, although they said much to each other. Finally the friend returned to his old seat. In a short while the three opponents could be seen together in a friendly bunch.

"Jimmie Rogers says I'll have to fight him after the battle today," announced the friend, and he again seated himself. "He says he don't allow no interfering in his business. I hate to see the boys fighting among themselves."

The youth laughed. "You're changed a good bit. You ain't at all like you was. I remember when you and that Irish fellow——" He stopped and laughed again.

"No, I didn't used to be that way," said his friend thoughtfully. "That's true enough."

"Well, I didn't mean——" began the youth.

The friend made another gesture of disapproval. "Oh, you needn't mind, Henry."

There was another little pause.

"The regiment lost over half the men yesterday," remarked the friend after a while. "I thought of course they was all dead, but, laws, they kept coming back last night until it seems, after all, we didn't lose but a few. They'd been scattered all over, wandering around in the woods, fighting with other regiments, and everything. Just like you done."

"So?" said the youth.

15

The regiment was standing at the side of a lane, waiting for the command to march. Suddenly the youth remembered the little packet in a faded yellow envelope, which the loud young soldier had entrusted to him. It made him start. He uttered an exclamation and turned toward his comrade.

"Wilson!"

"What?"

His friend, at his side in the ranks, was thoughtfully staring down the road. For some reason his expression at that moment was very meek. The youth, looking at him with sideways glances, felt prompted to change his purpose. "Oh, nothing," he said.

His friend turned his head in some surprise. "Why, what was you going to say?"

"Oh, nothing," repeated the youth.

He resolved not to deal the little blow. It was not necessary to knock his friend on the head with the misguided packet.

He had been afraid of his friend, for he saw how easily questions could make holes in his feelings. Lately, he had assured himself that the changed comrade would not pester him with curiosity. But he felt certain that during the first rest, his friend would ask him to tell about his adventures of the day before.

He was glad that he had a small weapon with which he could lay his comrade low at the first sign of a cross-examination. He was master. It would be he who could laugh and be sarcastic.

The friend had, in a weak hour, spoken with sobs of his own death. He had delivered a sad speech for his funeral, and had doubtless in the packs of letters presented various souvenirs to relatives. But he had not died, and thus he had delivered himself into the hands of the youth.

The youth felt superior to his friend, but he adopted towards him an air of patronizing good humor.

His self-confidence was now entirely restored. Since nothing could now be found out, he did not shrink from an encounter with his comrades. He had performed his mistakes in the dark, so he was still a man.

Indeed, when he remembered yesterday, and looked at it from a distance, he began to see something fine there. He could even boast of his adventures.

His agonies of the past he put out of his sight. He told himself that it was only the doomed and the damned who complained about fate. A man with a full stomach and the respect of his fellows had no business to complain about the ways of the universe.

He did not give a great deal of thought to the battles that lay ahead. He did not need to make any plan for them. He had been taught that many of life's duties were easily avoided. The lesson of yesterday had been that punishment was late and blind. With these facts before him, he did not think he needed to worry about what might happen during the next twenty-four hours. He could leave much to chance. Besides, a faith in himself had secretly blossomed. There was a little flower of confidence growing within him. He was now a man of experience. He had been out among the dragons, he said, and he assured himself that they were not so hideous as he had imagined them. Also they did not sting effectively. A stout heart often resisted, and in doing so, escaped.

And, furthermore, how could they kill him, who was the chosen of gods and fated for greatness?

He remembered how some of the men had run from the battle. As he recalled their terror-struck faces, he felt scorn for them. They had surely been faster and more wild than was absolutely necessary. They were weak mortals. As for himself, he had fled tactfully and with dignity.

He was aroused from his reverie by his friend, who, having blinked at the trees for a time, suddenly coughed in an introductory way, and spoke.

"Fleming!"

"What?"

The friend put his hand up to his mouth and coughed again. He fidgeted in his jacket.

"Well," he gulped at last, "I guess you might as well give me back them letters." His face was flushed.

"All right, Wilson," said the youth. He loosened two buttons of his coat, thrust in his hand, and brought forth the packet. As he extended it to his friend, the latter's face was turned from him.

He had been slow to hand over the packet because he had been trying to think of a comment to make. But he was forced to allow his friend to escape unmolested, and for this gave himself considerable credit. It was a generous thing. His friend seemed to be greatly ashamed. As he watched him, the youth felt his heart grow stronger. He had never had to blush in such a manner for his acts. He was a person of extraordinary virtues. He thought, with pity: "Too bad! Too Bad! The poor devil, it makes him feel tough!"

After this incident, and as he thought of the battle scenes he had seen, he felt quite able to return home and make the hearts of the people glow with stories of war. He could see himself in a room telling stories to listeners. He could exhibit victories. They were insignificant; still, in a district where victories were infrequent, they might shine.

He saw his audience picturing him as the central figure in blazing scenes. And he imagined the alarm of his mother and the young lady at the seminary as they heard his reports. He would destroy their vague feminine belief that brave deeds on the field of battle were possible without risk of life.

16

A sputtering of musketry was always to be heard. Later, the cannon had entered the dispute. In the fog-filled air, their voices made a thudding sound.

The youth's regiment was marched to relieve a command that had lain for a long time in some damp trenches. The men took positions behind a curving line of rifle pits that had been dug, like a ditch, along the line of woods. Before them was a level stretch, dotted with short, deformed stumps. From the wood beyond came the dull popping of the skirmishers and pickets, firing in the fog. From the right came the noise of a terrific battle.

The men settled in behind the small embankment and relaxed while awaiting their turn. Many had their backs to the firing. The youth's friend lay down, buried his face in his arms, and almost instantly fell asleep.

The youth leaned against the brown dirt and peered over at the woods and up and down the line. Curtains of trees got in the way of his line of vision. He could see the low line of trenches for only a short distance. A few idle flags were perched on the dirt hills. Behind them were rows of dark bodies with a few heads sticking curiously over the top.

Always the noise of skirmishers came from the

woods on the front and left, and the din on the right had grown to frightful proportions. The guns were roaring without an instant's pause for breath. It seemed that the cannon had come from everywhere and were engaged in a stupendous argument. It became impossible to make a sentence heard. The youth wanted to make a joke—a quotation from a newspaper. He wanted to say, "All quiet on the Rappahannock," but the guns would not permit even a comment on their uproar. He never success-fully finished the sentence. But at last the guns stopped, and among the men in the rifle pits, rumors again flew like birds. They heard stories of hesitation and indecision on the part of their gener-als. They heard stories of disaster, with many proofs. The growing din of musketry on the right underlined the army's predicament.

The men were discouraged and began to mut-ter. They made gestures as if to say, "Ah, what more can we do?" They were bewildered by the alleged news, and could not fully understand a defeat.

Before the gray mists had been totally burned away by the sun, the regiment was retiring care-fully through the woods. The disordered, hurrying lines of the enemy could sometimes be seen down through the groves and little fields. They were yelling, shrill and exultant.

At this sight, the youth became greatly enraged. He exploded in loud sentences. "By jiminey, we're generalled by a lot of lunkheads."

"More than one fellow has said that today," observed a man.

His friend, recently awakened, was still very drowsy. He looked behind him until his mind took in the meaning of the movement. Then he sighed. "Oh, well, I suppose we got licked," he remarked sadly.

The youth had a thought that it would not be fair for him to condemn other men. He tried to restrain himself, but the words on his tongue were too bitter. He presently began a long and complicated denunciation of the commander of the forces.

"Maybe it wasn't all his fault—not all together. He did the best he knew. It's our luck to get licked often," said his friend in a weary tone. He was trudging along with stooped shoulders and shifting eyes, like a man who has been caned and kicked.

"Well, don't we fight like the devil? Don't we do all that men can?" demanded the youth loudly.

He was secretly surprised to hear himself saying this. For a moment his face lost its boldness, and he looked guiltily about him. But no one questioned his right to deal in such words, and soon he recovered his air of courage. He went on to repeat a statement he had heard going from group to group at the camp that morning. "The brigadier said he never saw a new regiment fight the way we fought yesterday, didn't he? And we didn't do better than many another regiment, did we? Well, then, you can't say it's the army's fault, can you?"

In his reply, the friend's voice was stern. "Of course not," he said. "No man dare say we don't fight like the devil. No man will ever dare say it. The boys fight like hell-roosters. But still—still, we don't have no luck."

"Well, then, if we fight like the devil and don't ever whip, it must be the general's fault," said the youth decisively. "And I don't see any sense in fighting and fighting and fighting, yet always losing through some darned old lunkhead of a general."

A sarcastic man who was tramping at the youth's side then spoke lazily. "Maybe you think you fought the whole battle yesterday, Fleming," he remarked.

The speech pierced the youth. Inwardly he was reduced to a miserable pulp by these accidental words. His legs trembled. He cast a frightened glance at the sarcastic man.

"Why, no," he hastened to say, "I don't think I fought the whole battle yesterday."

But the other seemed not to have any deeper meaning. Apparently, he had no information. It was merely his habit. "Oh!" he replied in the same tone of calm derision.

The youth, nevertheless, felt a threat. His mind shrank from going near the danger, and thereafter he was silent. The sarcastic man's words took from him all loud moods that would make him stand out. He suddenly became a modest person.

There was low-toned talk among the troops. The officers were impatient and snappy, their faces clouded with the tales of misfortune. The troops, sifting through the forest, were sullen. In the youth's company once a man's laugh rang out. A dozen soldiers turned their faces quickly toward him and frowned with vague displeasure.

The noise of firing dogged their footsteps. Sometimes it seemed to be driven farther away, but it always returned with increased boldness. The men muttered and cursed, throwing black looks in its direction.

In a clear space the troops were at last halted. Regiments and brigades, broken and detached through their encounters with thickets, grew together again. Lines were faced toward the pursuing bark of the enemy's infantry.

This noise increased to a loud and joyous burst. Then, as the sun threw illuminating rays into the gloomy thickets, it broke out in prolonged roarings. The woods began to crackle as if on fire.

"Whoop-a-dadee," said a man. "Here we are! Everybody fighting. Blood and destruction."

"I was willing to bet they would attack as soon as the sun got fairly up," savagely asserted the lieutenant who commanded the youth's company. He jerked without mercy at his little moustache. He strode to and fro with dark dignity in the rear of his men, who were lying down behind whatever protection they had collected.

A battery had trundled into position in the rear and was thoughtfully shelling the distance. The regiment, not attacked as yet, waited for the moment when the woods before them should be slashed by the lines of flame. There was much growling and swearing.

"Good God," the youth grumbled. "We're always being chased around like rats! It makes me sick. Nobody seems to know where we go or why. We just get fired around from pillar to post, and get licked here and get licked there, and nobody knows what it's done for. It makes a man feel like a damn kitten in a bag. Now, I would like to know what the eternal thunders we was marched into these woods for anyhow, unless it was to give the rebs a regular pot shot at us. We came in here and

got our legs all tangled up in these cussed briers, and then we begin to fight and the rebs had an easy time of it. Don't tell me it's just luck! I know better. It's this darned old——"

The friend seemed weary, but he interrupted his comrade with a voice of calm confidence. "It'll turn out all right in the end," he said.

"Oh, the devil it will! You always talk like a dog-hanged parson. Don't tell me! I know——"

At this time there was an interruption by the lieutenant, who vented some of his own dissatisfaction upon his men. "You boys shut right up! There's no need of your wasting your breath in long-winded arguments about this and that and the other. You've been jawing like a lot of old hens. All you've got to do is to fight, and you'll get plenty of that in about ten minutes. Less talking and more fighting is what's best for you boys. I never saw such gabbling jackasses."

He paused, ready to pounce on any man who might have the boldness to reply. No words being said, he resumed his dignified pacing.

"There's too much chin music and too little fighting in this war, anyhow," he said to them, turning his head for a final remark.

The day had grown more white, until the sun shed its full radiance on the forest. A sort of a gust of battle came sweeping toward that part of the line where the youth's regiment was. The front shifted a trifle to meet it squarely. There was a wait. In this part of the field, the intense moments that precede the storm passed slowly.

A single rifle flashed in a thicket in front of the regiment. In an instant it was joined by many others. A mighty song of clashes and crashes went sweeping through the woods. The guns in the rear suddenly involved themselves in a hideous brawl with another band of guns. The battle roar settled to a rolling thunder, like a single, long explosion.

In the regiment, there was a peculiar kind of hesitation in the men. They were worn, exhausted, having slept little and labored much. They rolled their eyes toward the advancing battle as they stood awaiting the shock. Some shrank and flinched. They stood like men tied to stakes.

17

This advance of the enemy made the youth fume with rage. He beat his foot on the ground. He scowled with hate at the swirling smoke that was approaching like a phantom flood. It was maddening that the foe would give him no rest, would give him no time to sit down and think. Yesterday he had fought and had fled rapidly. There had been many adventures. For today, he felt that he had earned a chance to rest and think. He could have enjoyed telling others about what he had seen or discussing with them the course of the war. It was also important that his body should have time to recover. He was sore and stiff from his experiences. He had had enough work, and he wished to rest.

But those other men seemed never to grow weary. They were fighting with their old speed. He had a wild hate for the foe. Yesterday, when he had imagined the universe to be against him, he had hated the universe. Today he hated the army of the foe with the same great hatred. He was not going to be tormented out of his life, like a kitten chased by boys, he said. It was not well to drive men into corners; at those moments, they could all develop teeth and claws.

He leaned and spoke into his friend's ear. He shook his fist at the woods. "If they keep on chasing us, by God, they'd better watch out. Can't stand too much."

The friend twisted his head and made a calm reply. "If they keep on chasing us, they'll drive us all into the river."

The youth cried out savagely at this statement. He crouched behind a little tree, with his eyes burning hatefully, and his teeth set in a dog-like snarl. The awkward bandage was still on his head. On the bandage, over his wound, there was a spot of dry blood. His hair was mussed, and some straggling locks hung over the cloth of the badge down toward his forehead. His jacket and shirt were open at the throat, and exposed his young, bronzed neck. Frequent swallowing could be seen at his throat.

The winds of battle had swept all about the regiment, until the one rifle, instantly followed by others, flashed in its front. A moment later the regiment roared forth its sudden response. A dense wall of smoke settled slowly down. It was furiously cut by the knifelike fire from the rifles.

To the youth, the fighters resembled animals tossed for a death struggle into a dark pit. It felt as if he and his fellows were cornered. They were always trying to push back the fierce attacks of slippery creatures. Their rifle firing seemed to have no effect on the bodies of their foes. It seemed as if the enemy could avoid the bullets. They came through, between, and around them with unopposed skill.

When, in a dream, it occurred to the youth that his rifle was useless, he lost sense of everything but his hate. He wanted only to smash the glittering smile of victory that he could feel on the faces of his enemies.

The blue, smoke-swallowed line curled and writhed like a snake that had been stepped on. It swung its ends to and fro in an agony of fear and rage.

The youth was not conscious that he was standing up. He did not know the direction of the ground. Indeed, once he even lost his balance and fell heavily. He was up again immediately. One thought went through the chaos of his brain at the time. He wondered if he had fallen because he had been shot. But the suspicion flew away at once. He did not think more of it.

He had taken up a first position behind the little tree, determined to hold it against the world. He had not thought it possible that his army could succeed that day. From this, he felt the ability to fight harder. But the throng had surged in all ways. He lost all sense of directions and locations, except that he knew where the enemy was.

The flames bit him, and the hot smoke broiled his skin. His rifle barrel grew so hot that normally he could not have held it. But he kept on stuffing cartridges into it, and pounding them with his clanking, bending ramrod. When he aimed at some charging form through the smoke, he pulled his trigger with a fierce grunt, as if he were hitting someone with his fist with all his strength.

When the enemy seemed to fall back before him and his fellows, he went instantly forward. When he was forced to fall back again, he did it slowly, in steps of angry despair.

Once, in his intense hate, he was almost alone. He was firing when all those near him had stopped. He was so absorbed that he was not aware of the lull.

He was brought back by a hoarse laugh. A sentence came to his ears in a voice of contempt and amazement. "You infernal fool, don't you know enough to quit when there ain't anything to shoot at? Good God!"

He turned and, pausing with his rifle thrown half into position, looked at the blue line of his comrades. During this moment of leisure, they seemed all to be staring with astonishment at him. They had become spectators. Turning to the front again he saw, under lifted smoke, a deserted ground.

He looked bewildered for a moment. Then his eyes showed a return of intelligence. "Oh," he said, comprehending.

He returned to his comrades and threw himself upon the ground. He sprawled like a man who had been beaten. His flesh seemed strangely on fire, and the sounds of the battle continued in his ears. He groped blindly for his canteen.

The lieutenant seemed drunk with fighting. He called out to the youth, "By heavens, if I had ten thousand wildcats like you, I could tear the stomach out of this war in less than a week!" He puffed out his chest as he said it.

Some of the men muttered and looked at the youth with awe. They had been watching him as he had gone on loading and firing and cursing without pause. They now looked upon him as a war devil.

The friend came staggering to him. There was some fright and dismay in his voice. "Are you all right, Fleming? Do you feel all right? There ain't nothing the matter with you, Henry, is there?"

"No," said the youth with difficulty. His throat seemed full of knobs and burrs.

These incidents made the youth think. He realized that he had been a barbarian, a beast. He had fought like a pagan who defends his religion. He saw that it was fine, wild, and in some ways, easy. By this struggle he had overcome obstacles that he had thought of as mountains. They had fallen like paper peaks, and he was now what he called a hero. And he had not been aware of the process. He had slept and, awakening, found himself a knight.

He lay and basked in the occasional stares of his comrades. Their faces were various shades of black from the burned power. They were reeking with perspiration, and their breaths came hard and wheezing.

"Hot work! Hot work!" cried the lieutenant. He walked up and down, restless and eager. Sometimes his voice could be heard in a wild laugh.

When he had a particularly profound thought on the science of war, he unconsciously addressed himself to the youth.

There was some grim rejoicing by the men. "By thunder, I bet this army will never see another new regiment like us!"

"You bet!"

> "A dog, a woman, and a walnut tree,
> The more you beat them, the better they be!

That's like us."

"Lost a pile of men, they did. If an old woman swept up the woods, she'd get a dustpanful."

"Yes, and if she'll come around again in about an hour, she'll get a pile more."

The forest was still filled with the noise of battle. From off under the trees came the clatter of musketry. Each distant thicket was like a porcupine with quills of flame. A cloud of dark smoke, as from smoldering ruins, went up toward the sun, now bright and gay in the blue sky.

18

The ragged line had a pause for some minutes. But during this pause, the struggle in the forest grew, until the trees seemed to shake from the firing and the ground to shake from the rushing of the men. The voices of the cannon were mingled in a long and interminable brawl. It seemed difficult to live in such an atmosphere. The chests of the men strained for a bit of freshness, and their throats craved water.

There was a soldier who had been shot through the body. During this lull, he cried out. Perhaps he had been calling out during the fighting also, but at that time no one had heard him.

"Who is it? Who is it?"

"It's Jimmie Rogers. Jimmie Rogers."

When they first saw him, there was a sudden halt, as if they feared to go near. He was thrashing about in the grass, twisting his body into many strange positions. He was screaming loudly. Their hesitation seemed to fill him with a tremendous contempt, and he damned them in shrieked sentences.

The youth's friend believed there was a stream nearby, and he obtained permission to go for some water. Immediately canteens were showered on him. "Fill mine, will you?" "Bring me some, too."

"And me, too." He departed, loaded down. The youth went with his friend. He wanted to throw his heated body into the stream and, soaking there, drink quarts.

They made a hurried search for the supposed stream, but did not find it. "No water here," said the youth. They turned without delay and began to retrace their steps.

From their position as they again faced toward the place of fighting, they could see more of the battle than when the smoke of the line had blurred their vision. They could see dark stretches winding along the land. On one cleared space, a row of guns was making gray clouds, which were filled with flashes of orange-colored flame. Over some foliage they could see the roof of a house. One window, glowing a deep murder red, shone squarely through the leaves. From the house a tall, leaning tower of smoke went far into the sky.

Looking over their own troops, they saw masses slowly getting into regular form. The sunlight made twinkling points of the bright steel. To the rear, there was a glimpse of a distant roadway as it curved over a slope. It was crowded with retreating infantry. From all the forest arose the smoke and bluster of the battle. The air was always filled with a roar.

Near where they stood, shells were flip-flapping and hooting. Occasional bullets buzzed in the air and splattered into the tree trunks. Wounded men and other stragglers were slinking through the woods.

Looking down an aisle of the grove, the youth and his companion saw a jangling general and his staff almost ride over a wounded man, who was crawling on his hands and knees. The general reined his horse, guiding it with skillful horsemanship past the man. The wounded man scrambled in wild haste. His strength evidently failed him as he reached a place of safety. One of his arms suddenly weakened, and he fell, sliding over upon his back. He lay stretched out, breathing gently.

A moment later the small group was directly in front of the two soldiers. Another officer, riding with the skillful abandon of a cowboy, galloped his horse to a position directly in front of the general. The two unnoticed foot soldiers made a little show of going on, but they lingered near in the desire to overhear the conversation. Perhaps, they thought, some great historical things would be said.

The general, whom the boys knew as the commander of their division, looked at the other officer and spoke coolly, as if he were criticizing his clothes. "The enemy's forming over there for another charge," he said. "It will be directed against Whiterside, and I fear they'll break through there unless we work like thunder to stop them."

The other swore at his restive horse, and then cleared his throat. He made a gesture toward his cap. "It'll be hell to pay stopping them," he said shortly.

"I presume so," remarked the general. Then he began to talk rapidly and in a lower tone. He frequently illustrated his words with a pointing finger. The two infantrymen could hear nothing, until finally he asked, "What troops can you spare?"

The officer who rode like a cowboy thought for an instant. "Well," he said, "I had to order in the

12th to help the 76th, and I haven't really got any. But there's the 304th. They fight like a lot of mule drivers. I can spare them best of any."

The youth and his friend exchanged glances of astonishment. The general spoke sharply. "Get them ready, then. I'll watch developments from here, and send you word when to start them. It will happen in five minutes."

As the other officer saluted and started away, the general called out to him in a sober voice, "I don't believe many of your mule drivers will get back."

The other shouted something in reply. He smiled.

With scared faces, the youth and his companion hurried back to the line.

These happenings had taken an incredibly short time. Yet the youth felt that in that time, he had grown older. New eyes were given to him. The most startling thing was to learn suddenly that he was very insignificant. The officer spoke of the regiment as if he were talking about a broom. Some part of the woods needed sweeping, perhaps. He merely pointed out a broom, not really caring what happened to it afterwards. It was war, no doubt, but it appeared strange.

As the two boys approached the line, the lieutenant saw them and swelled with anger. "Fleming—Wilson—how long does it take you to get water, anyhow? Where you been to?"

But he stopped talking when he saw their eyes, which were large with great tales. "We're going to charge! We're going to charge!" cried the youth's friend, hurrying with his news.

"Charge?" said the lieutenant. "Charge? Well, by God! Now, this is real fighting." Over his dirty face there went a boastful smile. "Charge? Well, by God!"

A little group of soldiers surrounded the two youths. "Are we, sure enough? Well, I'll be darned! Charge? What for? What at? Wilson, you're lying."

"I hope to die," said the youth, in a tone of angry protest. "Sure as shooting, I tell you."

And his friend spoke in re-enforcement. "Not by a blame sight, he ain't lying. We heard them talking."

They caught sight of two figures on horseback a short distance from them. One was the colonel of the regiment, and the other was the officer who had received orders from the commander of the division. They were gesturing at each other. The soldier, pointing at them, interpreted the scene.

One man had a final objection: "How could you hear them talking?" But most of the men nodded, admitting that previously the two friends had told the truth.

They settled back with airs of having accepted the matter. And they thought about it, expressing their feelings in a hundred different ways. Many tightened their belts carefully and hitched at their trousers.

A moment later, the officers began to bustle among the men. They pushed them into a more compact mass and into a better alignment. They chased stragglers, and they fumed at a few men who acted as if they had decided not to move. They were like critical shepherds struggling with sheep.

Soon, the regiment seemed to draw itself up

and heave a deep breath. None of the men's faces suggested deep thoughts. The soldiers were bent and stooped, like sprinters before the starting signal. Many pairs of glinting eyes peered from the grimy faces toward the curtains of the deeper woods. They seemed to be making calculations of time and distance.

They were surrounded by the noises of the monstrous argument between the two armies. The world was interested in other matters. Apparently the regiment had its small affair to itself.

The youth, turning, shot a quick, questioning glance at his friend. The latter looked at the youth in the same way. They were the only ones who shared a secret knowledge. "Mule drivers—hell to pay—don't believe many will get back." Still, they saw no hesitation in each other's faces. They nodded silently when a shaggy man near them said in a meek voice, "We'll get swallowed."

19

The youth stared at the land in front of him. Its leaves now seemed to hide powers and horrors. He was unaware of the orders that started the charge, although from the corners of his eyes he saw an officer, who looked like a boy on horseback, come galloping, waving his hat. Suddenly he felt a straining and heaving among the men. The line fell slowly forward like a toppling wall. With a gasp that was intended to be a cheer, the regiment began its journey. The youth was pushed and jostled for a moment before he understood the movement at all, but he quickly lunged ahead and began to run.

He fixed his eye on a distant clump of trees, where he had concluded the enemy were to be met. He ran toward it as a goal. He ran desperately, believing that it was mainly a question of getting over an unpleasant matter as quickly as possible. His face was drawn hard and tight. His eyes were fixed. And with his soiled uniform, his flushed face surmounted by the dingy rag with its spot of blood, and his wildly swinging rifle and banging equipment, he looked like an insane soldier.

As the regiment swung out into a cleared space, the woods in front of it awakened. Yellow flames leaped toward it from many directions. The forest made a tremendous objection.

The line lurched straight for a moment. Then the right wing swung forward. It in turn was surpassed by the left. Then the center moved to the front, until the regiment was a wedge-shaped mass. But an instant later, the opposition of the bushes, trees, and uneven places on the ground split the command and scattered it into separate clusters.

The youth, light-footed, was unconsciously out in front. He kept watching the clump of trees. From all places near it, the yell of the enemy could be heard. The little flames of the rifles leaped from it. The song of the bullets was in the air, and shells snarled among the treetops. One shell tumbled directly into the middle of a hurrying group and exploded in crimson fury. There was an instant's spectacle of a man throwing up his hands to shield his eyes.

Other men, punched by bullets, fell in grotesque agonies. The regiment left a trail of bodies.

They had passed into a clearer atmosphere. The new appearance of the landscape was like a revelation to them. They could clearly see some men working madly at a battery. The opposing infantry's lines were defined by the gray walls and fringes of smoke.

It seemed to the youth that he saw everything. Each blade of the green grass was bold and clear. The brown or gray trunks of the trees showed each roughness of their surfaces. And the men of the regiment, with their bulging eyes and sweating faces, running madly, or falling as if thrown headlong—all were taken in. His mind took a firm impression, so that afterward everything was pictured and explained to him, except why he himself was there. The men, pitching forward insanely, had burst into cheering, moblike and barbaric. It made a mad enthusiasm that, it seemed, would not be able to stop itself. It was the delirium that is blind to the odds, even in the face of despair and death. It is a temporary but sublime absence of selfishness.

Soon the straining pace ate up the energies of the men. As if by agreement, the leaders began to slacken their speed. The volleys directed against them seemed to have the effect of wind. Among some stolid trees, the regiment began to falter and hesitate. The men, staring intently, began to wait for some of the distant walls of smoke to move and reveal the scene to them. Since much of their strength and their breath had vanished, they returned to caution. They were become men again.

The youth had a vague belief that he had run miles. He thought, in a way, that he was now in some new and unknown land.

The moment the regiment stopped advancing, the splutter of musketry became a roar. Long fringes of smoke spread out. From the top of a small hill came level belchings of yellow flame that caused an inhuman whistling in the air.

The men, now that they were halted, could see some of their comrades dropping with moans and shrieks. A few lay under foot, quiet or wailing. And now for an instant the men stood, their rifles slack in their hands, and watched the regiment dwindle. They appeared dazed and stupid. They stared woodenly at the sights, and lowering their eyes, looked from face to face. It was a strange pause, and a strange silence.

Then, above the sounds of the commotion, arose the roar of the lieutenant. He strode suddenly forth, his childish face black with rage. "Come on, you fools!" he bellowed. "Come on! You can't stay here. You must come on." He said more, but much of it could not be understood.

He started rapidly forward, with his head turned toward the men. "Come on," he was shouting. The men stared at him with blank eyes. He was obliged to halt and retrace his steps. He stood with his back to the enemy and delivered gigantic curses to the men. His body shook from the weight and force of his profanity.

The friend of the youth rallied. Lurching suddenly forward and dropping to his knees, he fired an angry shot at the woods. This action awakened the men. They stopped huddling like sheep. They seemed suddenly to think of their weapons, and at once began firing. Urged on by their officers, they began to move forward. The regiment started unevenly with many jolts and jerks. The men stopped every few paces to fire, and in this manner moved slowly on from tree to tree.

The opposition in front of them grew as they advanced. It seemed that all ways forward were barred by the thin leaping tongues of rifle fire. To the right, an ominous noise could be dimly heard. The smoke made it difficult for the regiment to proceed with intelligence. As he passed through each curling mass of smoke, the youth wondered what would confront him on the farther side.

The regiment went painfully forward until a space opened between them and the enemy lines. Here, crouching behind some trees, the men held on desperately, as if threatened by a wave. They look wild-eyed, and seemed to be amazed at this furious disturbance they had stirred up. Their expressions also suggested that they did not feel responsible for being there. It was as if they had been driven. The whole affair seemed to be a mystery to many of them.

As they halted thus, the lieutenant again began to bellow profanely. Regardless of the threats of the bullets, he went about coaxing, scolding, and damning. His lips, which usually were in a soft and childlike curve, were now writhed into unholy shapes. He swore by all possible gods.

Once he grabbed the youth by the arm. "Come on, you lunkhead!" he roared. "Come on! We'll all get killed if we stay here. We've only got to go across that lot. And then——" The remainder of his idea disappeared in a blue haze of curses.

The youth stretched forth his arm. "Cross there?" His mouth was puckered in doubt and awe.

"Certainly. Just across the lot! We can't stay here," screamed the lieutenant. He poked his face close to the youth and waved his bandaged hand. "Come on!" He grappled with him as if for a wrestling bout. It was as if he planned to drag the youth by the ear on to the assault.

The private felt a sudden anger against his officer. He wrenched fiercely and shook him off.

"Come on yourself, then," he yelled. There was a bitter challenge in his voice.

They galloped together down the regimental front. The friend scrambled after them. In front of the regimental flag the three men began to bawl, "Come on!" They danced and twirled like tortured savages.

The flag swept toward them. The men wavered in indecision for a moment. Then with a long, wailing cry, the dilapidated regiment surged forward and began its new journey.

Over the field went the scurrying mass. It was a handful of men splattered into the faces of the enemy. Toward it instantly sprang the yellow tongues. A vast quantity of blue smoke hung before them. A mighty banging made ears useless.

The youth ran like a madman to reach the woods before a bullet could discover him. He ducked his head low, like a football player. In his haste his eyes almost closed, and the scene was a wild blur. Saliva stood at the corners of his mouth.

Within him, as he hurled himself forward, was born a love for his flag which was near him. It was a creation of beauty and strength. It was a radiant goddess that bent its form to him. It was a woman, hating and loving, that called him with the voice of his hopes. Because no harm could come to it, it seemed to him to have power. He kept near, as if it could be a saver of lives.

In the mad scramble he was aware that the color sergeant flinched suddenly, as if struck by a club. He stumbled, and then became motionless, save for his shaking knees.

The youth made a spring and clutched at the

pole. At the same instant, his friend grabbed it from the other side. They jerked at it, but the color sergeant was dead, and the corpse would not give up its trust. For a moment there was a grim encounter. The dead man, swinging with bent back, seemed to be stubbornly fighting for the possession of the flag.

It was past in an instant of time. They wrenched the flag furiously from the dead man. As they turned again, the corpse swayed forward with bowed head. One arm swung high, and the curved hand fell with heavy protest on the friend's unheeding shoulder.

20

When the two youths turned with the flag, they saw that much of the regiment had crumbled away. The discouraged remnant was coming slowly back. The men, having thrown themselves forward, had now exhausted their strength. They slowly retreated, with their faces still toward the woods, and their hot rifles still replying to the din. Several officers were giving orders, their voices screaming. "Where in hell you going?" the lieutenant was asking in a sarcastic howl. And a red-bearded officer, whose trumpet-like voice could plainly be heard, was commanding, "Shoot into them! Shoot into them, God damn their souls!" There was a mixture of screeches, in which the men were ordered to do conflicting and impossible things.

The youth and his friend had a small scuffle over the flag. "Give it to me!" "No, let me keep it!" Each was satisfied to let the other carry it. But each felt obliged to show, by offering to carry the flag, that he was willing to risk himself further. The youth roughly pushed his friend away.

The regiment fell back to the trees. There it halted for a moment to shoot at some dark forms that had begun to follow it. Soon it began to march forward again, dodging among the tree trunks. By the time the thinned-out regiment had again reached the first open space, they were receiving a fast and merciless fire. There seemed to be mobs all around them.

Most of the men were discouraged, their spirits worn by the confusion. They acted as if they were stunned. They accepted the attacking bullets with bowed and weary heads. They felt that they had tried to conquer an unconquerable thing. There was no point in struggling against walls. There was no point to battering themselves against granite. From this, there arose a feeling that they had been betrayed. They glared at some of the officers, particularly at the red-bearded one with the voice of a trumpet.

However, men in the rear of the regiment continued to shoot at the advancing foes. The enemy seemed resolved to make every trouble. The youthful lieutenant had his back toward them. He had been shot in the arm. It hung straight and rigid. Occasionally he would forget about it and try to emphasize an oath with a sweeping gesture. The increased pain caused him to swear with incredible power.

The youth went along with slipping feet. A scowl of shame and rage was on his face. He had expected to prove the officer wrong who had referred to him and his fellows as mule drivers. But he saw that it could not happen. His dream had collapsed when the mule drivers had hesitated in the little clearing, and had then had turned back. Now the retreat of the mule drivers was a march of shame to him.

He directed a gaze of hatred toward the enemy. But his greater hatred was toward the man who, not knowing him, had called him a mule driver.

He knew that he and his comrades had failed to do anything that might make the officer regret his words. He had pictured red letters of revenge: "We are mule drivers, are we?" And now he had to throw them away.

His pride made him keep holding the flag up. He urged his fellows, pushing against their chests with his free hand. To those he knew well, he made frantic appeals, begging them by name. Between him and the lieutenant, who was near to losing his mind with rage, he felt a subtle fellowship and equality. They supported each other in all kinds of hoarse, howling protests.

But the regiment was a machine run down. The soldiers who wanted to retreat slowly were continually shaken by the knowledge that others were speeding back to the lines. It was difficult to think of reputation when others were thinking of saving their skins. Wounded men were left crying on this black journey.

The smoke and flames blew noisily. The youth, peering once through a sudden rift in a cloud, saw a brown mass of troops. They appeared to be thousands. A fierce-hued flag flashed before his vision.

Immediately, as if the lifting of the smoke had been planned, the enemy troops burst into a yell. A hundred flames shot toward the retreating band. As the regiment doggedly replied, a gray cloud again came between the armies. The youth had to depend again upon his ears, which were buzzing from the mixture of musketry and yells.

The way seemed unending. In the clouded

haze, men became panic-stricken with the idea that their regiment was lost and was going in the wrong direction. Once the men at the head of the wild procession turned and came pushing back against their comrades. They screamed that they were being fired on from what they thought were their own lines. At this cry, a hysterical fear and dismay struck the troops. A soldier, who up to now had wanted to make the regiment into a little band that would proceed calmly amid the difficulties, suddenly sank down and buried his face in his arms. From another came a shrill cry filled with profane references to a general. Men ran back and forth looking for roads of escape. Bullets hit men regularly, as if they were following a schedule.

The youth walked into the midst of the mob. With his flag in his hands, he took a stand as if he expected someone to push him to the ground. Without realizing it, he adopted the stance of the flag bearer in the fight the day before. He wiped his forehead with a trembling hand. He breathed with difficulty. He was choking during this small wait for the crisis.

His friend came to him. "Well, Henry, I guess this is goodbye John."

"Oh, shut up, you damned fool!" replied the youth, and he would not look at the other.

The officers labored to beat the mass into a proper circle to face the enemy. The ground was uneven and torn. The men curled into depressions and fitted themselves snugly behind whatever would stop a bullet.

The youth noted with vague surprise that the lieutenant was standing silently with his legs far apart and his sword held like a cane. The youth wondered what had happened to his voice.

There was something curious in this little intent pause of the lieutenant. He was like a baby that fixes its eyes on a distant toy. His soft underlip quivered from words whispered to himself.

Some smoke curled slowly. The men, hiding from the bullets, waited anxiously for it to lift and disclose the condition of the regiment.

The silent ranks were suddenly aroused by the eager voice of the youthful lieutenant bawling out, "Here they come! Right onto us, by God!" His further words were lost in a roar of thunder from the men's rifles.

The youth's eyes had instantly turned in the direction indicated by the lieutenant. The haze disclosed a body of enemy soldiers. They were so near that he could see their faces. The types of faces seemed familiar. Also he noticed with dim amazement that their uniforms were rather cheerful in effect, being light gray, accented with a brilliant-hued facing. Moreover, the clothes seemed new.

These troops had apparently been going forward cautiously, their rifles held in readiness. Then the young lieutenant had seen them, and their movement had been interrupted by the volley from the blue regiment. They seemed to have been unaware of the nearness of their dark-suited foes, or they had taken the wrong direction. Almost instantly they were blocked from view by the smoke from the rifles of his companions. He strained to see what the volley had accomplished, but the smoke hung before him.

The two bodies of troops exchanged blows like

a pair of boxers. The fast, angry firings went back and forth. The curving front bristled with flashes. The youth ducked and dodged for a time and achieved a few unsatisfactory views of the enemy. There appeared to be many of them, and they were replying swiftly. They seemed to be moving toward the blue regiment, step by step. He seated himself gloomily on the ground with his flag between his knees.

But the blows of the enemy began to grow weaker. Fewer bullets ripped the air. Finally, when the men slackened to learn of the fight, they could see only dark, floating smoke. The regiment lay still and stared. Soon the smoke began to roll away, and the men saw a ground empty of fighters. It would have been an empty stage if it were not for a few corpses that lay thrown and twisted into fantastic shapes on the grass.

At the sight, many of the men in blue sprang from behind their covers and made an ungainly dance of joy.

Their eyes burned, and a hoarse cheer broke from their dry lips.

It had begun to seem as if events were trying to prove that they were powerless. The purpose of their battles had been to demonstrate that the men could not fight well. When they were about to give in to these opinions, the latest fight had showed them what they were able to do.

The driving force of enthusiasm was theirs again. They gazed about them with looks of pride, feeling new trust in the grim weapons in their hands. And they were men.

21

Soon they knew that no firing threatened them. All ways seemed once more opened to them. They could see the dusty blue lines of their friends a short distance away. In the distance there were many colossal noises, but in this part of the field there was a sudden stillness.

They perceived that they were free. The depleted band drew a long breath of relief and gathered itself into a bunch to complete its trip.

In this last length of journey, the men began to show strange emotions. They hurried with nervous fear. Some who had been steadfast in the grimmest moments now could not hide their anxiety. It was perhaps that they dreaded to be killed in unimportant ways after the time for proper battlefield deaths had passed. Or, perhaps, they thought it would be too ironical to get killed when they were on the verge of safety. With backward looks of distress, they hurried.

As they approached their own lines, there was some sarcasm from a gaunt and bronzed regiment that lay resting in the shade of trees. Questions floated to them.

"Where the hell you been?"

"What you coming back for?"

"Why didn't you stay there?"

"Was it warm out there, sonny?"

"Going home now, boys?"

One shouted in taunting mimicry: "Oh, mother, come quick and look at the soldiers!"

There was no reply from the bruised and battered regiment, except that one man challenged everybody to fist fights, and the red-bearded officer walked near and glared at a tall captain in the other regiment. But the lieutenant silenced the man who wished to fist fight. The tall captain, flushing at the little fanfare of the red-bearded one, was obliged to look intently at some trees.

The youth was deeply stung by these remarks. From under his creased brows he glowered with hate at the mockers. He thought of a few revenges. Still, many in the regiment hung their heads like criminals, so that the men trudged with sudden heaviness. It was as if their bent shoulders carried the coffin of their honor. The youthful lieutenant began to curse softly.

When they arrived at their old position, they turned to look at the ground over which they had charged.

The youth was astonished. He discovered that the distances they had covered were trivial and ridiculous. The trees, where much had taken place, seemed incredibly near. Now that he thought about it, he saw that the time, too, had been short. He wondered at the number of emotions and events that had been crowded into such little spaces.

It seemed, then, that there was bitter justice in the speeches of the veterans. He glanced scornfully at his fellows who strewed the ground, choking with dust, red from perspiration, misty-eyed, scruffy.

They were gulping at their canteens, eager to wring every drop of water from them. They wiped their swollen and watery faces with coat sleeves and bunches of grass.

However, to the youth there was considerable joy in thinking about his performance during the charge. Up to now, he had done little to admire himself for. Now there was much satisfaction in quietly thinking of his actions. He remembered bits of color that in the flurry had stamped themselves in his memory.

As the regiment lay heaving from its hot exertions, the officer who had named them as mule drivers came galloping along the line. He had lost his cap. His tousled hair streamed wildly, and his face was dark with annoyance and anger. His temper was displayed more clearly by the way he managed his horse. He jerked savagely at his bridle, stopping the hard-breathing animal with a furious pull near the colonel of the regiment. He immediately exploded in a bawling out that some of the men could overhear. They were suddenly alert, being always curious about black words between officers.

"Oh, thunder, MacChesnay, what an awful bull you made of this thing!" began the officer. He tried to speak in low tones, but his anger caused his voice to carry. "What an awful mess you made! Good Lord, man, you stopped about a hundred feet this side of a very pretty success! If your men had gone a hundred feet farther, you would have made a great charge, but as it is—what a lot of mud diggers you've got anyway!"

The men, listening with bated breath, now

turned their curious eyes upon the colonel. They were interested in this affair.

The colonel stood up straight and put one hand out, as if to give a speech. He looked as if his feelings had been hurt. It was as if a deacon had been accused of stealing. The men were wiggling in excitement.

But suddenly the colonel's manner changed from that of a deacon to that of a Frenchman. He shrugged his shoulders. "Oh, well, general, we went as far as we could," he said calmly.

"As far as you could? Did you, by God?" snorted the other. "Well, that wasn't very far, was it?" he added, with a glance of cold contempt into the other's eyes. "Not very far, I think. You were intended to make a diversion in favor of Whiterside. How well you succeeded your own ears can now tell you." He wheeled his horse and rode stiffly away.

The colonel, told to listen to the noises of battle coming from the woods to the left, broke out in vague damnations.

The lieutenant, who had listened with an air of powerless rage to the interview, spoke suddenly. "I don't care what a man is—whether he is a general or what—if he says the boys didn't put up a good fight out there, he's a damned fool."

"Lieutenant," began the colonel severely, "this is my own affair, and I'll trouble you——"

The Lieutenant made an obedient gesture. "All right, colonel, all right," he said. He sat down with an air of being content with himself.

The news that the regiment had been reproached went along the line. For a time the men were bewildered by it. "Good thunder!" they exclaimed, staring at the vanishing form of the general. They thought of it as a huge mistake.

Soon, however, they began to believe that their efforts had, in fact, been called light. The youth could see that this idea worried the entire regiment. The men were like punished animals, but rebellious all the same.

The friend, with a complaint in his eye, went to the youth. "I wonder what he does want," he said. "He must think we went out there and played marbles! I never see such a man!"

The youth was thoughtful about this annoyance. "Oh, well," he answered, "He probably didn't see nothing of it at all. He got mad as blazes, and concluded we were a lot of sheep, just because we didn't do what he wanted done. It's a pity old Grandpa Henderson got killed yesterday. He would have known that we did our best and fought good. It's just our awful luck, that's what."

"I should say so," replied the friend. He seemed to be deeply hurt by unfairness. "I should say we did have awful luck! There's no fun in fighting for people when everything you do—no matter what—ain't done right. I have a notion to stay behind next time and let them take their old charge and go to the devil with it."

The youth spoke quietly to his comrade. "Well, we both did good. I'd like to see the fool what would say we both didn't do as good as we could!"

"Of course we did," declared the friend firmly. "And I would break the fellow's neck if he was as big as a church. But we're all right, anyhow, for I heard one fellow say that we two fought the best in the regiment, and they had a great argument about it. Another fellow, of course, he had to up and say it was a lie. He seen all what was going on, and he never seen us from the beginning to the end. And a lot more struck in and says it wasn't a lie. We did fight like thunder, and they give us quite a send-off. But this is what I can't stand—these everlasting old soldiers, tittering and laughing, and then that general, he's crazy."

The youth exclaimed with sudden exasperation: "He's a lunkhead! He makes me mad. I wish he'd come along next time. We would show him what——"

He ceased because several men had come hurrying up. Their faces expressed a bringing of great news.

"O Flem, you just ought to heard!" cried one, eagerly.

"Heard what?" said the youth.

"You just ought to heard!" repeated the other, and he arranged himself to tell his news. The others made an excited circle.

"Well, sir, the colonel met your lieutenant right by us. It was damnedest thing I ever heard. And he says, 'Ahem! ahem!' he says. 'Mr. Hasbrouck!' he says, 'By the way, who was that lad what carried the flag?' he says. There, Fleming, what do you think of that? 'What was the lad what carried the flag?' he says. And the lieutenant, he speaks up right away. 'That's Fleming, and he's a jimhickey,' he says, right away. What? I say he did. 'A jimhickey,' he says. Those are his words. He did, too. I say he did. If you can tell this story better than I can, go ahead and tell it. Well, then, keep your mouth shut. The lieutenant, he says, 'He's a jimhickey.' And the colonel, he says, 'Ahem! ahem! he is, indeed, a very good man to have, ahem! He kept the flag away to the front. I saw him. He's a good one,' says the colonel. 'You bet,' says the lieutenant. 'He and a fellow named Wilson was at the head of the charge, and howling like Indians all the time,' he says. 'Head of the charge all the time,' he says. 'A fellow named Wilson,' he says. There, Wilson, my boy, put that in a letter and send it home to your mother, hey? 'A fellow named Wilson,' he says. And the colonel, he says, 'Were they, indeed? Ahem! ahem! My sakes!' he says. 'At the head of the regiment?' 'They were,' says the lieutenant. 'My sakes!' says the colonel. He says, 'Well, well, well,' he says. 'Those two babies?' 'They were,' says the lieutenant. 'Well, well,' says the colonel, 'they deserve to be major-generals,' he says. 'They deserve to be major-generals.' "

The youth and his friend had said, "Huh!" "You're lying, Thompson." "Oh, go to blazes!" "He never said it." "Oh, what a lie!" "Huh!" But despite this youthful scoffing, they knew that their faces were deeply flushed from pleasure. They traded a secret look of congratulation.

They quickly forgot many things. The past held no memories of errors and disappointment. They were very happy, and their hearts swelled with warm feelings for the colonel and the youthful lieutenant.

22

When the masses of enemy began to pour out of the woods, the youth felt serene self-confidence. He smiled briefly when he saw men duck from the long screeches of the shells. He calmly watched the attack begin against a part of the line on a nearby hill. He had opportunities to see part of the hard fight, since his view was not blocked by smoke from the rifles of his companions. It was a relief to see at last where the noises which had roared into his ears were coming from.

Off a short way he saw two regiments fighting a little separate battle with two other regiments. It was in a cleared space, wearing a set-apart look. They were giving and taking tremendous blows. The firing was incredibly fierce and rapid. These regiments seemed to have forgotten all larger purposes of war, and were slugging each other as if in a game.

In another direction, he saw a magnificent brigade going to drive the enemy from a wood. They passed out of sight, and soon there was a most awe-inspiring racket in the wood. The noise was tremendous. Having stirred this immense uproar, and apparently finding it too immense, the brigade soon came marching airily out again. Its fine formation was unchanged. There was no hint of speed in its movements. The brigade seemed to point a proud thumb at the yelling wood.

On a slope to the left a long row of guns cursed the enemy, who, down through the woods, were forming for another attack. The blasts from the guns made a crimson flare and a high, thick smoke. Occasional glimpses could be caught of the hardworking artillerymen. In the rear of this row of guns stood a house, calm and white among the bursting shells. A group of horses, tied to a long railing, were tugging frantically at their bridles. Men were running back and forth.

The battle between the four regiments lasted for some time. They struck savagely and powerfully at each other. The gray regiments faltered and drew back, leaving the dark-blue lines shouting. The youth could see the two flags shaking amid the smoke remnants.

Then there was a stillness. The blue lines shifted and changed a trifle and stared expectantly at the silent woods and fields before them. The hush was solemn and churchlike, except for a distant battery that, evidently unable to remain quiet, sent a faint rolling thunder over the ground. It was irritating, like the noises of ill-behaved boys. The men imagined that it would prevent them from hearing the beginning of the new battle.

Suddenly the guns on the slope roared out a message of warning. A spluttering sound had begun in the woods. It swelled with amazing speed until an endless roar was developed. To those in the midst of it, it was like the whirring and thumping of gigantic machinery. The youth's ears were filled up. They were not capable of hearing more.

On an incline over which a road wound, he saw wild and desperate rushes of men backward and forward. The opposing armies were two long waves that swelled to and fro. Sometimes, the yells and cheers of one side would proclaim victory, but a moment later the other side would be all yells and cheers. Once the youth saw a band of the enemy leap like hounds toward the blue lines. There was much howling, and presently it went away with a vast mouthful of prisoners. Again, he saw a blue wave dash with such thunderous force against a gray obstruction that it seemed to clear the earth of it and leave nothing but trampled sod. And always in their swift and deadly rushes to and fro, the men screamed and yelled like maniacs.

The armies fought over pieces of fence or secure positions behind trees as if they were golden thrones. There were desperate lunges at these chosen spots, and most of them changed hands often. The youth could not tell from the battle flags flying in many directions which side was winning.

His thinned-out regiment bustled fiercely when its time came. When assaulted again by bullets, the men burst out in a wild cry of rage and pain. They aimed their guns with intense hatred. Their ramrods clanged loud with fury as they pounded the cartridges into the rifle barrels. The front of the regiment was a wall of smoke penetrated by the flashing points of yellow and red.

Wallowing in the fight, they soon surpassed in stain and dirt all their previous appearances. With their swaying bodies, black faces, and glowing eyes, they were like strange and ugly fiends dancing heavily in the smoke.

The lieutenant, returning from a search for a bandage, produced new and horrendous oaths suited to the emergency. He swung strings of curse words like whips over the backs of his men. It was clear that his earlier efforts had not weakened his vocabulary in any way.

The youth, still the bearer of the colors, was deeply absorbed as a spectator. The crash and swing of the great drama made him lean forward, his face working in small twists. Sometimes he babbled, the words coming unconsciously from him in grotesque exclamations. He was so absorbed that he was not aware of his own breathing or of the flag hanging silently over him.

A formidable line of the enemy came within dangerous range. They could be seen plainly—tall, gaunt men with excited faces running with long strides toward a wandering fence.

At sight of this danger, the men suddenly ceased their cursing. There was an instant of strained silence before they threw up their rifles and fired a volley at the foes. There had been no order given. The men had immediately let drive their flock of bullets without waiting for a command.

But the enemy were quick to gain the protection of the wandering line of fence. They slid down behind it with remarkable quickness. From this position, they began briskly firing at the blue men.

These latter braced their energies for a great struggle. Often, white clenched teeth shone from the dusky faces. Many heads surged back and forth in the smoke. The enemy frequently shouted and yelped, but the regiment maintained a stressed silence. Perhaps, at this new assault, the men remembered that they had been called mud diggers. They were desperately intent on holding their ground and thrusting away the rejoicing body of the enemy. They fought swiftly and with savage expressions on their faces.

The youth had resolved not to budge, no matter what should happen. The scornful remarks that had been made about his regiment had generated a strange hatred in him. It was clear to him that his final revenge would be his dead body lying, torn and glittering, on the field. This was how he would get even with the officer who had said "mule drivers" and later "mud diggers." In all the wild graspings of his mind for someone to blame for his sufferings, he always seized on the man who had named him unfairly. It was his vague idea that his corpse would be a great and bitter reproach.

The regiment bled extravagantly. Grunting bundles of blue began to drop. The orderly sergeant of the youth's company was shot through the face. His jaw hung down, showing in the wide cavern of his mouth a pulsing mass of blood and teeth. He made attempts to cry out, as if he believed that one great shriek would make him well.

The youth soon saw him go rearward. He seemed to have all his strength. He ran swiftly, casting wild glances for help.

Others fell down around the feet of their companions. Some of the wounded crawled away, but many lay still, their bodies twisted into impossible shapes.

The youth looked once for his friend. He saw a fierce young man, powder-smeared and untidy, whom he knew to be him. The lieutenant, also, was unhurt in his position at the rear. He had continued to curse, but it was now with the air of a man who was using his last box of oaths.

For the fire of the regiment had begun to wane. The sturdy voice, which had come strangely from the thin ranks, was rapidly growing weak.

23

The colonel came running along back of the line. There were other officers following him. "We must charge them!" they shouted. "We must charge them!" they cried, as if they expected a rebellion against this plan by the men.

On hearing the shouts, the youth began to study the distance between him and the enemy. He made vague calculations. He saw that to be firm soldiers, they must go forward. It would be death to stay in the present place, and to go backward would honor too many others. Their hope was to push the foes away from the fence.

He expected that his companions, weary and stiffened, would have to be driven to this assault. But as he turned toward them, he saw with a certain surprise that they were giving quick and complete assent. There was an ominous, clanging overture to the charge when the bayonets were attached to the rifle barrels. At the yelled words of command, the soldiers sprang forward in eager leaps. There was new and unexpected force in the movement of the regiment. Its weakened condition made the charge appear like a spasm, a display of the strength that comes before a final feebleness. The men dashed in an insane fever of haste, racing as if to achieve sudden success before all strength should leave them. It was a blind and despairing rush by the collection of men in dusty and tattered blue, over green grass and under a bright blue sky. They were running toward a fence, dimly outlined in smoke, from behind which spluttered the fierce rifles of enemies.

The youth kept the bright colors to the front. He was waving his free arm in furious circles, the while shrieking mad calls and appeals. He was urging on men who did not need to be urged. It seemed that the mob of blue men were again grown suddenly wild with unselfishness. From the many firings toward them, it looked as if they would merely succeed in making a great sprinkling of corpses on the grass between their former position and the fence. But they were in a state of frenzy, and it made an exhibition of sublime recklessness.

He himself felt the daring spirit of a religion-mad savage. He was capable of a tremendous death. He thought of the bullets only as things that could prevent him from reaching the place of his endeavor.

He strained all his strength. He did not see anything except the mist of smoke cut by the little knives of fire, but he knew that in it lay a farmer's fence protecting the snuggled bodies of the gray men.

As he ran, a thought of the shock of contact came to his mind. He expected a great collision when the two bodies of troops crashed together. This became a part of his wild battle madness. He could feel the onward swing of the regiment around him, and he imagined a crushing blow that would flatten the resistance and spread amazement for miles. This dream made him run faster among his comrades, who were giving out hoarse and frantic cheers.

But soon he could see that many of the men in gray did not intend to wait for the blow. The rolling smoke disclosed men who ran, their faces still turned. These grew to a crowd, who retired stubbornly. Individuals turned often to send a bullet at the blue wave.

But at one part of the line there was a grim and stubborn group that made no movement. They were settled firmly down behind posts and rails. A flag, ruffled and fierce, waved over them, and their rifles sounded fiercely.

The blue whirl of men got very near, until it seemed that there would be a close and frightful scuffle. The little group of enemy soldiers expressed scorn for their attackers, which changed the meaning of the cheers of the men in blue. They became yells of rage, directed at individual persons. The cries of the two parties were now an interchange of scathing insults.

The men in blue showed their teeth. Their eyes shone all white. They launched themselves as at the throats of those who stood resisting. The space dwindled to nothing.

The youth had centered the gaze of his soul on that other flag. Its possession would be high pride. He plunged like a mad horse at it. He was resolved it should not escape. His own emblem was winging toward the other. It seemed there would shortly be an encounter of strange beaks and claws, as of eagles.

The swirling body of blue men came to a

sudden halt at close range and roared a swift volley. The group in gray was split and broken by this fire, but its riddled body still fought. The men in blue yelled again and rushed in upon it.

The youth saw, as through a mist, a picture of four or five men stretched on the ground, or writhing on their knees as if they had been struck by bolts from the sky. Tottering among them was the rival color bearer, whom the youth saw had been mortally wounded by the bullets of the last volley. He perceived this man fighting a last struggle, the struggle of one whose legs are grasped by devils. It was a ghastly battle. Over his face was the bleach of death, but set upon it were the dark and hard lines of desperate purpose. With this terrible grin of determination, he hugged his precious flag to him. He stumbled and staggered in his resolve to carry it to safety.

But his wounds made it seem that his feet were held fast, and he fought a grim fight. The first of the scampering blue men, howling cheers, leaped at the fence. The despair of the lost was in his eyes as he glanced back at them.

The youth's friend went over the obstruction in a tumbling heap and sprang at the flag as a panther at prey. He pulled at it and wrenched it free, swinging it with a mad cry of exultation. The color bearer, gasping, lurched over and, stiffening convulsively, turned his dead face to the ground. There was much blood on the grass blades.

At the place of success, there began more wild cheers. The men gestured and bellowed in an ecstasy. When they spoke, it was as if they considered their listener to be a mile away. What hats and

caps were left to them they often slung high in the air.

At one part of the line, four men had been leaped upon, and they now sat as prisoners. Some blue men were about them in an eager and curious circle. The soldiers had trapped strange birds, and there was an examination. A flurry of fast questions was in the air.

One of the prisoners was nursing a slight wound in the foot. He cuddled it, baby-wise, but he looked up from it often to curse with abandon straight at the noses of his captors. He sent them to red regions; he called on the deadly fury of strange gods. He was singularly free from the finer points of the conduct usually expected of prisoners of war. It was as if a clumsy clod had stepped on his toe and he believed it to be his privilege, even his duty, to use deep, resentful oaths.

Another, a boy, took his situation with great calmness and apparent good nature. He talked with the men in blue, studying their faces with his bright and keen eyes. They spoke of battles and conditions. There was a sharp interest in all their faces during this exchange of viewpoints. It seemed a great satisfaction to hear voices from where all had been darkness.

The third captive sat with a gloomy expression. He maintained a stern and cold attitude. To all advances, he made one reply without variation: "Ah, go to hell!"

The last of the four was always silent and, for the most part, kept his face turned away. From the views the youth received, he seemed to be completely demoralized. He felt shame, and with it a profound regret that he was, perhaps, no more to be counted in the ranks of his fellows. The youth could see no sign that the man was worrying about his future as a prisoner. All that could be seen was shame for captivity and regret for the right to fight.

After the men had celebrated, they settled down behind the old rail fence, on the opposite side from where their foes had been. A few shot carelessly at distant marks.

There was some long grass. The youth nestled in it and rested, supporting the flag on a convenient rail. His friend, joyful and glorified, holding his treasure with pride, came to him there. They sat side by side and congratulated each other.

24

The roarings that had stretched across the forest began to grow less frequent and weaker. The artillery continued booming in the distance, but the crashes of the musketry had almost stopped. The youth and his friend suddenly looked up, feeling uncomfortable at the fading of these noises, which had become a part of life. They could see changes going on among the troops. There was marching this way and that way. On the crest of a small hill was the thick gleam of many departing muskets.

The youth stood up. "Well, what now, I wonder?" he said. By his tone he seemed to be preparing to resent some new, awful noise. He shaded his eyes with his grimy hand and gazed over the field.

His friend also stood up and stared. "I bet we're going to get along out of this and back over the river," he said.

"Well, I swan!" said the youth.

They waited, watching. In a little while, the regiment received orders to go back to where its had come from. The men got up grunting from the grass, regretting to leave the soft resting place. They jerked their stiffened legs, and stretched their arms over their heads. One man swore as he rubbed his eyes. They all groaned, "O Lord!" They had as many objections to this change as they would have had to a proposal for a new battle.

They tramped slowly back over the field across which they had run in a mad scamper.

The regiment marched until it had joined the other regiments. The brigade, in column, aimed through a wood at the road. Immediately they were in a mass of dust-covered troops, and were trudging along parallel to what had been the enemy's lines.

They passed within view of a stolid white house, and saw in front of it groups of their comrades lying in wait behind a low wall. A row of guns were booming at a distant enemy. Shells thrown in reply were raising clouds of dust and splinters. Horsemen dashed along the line of entrenchments.

At this point of its march, the division curved away from the field and went winding off in the direction of the river. When the youth realized what this movement meant, he turned his head and looked over his shoulder toward the trampled and debris-covered ground. He breathed a breath of new satisfaction. He finally nudged his friend. "Well, it's all over," he said to him.

His friend gazed backward. "By God, it is," he agreed. They thought deeply and at length.

For a time, the youth's thinking was puzzled and uncertain. His mind was undergoing a subtle change. It took a while for it to cast off its battlefield ways and return to its usual way of thinking. Gradually his brain emerged from the clouds, and finally he was able to understand himself and his situation more clearly.

He understood then that the shooting was in the past. He had been in a land of strange upheavals and had come out of it. He had been where there was red of blood and black of passion, and he had escaped. His first thought was to rejoice at this fact.

Later he began to think about what he had done, his failures and his achievements. Thus, fresh from scenes where he had not thought at all, he struggled to recall all his acts.

At last they marched before him clearly. From his present viewpoint, he was able to look at them like a spectator, and to criticize them with some correctness.

He felt good about his memories, for in them it was his public actions that stood out. It was a pleasure to remember those things that had been seen by his fellow soldiers. In his mind, they marched past cheerfully, with music. He spent delightful minutes viewing the golden images of memory.

He saw that he was good. He recalled with a thrill the other soldiers' respectful comments about his conduct. He said to himself again the sentence of the young lieutenant: "If I had ten thousand wildcats like you, I could tear the stomach out of this war in less than a week."

Nevertheless, the memory of his flight from the first engagement came back to him. For a moment he blushed, and the light of his soul flickered with shame.

A ghost bothered his conscience. There loomed the memory of the tattered soldier—he who, pierced by bullets and faint for blood, had worried about the youth's imaginary wound; he who had lent his last strength for the tall soldier; he who, blind with weariness and pain, had been deserted in the field.

For an instant, a wretched chill of sweat was upon him at the thought that he might be detected. He let out a cry of sharp irritation and agony.

His friend turned. "What's the matter, Henry?" he demanded. The youth's reply was an outburst of oaths.

As he marched along the little roadway among his companions, this vision of cruelty brooded over him. It clung near him always, and darkened his view of the recent battle. Whichever way his thoughts turned, they were followed by the somber ghost of the man he had deserted in the fields. He looked stealthily at his companions. He felt sure that they could see evidence of this worry in his face. But they were plodding along in a ragged line, discussing the late battle.

"Oh, if a man should come up and ask me, I'd say we got a damn good licking."

"Licking—in your eye! We ain't licked, sonny. We're going down here a ways, swing around, and come in behind them."

"Oh, hush, with your coming in behind them. I've seen all of that I want to. Don't tell me about coming in behind——"

"Bill Smithers, he says he would rather have been in ten hundred battles than been in that hell of a hospital. He says they got shooting in the nighttime, and shells dropped plum among them in the hospital. He says such hollering he never see."

"Hasbrouck? He's the best officer in this here regiment. He's a whale."

"Didn't I tell you we would come around in behind them? Didn't I tell you so? We——"

"Oh, shut your mouth!"

For a time this recollection of the tattered man took all pleasure from the youth's mind. He saw his error, and he was afraid that it would stand before him all his life. He took no part in the talk of his comrades. Nor did he look at them, except when he suddenly suspected that they were seeing his thoughts and examining each detail of the scene with the tattered soldier.

Yet gradually he gathered the strength to put the sin at a distance. At last his eyes seemed to be opened to some new ways. He found that he could look back on his earlier beliefs and see them accurately. He was glad to discover that he now despised them.

With that attitude came self-confidence. He felt a quiet manhood, not aggressive but sturdy and strong. He knew that he would no more fear for the future, wherever it might lead. He had been to touch the great death, and found that, after all, it was only the great death. He was a man.

And so it happened that as he trudged from the place of blood and wrath, his soul changed.

It rained. The procession of weary soldiers became a bedraggled train, marching in a trough of liquid brown mud under a low, wretched sky. Yet the youth smiled, for he saw that the world was a world for him. He had rid himself of the sickness of battle. The nightmare was in the past. He had been an animal blistered and sweating in the heat and pain of war. He turned now with a lover's thirst to images of tranquil skies, fresh meadows, cool brooks—an existence of soft and eternal peace.

Over the river a golden ray of sun came through the hosts of leaden rain clouds.

REVIEWING
YOUR
READING

CHAPTER 1

FINDING THE MAIN IDEA

1. This chapter mostly tells about the soldiers' wish to
   (A) have the war end   (B) finally move into battle
   (C) be permanently assigned to a regiment   (D) get a
   break from fighting

REMEMBERING DETAIL

2. The rumor that the regiment is about to go into battle is
   started by
   (A) the tall soldier   (B) the loud soldier   (C) the youth
   (D) a corporal
3. The youth had been discouraged from enlisting in the
   army by
   (A) his girlfriend   (B) his father   (C) his mother
   (D) one of his classmates
4. The reality of war, as the youth has seen it so far,
   has been
   (A) months of monotonous life at a camp   (B) frequent
   death struggles   (C) occasional fighting   (D) Greek-
   like battles
5. The youth is wrestling with the question of whether or
   not he will
   (A) be able to load his ammunition in time   (B) run
   from a battle   (C) be able to kill a man   (D) be
   promoted to a higher rank

DRAWING CONCLUSIONS

6. You can guess that the war being fought is
   (A) World War II   (B) World War I   (C) the American
   Revolution   (D) the Civil War

USING YOUR REASON   _why did the youth /enlist_
7. The youth enlists in the army because
   (A) he is eager to get away from his mother   (B) he has
   a thirst for adventure   (C) he has always dreamed of
   being a soldier   (D) he cannot afford to go to college

8. The youth's mother is probably unhappy about his joining the army because
   (A) she'll now have to take care of the farm alone
   (B) she's afraid he'll fall in with the wrong crowd
   (C) she's afraid he will be killed   (D) she doesn't believe in patriotism

THINKING IT OVER

1. Why was the youth disappointed in his mother's farewell speech? How had he expected their parting to be?
2. In your opinion, why does Stephen Crane refer to Henry as "the youth"? What characteristics of youth does Henry display?

CHAPTER 2

FINDING THE MAIN IDEA

1. A good title for this chapter might be
   (A) "Only a Rumor"   (B) "The Long March"
   (C) "The Youth's Eternal Debate"   (D) "The Plan to Steal a Horse"

REMEMBERING DETAIL

2. The youth knows that the only way to find the answer to his question will be to
   (A) ask some of his comrades   (B) confront one of the generals   (C) actually fight in a battle   (D) think about it long enough
3. The columns of men marching are compared to
   (A) lines of smoke   (B) ropes   (C) snakes   (D) rivers
4. A fat soldier attempts to steal
   (A) a farm girl's horse   (B) an officer's horse
   (C) a comrade's rations   (D) the general's rifle

USING YOUR REASON

5. You can guess that the youth might feel better if he
   (A) gets a good night's sleep   (B) discovers even one soldier who feels as he does   (C) tries to blend in with the other men   (D) writes home about his problems

DRAWING CONCLUSIONS

6. You can guess that the youth's doubts
(A) make him wish he had never enlisted in the army (B) make him wish he were dead   (C) are only a minor concern to him   (D) come and go

IDENTIFYING THE MOOD

7. The general mood of the men as they march is
(A) cheerful   (B) nervous   (C) gloomy   (D) hopeless
8. The youth's mood throughout this chapter is
(A) cheerful   (B) relaxed   (C) sullen
(D) anxious

THINKING IT OVER

1. If the youth is afraid, why is he so eager to go into battle?
2. What is the "eternal debate" in which the youth is engaged? Why doesn't he talk things over with his comrades?

CHAPTER 3

FINDING THE MAIN IDEA

1. In this chapter, the author is most interested in
(A) showing the tension and anxiety before the battle   (B) discussing the landscape of the battlefield   (C) revealing conflicts between the soldiers
(D) showing how the youth has resolved his problem

REMEMBERING DETAIL

2. The dead soldier's poverty is given away by
(A) his tattered clothing   (B) his empty pockets
(C) a tear in one of his shoes   (D) his friends
3. The youth feels strangely threatened by
(A) the enemy   (B) his comrades   (C) cannon fire
(D) the landscape
4. The youth finds comfort in the idea that, in death, he will finally be
(A) free   (B) understood   (C) at peace   (D) alone

DRAWING CONCLUSIONS

5. When the author says the regiment "lost many of the marks of a new command," he means
    (A) many of the men had already been killed   (B) the men were no longer as polite to one another   (C) the men had become veterans   (D) the men had lost much of their original vigor and enthusiasm

6. The "invisible burden" the youth feels he alone is doomed to carry is
    (A) the fear that he might run   (B) the knowledge that they are all about to be sacrificed   (C) the knowledge that the generals are all stupid   (D) the knowledge that the regiment could have avoided this battle

USING YOUR REASON

7. Some soldiers scoffed at those who built protective barricades. They probably thought this action was a sign of
    (A) cowardice (B) ignorance (C) disrespect (D) caution

8. At the end of the chapter, the loud soldier
    (A) is secretly planning to leave the army   (B) is dying   (C) believes he will be killed in the upcoming battle   (D) is afraid

READING FOR DEEPER MEANING

9. More than anything, the youth seems to be involved in a difficult process of
    (A) self-deception   (B) self-discovery   (C) self-destruction   (D) self-denial

THINKING IT OVER

1. When does the youth come to realize that he is committed to the regiment? How does this make him feel? Explain your answer.

2. Why is the youth inwardly rebelling against the officers? Are they the true cause of the youth's anxiety, or simply scapegoats for the youth's fears about himself? Explain your answer.

CHAPTER 4

REMEMBERING DETAIL

1. The lieutenant of the youth's company was shot
   (A) in the foot   (B) in the head   (C) through the heart
   (D) in the hand
2. After the lieutenant is wounded, the new men in his
   company are impressed by
   (A) his bravery   (B) the skill with which he bandages
   his wound   (C) the way he swears afterwards   (D) his
   patriotism
3. What weapon or form of ammunition is not mentioned
   in this chapter?
   (A) a sword   (B) a bullet   (C) a cannon   (D) a shell

DRAWING CONCLUSIONS

4. One might conclude that, in this chapter, the Union
   army is
   (A) winning the battle   (B) losing the battle
   (C) neither winning nor losing   (D) not yet fighting

USING YOUR REASON

5. The imprinted expression on the faces of the fleeing
   men was probably one of
   (A) fear   (B) nervousness   (C) grief   (D) thrill

IDENTIFYING THE MOOD

6. The scene in this chapter might best be described as
   (A) relaxed   (B) chaotic   (C) gloomy   (D) humorous

READING FOR DEEPER MEANING

7. In this chapter, the flag seems to symbolize
   (A) the struggles of the troops   (B) the United States
   (C) the South   (D) truth

THINKING IT OVER

1. What happens in this chapter that might cause the youth
   to feel better about himself? Explain your answer.

CHAPTER 5

FINDING THE MAIN IDEA
1. The most important thing we learn in this chapter is that
   (A) the youth does not run when confronted with battle
   (B) many men die in war   (C) war is devastating
   (D) fighting in a battle requires rage and concentration

REMEMBERING DETAIL
2. As the enemy approaches, the first thing that the youth
   thinks about is
   (A) whether or not he will run   (B) whether or not he
   will be killed   (C) whether or not his rifle is loaded
   (D) his mother
3. Why does the youth stay and fight?
   (A) he is so frightened he cannot run   (B) he is blocked
   in by his comrades   (C) he suddenly feels a part of the
   cause   (D) his lieutenant will not let him run
4. What gives the youth assurance that his regiment is not
   being wiped out?
   (A) the constant noise of the guns firing and the men
   talking   (B) the sight of his regiment's flag
   (C) the enormous number of enemy dead   (D) the officers' encouragement

DRAWING CONCLUSIONS
5. You can conclude that once the youth stopped worrying
   about himself
   (A) everyone else stopped worrying about him, too
   (B) the regiment fought better   (C) he became a better,
   more focused soldier   (D) he felt closer to God

USING YOUR REASON
6. When the author refers to the youth as working "like a
   carpenter who has made many boxes," he means
   (A) the youth's fighting became a job that he did automatically   (B) fighting requires the same skill and pre-
   cision that carpentry does   (C) the youth feels boxed in
   by his comrades   (D) both fighters and carpenters use
   their hands in their work

7. The youth's attitude in this chapter has become that of a
   (A) loner   (B) follower   (C) leader   (D) team player

THINKING IT OVER

1. How do you explain the youth's ability to shoot
   automatically when the need arises?
2. What do you think transforms the youth from a man to a
   "member"? Explain your answer.

CHAPTER 6

FINDING THE MAIN IDEA

1. This chapter is mostly about
   (A) the youth bragging about how well he fought in the
   last battle   (B) the defeat of the enemy   (C) the youth's
   mistaken belief that the army is being defeated
   (D) the courage of the enemy soldiers

REMEMBERING DETAIL

2. The sight and sounds of the enemy approaching caused
   the youth to
   (A) run   (B) begin shooting wildly   (C) show
   uncommon courage   (D) freeze
3. At the beginning of the chapter, the youth is proud of
   himself because
   (A) he managed to avoid injury in the last battle   (B) he
   learned to fire a cannon   (C) he had stayed and fought in
   the last battle   (D) he has been awarded a medal of courage
4. The youth compares the approaching enemy to
   (A) a tired horse   (B) a freight train   (C) a whirlwind
   (D) a fearsome dragon
5. The youth believes the soldiers who continue to fight in
   the face of destruction are
   (A) courageous   (B) delirious   (C) fools   (D) heroes

DRAWING CONCLUSIONS

6. The fact that the youth stayed and fought in the previous
   chapter, but ran in this chapter, proves
   (A) courage is not a predictable quality   (B) the youth is
   more of a coward than he thought he was   (C) this battle
   was worse than the previous one   (D) the youth is indecisive

USING YOUR REASON

7. At the beginning of the chapter, the youth's regiment feels unprepared to fight the enemy because
   (A) they have not been given orders from their officers
   (B) they haven't mentally or physically recovered from the last battle   (C) they've lost a lot of men in the last battle   (D) their wounds are not completely healed yet

8. The soldier who said "I wish Bill Smithers had stepped on my hand, instead of me stepping on his," probably said it because
   (A) he is sympathetic toward Bill Smithers   (B) he feels responsible for Bill Smithers's pain   (C) he knows Bill Smithers is safe inside a hospital, while he, the soldier, now has to fight   (D) Bill Smithers is his friend

IDENTIFYING THE MOOD

9. At the beginning of this chapter, the youth feels a great sense of
   (A) dread   (B) remorse   (C) fear   (D) satisfaction

THINKING IT OVER

1. Why does the youth "run like a rabbit" even before he really sees the enemy?

2. What news does the youth believe he should let the generals in on? Does the youth's news turn out to be accurate? Explain.

CHAPTER 7

REMEMBERING DETAIL

1. The youth convinces himself that running was
   (A) a cowardly act   (B) a silly mistake   (C) a correct and wise action   (D) good exercise

2. To be alone, the youth takes a walk in a
   (A) graveyard   (B) shrine   (C) church   (D) forest

3. The youth throws a pine cone at
   (A) a squirrel   (B) a horse   (C) an enemy soldier
   (D) one of his comrades

4. The youth believes Nature gives him a sign that
(A) war is evil   (B) when confronted with danger, you should run to save yourself   (C) humans are the only animals that fight among themselves   (D) Nature will go on, even in the midst of war

DRAWING CONCLUSIONS

5. You can conclude that most of the fighting the youth has done so far has been with
(A) the enemy   (B) his comrades   (C) the officers (D) his own conscience

USING YOUR REASON

6. Why does the youth feel he has been wronged?
(A) because he had done the smart thing and had run, but no one except him recognized it as smart
(B) because he had not been allowed to take part in the fighting   (C) because he had felt brave enough to lead the front, but wasn't allowed to   (D) because he had run, and therefore, was not invited to the victory celebration

IDENTIFYING THE MOOD

7. To the youth, the woods represent
(A) mystery   (B) peace and serenity   (C) despair (D) death

THINKING IT OVER

1. How does the youth justify running away from the battle? Do you agree with his reasons? Why or why not?
2. Is the author's description of the dead man too graphic? Why do you think Crane included so many details?

CHAPTER 8

FINDING THE MAIN IDEA

1. This chapter mainly focuses on
(A) the youth and the procession of wounded soldiers
(B) a dead soldier   (C) the youth in the forest
(D) the youth's determination to fight

REMEMBERING DETAIL

2. The youth joins a group of soldiers who are
   (A) heroes   (B) dead   (C) wounded   (D) resting
3. A wounded officer is being carried along by
   (a) two privates   (B) the youth   (C) the tattered soldier
   (D) the ghostly soldier
4. The youth is engaged in conversation by
   (A) an officer   (B) the ghostly soldier   (C) two
   privates   (D) the tattered soldier

USING YOUR REASON

5. In the sentence, "Listening to this present din, he was
   doubtful if he had seen real battle scenes," you can tell
   that "din" means
   (A) loud noise   (B) speech   (C) family room
   (D) complaint
6. The ghostly soldier's teeth are clenched because
   (A) he is angry   (B) he has a toothache   (C) he is in
   great pain   (D) he does not want to speak

IDENTIFYING THE MOOD

7. You can guess that the youth avoids the wounded
   soldier's question because he feels
   (A) guilt and shame   (B) tired and weary   (C) pain
   (D) dazed

THINKING IT OVER

1. The author notes that it is good that soldiers take
   themselves very seriously. Otherwise, he says, they
   would surely run. What does he mean by these
   statements?
2. The youth sees the tattered soldier as a symbol of
   courage. This causes him to feel tortured by an inner
   conflict. What conflict is this? Do you sympathize with
   the youth? Why or why not?

196

CHAPTER 9

FINDING THE MAIN IDEA
1. A good title for this chapter might be
   (A) "The Youth's Guilt Shows Through"   (B) "The Death of a Soldier"   (C) "Jim's Wounds"   (D) "Jim's Strange Dance"

REMEMBERING DETAIL
2. A "red badge of courage" is
   (A) a medal (B) an award (C) a wound (D) a document
3. The ghostly soldier turns out to be
   (A) Jim Conklin   (B) Bill Smithers   (C) the loud soldier   (D) the lieutenant of the youth's regiment
4. The ghostly soldier pleads with the youth to
   (A) take him back to his camp   (B) leave him alone   (C) give him first-aid   (D) go get help

DRAWING CONCLUSIONS
5. You can tell that the youth and the ghostly soldier are
   (A) friends   (B) enemies   (C) brothers   (D) from the same hometown

USING YOUR REASON
6. The ghostly soldier probably knows he is
   (A) wounded   (B) dying   (C) slowing down the line   (D) weak
7. The ghostly soldier had struggled to a chosen place to meet
   (A) his girlfriend   (B) medics   (C) death   (D) his commander

IDENTIFYING THE MOOD
8. The tone of this chapter is
   (A) happy   (B) sad   (C) angry   (D) suspenseful

THINKING IT OVER
1. The youth wishes that he, too, had a "little red badge of courage." Why does the youth wish this? Do you agree with this definition of a wound? Why or why not?
2. In your opinion, what is the significance of Jim's death? What does it mean to the youth?

197

CHAPTER 10

REMEMBERING DETAIL

1. The tattered soldier has been shot
    (A) on the shoulder and the leg   (B) on the arm and the
    leg (C) on the head and the leg   (D) on the head and
    the arm
2. When does the tattered soldier realize he has been shot?
    (A) after his friend, Tom Jamison, tells him so
    (B) after he is told by the enemy soldier who shot him
    (C) when he sees that he is covered with blood
    (D) the following morning
3. Which question asked by the tattered soldier bothers the
    youth most?
    (A) "I wonder where he got his strength from?"
    (B) "Where is it [your wound] located?"   (C) "Why
    partner, where you going?"   (D) "Are you hurt much?"
4. The tattered soldier tells the youth that the worst
    wounds are those that are
    (A) on the inside   (B) bleeding a lot   (C) gangrenous
    (D) open

USING YOUR REASON

5. When the tattered soldier says, "There's two of
    them—little ones—but they're beginning to have fun
    with me now," he is referring to
    (A) bees   (B) wounds   (C) pains   (D) children
6. The youth wishes the tattered soldier would
    (A) be his friend   (B) stop talking about the war
    (C) leave him alone about his injuries   (D) help him
    treat his wounds

THINKING IT OVER

1. What is the "ghost of shame" that continues to torment
    the youth? Why does the youth find it so hard to face
    this ghost?
2. Given the tattered soldier's condition at the end of the
    chapter, what do you believe will happen to him?
    Explain your opinion.

CHAPTER 11

FINDING THE MAIN IDEA
1. The purpose of this chapter is to show
   (A) the youth's happiness at still being alive   (B) the youth's constant guilt and bitterness after having run   (C) that the youth may become a liar   (D) how the youth finds self-respect

REMEMBERING DETAIL
2. The youth is comforted by the sight of
   (A) his regiment   (B) his old friend Jim Conklin
   (C) members of the army retreating   (D) his rifle
3. Rather than admitting that he has run, the youth considers
   (A) making up a story to tell his regiment   (B) asking for a discharge from the army   (C) changing regiments
   (D) blaming his actions on another soldier
4. The youth is afraid that once he returns to his camp, his comrades will
   (A) try to pick a fight with him   (B) ignore him
   (C) ask him where he has been   (D) ridicule him

USING YOUR REASON
5. Seeing soldiers march bravely into battle makes the youth believe that
   (A) these soldiers must be superior to him   (B) they are all crazy   (C) he will one day be like them   (D) they will defeat the enemy
6. Although the youth doesn't want to be in the battles, he does want to
   (A) see and know about them   (B) stay in the army
   (C) tell of them   (D) help the wounded

IDENTIFYING THE MOOD
7. Which of these emotions does the youth *not* feel toward himself?
   (A) pity   (B) guilt   (C) anger   (D) pride

THINKING IT OVER

1. Why does the youth argue that a defeat would excuse his actions?
2. The youth needs to feel that it was morally right for him to run. Why is moral justification so important to him?

CHAPTER 12

REMEMBERING DETAIL

1. In this chapter, the youth is amazed to see that
   (A) the soldiers who at first appeared brave are now retreating   (B) the road is cluttered with wagons and men   (C) he no longer is afraid   (D) the enemies are friendly
2. The youth is hit on the head by
   (A) a shell   (B) a retreating soldier   (C) an enemy officer   (D) a flying brick
3. The knock on the head affects the youth's
   (A) sight   (B) hearing   (C) balance   (D) speech
4. As the man who helped the youth is leaving, the youth realizes
   (A) he is from the South   (B) he never saw the man's face   (C) the man is his long-lost brother   (D) the man is badly hurt

USING YOUR REASON

5. In the sentence, "He knew at once that the steel fibers had been washed from their hearts," steel fibers stand for
   (A) tendons   (B) mercy   (C) fear   (D) courage
6. The youth probably regards the cheery soldier as
   (A) a meddler   (B) a savior   (C) a threat
   (D) an enemy

DRAWING CONCLUSIONS

7. The skill and ease with which the cheery soldier helps the youth suggests the man is probably
   (A) a veteran   (B) one of the youth's officers
   (C) a new soldier   (D) a doctor

200

1. After being injured, how does the youth compare himself to Jim, the tall soldier? In your opinion, does the youth have the right to make a comparison between himself and the soldier? Explain your answer.

CHAPTER 13

FINDING THE MAIN IDEA

1. This chapter is mostly about
(A) the youth's return to battle   (B) the youth's return to his regiment   (C) how the youth has changed   (D) the youth's depression

REMEMBERING DETAIL

2. Back at camp, the youth is halted by the sentinel. Who is the sentinel?
(A) the tall soldier, Jim Conklin   (B) the loud soldier, Wilson   (C) Simpson   (D) the corporal
3. The youth tells his regiment that he has been
(A) hiding   (B) in the forest   (C) shot in the head
(D) unconscious
4. Both Wilson and the corporal tell the youth that they thought he was
(A) dead   (B) a ghost   (C) more courageous
(D) fighting with another regiment

USING YOUR REASON

5. A sentinel is a(n)
(A) officer   (B) youth   (C) one hundred-year-old man
(D) guard
6. The corporal tells the youth that in the morning, he'll feel as though a number ten hat wouldn't fit. What does the corporal mean?
(A) the youth's head will feel shrunken   (B) the youth's wound will make it impossible for him to wear a hat
(C) the youth's head will feel big and swollen   (D) the youth will be fitted for a new hat in the morning

DRAWING CONCLUSIONS

7. You can tell that the youth did not have the nerve to
   (A) go to sleep   (B) fight in tomorrow's battle   (C) tell
   the truth   (D) drink the coffee his friend has made

IDENTIFYING THE MOOD

8. By the end of the chapter, how does the youth feel
   toward Wilson?
   (A) angered   (B) humbled   (C) suspicious   (D) shocked

THINKING IT OVER

1. On the first page of this chapter, how does the youth
   appear to face up to his problem of courage?
2. Why is it ironic that the youth is treated with such
   respect and consideration after his return? How do you
   think the youth feels about himself? Explain your
   answer.

CHAPTER 14

FINDING THE MAIN IDEA

1. A good title for this chapter might be
   (A) "The Thousand-Year Sleep"   (B) "The Youth's
   New Attitude"   (C) "Wilson's New Attitude"   (D) "A
   Fight Breaks Out"

REMEMBERING DETAIL

2. When the youth awakens, he believes he is surrounded
   by
   (A) his family   (B) friends   (C) corpses   (D) insects
3. How does Wilson handle the three soldiers who seem
   ready to break into a fight?
   (A) he encourages the fight   (B) he warns that he will
   tell the generals   (C) he reminds them that it is point-
   less to fight among themselves   (D) he bets on the
   winner
4. Wilson, the loud soldier, is now referred to as
   (A) the instigator   (B) the doctor   (C) the nurse
   (D) the friend

USING YOUR REASON

5. By morning, the youth's wound is
   (A) feeling much better   (B) much more painful
   (C) completely healed   (D) infected
6. It is probable that Wilson's attitude has changed because
   (A) he is getting older   (B) facing death almost daily
   has given him a new appreciation of life   (C) he has
   found religion   (D) a comrade advised him to be nicer

IDENTIFYING THE MOOD

7. Wilson's attitude toward the youth reflects
   (A) hostility   (B) indifference   (C) arrogance
   (D) compassion

THINKING IT OVER

When the youth returns to the regiment, he finds that
Wilson has changed. In what ways is he different? Do
you believe the changes in Wilson are permanent or
temporary? Explain your belief.

CHAPTER 15

FINDING THE MAIN IDEA

1. The most important thing we learn in this chapter is that
   (A) the youth feels sorry for Wilson   (B) Wilson did
   not die   (C) the youth has regained his self-confidence
   (D) the regiment is about to fight another battle

REMEMBERING DETAIL

2. In this chapter, the youth remembers that he still has
   (A) Wilson's packet of letters   (B) a head wound
   (C) not fought in a battle   (D) doubts
3. Wilson had believed he was going to be
   (A) transferred to the Rebel army   (B) wounded
   (C) awarded a medal of honor   (D) killed in combat
4. If necessary, the youth will use the packet of letters as a
   (A) shield against bullets in battle (B) weapon against
   Wilson (C) way out of the army (D) reminder of the war

USING YOUR REASON

5. The last paragraph of this chapter implies that
(A) more women should join the army   (B) war is more disastrous than most women think   (C) most women really enjoy war stories   (D) bravery is mostly a male characteristic

IDENTIFYING THE MOOD

6. In this chapter, the youth has an air of
(A) kindness   (B) obedience   (C) cockiness
(D) respectfulness
7. How does Wilson feel when he has to ask the youth for the letters back?
(A) embarrassed   (B) angry   (C) glad   (D) relieved

THINKING IT OVER

1. In the last chapter, we found that Wilson had changed. Now the youth has changed, too. What changes have taken place in the youth? What accounts for the youth's new outlook?
2. Which do you prefer, the old Henry or the current Henry? Why do you feel as you do?

CHAPTER 16

FINDING THE MAIN IDEA

1. This chapter is mostly about
(A) the youth's friendship with Wilson   (B) the way the youth fights   (C) the games the men play while waiting to fight   (D) the men trying to decide whom to blame for their losses

REMEMBERING DETAIL

2. The men are discouraged by rumors that
(A) they have suffered another defeat   (B) they will have to fight two more battles today   (C) another one of their officers has been killed   (D) they will have to fight in bad weather
3. The youth is quick to blame their defeats on
(A) the soldiers   (B) the bravery of the enemy   (C) the geography   (D) the poor leadership of the generals

4. For a moment, the youth is afraid his secret has been revealed by
   (A) Wilson   (B) a sarcastic soldier   (C) an enemy soldier
   (D) a lieutenant

DRAWING CONCLUSIONS
5. You can tell that morale among the men is
   (A) low   (B) high   (C) the same as it would be if they were winning   (D) growing

USING YOUR REASON
6. The youth probably feels like making a joke because
   (A) he secretly wants to become a comedian   (B) he wants to see if the men will get the punchline
   (C) he wants to relieve the tension before the battle
   (D) he cannot think of other conversation to make
7. When Wilson says, "It's our luck to get licked often," he means
   (A) bad luck   (B) good luck   (C) fate
   (D) punishment

THINKING IT OVER
1. Is it surprising that the youth should be the person who speaks out so boldly against the way the fighting is being managed? What is the irony in this situation?
2. When the accidental bump on the head provides the youth with his own "red badge of courage," he is able to pretend that his courage has been tested. Do you believe the youth will get a real chance to prove his courage? Predict what will happen to the youth by the end of the book.

CHAPTER 17

FINDING THE MAIN IDEA
1. This chapter mostly concentrates on
   (A) the advances made by the enemy   (B) the youth's performance in the battle   (C) Wilson's frustration at having to fight so often   (D) the youth's feelings toward the officers

REMEMBERING DETAIL

2. Yesterday the youth had felt hatred for the universe. Today he feels a wild hatred for
   (A) the war   (B) Wilson   (C) the enemy   (D) the North

3. Once, when the youth falls, he wonders if he
   (A) will be paralyzed   (B) has tripped   (C) was pushed   (D) has been shot

4. The youth continues to fire because
   (A) he can still see the enemy approaching   (B) of his determination to win the war   (C) he doesn't realize the enemy has retreated   (D) he wants to impress his lieutenant

USING YOUR REASON

5. The youth's regiment has a reputation of being
   (A) crybabies   (B) easily injured   (C) good fighters   (D) poor fighters

6. The last sentence of the chapter serves as a reminder of
   (A) the weather conditions   (B) the beauty of nature amidst the ugliness of war   (C) the approaching summer season   (D) the color of smoke

IDENTIFYING THE MOOD

7. The word that best describes the regiment's attitude after the battle is
   (A) disappointed   (B) triumphant   (C) dismal   (D) anxious

THINKING IT OVER

What does the author mean by "It was not well to drive men into corners; at those moments, they could all develop teeth and claws"? How might men react when faced with such a situation?

CHAPTER 18

FINDING THE MAIN IDEA
1. The most important thing we learn is this chapter is that
(A) Jimmie Rogers has been shot   (B) all of the
soldiers want water   (C) the youth's regiment is going
to charge the enemy   (D) the men do not believe Henry
and Wilson

REMEMBERING DETAIL
2. After finding that Jimmie Rogers has been shot, the
youth and Wilson are sent to
(A) get the doctors   (B) go get water   (C) ask the
enemy to hold their fire   (D) get a first-aid kit
3. Whom do Henry and Wilson overhear talking?
(A) two privates   (B) three foot soldiers   (C) two
officers   (D) an officer and a foot soldier
4. The youth is startled by the revelation that, in the war,
he is as insignificant as a
(A) broom   (B) needle   (C) tent   (D) canteen

DRAWING CONCLUSIONS
5. You can guess that charging the enemy is
(A) something this regiment is accustomed to doing
(B) a major assignment for the regiment   (C) an easy
task   (D) what the youth has always wanted to do

USING YOUR REASON
6. Jimmie Rogers is thrashing about in the grass because
(A) he is in great pain   (B) his back itches
(C) he is crazy   (D) his clothes are on fire
7. The lieutenant can tell something is wrong by
(A) the way the men are staring at Henry and Wilson
(B) Henry's and Wilson's hurried speech   (C) Henry's
and Wilson's screams   (D) the look in Henry's and
Wilson's eyes

IDENTIFYING THE MOOD

8. Which is probably *not* an emotion the men feel after hearing Henry's and Wilson's news?
   (A) fear (B) uncertainty (C) nervousness (D) humor

THINKING IT OVER

When Henry and Wilson present the news that their regiment will charge the enemy, what secret knowledge do they omit? Why might they have omitted this part? In your opinion, was it admirable and wise to make this omission, or was it foolish? Explain your answer.

CHAPTER 19

FINDING THE MAIN IDEA

1. The most important event in this chapter is that
   (A) the color sergeant is killed (B) many men die during the charge (C) Wilson rallies the men forward (D) the youth finds within himself a new love and respect for the flag

REMEMBERING DETAIL

2. How does Wilson reawaken his comrades to action?
   (A) by calling them names (B) by threatening to shoot them himself (C) by firing a single rifle shot into the woods (D) by sending a complaint to the general
3. Near the end of the chapter, which two soldiers lead the regimental front?
   (A) Wilson and the color sergeant (B) Henry and the color sergeant (C) Henry and Wilson (D) Henry and the lieutenant
4. After the color sergeant is killed, Henry and Wilson take up his
   (A) flag (B) rifle (C) uniform (D) sword

DRAWING CONCLUSIONS

5. You can guess that, after seeing so many comrades killed, the regiment feels
   (A) a great sense of pride toward their cause (B) bitter (C) hesitant to carry on with the charge(D) tremendous courage

USING YOUR REASON

6. The word "charge," as used in the context of this and the previous chapter, means
   (A) to assign responsibility   (B) to accuse   (C) to pay by credit   (D) to attack

7. The "yellow tongues" mentioned in this chapter are
   (A) flags   (B) the flames from the enemy's rifles
   (C) the men's tongues hanging from their mouths as they charge   (D) scorched blades of grass

THINKING IT OVER

1. After describing the frenzied fighting of the regiment, Crane says the men ". . . returned to caution. They were become men again." What do these sentences imply?

2. Note the figurative language used in describing the flag. Give at least two examples of simile or metaphors that describe the flag. What is the flag symbolic of? When does it become a symbol of all that the youth loves?

CHAPTER 20

REMEMBERING DETAIL

1. In this battle, the youth had hoped to prove
   (A) that he can fight, even with a head wound   (B) that he and his comrades are not mule drivers   (C) that although his comrades may be mule drivers, he is not one   (D) his devotion to Wilson

2. The author refers to the battle-worn regiment as a
   (A) run down machine   (B) worn out automobile
   (C) loaded down mule   (D) raging bull

3. Throughout the assault, the youth continues to
   (A) seek refuge   (B) carry the flag   (C) call for reinforcements   (D) stay close to the ground

4. At one point, the enemy appears so near that the youth can see their
   (A) rifles   (B) flags   (C) generals   (D) faces

DRAWING CONCLUSIONS

5. In most cases, the troops are unable to assess the damages until
   (A) the next day   (B) a written report is given   (C) the smoke clears   (D) they count the number of casualties

USING YOUR REASON

6. At the end of the battle, the youth sees that his regiment has
   (A) been defeated   (B) held back the enemy
   (C) retreated   (D) been firing upon itself

7. After the battle, the youth believes he and his comrades have
   (A) fought disgracefully   (B) fought admirably
   (C) suffered too many losses   (D) demonstrated that they are the best regiment of both armies

IDENTIFYING THE MOOD

8. After the battle, which emotion is probably *not* felt by the youth's regiment?
   (A) pride   (B) triumph   (C) enthusiasm   (D) sorrow

THINKING IT OVER

1. It has been said that the change in the youth is mostly a spiritual one. What does this mean? Does the youth show signs of a new maturity in this chapter? If so, what are they?

2. The chapter ends with the sentence, "And they were men." What is the significance of this sentence? Why is this more meaningful than just stating they were *better soldiers?*

CHAPTER 21

FINDING THE MAIN IDEA

1. The most important thing we learn in this chapter is that
   (A) the colonel is scolded   (B) the men had not covered as much ground as the youth believed they had   (C) the regiment did not fight well   (D) the youth conducted himself honorably during the charge

REMEMBERING DETAIL

2. According to the scolding officer, the youth's regiment had stopped short of success by
(A) one hundred yards   (B) one hundred feet   (C) one thousand feet   (D) two hundred feet

3. Who comes to the colonel's defense?
(A) the lieutenant   (B) Henry   (C) Wilson   (D) the sarcastic soldier

4. At the end of the chapter, Henry and Wilson learn that they have been
(A) reported for insubordination   (B) given leave
(C) praised   (D) scolded

5. The colonel had declared that Henry and Wilson deserve to be
(A) color sergeants   (B) lieutenants   (C) jimhickeys
(D) major-generals

DRAWING CONCLUSIONS

6. The fact that the youth perceived the charge as taking much longer and covering more ground than it actually did indicates
(A) combat distorts one's sense of time and space
(B) the regiment was tricked   (C) the youth was not really paying attention   (D) the youth was fighting on a different battlefield than he thought he was

USING YOUR REASON

7. For the youth to have been called a "jimhickey" was
(A) a disgrace   (B) an insult   (C) a compliment
(D) nonsense

8. The praise that Henry and Wilson received will probably
(A) cause more competition between them   (B) make them closer friends   (C) cause them to become snobs
(D) not change them at all

IDENTIFYING THE MOOD

9. After being scolded by the officer on horseback, you can imagine the regiment feels
(A) pride and joy   (B) anger and humiliation
(C) happiness and contentment   (D) warmth and affection

10. After hearing that they were praised, you can imagine that Henry and Wilson feel

(A) nervous   (B) proud   (C) angry   (D) sad

THINKING IT OVER

How do you think the youth will handle the news that the colonel praised his performance in battle? Will he be boastful or modest about the news? Would the "old" Henry have been boastful or modest? Explain your answers.

CHAPTER 22

REMEMBERING DETAIL

1. From the youth's view, which side is winning the battle in this chapter?

(A) the North   (B) the South   (C) he cannot tell
(D) there is no battle

2. The youth is something of a spectator in this battle since he

(A) bears the flag   (B) has been injured   (C) chose to sit this battle out   (D) was ordered not to fight

3. Who has been shot through the face?

(A) the youth   (B) Wilson   (C) the lieutenant
(D) the orderly sergeant

USING YOUR REASON

4. The bearer of the colors

(A) carries the uniforms   (B) carries the flag
(C) guards the front   (D) shouts the commands

5. It is the youth's idea that his dead body will be his final revenge. He probably feels that

(A) his death will prove that he sacrificed all to the cause, thus marking him as a great soldier after all
(B) his ghost can haunt the officer after he is dead
(C) the officer is frightened by corpses   (D) the officer doesn't recognize the good deeds of soldiers until after they have been killed

IDENTIFYING THE MOOD

6. The youth's tone in resolving that "he will not budge, no matter what," is

(A) uncertain (B) determined (C) fearful (D) mocking

THINKING IT OVER

Crane's style of writing appeals greatly to the senses—touch, hearing, taste, smell, and sight. In your opinion, which sense does he appeal most to in this chapter? Find at least two examples to support your answer. Tell why you chose these examples.

CHAPTER 23

REMEMBERING DETAIL

1. The enemy had positioned themselves behind
(A) a white house (B) a fallen tree trunk
(C) a farmer's fence (D) a brick wall

2. When his regiment is ordered to charge the enemy, the youth is surprised to see that the men
(A) protest (B) charge the lieutenant instead
(C) willingly carry out the order (D) are weeping

3. The youth had resolved to capture
(A) a few prisoners (B) the enemy general's horse
(C) the battle scene on film (D) the enemy's flag

4. The charge in this chapter turns out to be
(A) successful for Henry's regiment (B) unsuccessful for Henry's regiment (C) rescheduled (D) a big mistake

5. The regiment captured four
(A) wounded soldiers (B) prisoners (C) flags
(D) hours of rest

DRAWING CONCLUSIONS

6. You can guess that the youth will now
(A) have more doubts about his abilities than ever before (B) be dishonorably discharged from the army
(C) continue to feel confidence in his abilities
(D) go back home to his mother

7. The youth has now become
   (A) hard to get along with   (B) a major-general
   (C) a leader of troop spirit   (D) badly injured
8. Fighting unselfishly means being willing to
   (A) give your life, if necessary   (B) share your
   weapons   (C) be kind to the enemy   (D) put your own
   wants and needs first

THINKING IT OVER

What is your overall opinion of the youth now, and why
do you feel as you do? Can you in any way relate to the
youth's experiences, even though you have not been to
war? Explain your answer.

CHAPTER 24

FINDING THE MAIN IDEA

1. A good title for this chapter might be
   (A) "The Final March"   (B) "The Youth Finally Finds
   Himself"   (C) "Walking in the Rain"   (D) "The Youth
   Remembers the Tattered Soldier"

REMEMBERING DETAIL

2. As he marches, the youth reflects on
   (A) his experiences in the war   (B) his home
   (C) his relationship with his mother
   (D) his relationship with his girlfriend
3. The ghost that bothers the youth's conscience is
   (A) the remembrance of Jim Conklin
   (B) the remembrance that he ran   (C) the remembrance
   of deserting the tattered soldier   (D) the remembrance
   of his lieutenant's death
4. The youth feels that he finally has
   (A) become a soldier   (B) earned his "red badge of
   courage"   (C) come to understand life
   (D) become a man

DRAWING CONCLUSIONS

5. You can conclude that the youth now feels a greater sense of

(A) self-respect (B) self-hatred (C) hostility
(D) shame

USING YOUR REASON

6. The youth's comment to Wilson, "Well, it's all over," means

(A) they are about to be killed (B) they are leaving the battlefield (C) they are ending their friendship (D) they no longer have faith in life

7. What symbolizes the peaceful existence that lies ahead for the youth?

(A) the rain (B) the march back to the river
(C) the sunshine breaking through the clouds
(D) the fading of the musketry fire

THINKING IT OVER

1. In your opinion, what does Crane mean by the following passage:

"He knew that he would no more fear for the future, wherever it might lead. He had been to touch the great death, and found that, after all, it was only the great death. He was a man."

2. Does the plot of *The Red Badge of Courage* revolve around the youth's conflict with others, with his environment, or with himself? Explain.

3. Does Crane come to any definite conclusions in this book, or does he let you draw your own conclusions? What would you say is a logical conclusion to be drawn from the youth's story?

Ngambika
Studies of Women in African Literature

edited by
Carole Boyce Davies & Anne Adams Graves

Africa World Press, Inc.

P.O. Box 1892
Trenton, New Jersey 08607

896
Nga
c.1

Africa World Press, Inc.
P.O. Box 1892
Trenton, N.J. 08607

Typeset by TypeHouse of Pennington

Cover design by Adjoa Jackson-Burrowes

Library of Congress Catalog Card Number: 85-71385

ISBN: 0-86543-017-9   Cloth
       0-86543-018-7   Paper

For Mariama Bâ
1929 - 1981
African woman writer,

Whose commitment and African feminism
made works such as this one necessary.

Acknowledgments

The Tshiluba phrase *Ngambika* (the 'g' is silent—pronounced Nambika) which we have used as our title was suggested by Elizabeth Mudimbe-Boyi as the equivalent of "Help me to balance/carry this load". The editors extend to her sincere acknowledgments. A number of colleagues and friends, especially the contributors, have supported this effort in a number of ways. We cannot mention them all by name but extend sincere thanks for their encouragement. Elizabeth Robinson of Africa World Press provided knowledgeable and painstaking copy-editing for which we are grateful. Her attention to detail and thoughtful suggestions contributed immensely to the realization of this work.

"Maidens, Mistresses and Matrons: Feminine Images in Selected Soyinka Works" which originally appeared in *Interdisciplinary Dimensions in African Literature* (Washington, D.C.: Three Continents Press, 1985). Reprinted with permission of Editor, Stephen Arnold and Three Continents Press.

Preface

In attempting to redress the relative inattention to women in African literary scholarship, the criticism in the present anthology is concerned with expanding and augmenting the interpretation of the whole body of African literary creativity. This objective involves both a re-reading of earlier writings, produced entirely by men, and a balanced reading of the more recent writings by women and by men. Therefore, the editorial and ideological orientation here is not just around the works of women writers (and critics), but around *African* writers whose works constitute the developing canon of African literature. (Indeed, any study devoted to women in the African novel that ignored Sembène and Ngugi simply because of their gender would be chauvinistically self-defeating.) What the critics assembled in this collection share, however, is a concern that the perspective and characterization of women heretofore relegated to the critical shadows, be brought into focus in whatever form they may manifest themselves in the works. To be sure, in a mature criticism of the developing canon the absence of a feminine perspective or the stunted characterization of women is as demanding of critical attention as is the more complete presentation of the feminine presence.

There is by now no need to defend the conscious and unapologetic commitment (indeed, urgency) that underlies the inspiration of most African writers—and most especially women writers. By the same token, the current efforts, as reflected in this collection of essays, to redress the relative omission of women in the criticism employs methodological approaches that are consciously and unapologetically devoted to the *substance*—social, political, psychological—of women's presence in the literature. This concentration, while in no way ignoring the place of questions of structure in the criticism, speaks to the primacy of the feminine as subject matter itself in the critics' view as well as in the view of many of the authors, particularly in recent years. Attention is in fact devoted to structural questions, for example by Naana Banyiwa-Horne and Elaine Savory Fido, as it bears on the content that is the focus of the discussion at hand. This collection of essays is, we feel, characterized by the range and diversity of approaches that the complexity of the subject matter of the feminine presence necessarily comprehends. The approaches employed are discussed in detail below as the basis for the ordering of the essays in the book.

The range and diversity of approaches contributed by these scholars to the analysis of the feminine in African literature signals, among other things, the fact that there is active debate in the community of scholars over the subject. Perhaps the single most productive discussion generated in the debate is the challenge to formerly promulgated roles and role categories for women in the few earlier studies published, such as those established by Kenneth Little in *The Sociology of Urban Women's Image in African Literature* (1980). The essays in the present collection, either directly or indirectly, repudiate such men-centered roles for women without, however, repudiating the fact that the women's lives obviously include men. Such re-definitions of the women's roles apply not only to the works written by women, as one would assume, or even to the most recent works by men. But, as several of these essays articulate, revised, women-centered definitions of women's roles apply to some earlier works as well, for example Sembène's, as Brenda Berrian demonstrates. Thus, in place of role-categories such as girlfriends, mistresses, and prostitutes, we can recognize prophets, decision-makers, heroines, martyrs, and challengers of the status quo. The issue in this book, then, is the opening up of the critical perspective, to look at woman in African literature standing on her own rather than in the shadow of the men with whom she shares the literary stage. If a legitimized re-definition of the feminine presence is the single new issue added by this book to African literary criticism, its contribution to the canon is made, and our efforts are justified.

The eighteen essays in this anthology must be viewed as a selection, rather than an overview or comprehensive study, of critical analyses of literature about the African woman. While the number and stature of authors and works included here are appropriately representative, the articles in this collection do not attempt to cover the waterfront of this fertile field of literary criticism. In the ethnographic, geographic, and cultural range of the literature discussed much of the diversity of the African experience is reflected. The works under study come from the several areas of the continent—East, West, Central, South, and the Maghreb—and represent Franchphone and Anglophone (though unfortunately not Luso-phone) as well as one indigenous language group; Muslim, Christian, indigenous African belief systems; urban and village settings; traditional and modern values and lifestyles; mythological, folkloric, and European literary-influenced content. Titles evoked by this literary topography are, for the most part, familiar to the Africanist: the Ghanaian Ama Ata Aidoo's short-story collection *No Sweetness Here* and her novel *Our Sister Killjoy*, for the urban and the rural, the traditional and the modern, the African in Europe; the Kenyan Ngugi wa Thiong'o's novels, *The River Between*, *A Grain of Wheat*, *Petals of Blood* and *Devil on the Cross*, for the Christianity-indigenous belief encounter, the traditional and modern lifestyles and values, the mythological and folkloric; Hausa women writing Hausa poetry who, as Muslims, attempt a balancing act between the traditional and the modern; the Senegalese novelist Mariama Bâ's *Une si longue lettre* and *Un chant écarlate* present likewise the Muslim tradition facing modernity.

The genres of short story, novel, drama, poetry, and biography are included, from works by both women and men authors, spanning the periods of colonial, independence, and post-independence writing: from Camara Laye's *L'enfant noir* (1956) of the Négritude era and Achebe's pioneering *Things Fall Apart* (1959), through Sembène's *Voltaïque* (1962), *Les Bouts de bois de Dieu* (1971), and *Xala* (1973) of the independence and early post-independence years; to Buchi Emecheta's *Double Yoke* (1983); and including the entire oeuvre of Ayi Kwei Armah, a representative selection of Soyinka's prose and drama; and Christopher Okigbo's poetry volume *Labyrinths*. The majority of the articles treat, however, prose fiction.

The differences in topical focus in the articles provide both depth and breadth of analysis of individual writers and of the works treated. The essays range in coverage from the examination of a narrowly defined issue presented in a single work, or in all the works of a single author, to a wider, sometimes evolutionary, consideration of a theme across two or several works by different writers, and even to an analysis of the comprehensive corpus of a delimited community of authors; two papers focus on the writings from specific ethnic groups. Although the crucial point of the anthology is the literature's treatment of the African woman per se, the primary attention devoted, in a few of the pieces, to the complexities of men's consciousness regarding women gives support to the underlying truth that woman's consciousness of herself—in literature as in life—cannot be considered in a vacuum.

While writers of the stature of Ngugi, Achebe, Aidoo, Sembène, Armah, and Soyinka are indeed present, as well as some who are less widely read, such as Flora Nwapa and Henri Lopès, the absence of studies on Beti, Ogot, Head, Farah, Mudimbe and others who also provide important sources for critical analyses of the African woman in literature, is recognized here by the editors as legitimizing rationale for on-going work in this area. Another, regrettably unavoidable, absence is more work by Francophone African women. Although Mariama Bâ is represented here, there are, besides Aminata Sow Fall no others who have attained any visibility as published writers. And the death, in 1981, of the Noma Prize-winning Bâ only makes the situation ironically more remarkable. However, we are beginning, happily, to see works appearing by other Francophone women, for example from Benin and from Congo. There is hope, therefore, that the ranks will increase, thus raising the volume of the literary voice of the African woman.

The organization of the papers into the three sections: "Defining 'Woman's Place': Female Portraiture in African Literature," "Towards a Critical Self-Definition of the African Woman: Writers and African Woman's Reality," and "Social and Political Themes: Women's Issues in African Literary Criticism," represents less a focus on differences in subject matter than an emphasis on common approaches to the treatment of the subject matter. Indeed, the examination of some authors and some works in several articles—as is evident in the titles—is an indication of obvious overlap of subject matter among the eighteen articles.

The first and second sections are similar to each other in that the articles in both focus on the depictions and perceptions of African women from several viewpoints. What distinguishes Part I from Part II is the relative presence or absence of the woman's own perception of herself, according to the analysis of the works studied in each paper. The studies in Part I examine the depiction of women from the male perspective or that of the general society, which is by and large dominated by the male perspective anyway. Whether the images are positive or negative, sympathetic or unsympathetic, traditional or modern, the perspective is that from which others view the woman. The articles in the second section, by contrast, present the woman's own conscious self-perception, whether as a model of the traditional African woman who knows fulfillment in her life, or as an individual questioning and challenging herself and the other people and forces that participate in the determination of the course of her life. Emphasis in Part III is on thematic analysis of literary presentation of political and social institutions in African societies as they influence women's thoughts and actions, happiness and unhappiness, life and death, or as women serving their roles in these institutions influence the condition of others' lives. Marriage in its many forms—polygamous/monogamous, interracial, intergenerational, sight-unseen arranged, divorce—is one such institution treated in this section. Other aspects of the domestic institution of family that are presented in this section include motherhood (and grandmotherhood), child custody and in-law relationships. Social practices and other institutionalized behavior based in religious and historical/mythological traditions are also examined as they affect or are affected by women. While the discussions of the institutions present them primarily in their social contexts, their significance in relation to the political structures on which the societies rest is central to the perspective of some of the essays in the section on social and political themes.

A reading of the eighteen pieces in this collection will reveal an interconnectedness that is manifested not only in the overlap among articles, as acknowledged at the outset, but also some disagreement—criticism in some articles of writers and works handled in others. Indeed, alternative ordering of the articles among the three sections is possible. We consider this not only acceptable but salutary. For feminist critical theory as applied to African literature is being developed through collections such as this, just as the canon of African literature itself is still being developed through the continued production of works such as those studied here. What is of importance now is correcting the faulty vision through which the African woman in literature has been seen. Her presence as reflected in the literature must be fully recognized and appreciated as an integral part of what Africa is going to become. Mariama Bâ draws a future picture of the African women in literature thus:

> The nostalgic songs dedicated to African mothers which express the anxieties of men concerning Mother Africa are no longer enough for us. The Black woman in African literature must be given the dimension that her role in the liberation struggles next to men has proven to be hers, the dimension which coincides with her proven contribution to the economic development of our country.*

Anne Adams Graves

---

*Cited in Hans Zell, Carol Bundy, and Virginia Coulon, eds. A New Reader's Guide to African Literature (New York: Holmes & Meier, 1983) p. 358.

Table of Contents

Introduction: Feminist Consciousness and African Literary Criticism

Carole Boyce Davies

African written literature has traditionally been the preserve of male writers and critics. Today, however, accompanying an ever-growing corpus of literature by African women writers, a new generation of critics, most of them women, is impacting on this male-dominated area. The perspectives of these critics exhibit a double influence, and consequently a tension of sorts. On the one hand there is a grounding in the need to liberate African peoples from neo-colonialism and other forms of race and class oppression, coupled with a respect for certain features of traditional African cultures. On the other, there is the influence of the international woman's movement and the recognition that a feminist consciousness is necessary in examining the position of women in African societies. The tension involved in this double allegiance provides a nexus from which this criticism grows.

In examining the relative scarcity of women in African written literary tradition a few points reveal themselves. First of all, there is ample evidence of women's creativity in the production of oral literature, as there is nothing inherently male about literary creativity. According to Finnegan,

> The limitations on this general mastery of the art of storytelling arise from local conventions about the age and sex of the narrators. In some

1

> societies, it appears, these are quite free; in others there is a definite
> emphasis on one or another category as being the most suitable one for
> a storyteller. In some areas it is the women, often the old women, who
> tend to be the most gifted . . . Elsewhere it is the men who tend to be
> the more expert . . .[1]

The available research makes it clear that there was equal billing for male
and female in the oral literary tradition and that while there was specialization
in certain genres according to gender, there was no large scale exclusion of
one group from the creative process.

As opposed to that, the first African writers to achieve prominence were
male. Reasons for this are obvious. The selection of males for formal
education was fostered by the colonial institutions which made specific
choices in educating male and female. Then too, the sex role distinctions
common to many African societies supported the notion that western
education was a barrier to a woman's role as wife and mother and an
impediment to her success in these traditional modes of acquiring status.
With few exceptions, girls were kept away from formal and especially
higher education.[2] The colonial administrations were therefore willing
accomplices because they imported a view of the world in which women
were of secondary importance. Clearly then, European colonialism, as well
as traditional attitudes of and to women, combined to exclude African
women from the educational processes which prepare one for the craft of
writing.

The criticism of African literature was subject to similar historical
realities. The earliest critics of African literature were European academicians
who communicated the Western male-oriented mode of creating and
evaluating literature. The first critical works were authored by European
and American critics in the 1950's and '60's (Janheinz Jahn, Ulli Beier,
Gerald Moore and others)[3] who, while they performed an invaluable service
in the development of a written literary tradition, maintained the Western
critical manner of approaching literary texts solely from the point of view of
male experience. This Ellman appropriately defines as "phallic criticism"[4]
as it excludes a host of woman-oriented configurations. The second school
of critics of African literature, continental Africans like writers Ezekiel
Mphalele, Eldred Jones, and Eustace Palmer[5] and Caribbean critics, like
Oscar Dathorne and John Ramsaran,[6] to a large extent maintained this
reductionism as it relates to women in the literature.

Most of the women who appear as contributors in the early anthologies
and journals are bibliographers like Margaret Amosu.[7] The few women
critics, Lilyan Kesteloot, Molly Mahood[8] and later Omolara Ogundipe-
Leslie,[9] for example, had to utilize the same critical apparata as their male
contemporaries. This meant turning a blind eye to women in African
literature. Even when the first major African women writers appeared—

Ama Ata Aidoo (1965), Flora Nwapa and Grace Ogot (1966)—the same type of alliance which was created by male critics and writers was not formed between the women critics and writers. Instead, without the benefit of a feminist focus, there was a reluctance to bring the works of African women writers under serious but sensitive critical evaluation.

Review of the Relevant Literature

Early criticism, largely written by male critics about male writers, as we have established above, viewed women as tangential to the discussion of men in the literature. A survey of African literary criticism, at this point, reveals little more than passing reference within general discussions. In cases where the main character is female, there is no evaluation of the female image and/or the writer's treatment of the female character. It must be noted that much of the early literature deals with the social and political implications of colonialism and man's struggle within, and away from, its confines. Women are usually made peripheral to all of that and function either as symbols or as instruments for the male hero's working out of his problems. Rafika Merini's title, "Women in Man's Exploration of His Country, His World" in this work, is an appropriate summation of this pattern. The standard critical approach follows this pattern to a large extent.

The first work to identify a female presence in African literature is Wilfred Cartey's *Whispers from a Continent*[10] which uses mother and child as its larger thematic and symbolic focus. It starts with "The Movement Away" from Mother Africa and works through "The Movement Back" which Négritude represents. His usage of mother as symbol for Africa, earth and nature popularized by the Négritude poets continues the mythologization of motherhood. When women are discussed, in line with the works he selects, it is only from the point of view of male experience. Cartey nonetheless, importantly, sees this symbolic mother-child relationship as central to the literature and to any discussion of African literature.

Criticism which employs the sociological approach has so far focused the most attention on women in African literature. E.M. Obiechina's *Culture, Tradition and Society and the West African Novel*,[11] because it does examine culture, gives minute space to a discussion of women as characters and provides some additional information on other minor aspects of women's lives. The first major discussion of women in the literature, however, comes from G.C.M. Mutiso in his essay "Women in African Literature".[12] In this work, he discusses a few notable women characters like Jagua Nana, Lawino, Efuru, Simi, and concludes that the most memorable women in African literature are city types with loose morals and political roles who are free from the bondage of traditional mores but for whom this freedom is a mixed blessing. Kenneth Little's *The Sociology of Urban Women's Image in African Literature*[13] is the most problematic of this group. It seems a development of the Mutiso study in that it lists the same categories of women. There is much overlap in these categories and much is left out. The major weaknesses of the Little study particularly are its overwhelming male bias along with several inaccuracies and its definition of women almost exclusively according to their relationships with men: 1) girl friends and good time girls; 2) wives; 3) free women; 4) mothers; 5) courtesans and prostitutes, and finally 6) political women and workers.

A much more important contribution is Arlette Chemain-Degrange's *Emancipation Féminine et Roman Africain*.[14] It examines female images in the works of Francophone male novelists who dominate this genre. Dividing her examination of the images of the Black woman into the pre-independence and post-independence periods, she concludes that three basic representations recur: the woman with the heart of gold, the suffering woman and the diligent, active woman working hard for change. She concludes that although women have been silent until recently, a number of male authors are able to envisage female emancipation without terror. Mongo Beti, Ferdinand Oyono, Sembène Ousmane, Henri Lopès and Ahmadou Kourouma have contributed to the promotion of women, convinced that the liberation of Africa is directly connected to the liberation of women. The Chemain-Degrange work is a fairly comprehensive study of this subject, and especially valuable since it concentrates on the Francophone African literature which often takes second place in examinations of African literature.

Anne Lippert's doctoral dissertation, "The Changing Role of Women as Viewed in the Literature of English Speaking and French Speaking West Africa"[15] does attempt some integration of the two language areas. But it is limited to West Africa unlike the Chemain-Degrange work which is continental in emphasis. Lippert's divisions are the "Traditional Role of Women in the Novel" under which she discusses the characterization of the young girl, the wife and the mother, all of whom (except some of the depictions of the wife) tend to be idealized, and "The Changing Roles of Women in the Novel", under which she delineates the prostitute, the political woman and the educated woman. A similar work is Sonia Lee's "L'Image de la femme dans le roman Francophone de l'Afrique occiden-tale."[16] This unpublished dissertation compares female characterization in the works of male and female writers, exploring the question of happiness for women.

The most impressive work to date is Lloyd Brown's *Women Writers in Black Africa*[17] in which he identifies "The Woman's Voice in African Literature" and goes on to study five major African women writers: Bessie Head, Efua Sutherland, Ama Ata Aidoo, Flora Nwapa, Buchi Emecheta. His basic position is that all of these writers have made significant contributions to their genres yet remain beyond the pale of criticism. In his introduction, he explores the idealistic images of women, symbolism of women in the literature and the question of persistent neglect. Brown makes some penetrating conclusions about the way these writers express the African women's sense of self in relation to tradition and society. Its limitations are that it deals primarily with English-speaking writers and that each of his writers has since published other major works. A more recent work in this vein is Oladele Taiwo's *Female Novelists in Modern Africa*.[18] Most attention is directed to Emecheta but, although he includes a larger cross-section of writers than does Brown, most reviewers identify several biases and inappropriate analyses.

The minor studies include Marion Kilson's "Women and African Literature"[19] which is a study of the short stories of Ama Ata Aidoo and Grace Ogot. In it she contrasts the images of women in both authors' works based on the status of women as protagonists, the racial and cultural status of women, their economic, domestic and leisure roles, and the life cycles of women. The Kilson essay, though somewhat tentative, is a valuable comparison of two African women writers. Roseann P. Bell's "The Absence of the African Woman Writer"[20] identifies several unexamined African women writers while Yinka Shoga's "Women Writers and African Literature"[21] is a brief overview of genres and writers. She posits that African women's lives as childbearers and childrearers, and the entire social situation which subordinates them, impede literary creativity. The requirements described by Virginia Woolf in "A Room of One's Own" seem to have no place in the African woman's life. Yet, she concludes "these pioneers . . . have begun a respectable and inclusive tradition for their daughters-in-art." In this connection it may be useful to examine Alice Walker's conclusions on writing as *work* as they relate to African women. In her article on Buchi Emecheta, "A Writer Because of, Not in Spite of, Her Children,"[22] she states in praise of Emecheta's creativity: "she integrates the profession of writer into the cultural concept of mother/worker that she retains from Ibo society. Just as the African mother has traditionally planted crops, pounded maize, and done her washing with her baby strapped to her back, so Adah can write a novel with her children playing in the same room." Anne Lippert's "Women Characters and African Literature"[23] is limited to Nigerian writers and is a brief look at the characterization of women. Obviously an excerpt from her dissertation discussed above, she uses similar categories as Mutiso and Little.

The landmark work *Sturdy Black Bridges*[24] which examines Black women's images in literature has representative essays and creative work from Africa, the Caribbean and Afro-America. Of importance to our discussion are the essays by Andrea Benton Rushing, Marie Linton Umeh, Karen Chapman and Sonia Lee.[25] The Rushing study remains so far the only major study of women in African poetry but it is dated in the sense that in her attempt to locate symbols and images specific to African culture, there is a tendency towards the acceptance of the glorification of motherhood and other prescribed female roles which is at the core of most African poetry. Her conclusion is, however, a plea for the voices of African women writers who are most equipped to tell of their realities. A growing number of African women writers, in both poetry and prose, are however demystifying this traditional romanticization of motherhood. For one thing, it disregards the childless woman and mythologizes the tedia involved in motherhood. Sonia Lee shows how Sembène allows his women characters greater self-awareness and in doing so links their freedom with Africa's freedom. Karen Chapman examines Aidoo's *The Dilemma of a Ghost*[26] for form, language and theme. Marie Linton Umeh's study "The African Heroine" begins the call for more heroic portrayals of African women.

Another significant contribution is Maryse Condé's "Three Female Writers in Modern Africa: Flora Nwapa, Ama Ata Aidoo and Grace Ogot".[27] In many ways it is a challenge to women writers to be more forthright in the examination of their societies and in their presentation of women characters. Recently there has been a movement away from the examination of feminine images[28] in the literature of male African writers to an increasing number of essays on individual African women writers.[29] Many of the earlier essays, such as those by Brown and Little[30] have been incorporated into the larger works by the same authors discussed above.

All of these works are of value to any study of women in African literature as they are important bases for present and future work. The criticism at this point seems to be crystallizing itself and defining its foci. In many ways, the pattern is similar to what occurred in mainstream feminist criticism which moved from the early identification of biases in male writers to an exploration of the works of women writers who have remained outside of the purview of literary criticism. The papers in this collection mark this transition.

Some Notes on African Feminism

The social and historical realities of African women's lives must be considered in any meaningful examination of women in African literature and of writings by African women writers. A number of works have examined African women from a variety of perspectives. Several statements have come from African women themselves in recent years. The only formulation of a feminist theory for African women, however, comes from Filomina Steady who, after examining the commonalities of experience and response of African women in Africa and the diaspora, defines an African feminism. In her introduction to *The Black Woman Cross-Culturally*,[31] she posits that this African brand of feminism includes female autonomy and cooperation; an emphasis on nature over culture; the centrality of children, multiple mothering and kinship; the use of ridicule in African woman's worldview. A number of traditional rights and responsibilities of women allow her to conclude that the African woman is in practice much more a feminist than her European counterpart.

> True feminism is an abnegation of male protection and a determination to be resourceful and reliant. The majority of the black women in Africa and the diaspora have developed these characteristics, though not always by choice . . . (pp. 35-36)

Steady's position is perhaps the most appropriate start for our discussion especially since she examines the socio-economic and class factors which contribute to African woman's oppression (economic exploitation and marginalization) and her responses to this oppression (self-reliance). There are a few debatable points in the Steady definition, however. Many will argue that assuming a nature over culture posture for African women denies her participation in the shaping of human culture and renders her an inert, unintelligent "vessel", not a creative person in her own right. Additionally, the discussion too quickly glosses over certain traditional inequities which continue to subordinate African women. (While acknowledging their existence, Steady devotes only a footnoted paragraph to these inequities in favor of extensive discussion of what makes black women's situation different.) Among them, lack of choice in motherhood and marriage, oppression of barren women, genital mutilation, enforced silence and a variety of other forms of oppression intrinsic to various societies which still plague African women's lives and must inevitably be at the crux of African feminist theory.

Steady's introduction, nonetheless, is still, so far, the most comprehensive detailing of the various facets of African women's experience. A closer examination of the African woman's situation vis a vis the layers of oppression that have to be torn away is offered by Molara Ogundipe-Leslie's "African Women, Culture and Another Development" which locates the condition of women in Africa within the socio-economic realities of culture and development. She makes the point (extending Mao-Tse Tung's "mountain on the back" metaphor) that African women have additional burdens bearing down on them: 1) oppression from outside (foreign intrusions, colonial domination etc.); 2) heritage of tradition (feudal, slave-based, communal, 3) her own backwardness, a product of colonization and neo-colonialism and its concomitant poverty, ignorance etc.; 4) her men, weaned on centuries of male domination who will not willingly relingquish their power and privilege; 5) her race, because the international economic order is divided along race and class lines; 6) her self. While she spends less time detailing the nature and scope of the last four "mountains" than she does on the first two, Ogundipe-Leslie makes it clear that the most important challenge to the African woman is her own self-perceptions since it is she who will have to define her own freedom:

> The sixth mountain on the woman's back—herself—is the most important. Women are shackled by their own negative self-image, by centuries of the interiorization of the ideologies of patriarchy and gender hierarchy. Her own reactions to objective problems therefore are often self-defeating and self-crippling. She reacts with fear dependency complexes and attitudes to please and cajole where more self-assertive actions are needed . . . [32]

Progressive African women see the women's struggle as even more difficult than the obvious struggles for national liberation where the enemy is easily recognized. As Gwendolyn Konie describes it:

> The struggle for equal rights between the sexes is going to prove even more difficult than that of de-colonization because in essence it is a struggle between husband and wife, brother and sister, father and mother.[33]

And Annabella Rodrigues who participated in the FRELIMO struggle for Mozambican liberation identifies polygamy, initiation rites and *lobolo*, or dowry, as the most difficult of traditions to eliminate and the most oppressive to women and says,

> It is easier to eliminate the colonial, bourgeois influences that were imposed on us and identified with the enemy than to eliminate generations of tradition from within our own society.[34]

Inevitably, the question of national reconstruction along more egalitarian lines enters and has to be hinged to women's lives in African nations. The positions of more radically feminist organizations like C.A.M.S. Internationale (La Commission Internationale Pour l'Abolition des Mutilations Sexuelles), a Dakar-based organization which includes membership from Afro-America, the Caribbean, Africa and Europe, have to be considered here. Founded in 1979, it proposes to work toward enhancing woman's status in society through the abolition of sexual mutilation, institutionalized polygamy, obligatory motherhood, the mandatory wearing of clothing of constraint and illiteracy of women. CAMS insists that Third World Women ought not wait for a revolution initiated by men to institute certain changes in women's lives. ("Nous n'avons plus à attendre une révolution introduite et toujours menée par les hommes. Nous prenons en charge notre propre lutte sans devinir, comme toujours, la section féminine de la révolution des hommes, par les hommes.")[35]

A genuine African feminism can therefore be summarized as follows. Firstly, it recognizes a common struggle with African men for the removal of the yokes of foreign domination and European/American exploitation. It is not antagonistic to African men but it challenges them to be aware of certain salient aspects of women's subjugation which differ from the generalized oppression of all African peoples.

Secondly, an African feminist consciousness recognizes that certain inequities and limitations existed/exist in traditional societies and that colonialism reinforced them and introduced others. As such, it acknowledges its affinities with international feminism, but delineates a specific African feminism with certain specific needs and goals arising out of the concrete realities of women's lives in African societies.

Thirdly, it recognizes that African societies are ancient societies, so logically, African women must have addressed the problems of women's position in society historically. In this regard there already exist, in some societies, structures which given women equality. According to van Sertima, the colonial period and immediate pre-colonial period are not the only indices by which one evaluates traditional African society.[36] Revised historical records are indicating that African women in the pre-colonial period and in antiquity were competent rulers, warriors and participants in their societies.[37] In fact the mythology of several peoples shows women in leadership positions (See Nama's discussion on the "Daughters of Moombi"[38] in Gikuyu culture in this work for example).

Fourthly, African feminism examines African societies for institutions which are of value to women and rejects those which work to their detriment and does not simply import Western women's agendas. Thus, it respects African woman's status as mother but questions obligatory motherhood and the traditional favoring of sons. It sees utility in the positive aspects of the extended family and polygamy with respect to child care and the sharing of household responsibility, traditions which are compatible with modern working women's lives and the problems of child care but which were distorted with colonialism and continue to be distorted in the urban environment. African feminist author Buchi Emecheta was soundly attacked for daring to suggest that polygamy worked in many ways to women's benefit.[39] The CAMS colloquium examined both monogamy and polygamy, soundly criticizing the latter but not totally endorsing the former. The debate lingers as within both marital systems women may be dominated. What should be attacked is the privilege that is accorded to males in marriage in general and the concomitant loss of status that is the females'. The excesses of polygamy which most offend women include the man's prerogative to be catered to by several women, the fact that *he* usually has the *choice*, the rejection of women and the competition between them which his choices generate. Omolara Ogundipe-Leslie, in discussing the Nigerian situation says, "the woman as daughter or sister has greater status and more rights in her lineage. Married, she becomes a possession, voiceless and often rightless in her husband's family, except for what accrues to her through her children."[40] There are, however, other forms of male-female relationships which work favorably in Africa and these need adequate examination. Importantly, no system should be institutionalized and mandated, and the woman's right to choose, without censure, should be respected.

Fifthly, it respects African woman's self-reliance and the penchant to cooperative work and social organization (networking) and the fact that African women are seldom financially dependent but instead accept income-generating work as a fact of life. It rejects, however the over-burdening, exploitation and relegation to "muledom" that is often her lot.

Sixthly, an African feminist approach has to look objectively at women's situation in societies which have undergone a war of national liberation and socialist reconstruction. Urdang's[41] essay on the steps taken to equalize the sexes in Guinea Bissau is of immense value. So are the essays in *Third World. Second Sex. Women's Struggles and National Liberation.*[42] Women who have participated fully in struggles for national liberation often find that in the national reconstruction phase, a new and more sustained struggle has to be waged with and against the men along whose sides they fought.

Finally, African feminism looks at traditional and contemporary avenues of choice for women. It is important to state here that anthropologists (largely white and male) who were the first to study African women's roles took as norm outward demeanors of submissiveness and failed to extricate other modes by which African women access power. Many of these power mechanisms surface in times of crisis. New studies by African women anthropologists and sociologists are beginning to reveal more accurate findings as these women scholars are able to enter the African women's world in ways in which the male (and white) anthropologists could not.[43] Above all, African women themselves are beginning to tell their own stories.[44] All of this must contribute to the development of a true African feminist theory.

The obvious connection between African and Western feminism is that both identify gender-specific issues and recognize woman's position internationally as one of second class status and "otherness" and seek to correct that. An International Feminism[45] to which various regional perspectives are contributed seems acceptable to African women while the European/American model is not. The failure of Western feminists to deal with issues that directly affect Black women and their tendency to sensation-alize others create antagonisms[46] as does the fact that white women are often partners in the oppression of both African women and men (South Africa as the most overt example). The term "feminism" often has to be qualified when used by most African and other Third World women. The race, class and cultural allegiances that are brought to its consideration cause the most conflict. Yet, although, the concept may not enter the daily existence of the average woman, and although much of what she understands as feminism is filtered through a media that is male-dominated and male-oriented, African women recognize the inequities and, especially within the context of struggles for national liberation, are challenging entrenched male dominance.

Theoretical African feminism understands the interconnectedness of race, class and sex oppression.[47] Consequently it realizes that there are white men and women, and definitely Black men who seek to overturn the oppressive structures of their societies. Thus, it of necessity has a socialist orientation. Kenyan writer/critic Micere Mugo's position is perhaps the best summary of this interconnectedness. In a 1976 interview she stated:

> First of all, let me note that we cannot only speak of women's oppression by men. In capitalist systems, women tend to be exploited by the very nature of the society, particularly the working and peasant women, just as men are exploited. The difference is that women are hit particularly hard. Their most obvious hardship is being educationally disadvantaged. Then you have forms of abuse that cut across class lines: sexual abuse, wife-beating and the fact that men take advantage of the woman's role as child-bearer. But I won't give the impression that I foster any illusions. Sexual abuse, rape etc. do take place in socialist societies, but I believe statistics will bear me out that the degree of such abuses is less than in capitalist societies, whose conditions of maldistribution and ownership tend to breed many social problems.[48]

For this reason she projects "a system where all the oppressive institutions are dismantled—politically, socially for the sake of men and women. . . . a society which actively encourages the idea of collective responsibility." Micere Mugo's own creative work, her collaborative work with writer Ngugi wa Thiong'o and her own activism which led to her exile from Kenya demonstrates the inextricable link between an African feminist consciousness and a socialist orientation—both commited to total freedom of all people. Omolara Ogundipe-Leslie's argument as expressed in "Not Spinning on the Axis of Maleness" and "The Female Writer and Her Commitment" cited earlier (fn.9) is another articulation of this position. African men who challenge the traditional social and political dominance of patriarchy and who support women's issues are obvious partners. Among writers, Ngugi wa Thiong'o is probably the most brilliant example, seeing the woman's struggle as inextricably entertwined with the total struggle. In a 1982 interview, on his novel *Devil on the Cross* and in *Detained: A Writer's Prison Diary* Ngugi describes women as the most exploited and oppressed section of the entire working class, "exploited as workers and at home, and also by "backward elements in the culture, remnants of feudalism.' " As a result, he says, "I would create a picture of a strong, determined woman with a will to resist and to struggle against the conditions of her present being."[49]

The very fact that it is necessary to qualify feminism or limit it with the word "African" indicates implicitly the relationship between the two. In the main, therefore, African feminism is a hybrid of sorts, which seeks to combine African concerns with feminist concerns. This is the nature of the "balancing" which has to take place.

The term "womanism" defined by Alice Walker and which comes directly out of African-American and Caribbean culture is inextricably entwined in the definition of African feminism. It too is a qualification, a search for new terminology to adequately convey Black women's feminism and a recognition of the limitation of the term "feminism" for our purposes. A womanist, she says, in part, is "a black feminist, or feminist of color . . . committed to survival and wholeness of entire people, male and female . . . [but who] loves herself. Regardless."[50] Seriousness, capability, self-reliance, love of culture, love of SELF are indicated. There may be some differences in orientation but in much the same way for African feminists, the double allegiance to woman's emancipation and African liberation becomes one.

Defining an African Feminist Critical Approach

African feminist criticism is definitely engaged criticism in much the same way as progressive African literary criticism grapples with decolonization and feminist criticism with the politics of male literary dominance. This criticism therefore is both textual and contextual criticism: textual in that close reading of texts using the literary establishment's critical tools is indicated; contextual as it realizes that analyzing a text without some consideration of the world with which it has a material relationship is of little social value. So the dichotomy between textual and contextual criticism, the perennial argument about form and content, common in literary circles finds some resolution here.

Our task here is to identify critical approaches and standards and criteria which have been applied so far to the study of African literature from a feminist perspective and which can be utilized and built upon for further examination of women in/and African literature. In a larger sense, African literary criticism, in general, if it be unbiased in the future will have to come to grips with issues such as the treatment of women characters and the growing presence of African women writers.

The African feminist theoretical framework previously outlined, along with the work of feminist theorists, combine in a unique fashion in this approach. Again, the "balancing act" described above applies. African feminist critics must take what is of value from both mainstream feminist criticism and African literary criticism, keeping in mind that both are offshoots from traditional European literary criticism and in some cases its adversaries. The result then is not reduction but refinement geared specifically to deal with the concrete and literary realities of African women's lives.

It is important to underscore the fact that a substantial amount of literature exists on the development of a feminist aesthetic[51], on one hand, and a Black/African aesthetic[52] on the other. The work of Black feminist critics[53] in the United States also provides an important focus especially when examining African women writers and the question of their exclusion from the literary canon(s).

For this reason, Katherine Frank's "Feminist Criticism and the African Novel"[54], the only published work known to this writer to deal directly with this subject, loses by not understanding the critical connection between feminist criticism and African literature by not taking into consideration how African-American feminists apply feminist theory to Black literature. There, the geo-cultural differences notwithstanding, lies the link—in the explorations of Deborah Mc Dowell, Barbara Christian, Mary Helen Washington, Alice Walker, Barbara Smith and others. For example, her questions about whether "gender or race is the most significant defining characteristic of a writer" is already answered. For Black/African feminists never make that distinction. It is not a question of either/or, but one of an acceptance of BOTH and the balances and conflicts that go with that twin acceptance. Frank, moreover is guilty of some gross distortions in the way in which she interprets feminism, for example her conclusion: "Feminism, by definition, is a profoundly individualistic philosophy: it values personal growth and individual fulfilment over any larger communal needs or good" (p.45) is just the kind of conclusion that some retrograde males have made. Quite to the contrary, feminism is not individualistic but openly speaks of "sisterhood" and the need for "women" to advance in society to be on at least an equal level with men for the society's overall good. Frank also, much like Ojo-Ade in his "Female Writers, Male Critics"[55] reads feminism solely as a Western import forgetting the African-American women, like Sojourner Truth's contribution to feminism and the many African women in history whose lives and deeds can be clearly read as "feminist". Frank, nonetheless has made an important contribution to the discussion and importantly delineates the various types of feminist literary theory which can be applied. For example, she sees the need for a literary history of African women writers which would account for the "lost lives" in African literary history. Our position is that women writers are not simply seeing themselves in conflict with traditionalism but are pointing out to society where some of the inequities lie and thereby are directly involved in a struggle to reshape society.

African feminist criticism so far has engaged in a number of critical activities which can be conveniently categorized as follows: 1) Developing the canon of African women writers; 2) Examining stereotypical images of women in African literature; 3) Studying African women writers and the development of an African female aesthetic; and 4) Examining women in oral traditional literature.

1. *Developing the Canon of African Women Writers.*

In a sense this task is two-fold—the development of a canon of African women writers and a parallel canon of critical works with the final aim of expanding the African literary canon. To this end, it encourages women writers, yet challenges their work by providing criticism which is not punitive but challenging and which seeks to elucidate the woman writer's view of the world.[56] In this instance it is one with feminist critics in the discovering of writers considered by establishment to be minor or unimportant. It re-evaluates dismissed women writers by providing critical studies which reveal specific woman-oriented configurations. An excellent example is the case of Flora Nwapa, clearly a victim of literary politics. Cavalierly dismissed by many critics[57] as unimportant, after re-vision she is credited with recreating that oral culture that African society is noted for and making important contributions to her genre. Ernest Emenyonu's rebuttal, "Who Does Flora Nwapa Write For," which explores Nwapa's aesthetic connections with Igbo oral culture,[58] Lloyd Brown's work on Nwapa in his *Women Writers of Black Africa*, and Naana Banyiwa-Horne's essay in this collection are examples of the reassessment of this writer. Published in the same year (1966), Nwapa's *Efuru*, which has a similar plot as Elechi Amadi's *The Concubine*, has not received the same critical acceptance as Amadi's book. Yet while the former provides a resolution which is favorable to women or at least shows the protagonist grappling with the conflicts, Amadi, without any more significant creative ability than Nwapa, shows woman simply as object, unable to exert any control over her life.

2. *The Examination of Female Stereotypes and Images in the Works of African Writers.*

The approach here is the identification of negative and positive images. African women writers have been attacked for dwelling on the "woman as victim" image and African male writers for locking women into postures of dependence and for defining women only in terms of their association with men. Clearly the study of images of women is not a "dead-ended" enterprise nor one exhausted by Little, as Frank puts it, for Little himself has done questionable work. The study of images is an important developmental step in feminist criticism. It represents the first realization that something is wrong and is usually the first rung of consciousness for the critic. Beyond that it becomes a challenge to established male writers to recognize distortions just as it is for racist writers to recognize and correct racial caricatures. For women writers the "woman as victim" character performs a political function, directly stimulating empathetic identification in the readers and in a sense challenging them to change. Nnu Ego in Emecheta's *The Joys of Motherhood* is the best example. It is such an excellent example of the undesirable "long-suffering" character presented by a woman writer to make a statement on the depths to which women's lives can descend. A positive image, then, is one that is in tune with African historical realities and does not stereotype or limit women into postures of dependence or submergence. Instead it searches for more accurate portrayals and ones which suggest the possibility of transcendence. Writers like Ngugi wa Thiong'o and Ousmane Sembène have demonstrated this possibility in their creation of characters like Waaringa and N'Deye Touti. Flora Nwapa, Ama Ata Aidoo, Mariama Bâ, Buchi Emecheta and other women writers have worked to provide truthful assessments of women's lives, the positive and negative and to demonstrate the specific choices that women must often make. Thus African feminist critics seek to make writers conscious of unrelenting, uniformly undesirable stereotypes and other shortcomings in female portraiture. Included here also is making visible the "invisible woman", or audible, the mute, voiceless woman, the woman who exists only as tangential to man and his problems. Additionally it explores the idealization of women and motherhood in the Négritude vein—woman as supermother, symbol of Africa, earth as muse, how this supports or distorts the creation of a female mythos and how it conforms to the realities of women's lives.

3. African Women Writers and the Development of an African Female Aesthetic.

An important cornerstone of this criticism is the examination of the works of African women writers. It looks at the themes and topics which engage women writers, their language, characterization, the forms they use, images and the like. It demands new examinations into the principles of composition, thought and expression of African women writers. New studies of oral literature from this perspective are necessary, and this is discussed separately below. In the case of written literature, previous work of African-American feminist critics who are still working in this area, provide valuable examples. Mary Helen Washington, for example, in her introduction to *Black Eyed Susans*[59] provides an excellent summation of the themes which are common to African-American women's writing: Growing up Black and Female; The Intimidation of Color; The Black Woman and the Myth of the White Woman; The Black Mother-Daughter Relationship; The Disappointment of Romantic Love; Reconciliation between Black men and women. How similar are these to themes in African women's writing?

My examination of African woman's literature reveals some concerns are similar and others that are unique to African women: 1) motherhood (the presence or absence of it/its joys and pains); 2) the vagaries of living in a polygamous marriage; 3) the oppression of colonialism and white rule; 4)

the struggle for economic independence; 5) the achievement of a balance
between relationships with men and friendships with other women; 6) the
fickleness of husbands; 6) the importance of having a support system,
particularly in the urban environment; 7) the mother-daughter conflict or
relationship; 8) the mother-son relationship; 9) above all, the definition of
self or the development of a separate self over and beyond, but not separate
from, tradition or other "man-made" restrictions. While there are similarities
arising out of women's lives internationally, and while some of these themes
also appear in the works of male writers, like Nuruddin Farah, the literature
reveals that there are differences which point to the specific types of
oppression African women face in the various cultures. For example,
although we are dealing with the literature of two groups of Black women,
each group has both distinct and common political and cultural realities
which inform its literary concerns.

Comparative assessments of the two bodies of literature and with
women's writing in other parts of the world may throw light on the
uniqueness of the African woman's literary experience or its participation
in an overall female aesthetic. For example, one finds the recurrence of
certain forms like the epistolary form, the journal, the letter and other modes
of story narration which appear here as in other women's works. Also, the
inclusion within the narrative of "small talk" is often considered a weakness
in women writers who have not "mastered form". But Pauline Nalova
Lyonga in her recent dissertation "Uhamiri. A Feminist Approach to
African Literature"[60] demonstrates a thematic and formal continuity
between African women's oral and written literature. Importantly, if we are
to apply the critical criteria of the literary establishment which is European
and male dominated, many of these African female forms are dismissed as
weaknesses. The same battle that African literary theorists had to wage to
make the European/American critics realize that other African-based
aesthetic criteria have to be applied to African literature, in effect has to be
waged for African women writers.

4. Women In/And African Oral Literature and Comparative Studies

The examination of women in oral literature and/or of the aesthetics of oral
literature created by women as compared to that created by men is another
task which so far has not been sufficiently attacked. This critical inquiry is
in some ways subsumed in the previous category but important enough to
stand on its own. Finnegan's work raises some concerns but obviously was
not geared to that endeavor, so it contains relatively little material of
relevance to us. There is, however, some available material with which
critics can work.[61] A few interesting studies have been done on women in the
mythology and how that carries over into the written literature.[62] Several
studies of the oral literature of specific groups include some discussion of

women as creator/performer and as subject.[63] Several researchers (sociologists, anthropologists) have found it important to look at women's oral literature in addition to their main interests and some work is being done exclusively on African women's oral literature.[64] But there remains much more to be done. There is an overall male bias in approaching oral literary studies (as is the case in written literary studies) which assumes that the artist is always male and which consequently overlooks a large body of material or does not look for specific aesthetic features common to women when women's work is included.

All of the above cut across a number of time periods, (pre-colonial, colonial and neo-colonial contexts), political systems (socialist and capitalist states) and settings (rural and urban locales). A number of areas remain uncovered: Language, symbolic structure and how these are revealed in the works of male and female African writers is a relatively unexplored area. Additionally, in defining an African female aesthetic, it may be worthwhile to make comparisons with the art of African women and its images of women and the female characterizations of African male artists.

Any exposition of a critical approach such as this one must lay claims to incompleteness. It is a step towards a larger end rather than the end itself. This introduction represents a summary of the currents in African feminist criticism and the directions it can take. Inevitably it is derivative and its tasks in many ways are identical to the tasks of mainstream feminist theorists and African literary theorists. Obviously, it must utilize the philosophical developments of both and arrive at a necessary synthesis. The contributors in this volume are all engaged in this task, though they are not alone as several important papers emerge each year. Another collection entitled *Critical Perspectives on Women Writers from Africa*[65] edited by Brenda Berrian and Mildred Mortimer is in press. Many of the papers in this collection were presented at forums like the African Literature Association annual conferences and women's conferences which give time and space to the presentation of women's issues in literary criticism. Each of the areas outlined above must, of necessity be expanded upon and developed. A host of research possibilities reveal themselves. This is only a beginning.

NOTES

1. Ruth Finnegan, *Oral Literature in Africa*, (London, Oxford University Press, 1970), pp. 375-376. The written African literature is correctly defined as "Modern Written Literature" in recognition that Africa has a long and distinguished oral literary tradition referred to as oral literature and, more recently, "orature".

2. Ama Ata Aidoo, for example, describes her somewhat unique position coming from one of those families which saw Western formal education as important for all and especially for women, in "To Be A Woman", *Sisterhood is Global*, ed. by Robin Morgan (New York, Anchor/Doubleday, 1984), p.259.

3. See for example works like Ulli Beier ed. *Introduction to African Literature* , (London, Longman, 1967); Janheinz Jahn, *Approaches to African Literature* (Ibadan University Press, 1959); and several other books and journals which were published in the 1950's and 1960's.

4. Mary Ellman, *Thinking About Women* (New York, Harcourt Brace Jovanovich, 1968), pp. 28-54.

5. Novelist Ezekiel Mphalele has published several articles on African literature along with his book *The African Image* (London, Faber, 1962); Eldred Jones has edited a number of volumes of *African Writing Today* but is only now (Vol. 15 forthcoming) devoting space to women in African literature; Eustace Palmer, *An Introduction to the African Novel* (London, Heinemann, 1972) follows the Western critical mold exclusively. A range of perspectives exist among African critics of the late 70's and 80's however.

6. O.R. Dathorne, *African Literature in the Twentieth Century* (Heinemann, 1976) had published several other essays and monographs on African literature before this work which does contain some limited discussion of African women writers; John Ansuman Ramsaran, *New Approaches to African Literature* (Ibadan University Press, 1965).

7. Margaret Amosu is the only woman to appear in Ulli Beier's *Introduction to African Literature* cited above. Her contribution is a "Selected Bibliography of Critical Writing", pp. 265-270. She had earlier published "A Preliminary Checklist of creative African Writing in the European Languages" (University of ibadan, 1964).

8. Lilyan Lagneau-Kesteloot who is one of the few European women critics of the 60's wrote an article "Problems of the Literary Critic in Africa.", *Abbia*, 8, (1965), pp. 29-44 but does not discuss the woman as critic. Molly Mahood for some years taught at Ibadan and was a mentor of teacher/critics like Oyin Ogunba. Among her works are "Drama in Newborn States, *Presence Africaine* 60 (1966), pp.16-33.

9. Omolara Ogundipe-Leslie's work, like other African women critics writing in the late sixties and early 1970's had been geared completely to mainstream criticism. In the late 70's, however, her critical orientation became first Marxist and then Marxist/feminist. Recently, however, she published an essay, "Not Spinning on the Axis of Maleness" in *Sisterhood is Global*, pp. 498-504. This is an important step for it is the first feminist statement that has come from this critic. It is directed at an international audience and should have some bearing on future critical works by her and contribute to African feminist literary theory. A short piece "The Female Writer and Her Commitment" appeared in *The Guardian* (Lagos), December 21, 1983, p. 11. Ms. Ogundipe-Leslie has for years had to struggle almost singly in a male-dominated academic climate which Ama Ata Aidoo also describes.

10. (New York, Random House, 1969).

11. (London, Cambridge University Press, 1975).

12. *East Africa Journal,* 3:3 (March, 1971), 4-14; later included in his *Socio-*

Political Thought in African Literature (London: McMillan Press, Ltd., 1974).

13. (New Jersey, Rowman, 1980).
14. (Dakar, Les Nouvelles Editions Africaines, 1980).
15. Ph. D. dissertation for Indiana University. 1971.
16. Ph. D. Dissertation for University of Massachusetts, 1974.
17. (Connecticut, Greenwood Press, 1981).
18. (London, McMillan, 1984).
19. *Journal of African Studies* 4 (1970), 161-166.
20. *CLA Journal* 21:4 (1978), 496.
21. *Afriscope* 3:10 (October, 1973), 44-45.
22. From *In Search of Our Mother's Gardens. Womanist Prose* (San Diego, Harcourt Brace Jovanovich, 1983), pp. 66-70.
23. Her essay also appears in *Afriscope*, 3:10 (October, 1973), 45-46, 49.
24. Edited by Roseann P. Bell, Bettye J. Parker and Beverly Guy-Sheftall (New York, Anchor Press/Doubleday, 1979).
25. Andrea Benton Rushing, "Images of Black Women in Modern African Poetry: An Overview." (pp. 18-24); Marie Linton-Umeh, "The African Heroine", (pp. 393-51); Sonia Lee, "The Awakening of Self in the Heroines of Ousmane Sembene, (pp. 52-60); also Karen Chapman, "Introduction" to Ama Ata Aidoo's *Dilemma of a Ghost*", pp. 25-38.
26. (New York, Collier, 1971). First published in London in 1965). Among African women writers, Ama Ata Aidoo has perhaps had the most critical attention. Yet the criticism is not commensurate with her output and talent when compared with that accorded male writers with similar or lesser work.
27. Condé's article is in *Presence Africaine* (2:82, 1972), 132-143.
28. For example, Kathleen Staudt, "The Characterization of Women by Soyinka and Armah," *Ba Shiru* (8:2, 1977), 63-69. Another essay "Symbolic Characterization of Women in the Plays and Prose of Wole Soyinka" by Adetokunbo Pearse appears in *Ba Shiru* 9:1&2 (1978), 39-46.
29. Many of these essays will be listed in the bibliography of criticism.
30. See fns. 13 & 16 above.
31. (Cambridge, Mass., Schenckman Publishing Company, Inc., 1981), pp. 7-41.
32. *The Journal of African Marxists* 5(February, 1984):89 pp. 35-36.
33. In *Sisterhood is Global*, p. 744.
34. In Miranda Davies, ed. *Third World—Second Sex. Women's Struggles and National Liberation* (London, Zed Books, 1983), pp. 131-132. Jane Ngwenya a political activist from Zimbabwe had much earlier made similar points in an interview "An African Woman Speaks", *Encore*, June 23, 1975, p. 48. Grace Akello, *Self Twice Removed*, a report on Ugandan women published by Change, an International Women's Research Organization in 1982 and reported in "Struggling Out of Traditional Strait-jackets", *New African*, January, 1983.
35. Le Soleil (Dakar), 29 decembre 1982. "We no longer have to wait for a revolution introduced and always led by the men. We are taking charge of our own struggle without becming, as always, the female section of the revolution of and for men." (my translation).
36. See his *They Came Before Columbus* (New York, Random House, 1976) and

Blacks in Science: Ancient and Modern (Available through African Studies Department, Rutgers University), 1983.

37. John Henrik Clarke, "African Warrior Queens" in *Black Women in Antiquity* ed. by Ivan Van Sertima (New Brunswick, Transaction Books, 1984), pp. 123-134. Caroline Ifeka-Moller, "Female Militancy and Colonial Revolt. The Woman's War of 1929, Eastern Nigeria, in *Perceiving Women* ed. Shirley Ardener (New York, John Wiley & Sons, 1975), pp. 127-157. A paper "Slavery and Women in The Pre-Colonial Kingdom of Dahomey" by Boniface Obichere (Institute of African Studies, University of ibadan, 1976) demonstrates that women participated equally in the political, social and economic life of pre-colonial Dahomey.

38. African woman writer, Charity Waciuma also has an autobiographical work entitled *Daughter of Mumbi* (Nairobi, East African Publishing House, 1969).

39. African Studies Meeting, (California) October, 1984. African women in the audience, some feminists, were appalled at Emecheta's stand on polygamy. One has to admit, however, that Emecheta, who has written several novels which show polygamy in negative light would not have come to her position casually.

40. "Not Spinning on the Axis of Maleness" in *Sisterhood is Global*, pp. 500-501.

41. Stephanie Urdang, "The Role of Women in the Revolution of Guinea-Bissau." in Steady, pp. 119-139.

42. (London, Zed Press, 1983); Essays in *Sisterhood is Global* also provide views on women in countries undergoing socialist reconstruction. Some describe it as the second struggle. Others like Jane Ngwenya, "Women and Liberation in Zimbabwe", pp. 78-83 say that suffering and fighting together erodes sexual prejudices and stereotyping. More long-term study will show if this is sustained.

43. See for example D. M. Hull's bibliography "African Women in Development: An Untapped Resource" (Moorland-Spingarn Research Center, Howard University, April, 1983) which lists a number of works by African women specifically and by women in general. Audrey Smedley, "Motherhood and Women in Patrilineal Societies" presented at the ASALH Conference, Detroit, Michigan, 1983, part of a major work being prepared on women and patriliny, holds that by assuming women have no say in the shaping of the kind of society they live in, we bring a male-oriented approach to examining African societies. African and African-American anthropologists like Bolanle Awe and Niara Sudarkasa, are providing important information on women in African societies. The essays in Steady's *The Black Woman Cross-Culturally* are additional examples.

44. African women writers are making statements on the social organization of their societies, in addition to their creative writing. A number of interviews with African women are being published.

45. *Sisterhood is Global* is subtitled "The International Women's Movement Anthology". The extent of contributions to this and other similar volumes indicates the validity of international feminism.

46. The AAWORD Statement on Genital Mutilation in *Third World-Second Sex*, pp. 217-220 is a case in point. Steady's introduction is in many ways a rebuttal to Western feminism.

47. See for example, Lillian Robinson's *Sex, Class and Culture* (Bloomington,

Indiana University Press, 1978), Angela Davis, *Women, Race and Class* (New York, Random House, 1983), Lise Vogel, *Marxism and the Oppression of Women. Toward Unitary Theory* (New Jersey, Rutgers University Press, 1983); Bonnie Thornton Dill, "Race, Class and Gender: Prospects for an All-Inclusive Sisterhood," *Feminist Studies* 9 (1983), 131-150.

48. "Dr. Micere Mugo, Kenya's outspoken Intellectual and Academic Critic, Talks to Nancy Owano," *Africa Woman* 6(September to October, 1976), pp. 14-15.

49. Profile: "Ngugi: My Novel of Blood, Sweat and Tears." *New AFrican* (August, 1982), p. 36. The works cited are published by Heinemann (London) African Writers Series Nos. 200 (1982) and 240 (1983) respectively.

50. The definition of "womanist" is a preface to her *In Search of Our Mothers Gardens: Womanist Prose*, op. cit., pp. xi-xii.

51. Among them are essays in Cheryl L. Brown and Karen Olson, *Feminist Criticism* Essays on Theory, Poetry and Prose (New Jersey, The Scarecrow Press, Inc., 1978). Cheri Register's Review essay, "Literary Criticism" in *Signs* (Winter, 1980) is a fairly comprehensive sampling of the issues and theorists of feminist criticism. Essays in Elizabeth Abel, ed., *Writing and Sexual Difference* (University of Chicago Press, 1982) and Elaine Showalter, *Feminist Criticism* (New York, Random House, 1985) are additional examples.

52. See Addison Gayle, *The Black Aesthetic* (New York, Doubleday, 1971); Carolyn Fowler's introduction to her *Black Arts and Black Aesthetics - A Bibliography* (Atlanta, First World Foundation, 1984); Zirimu and Gurr, *Black Aesthetics* (Nairobi, East African Publishing House, 1973); Wole Soyinka, *Myth, Literature and the African World* (London, Cambridge University Press, 1976); Chinweizu et al, *Towards the Decolonization of African Literature* (Washington, D.C. Howard University Press, 1983); Johnson, Cailler, Hamilton and Hill-Lubin, *Defining the African Aesthetic* (Washington, D.C. Three Continents Press, 1982).

53. Section Five of *But Some of Us Are Brave*, edited by Gloria T. Hull, Patricia Bell Scott and Barbara Smith (New York, The Feminist Press, 1982) is devoted to literature and contains Barbara Smith's "Toward a Black Feminist Criticism", pp. 157-175 which is also published separately in booklet form and distributed by The Crossing Press, 1982. Deborah McDowell, "New Directions in Black Feminist Criticism", *Black American Literature Forum* 14:4 (Winter, 1980), 153-159; Claudia Tate's *Black Women Writers at Work* (New York, Continuum, 1983), Alice Walker's essays in *In Search of Our Mothers Gardens*, Mary Helen Washington's many essays and a number of other works address this issue. Toni Cade Bambara's *The Black Woman. An Anthology* (New York, New American Library, 1970) includes essays like Francis Beale's "Double Jeopardy: To Be Black and Female" which discuss the particular situation of Black American women. Deborah Mc Dowell is preparing an extensive manuscript on feminist criticism as applied to African-American literature. Barbara Christian, *Black Feminist Criticism. Perspectives on Black Women Writers* (New York, Pergamon Press, 1985) includes Buchi Emecheta in her study.

54. Katherine Frank, "Feminist Criticism and the African Novel," *African*

Literature Today 14 (London, Heinemann, 1984), 34-48.

55. Although it has a catchy introduction and conclusion, Femi Ojo-Ade's, "Female Writers, Male Critics" does not deal with criticism but is a study of Flora Nwapa and Ama Ata Aidoo. Ojo-Ade is well recognized for an overtly belligerent, condescending-to-female-writers-and-critics language and oral style of presentation which contradicts some of the points he makes in his conclusion "Criticism, Chauvinism, Cynicism . . . Commitment". While he seems to be arguing for fairness to women here, his tone may betray his true attitude to this subject. Most Black women welcome men as fellow explorers in this field and rarely descend to the gross abuses he suggests, in his final paragraph, that are levelled against male critics. It seems instead a rehashing of some of the early stereotypical language of "women's liberation."

56. Carole Boyce Davies and Elaine Savory Fido, "African Women Writers" in *African Literature in the Twentieth Century* ed. by Oyekan Owomoyela (University of Nebraska Press, forthcoming). This chapter attempts a literary history of African women writers which approaches the works from a womanist critical perspective. Roseann P. Bell had earlier called for a "mutual" supportive and critical system sympathetic to our needs" in "The Absence of the African Woman Writer," op. cit., p. 498.

57. See Eustace Palmer's review "Elechi Amadi and Flora Nwapa" in *African Literature Today* 1-4 (1968-70), 56-58.

58. Ernest N. Emenyonu, "Who Does Flora Nwapa Write For?" *African Literature Today* 7 (London: Heinemann, 1975): 28-33.

59. (New York, Anchor/Doubleday, 1975).

60. Unpublished Ph. D. Dissertation, University of Michigan, 1985.

61. Elizabeth Gunner, "Songs of Innocence and Experience: Women as Composers and Performers of *Izibongo*, Zulu Praise Poetry," in *Research in African Literatures* 10:2 (1979), 239-267. Harold Scheub, *African Oral Narratives, Proverbs, Riddles, Poetry and Song* (Boston, G. K. Hall, 1977) is a comprehensive bibliography of African oral literature. A number of dissertations and theses and other collections contain material which is rarely used and which needs to be reviewed for women's contributions.

62. Chidi Ikonne, "Women in Igbo Folktales" presented at the 1982 (Howard) ALA conference is an example. So is Nama's paper on women in Gikuyu mythology in this work.

63. Examples are Marion Kilson, *Royal Antelope and Spider: West African Mende Tales*. (Cambridge, Mass: The Press of Langdon Associates, 1976). See also Donald Cosentino's review in *Research in African Literatures* 10 (1979): 296-307 which discusses the question of woman as performer and makes reference to his own collection and to Mama Ngembe, a highly reputed oral artist. Thirty-nine of the forty stories included in Harold Scheub's *The Xhosa "Ntsomi"* (Oxford, Clarendon Press, 1975) were told by women. See Jeff Opland's review of A. C. Jordan, *Tales From Southern Africa* (Berkeley, University of California Press, 1978) in the same issue of *RAL* pp. 307-314.

64. For example Beverly B. Mack *"Waka Daya Ba Ta Kare Nika':* One Song Will Not Finish the Grinding: Hausa Women's Oral Literature" in *Contemporary African Literature* ed. by Wylie et al. (Three Continents Press, 1983), 15-46; Enoch T. Mvula, "Tumbuka Pounding Songs in the Management of

Familial Conflicts" *Cross Rhythms* 2 ed. by Daniel Avorgbedor and Kwesi Yankah (Indiana University, Department of Folklore, The Trickster Press, 1985), 93-113. Mvula is doing some further research on African women's oral literature in East Africa.

65. (Washington, D.C. Three Continents Press, forthcoming). Brenda Berrian's *Bibliography of American Women Writers and Journalists* (Three Continents, 1985) will contribute significantly to the study of African women writers and definitely establishes that there is a substantial body of literature by African women.

PART ONE
Defining 'Woman's Place': Female Portraiture in African Literature

Part I "Defining 'Woman's Place': Female Portraiture in African Literature", looks at roles/depictions/characterizations—in short, the "place" given to women in novels, primarily, from the 1950s, which produced the earliest of the works of African literature in the European mold, to the very recent. Those images of the African woman as discussed in the papers—whether from the Négritude movement with its romanticization of women or from the more recent years in which she is depicted with greater fidelity—the images are, in the evaluations presented in the articles, less than whole, incompletely formed, images imposed on women by others, or otherwise unrealistic. All, however, are seen through the eyes of males who are the dominant figures in the literary works as well as in the lives of the women characters in those works. Whatever the depiction, whatever the sentiment that generates it, it is someone else's image of the woman, as he (they) see(s) and interact(s) with her, whether idealized, loved, pitied, or castigated. An overview of such portraiture in literature from the colonial era is the subject of Esther Smith's article. The nearly universal depiction of women is in the role of mothers, whose place in the survival of the African family in the face of colonialism is presented as critical, according to Smith. Her analysis substantiates the concept of the supremacy

25

of motherhood in the cosmology of most African peoples. Quite the contrary view of the mother's (and wife's) position is presented in Rafika Merini's paper on Driss Chraïbi's Succession Ouverte. *Merini points up the powerlessness of the wife/mother in the Moroccan Muslim society as depicted by Chraïbi, showing, for example, that women never speak for their own interests separate from those of their men. But her position as wife and mother is, of course, not the sole characterization of woman in African literature. Besides this concentration on her domestic relationships there is also attention given to woman's reaction and adaptation to the westernizing influences of colonialism. Karen Smyley-Wallace's article discusses the alienation of women in Abdoulaye Sadji's* Nini *and in Sembène's* God's Bits of Wood, Xala, *and "Black Girl." Smyley-Wallace shows that these women's obsession for the Europeanization of themselves, in one form or another, causes irreversible and sometimes tragic alienation.*

The unsatisfying and unrealistic self-image discussed by Smyley-Wallace is but one side of a coin whose reverse side can be described as the incomplete re-creations of historical and mythological heroines, as discussed by Carole Davies in her paper "Maidens, Mistresses, and Matrons: Feminine Images in Selected Soyinka Works." Although the contemporary versions of the heroines Soyinka creates are engaged as well as engaging, Davies sees them as confined to the state of being objects, rather than subjects. Across the dramatic and prose works she refers to for her analysis Davies is able to conclude at least that Soyinka's women characters who are modeled on heroines from Yoruba history succeed better than do those based on characters from the mythology. A qualitative distinction among women characters is also seen across the several works of another writer of equal stature, as presented in Abena Busia's "Parasites and Prophets: The Use of Women in Ayi Kwei Armah's Novels." In this article Armah's entire oeuvre of five works is studied for what Busia sees as remarkable evolution, from his first, The Beautyful Ones Are Not Yet Born *to his most recent* The Healers. *Recognizing that Armah's major women characters are in a position of having to choose between a role of "earth mother" or "public servant," Busia concludes that by his fifth novel the writer has reached a resolution between those two positions. This discussion by Busia, in its presentation of the gradual emergence of woman from a unidimensional, externally viewed character to a multi-faceted self-motivated person, can be viewed as a bridge to Part II with its decidedly feminine-centered perspective.*

A.A.G.

Images of Women
in African Literature:
Some Examples of Inequality
in The Colonial Period

Esther Y. Smith

Studies of inequality in colonial Africa rarely focus on the status of women. Studies of women in African literature rarely focus on the colonial period, and when they do, tend to show either strong mother figures in traditional society, or rootless young women pursuing individualistic and materialistic goals in modern society. Reductionist reflections of monolithic or dualistic images of women in African literature, however, shatter to pieces with the press of data from the vast and diverse body of African literature. This study focuses on images of women in African novels which deal with the colonial period. It outlines some of the many different images of women which reflect some of the many faces of Africa and facets of inequality in the colonial period. It is a brief look at that vast and complex tableau which can only suggest productive ways of exploring images of women in African literature. It is in no way intended as an exhaustive or definitive study.

The primary data are limited to fictional sources from West and East Africa dealing with the colonial period. Limitations of genre have been imposed not only for reasons of space allotted, but in the interest of

27

consistency. A number of scholars have pointed out the relatively limited amount of drama, and the limited range of images of women in poetry from Africa, as compared to the fictional modes. Karen Chapman analyzes reasons for this lag in dramatic literature in her perceptive introduction to the Ghanaian drama, *The Dilemma of a Ghost* by Ama Ata Aidoo.[1]

> Black-African theater (and also film), still young and still forming, is a first fruit of Independence; few of its makers are yet middle-aged. More than any other literary form, theater requires for its life a physical continuity of institutions and audience, an atmospheric "place" where talent (and learning) congregates, collides, and grows old in the practice of skills; not less important, it requires a supportive community physically hooked on theatergoing. Until almost 1960, a gifted African writer had no such place to go . . .[2]

In poetic genres, Andrea Rushing points out that images of women are limited to two. Most poems reflect a vision of the strong, traditional "mother-is-gold" figure. Exceptions reflect what happens to young women cut off from their roots by the impact of colonialism, wanderlusting around in their pursuit of the big men in the big city. In her essay on "Images of Black Women in Modern African Poetry," Rushing compares this narrow focus with the broad range of images of women in modern African fiction, and offers some explanations.

> Unlike the images of African women in contemporary West African fiction, very few poetic images mirror the social change stalking Africa. One looks almost in vain for poems (like the short stories in Ama Ata Aidoo's *No Sweetness Here*), about urban women working, living alone, rejecting polygamy, deciding to have small families, agonizing over the crises of romantic love, snapping their ties to the extended family, playing critical roles in the past and present liberation struggles. On the one hand poetry, with its terse and vivid imagery, is the wrong place to go for full-scale realistic and naturalistic representations. On the other, almost all modern African poetry is written by men . . .[3]

This study will focus on images of women in novels about Africa during three stages of colonization: the first contacts with Europeans; colonial government in full control; and movements towards independence. In addition, a brief look at images of women and inequality in fiction dealing with traditional African societies and a glimpse at those about newly independent African countries will bracket the study of colonial times, providing those images of women with a perspective of historical depth.

In narrative genres of traditional oral literature from Africa, as in those from around the world, images of women show the good and the evil, the weak and the strong, the queens and heroines with magical powers, as well as the wives and mothers of more ordinary resources. The mother of the hero in *Sundiata, An Epic of Old Mali*[4] is unfailingly strong and courageous in protecting her children from danger and in fostering Sundiata's growth to heroic leadership. Sogolon is endowed with extraordinary powers which enable her to counteract the effects of her jealous co-wife's evil-doings. The machinations of Sassouma, the wicked co-mother, reflect the psychological realities of inequality in polygamous relationships.

The motif of jealousy and inequality in polygamous families is frequent in modern fiction about traditional society. Ousmane Sembène's psychological study of inequality in polygamy in "Her Three Days," is analyzed by Sonia Lee:

> The young woman, Noumbe, is the main protagonist of "Ses trois jours," a story in the collection *Voltaïque* (1962). Noumbe is the third wife of Moustaphe, who has very recently taken a fourth wife. Following the law of the Koran, the husband must treat his four wives equally in all ways and spend the same amount of time with each of them. But Sembene confronts us with reality: Husbands do not treat their wives with equal fairness, and the new wife is almost always the favorite . . .Noumbe remembers how it was to be the favorite and remembers also how she kept the husband beyond her own three days just as the new wife is doing now. She remembers how she cheated the other wives, how she tried to drain the husband of his strength so he would be "no good" to the next woman whom he was to visit. Now it is her turn, and she sees for the first time the viciousness of the competition. Noumbe realizes that she and the other wives are fighting a losing battle and that the husband is always the winner.[5]

Other aspects of inequality in traditional marriages are reflected in images of the barren woman. Pokuwaa, the central figure in *A Woman in Her Prime* by Asare Konadu,[6] is a very successful woman as a farmer, but she is in desperation over her inferior status and dismal future as childless woman. After years of rituals for the treatment of infertility, she ultimately puts a stop to the sacrifices and medicines which are poisoning her existence and finds a new peace through this rebellious act of acceptance of her state. In a tidy little ending, Pokuwaa finally gets pregnant and they all live happily ever after.

Another barren female character who finally conceives is Agom, the number one wife in *Highlife for Lizards* by Onuora Nzekwu.[7] Her new worry is that her child be a boy, so that she may enjoy higher status among her husband's people and finally earn the right to be buried there, for if she produces only female children, her body will be conveyed back to her relatives when she dies.

In contrast to these images which show women's unequal or inferior status, there are also the women of superior abilities like Adebisi, in *The Brave African Huntress*, by Amos Tutuola.[8] Marie Linton-Umeh, in her essay on "The African Heroine,"[9] shows that Adebisi uses magical powers to achieve greatness in the non-traditional role of hunter, out-doing all her brothers and freeing them from the evil beasts which she alone is able to eradicate.

These images of women in narratives dealing with traditional African society, including the jealous co-wives, the barren women, the mothers hoping for sons, and the heroines whose extraordinary abilities lift them to positions of leadership, recur repeatedly in novels about the colonial period. Images of women dealing with those aspects of inequality, in addition to those introduced by colonialist oppressors will emerge from the following analysis of novels situated in the first stages of colonialism, in the period of colonialism in full sway, and during colonialism under siege by movements for independence.

The image of the mother in *The African Child* by Camara Laye is reminiscent in a number of ways of that earlier Malinké mother, Sogolon, the mother of Sundiata: strong in her devotion to duty, and possessed of extraordinary powers in the protection of her son. Camara's highly autobiographical account of a child growing up in a peaceful town in Guinea seemingly unspoiled by the incursions of colonialism projects a strong image of the mother, given equal weight (if not strictly equal time) with the father figure. His mother is strong in her respect for tradition, in the respect she has for others and for herself, and in the great esteem in which she is held by her husband and by all. She is seen as the conserver of ancestral and Muslim traditions: teaching her children respect for family prayers, totems, medicines and rituals; sending her son and daughter to Koranic school, as well as to the government elementary school; serving meals to the men and women separately, but receiving thanks and a bow from all who had eaten. She is seen, also, as proprietor of extraordinary spiritual powers inherited from her smith family: gifts of healing; gifts of extra-sensory perception vis-à-vis her loved ones' troubles; and a special protective relationship with the crocodile, totem of her clan. She plays an important protective role: teaching her child not to play with snakes; checking on him to make sure he was well after the circumcision; chiding her husband about ruining his eyes by forging too much gold; and refusing to give permission for her son to go to Paris for his higher education. If there is any way at all in which this ideally equal partner in the home may be seen to be unequal, it is only that she is unequal to the task of preventing her son's going to France. She realizes, finally, with overflowing grief, that she has to let him go, that nothing will stem the tide of change which colonialism is bringing to their land.

Emile Snyder, in his essay on "Modern African Literature," analyzes the role of the mother on a heightened symbolic plane.[10]

> The image of the African mother is central to an understanding of Camara Laye's novel L'Enfant Noir . . .It is she who keeps the family traditions together because she respects them, while dispensing them. It is she who raises her son along the path of the ancestor's ways, so that even later, while a student in Paris, the son sees in the recalled image of his mother a reflection of the dignity of African life.[11]

In contrast to the central position played by the mother figure in *The African Child*, women play very minor parts in Chinua Achebe's novel about the coming of colonialism in Nigeria, with its apocalyptic title, *Things Fall Apart*.[12] The three wives of Okonkwo are merely numbered as part of his acquisitions in the end of the first chapter:

> Okonkwo was clearly cut out for great things. He was still young but he had won fame as the greatest wrestler in the nine villages. He was a wealthy farmer and had two barns full of yams, and had just married his third wife. To crown it all he had taken two titles and had shown incredible prowess in two inter-tribal wars.[13]

His wives are introduced by name, rank, and snippets of character only little by little. Ojiugo, the youngest, is beaten severely (p. 31) for forgetting her husband's dinner hour. Nwoye's mother, the first wife, tries to cover for her. She is always referred to as Nwoye's mother, which should be a term of respect, except that Okonkwo hates what he perceives as Nwoye's "weak character." Ekwefi, his second wife, is not introduced by name until later (p. 40), and much later we learn how it was that she left her first husband to come and live with Okonkwo (p. 103). There are brief glimpses of the wives preparing food for their husband, and helping each other get ready for various big events; but Ekwefi is the only wife whose character is at all developed.

Ekwefi receives more than her equal share of attention from Okonkwo, partly because of her irresistible love for the wrestling hero, but also because of her "changeling" child, her daughter, Ezinma, cherished as the child who finally decided to stay, after Ekwefi had lost ten children, most of them in infancy. Ezinma is a neverending source of delight to Okonkwo for her intelligence, understanding and spunk, and he never ceases wishing under his breath that she had been born a boy.

References by Okonkwo, as well as by other men in the village, to the inferiority of women recur with sufficient regularity to act as a leit-motif, setting the tone for images of inequality perceived through the insecure

defensiveness of Okonkwo. Early in the novel, for example, we see
Okonkwo worried about supporting his father's household, as well as his
own:

> His mother and sisters worked hard enough, but they grew women's
> crops, like coco-yams, beans and cassava. Yam, the king of crops, was
> a man's crop.[14]

Later on in the novel, he curses his own weakness with the worst insult he
can think of:

> "When did you become a shivering old woman," Okonkwo asked
> himself, "you, who are known in all the nine villages for your valor in
> war? How can a man who has killed five men in battle fall to pieces
> because he has added a boy to their number? Okonkwo, you have
> become a woman indeed."[15]

In yet another scene, Okonkwo discusses cultural differences stranger than
fiction with a neighbor:

> "The world is large," said Okonkwo. "I have even heard that in some
> tribes a man's children belong to his wife and her family."
>
> "That cannot be," said Machi. "You might as well say that the
> woman lies on top of the man when they are making children."[16]

Near the end of the novel, in a supreme irony, Okonkwo names one of his
children "Mother is Supreme," based on an Igbo aphorism. The fact that
this was done merely out of politeness to his mother's kinsmen, where he
had been exiled, was revealed two years later when he named his next child
"Nwofia," "Begotten in the Wilderness."[17]

These images of women during the early stages of colonialism, whether
functioning in a secondary role in the novel as in *Things Fall Apart*, or
playing a major role as in *The African Child*, all function similarly in their
society as conservers of tradition. Through good times and adversity,
women struggle to protect their children from dangers perceived in the
coming of colonialism.

In contrast, the images of women in the following examples of novels
about colonialism at its height reflect a new strategy for dealing with the
aliens and their culture: the politics of so-called accommodation. No longer
able to protect themselves and their children from the dangers of colonialism,
Africans practice the politics of survival with a new approach. By
cooperating to a certain extent with the colonial oppressors, they acquire
sufficient knowledge of alien ways to survive their destructiveness.

The image of the Most Royal Lady in *Ambiguous Adventure* by Cheikh Hamidou Kane[18] reflects the strategy of a powerful Fulani aristocrat of what is today Senegal in dealing with the incursion of French civilization:

> "I have done something which is not pleasing to us and which is not in accordance with our customs. I have asked the women to come to this meeting today. We Diallobé hate that, and rightly, for we think that the women should remain at home. But more and more we shall have to do things which we hate doing, and which do not accord with our customs. It is to exhort you to do one of those things that I have asked you to come to this meeting today.
>
> "I come here to say this to you: I, Most Royal Lady, do not like the foreign school. I detest it. My opinion, nevertheless, is that we should send our children there."[19]

The imposing "queen mother" figure then explains her strategy with powerful earth imagery symbolic of her role as the practical preserver of ancient and Islamic traditions. She compares the children to the seeds which are buried, "killed" in a sense, in the period of hibernation, in order to spring up after the rainy season as the fertile new generation.

The image of the Most Royal Lady is comparable in some ways to that of the mother of *The African Child*. Tall, strong, and dignified in her bearing, she is equally committed to the ancient and to the Islamic traditions of her people.

> The Most Royal Lady, who could well have been six feet tall, had lost none of her impressive bearing, in spite of her age.
>
> The little white gauze veil clung to the oval of a face full of contours . . . it was like a living page from the history of the Diallobé country. Everything that the country treasured of epic tradition could be read there. All the features were in long lines, on the axis of a slightly aquiline nose. The mouth was large and strong, without expression. An extraordinarily luminous gaze bestowed a kind of imperious lustre upon this face. All the rest disappeared under the gauze, which, more than a coiffure would have done, took on here a distinct significance. Islam restrained the formidable turbulence of those features, in the same way that the little veil hemmed them in.[20]

The Most Royal Lady, however, is more than equal to the tasks she undertakes as preserver of traditions. As older sister of the chief of the Diallobé, is was she who had pacified the peoples of the North by her firmness. "The chief of the Diallobé was by nature more inclined to be peaceable. Where he preferred to appeal to understanding, his sister would cut through on the path of authority. 'My brother is not a prince,' she was in the habit of saying, 'he is a sage.'"[21] The most powerful example of this image of strength, however, is her victory over rulers and people alike, in persuading them of the practical necessity of cooperating with the colonial government: seeking self-preservation through calculated self-destruction, by sending their children to the colonialist schools.

Unlike the Most Royal Lady, the female characters in *Houseboy* by Ferdinand Oyono[22] play secondary roles in the novel as well as in their society. They are comparable in some ways to the non-aristocratic, female folk in *Things Fall Apart*. They in no wise attempt to interact with their men on any plane of equality, but rather deal with them from a seemingly supportive stance, in the background of the main action. Behind the scenes, however, the women in *Houseboy* play the politics of collaboration, secretly undermining the power of the colonial oppressors.

The image of women in Oyono's sardonic novel about colonialism at its most brutal heights reflects the politics of intimacy at its most devastating depths. Similar strategies of sexual politics are employed by the African women who are wise and very practical, and by the European women who are silly, vapid, and blindly prejudiced. The degree of their comparative success seems to reflect the quality of their strength of character.

Kalisia, the beautiful, self-sufficient young African woman drifts into the employ of the Commandant with the same earthy, bright insouciance with which she has moved from man to man, black and white, loving and leaving them with a carelessness that bespeaks a viable strategy of survival. Hers is in no way the image of a hapless, helpless creature shunted from man to man in the psychology of dependency. Her actions and reactions rather reflect the feisty image of the successful entrepreneur, very much in control of all her undertakings, and of her choice of clientele.

Sophie, the African mistress of the agricultural engineer, employs a similar strategy of survival, but at times suffers from lack of control over the humiliations she sustains at the hands of the colonials. Hurting physically as well as emotionally one day as she was being jounced all over the back of a truck, Sophie breaks down to Toundi, the young protagonist of *Houseboy*:

> A violent swerve nearly flung us over the side. "Christ," cried Sophie. 'What have they got that I haven't got?' She turned towards me. Two big tears were rolling down her cheeks. I laid my arm on hers. She wiped her eyes with her cloth.
> 'What lovely manners they've got, these whites . . .even if it's only among themselves . . .my arse is just as delicate as the arses of the ladies they have up there in the driver's cabin. . . . '[23]

Another day, Sophie is furious with herself for missing a chance to pick the engineer's pocket for the keys to his strongbox. She explains to Toundi that she's "sick and tired of hearing 'Sophie, don't come today. I've got a European coming to see me at the house', 'Sophie, you can come, the

European has gone', 'Sophie, when you see me with a white lady don't look at me, don't greet me' and all the rest."[24] She continues to wait for her big chance, however, and finally leaves the engineer with nothing in his cashbox and even less understanding of how this could have happened.

Like the African women, the wives of the colonial administrators also control their men by playing up the dependency role, flattering their insatiable and fragile egos with ostensible supportiveness. Behind the scenes, they are vicious in their betrayals of their men, of each other, and of the Africans they victimize as scapegoats. Their petty politics of manipulation through collaboration reflect the narrow minds and shallow souls of the oppressors. The colonial women are playing the same game, but for much smaller stakes than the African women who put their lives on the line in the politics of survival.

These images of women in novels about the hey-day of colonialism in Africa, whether reflecting those dealing from a position of strength as in *Ambiguous Adventure*, or from a secondary position as in *Houseboy*, all demonstrate the same strategies of survival characteristic of oppressed people. They collaborate and accommodate and seemingly accept the power of the colonizers, while studying the situation and biding their time, until the time comes for more direct action.

It is in the novels dealing with the final stages of colonialism in Africa, under siege by movements for independence, that images of women reflect a new, active response to inequality. In *God's Bits of Wood* by Ousmane Sembène,[25] the march of the women in support of the railway strike on the Dakar-Niger line from October, 1948 to March, 1949 is described by A. Adu Boahen in the "Introduction" as a critical point in the colonial period: "the point of the beginnings of mass African nationalist movements and political parties."[26]

The images of women in this dramatic fictionalized account of that historical event reflect a broad spectrum of ages, classes, ethnic groups, occupations and degrees of political awareness. There are many of them, of which ten are composed with a judicious and dramatically effective choice of detail by the master of African cinema of commitment, Ousmane Sembène.

The first we meet are a young schoolgirl, Ad'jibid'ji, and her old grandmother, Niakoro, representing the future generation and the passing generation of African women. The grandmother expresses her malaise about the fastpaced events which have left her far behind. She scolds the child about running messages to and from the meetings of the strikers, as well as about running off to the colonial school.

"Why are you always poking your nose in the affairs of men? They are preparing a strike, and that's not a thing for you . . .

"What use is the white man's language to a woman? To be a good mother you have no need of that . . .I have never heard of a white man

who had learned to speak Bambara, or any other language of this
country. But you rootless people think only of learning his, while our
language dies . . .In my time we learned only some verses of the
Koran for our prayers."[27]
  . . .It was this that disturbed and haunted her. In her time the young
people undertook nothing without the advice of their elders, but now,
alone, they were deciding on a strike . . .and she had seen one. A
terrible strike . . .it had taken a husband and a son from her, but no one
even came to seek her advice. Were the ways of the old time gone
forever?[28]

In contrast to the old Niakoro, sitting alone in the courtyard reflecting on
how changing times had changed her people, we see Ramatoulaye, the
capable bustling organizer of her district. "Her responsibilities had become
very great, because the house of which she was the eldest was large: there
were no less than twenty of 'God's bits of wood.'"[29] This expression was the
traditional method, used by the strikers and their supporters, to count heads
without drawing the attention of any unfriendly spirits who might happen to
be listening for names.
  Others who joined the march included Mame Sofi, wife of the guard at
union headquarters, who cooperated with her co-wife Bineta in organizing
activities. There was N'Deye Touti, the committed young student whose
love for strike leader Bakayoko would have led her to abandon her
principles and become his second wife, had his stronger stance against
polygamy not prevailed. We see a very young girl, Anta, the "little
watcher" standing sentinel before the unsuspecting eyes of the enemy while
her mother, Houdia M'Baye hustles food for neighbors involved in the
strike. The most developed and consequently most powerful character is
Penda. This radical young woman was chosen to lead the women's march
because of her self-reliance and objective distance from her neighbors, as
evidenced by incidents of sexual liberation which had everybody talking.
As we see her grow from strength to strength, we trace as well the
development of her seemingly passive but calm and effective counterpart,
Maïmouna, the blind market woman. An established figure in the community,
her compassion for one of the strikers leads her to another type of sexual
liberation, and motherhood of illegitimate twins, Maïmouna's calm commitment to the march, in spite of hunger, cold, pain, exhaustion and the
sacrifice of one of her children to the trampling horde of marchers,
combined with Penda's active, militant command, and ultimate sacrifice of
her own life to the soldiers' bullets, rally the thousands of women from every
walk of life, and every village and language along the march from Thiès to
Dakar. In the face of the staggering odds facing this act of revolt against
colonial opression, the differences of languages, the distance to be covered,
the poverty and the sheer starvation, the participants supported and rallied

one another to renewed commitment to their common cause.

> Someone would say, "Let's go to see so-and-so. Perhaps she still has
> a little millett." But most of the time so-and-so could only answer 'No, I
> have nothing more. Wait, and I'll come with you." Then, carrying a
> baby against a flaccid breast, she would join the procession . . .
> And the men began to understand that if the times were bringing
> forth a new breed of men, they were also bringing forth a new breed of
> women.[30]

A similar change in the images of women reflecting the changing times, as colonialism reached its last bloody throes in Africa, can be seen in roles of the women characters in *A Grain of Wheat* by Ngugi wa Thiong'o.[31]

Instead of a single dramatic event like the march of the women in Senegal, in Kenya we see the bloody and protracted struggles of the "Mau-Mau" freedom fighters, and the complex levels of awareness and involvement on the part of the women. The two poles of that broad spectrum of involvement are represented by the characters of Wambui and Mumbi.

Wambui becomes a leader of women's revolutionary activities, participating fully in the risks and decisions of the movement. It is she who is chosen by General R(ussia) to be the judge of Mugo the traitor in the dramatic but painfully anticlimactic aftermath of the fight for freedom. It is therefore she who feels most acutely the grey muddied emotions facing all the women and men who have survived the days of bold action in the cause of right, to face the years of painful healing of a society torn assunder by accommodation to and revolution against colonial opression.

> Wambui sat on and watched the drizzle and the grey mist for a few
> minutes. Darkness was creeping into the hut. Wambui was lost in a
> solid consciousness of a terrible anti-climax to her activities in the
> fight for freedom. Perhaps we should not have tried [Mugo], she
> muttered. Then she shook herself, trying to bring her thoughts to the
> present. I must light the fire. First I must sweep the room. How dirt can
> so quickly collect in a clean hut! But she did not rise to do anything.[32]

Her counterpart, Mumbi, represents the collaborators, those whose lives were more liveable as long as the oppressor was in control, and who now face the painful process of reintegration into a community which was always hostile, but which is now free of fear of the oppressor/protector. Mumbi is the wife of Gikonyo, one of the freedom fighters now released from detention camp and convalescing in the hospital. It will take hime time to learn of the extenuating circumstances which led his wife to accept food from Karanja, and to become the mother of Karanja's child—Karanja, his old friend—Karanja, the collaborator.

For her part, Mumbi will also need time to open herself up to her husband, to try to bridge the chasm wreaked by the effects of colonialism. As she speaks to him, he hears a message behind her words, and sees behind her face the image of a changing Mumbi.

> 'No, Gikonyo. People try to rub out things, but they cannot. Things are not so easy. What has passed between us is too much to be passed over in a sentence. We need to talk, to open our hearts to one another, examine them, and then together plan the future we want. But now, I must go, for the child is ill.
> 'Will you—will you come tomorrow? he asked, unable to hide his anxiety and fear. He knew, at once, that in future he would reckon with her feelings, her thoughts, her desires—a new Mumbi.[33]

In the changing images of women in African novels about the colonial period, from the mother protecting her children and her culture against the first incursions of alien ways, to those who sought more practical approaches to preservation through accommodation with colonialism in full sway, to those who found themselves changed by the roles they played in the nationalist struggles against colonialism, reflections of African women's responses to inequality mirror the progressive movements characteristic of the psychology of oppression.

In order to lend a perspective of historical depth to images of women in novels dealing with colonial times, it would be productive to take a look at those in novels about Africa since independence. Many of these depict women in traditional supportive roles, but with a new dimension of political significance. The women in *A Man of the People*[34] by Chinua Achebe resemble the wives, mothers and lovers in novels about traditional and colonial times, but with one important difference. Their relationships with "Chief the Honourable Micah A. Nanga, M.P." all have political ramifications. His wife is as unhappy as any other might be about her husband's relationships with other women, but when his political career is threatened by those who wanted to break up his pending marriage to Edna, the beautiful young second-wife-to-be, Mrs. Nanga betrayed them. Elsie, the girlfriend of the narrator Odili, is seduced by the old man's power and prestige, and even the village women playing traditional roles as dancers and singers of praise songs are now mobilized for the political campaign.

> Five or six dancing groups were performing at different points in the compound. The popular 'Ego Women's Party' wore a new uniform of expensive accra cloth. In spite of the din you could still hear as clear as a bird the high-powered voice of their soloist, whom they admiringly nicknamed 'Grammar-Phone'. . . .

She was now praising Micah's handsomeness, which she likened to the perfect, sculpted beauty of a carved eagle, and his popularity which would be the envy of the proverbial traveller-to-distant-places who must not cultivate enmity on his route.[35]

The note of warning here might well have been heeded by the narrator. As a traveller-to-be, he needed to beware of incurring the enmity of so popular a man of the people. Whatever Chief Nanga's limitations regarding fiscal responsibility, morals, and service to his constituency, he knew how to win friends and influence his people.

In addition to the images of women playing traditional roles, those of women with their own careers also take on a new political significance. One of the most frequent examples is that of the market women whose importance goes far beyond that of the traditional small trader using the egg money for extra household expenses. In *The Ashanti Doll*[36] by Francis Bebey, the central characters are Ghanaian market women shown after giving their vast resources and powerful organization to elect "the Doctor" as Prime Minister. They are disgruntled by his neglect of their interests in policy decisions affecting commerce.

> "You have to take my place here, child of my heart, that's essential. I thought you had understood that long ago. You know, to be a market woman is important. She is a person who has a real part to play in the life of the country. She is the backbone of the country, child of my heart."
>
> "Yes, she makes up the country and then lets herself be governed by idiots more cunning than herself. Why isn't there a market woman in an important position in our country?"
>
> "But, Edna, you can't be both at the market and in an office at the same time!"
>
> "Especially if you can neither read nor write, nor do any of the things that people generally do in offices."
>
> "That may be a good reason. But that doesn't prevent the market women being active in every sphere in the country and their union being the most important. My child, face facts: could the Doctor, for example, ever have come to power without the agreement, without the active support of the market women?"
>
> "Mom, that's true. However, you must admit that, since he's been in power, the Doctor hasn't done much to show the market women that he's grateful for the campaign they waged on his behalf. I would even say that quite the reverse is true, if I think of your own grievances, and that the life of the market women has hardly improved since the Doctor formed his government."

"Because he included in his government only members of his family or men of his party. That's politics, child of my heart, what can you do about it?"[37]

What Mom decided to do about it was to organize a demonstration by the market women in support of a member of their union. Mrs. Amiofi's commercial license had been illegally revoked for political reasons. Because of her association with a leading member of the opposition party, when he was arrested her permit was revoked without any justification whatsoever.

The influence of the market women's union in the eventual erosion of support for the Doctor (Nkrumah) and his removal from office are referred to but not depicted in this novel dealing with early years of independence.

> In these circumstances, it must be recognized that questions like the Amiofi affair demonstrated clearly to the Doctor that his team and his Party were less imbued with the same idea of democracy, and therefore gradually sharpened his authoritarian tendencies, leading to crises which were to culminate, later, in the historic outcome which is familiar to the reader.
>
> But let us return to the days when an injustice done to a market woman still profoundly troubled the Prime Minister.[38]

In addition to the expanded political role of market women, another changing image of women with political ramifications is that of the "good-time" girls. Beyond the traditional roles of village beer-makers and single women, the introduction of prostitution is shown as a legacy of colonialism in post-independence Africa.

For example, in *Ripples in the Pool* by Rebeka Njau,[39] Selina represents the debilitating aftermath of colonialism on some independent young women pursuing an education or career, sidetracked by the easy money and good times offered by foreigners in the big city. Similarly, in *Petals of Blood* by Ngugi wa Thiong'o,[40] the political ramifications of Wanja's slide into prostitution are presented in heavy ideological terms:

> "KCO and Imperialism stand for the rich against the poor. They take from the poor and that's why they hate to see the poor organize and you are helping them. . .Whatever you are, you have chosen sides . . .we must struggle for a world . . .in which the wealth of our land shall belong to us all, in which we shall all be workers for one another's happiness and well-being."
>
> She had chosen. This she could not now hide from herself . . .In doing so she had murdered her own life and now she took her final burial in property and degradation as a glorious achievement. She

tried to look at this coolly, without this time shifting the blame onto others.

She could not now return to a previous state of innocence. But she could do something about her present circumstances.[41]

Wanja sees suddenly that she does have other options. She chooses to turn her back on a lucrative trade, and to take a strong stand against the perpetrators of economic oppression in her town.

Also noteworthy in this period of renewal of images of women in African literature is the entry of African women writers into the publishing market. In Ama Ata Aidoo's short stories *No Sweetness Here*,[42] modern Ghanaian women in the village and in the city lead complex lives in which many seemingly picayune details take on a political significance. In the lead story entitled significantly "Everything Counts," the wig assumes a symbolic importance representing the temptation of facile materialism and imitation of Western mores:

'But what has wearing wigs got to do with revolution?' 'A lot sister,' they would say. 'How?' she would ask, struggling not to understand. 'Because it means that we have no confidence in ourselves.[43]

Aidoo's works depict the delicate balance in daily decision-making by women in Africa as elsewhere today. The complex images of women in this collection reflect conflicting objectives juggled by women pursuing what they find of value in traditional and modern roles.

In comparison with these images of women in novels from East and West Africa, it is instructive to see the politicization of women's roles in novels by South African writers in exile. Examples from South Africa were omitted from this study of novels about colonial times vis-à-vis traditional and post-independence societies. The struggle for liberation has yet to see African peoples there in control of their destiny.

Yet, images of women in traditional supportive roles, as well as independent entrepreneurs and urban free women also carry important political overtones in novels about southern African peoples still in colonial bondage. A glimpse of several novels by South African authors reveals images similar to those from post-independence African nations. In *A Wreath for Udomo*[44] by Peter Abrahams, for example, we see again the powerful market women at work in support of an aspiring politician. Selina the market woman plays a major role in the rise and fall of Udomo's regime in the early years of independence.

Similarly, political ramifications complicate the entrepreneurship of loose women in South African fiction. For example, in "Life,"[45] a short story by Bessie Head, the central character is a woman named Life who returns to Botswana from Johannesburg and causes considerable social upheaval in her quiet village by opening a house of prostitution. Even her beer-making women friends were taken aback because no one had ever thought of sex for sale, and the novelty of it turns the village upside down until Life's untimely death. In contrast, in *Mine Boy*[46] by Peter Abrahams, women like Leah who make illegal beer in Johannesburg also play a strong supportive role in tending the wounds of bodies and souls of victims of apartheid.

Even marriage becomes a political act in *Maru*[47] by Bessie Head. The wedding of Margaret Cadmore (a Masarwa, or Bushman) to Maru (the chief of the ruling Batswana of the village) opens a new perspective of freedom for the enslaved people of her ethnic group.

> When people of the Masarwa tribe heard about Maru's marriage to one of their own, a door silently opened on the small, dark airless room in which their souls had been shut for a long time. The wind of freedom, which was blowing throughout the world for all people, turned and flowed into the room.
>
> People like the Batswana, who did not know that the wind of freedom had also reached people of the Masarwa tribe, were in for an unpleasant surprise because it would be no longer possible to treat Masarwa people in an inhuman way without getting killed yourself.[48]

This complex collage of images of women in African fiction reflects complex realities, but if an image is worth a thousand words, the tableau of a thousand women in the vast panorama of African literature projects a powerful picture. Beyond the inequalities seen in novels about traditional, colonial or post-independence societies, these images communicate a strength of purpose of women more than equal to the tasks they set themselves, vis-à-vis families, friends, careers, communities and nation.

NOTES

1. Christina Ama Ata Aidoo, *The Dilemma of a Ghost* (New York: Collier, 1965).
2. Karen Chapman, Introduction to *The Dilemma of a Ghost*, by Christina Ama Ata Aidoo (New York: Collier, 1965), pp. 7-8.
3. Andrea B. Rushing, "Images of Black Women in Modern African Poetry: An Overview" in *Sturdy Black Bridges: Visisions of Black Women in Literature*, edited by Roseann P. Bell, Bettye J. Parker, and Beverly Guy-Sheftall (Garden City, NY: Anchor, 1979), pp. 18-24.
4. D. T. Niane, ed., Sundiata: *An Epic of Old Mali* (London: Longman, 1965).
5. Sonia Lee, "The Awakening of the Self in the Heroines of Ousmane Sembène," in *Sturdy Black Bridges*, Bell *et al*, eds., pp. 54-55.

6. S. Asare Konadu, *A Woman in Her Prime* (London: Heinemann, 1967).
7. Onuora Nzekwu, *Highlife for Lizards* (London: Hutchinson, 1965).
8. Amos Tutuola, *The Brave African Huntress* (London: Faber and Faber, 1958).
9. Marie Linton-Umeh, "The African Heroine," in *Sturdy Black Bridges*, Bell *et al.*, pp. 42-44.
10. Emile Snyder, "Modern Africa in Literature," in *Africa* edited by Phyllis M. Martin and Patrick O'Meara (Bloomington, Indiana: Indiana University Press, 1977), pp. 331-347.
11. Ibid., p. 334.
12. Chinua Achebe, *Things Fall Apart* (Greenwich, Conn: Fawcett Crest, 1959).
13. Ibid., pp. 11-12.
14. Ibid., p. 25.
15. Ibid., pp. 62-63.
16. Ibid., p. 71.
17. Ibid., p. 151.
18. Cheikh Hamidou Kane, *Ambiguous Adventure* (New York: Collier, 1969), copyright 1963 by Walker and Co., first published in French as *L'aventure ambiguë* in Paris by René Julliard in 1962.
19. Ibid., p. 41.
20. Ibid., p. 19.
21. Ibid.
22. Ferdinand Oyono, *Houseboy* (London: Heinemann, 1966), African Writers Series, John Reed, translator; first published in French as *Une Vie de Boy* in Paris by Editions Julliard, in 1960.
23. Ibid., p. 45.
24. Ibid., p. 31.
25. Ousmane Sembène, *God's Bits of Wood* (Garden City, New York: Anchor, 1970), translated by Francis Price, originally published in French as *Les Bouts de bois de Dieu.*
26. Ibid., p. 13.
27. Ibid., p. 37.
28. Ibid., p. 34.
29. Ibid., p. 84.
30. Ibid., p. 76.
31. James Ngugi, *A Grain of Wheat* (London: Heinemann, 1967).
32. Ibid., pp. 275-76.
33. Ibid., p. 280.
34. Chinua Achebe, *A Man of the People* (Garden City, NY: Doubleday Anchor Books, 1967).
35. Ibid., p. 1.
36. Francis Bebey, *The Ashanti Doll* (London: Heinemann, 1978).
37. Ibid., p. 20.
38. Ibid., p. 134.
39. Rebeka Njau, *Ripples in the Pool* (London: Heinemann, 1975).
40. Ngugi wa Thiong'o, *Petals of Blood* (London: Heinemann, 1977).
41. Ibid., pp. 327-328.
42. Ama Ata Aidoo, *No Sweetness Here* (Garden City, NY: Doubleday, 1971).

43. Ibid., p. 2.
44. Peter Abrahams, *A Wreath for Udomo* (New York: Alfred A. Knopf, 1956).
45. Bessie Head, "Life" in *The Collector of Treasures* (London: Heinemann, 1977), pp. 37-46.
46. Peter Abrahams, *Mine Boy* (New York: Macmillan, 1970).
47. Bessie Head, *Maru* (New York: McCall Publishing Company, 1971).
48. Ibid., p. 126-127.

Women in a Man's Exploration of His Country, His World: Chraïbi's Succession Ouverte

Rafika Merini

While it has been said that the works of North African writer, Driss Chraïbi are preoccupied with women[1], it is my thesis that that is so only in a limited way. While accepting the statement that women play a major role in his fiction, I would argue that women do not have the author's full, dedicated attention, but are often limited to being communication channels for his deviated cult of the mother and his own angst. The mother figure and/or the cult of the mother is definitely a central issue in the North African psyche, and is certainly evidenced in Chraïbi's semi-autobiographical work *Succession Ouverte* as well as in *Le Passé Simple* and *La Civilisation, ma Mère! . . .* [2] where it is a recurrent theme. However, I would argue that Chraïbi's literature keeps tugging at this concern without eludicating it. A. Bouhdibi characterizes the cult of the mother as "une des clés maîtresses pour la compréhension de la personnalité de base des sociétés arabo-musulmanes" ["one of the key factors in the understanding of the basic personality of Arabo-Muslim societies"][3].* I will be more concerned, however, with how the author uses this theme with a different ultimate result in mind than simply understanding Arab cultures. In *La civilisation, ma Mère! . . .*, both mother and son evolve from a restricted world to one where

*Translations are the author's.

45

their fantasies are given full expression; the mother's troubles strangely parallel the son's, and the hero frees himself at the same time that he frees his mother. Would it then be appropriate to speak of an Oedipal complex "mal resolu" with J. Déjeux?[4] That is not a possibility which I propose to explore here, although it could be one of the major obstacles in the coverage of the female condition by male authors. That theory would also explain the focus on the mother as a facade, an excuse for focusing on one's self. My assumption is that women are not usually portrayed to objectively represent themselves, rather, they are used to convey what the author needs to say about himself and his malaise.

Underdevelopment (comprising the search for identity) constitutes the second and most important unifying theme of *Succession Ouverte*. This theme forms a looking glass through which a whole society is analyzed: the "Seigneur" (the father/patriarch) is the live illustration of it. He represents a once powerful society which crumbled and left behind poverty, lethargy, pharisaism, and corruption. The mother, who remains as nameless as she is powerless, is the woman whose odyssey the writer will manipulate to metaphorically convey his own feelings of helplessness, frustration and despair sprung from a common background.

The son in revolt talks through his mother, by a strange procuration. In a skilled twist, their destinies are joined in the author's mind. It is this confusion which detracts from the socio-literary value of *Succession Ouverte*. Both the mother and the son suffer under the same yoke. They both have had to, and still will have to (in spite of his death) bend to the wishes of the "Seigneur," their lord and master who presides on top of their culture, its weight crushing them. Driss, stricken by this realization acknowledges: "il a fallu qu'il meure pour que je réalise soudain que j'étais un être vivant". ["It was necessary that he die for me to come to the sudden realization that I was a living being."] (Pt. II, Ch. xi; p. 182). The nearly unbearable malaise engendered by the situation is pervasive. But the author would be more convincing if he did not put the general disarray in masculine terms as a rule. The mother passively complies. Ignoring herself and her feelings the way society ignores her, she merely becomes the mirror of her son's agony. Her pain is compounded by the fact that there is no escape for her aggravations and affliction. As for similarities, we see them both clinging to the same pain-inducing roots, their fate hanging from a thin weathered thread. The mother's persistent good will only leads to acute feelings of uselessness, lack of importance and influence.

From an exclusively literary standpoint, there is nothing wrong with this. It makes the novel more complex and fascinating, especially when one knows what a crucial part Chraïbi's own mother played in his past and the large place she still claims in his private world. It is when the socio-critical values inherent in this kind of literature are introduced that one is forced to take the author to task. Chraïbi is a feminist. He is one of a handful of male

North African authors dealing with women's status. His contribution is unique. His influence—although I concede that his number of North African readers might be quite small at the present time—is great among those who do read his works. They themselves are often highly placed and have influence (or sheer power) over others. That is why, although I greatly enjoy and appreciate Chraïbi's work, as a feminist and a socio-literary critic I must raise a few questions, hoping that I can contribute something of value to it.

The climax mentioned at the beginning finds the mother portrayed by the author as being utterly unable to directly express her feelings. We guess what they might be through what her son feels looking at her after a sixteen year separation and his father's death.[5] The extreme hardening in the hero—Chraïbi's lack of disinterestedness notwithstanding—amounts to a very dramatic and effective description of what any Moroccan woman would inspire in a loving son at her husband's death when the latter had always treated her like a child. She has spent her life in a children's (her children's) world, cut-off from everything else, voiceless and vacant (except when pregnant; which happens to her more than a half-dozen times). From what we already know about Moroccan women in general, Ferdi's mother is genuine. Why not let her speak for herself at this, the most revealing and intense moment of the book? The author's main concern must then be construed to be his own feelings transmitted through the male hero's character.[6] This is only another instance of women given second place. Again, they are made to be the means and not the end.

We are told that for years, she was "espiègle et vive au dépit de n'importe quelle souffrance," ["mischievous and spirited whatever pain and suffering she was going through"] (Pt. I, Ch. iii; p. 68) but we cannot believe it. It just does not fit in with all we know about her. After all, *Succession Ouverte* is not *La Civilisation, ma Mère!* . . . where fantasy and wishful thinking are the avowed rule. Once more, reality has been shirked.

When we read ". . . . je savais que quelque chose était mort en elle," ["I knew that something inside her was dead"] it strikes us as such an understatement and stereotypical way of expediting the action that the author's whole description seems preposterous (Pt. I, Ch. iii; p. 72). We see through the author's underhanded trick when he adds a few pages later: "J'évitais soigneusement ses yeux" ["I carefully avoided her eyes"] (Pt. I, Ch. iii; p. 77). There is no need for further clarification. In my eyes, it seems that Driss is primarily engrossed by his own lingering dependence on the "Seigneur". His brother Nagib is not only speaking for himself when he posits: "Il était notre maître maî de fer, mais aussi notre nourricier et notre dignité" ["He was Master with the iron grip, but also our provider and the source of our dignity"] (Pt. II, Ch. v; p. 109). Driss and his brothers have been caught in the same trap as their mother. Do they have a future of their own or will they forever be living in the past? Nagib's embittered questioning restates the ultimate question: when will Moroccans shake off the yoke of the past? This question is an anguished one since its answer seems to be: never. It is reflected in the mother's eyes that Driss refuses to look at, while inwardly staring at them. They contain ". . . une intense angoisse . . . " ["an intense anxiety . . . "] (Pt. I, Ch. iii; p. 67). In a face drained of all life, they hurt and shame him not only because of what she has been through as a woman, but also because of the shackled and decaying culture behind them. Driss is still a part of her (as she is a part of him), and a part of his culture, inescapably.

Nagib, who bought all of his society's values, revered and loved the old man so much that he pictures everyone including his family as undeserving pests who helped cause the fall of his father, for him a kind of Hercules, a superior being and protector to whom life itself, as well as other beings, should have deferred.[7] Driss shares these feelings somehow until the sick "Seigneur" comes back. He is "inside" the tape recorder, not weakened at all, not disarmed in the least, still carrying his final instructions for his sons, their mother and all his other dependents. He now will tell them how to live out the rest of their lives. Driss thinks this whole set-up is hilarious but it is not so for anyone else, so he acquiesces. Nagib's brawn at the service of God (and the "Seigneur") will suffice indeed to convince him that the situation must be taken seriously. Meanwhile, he has been healed and freed: "Mais j'étais déchaîné, exorcisé" ["But I was freed of my chains, exorcised"] Pt. II, Ch. vi; p. 124.)

The mother best exemplifies again the ambient atmosphere of dread and muted revolt. She is "the Moroccan mother" or "ras el mehna," the root and receiver of all pain and suffering scrutinized from outside.

> "Tassée dans un coin, ma mère pleurait sans bruit et sans larmes, comme seules peuvent le faire des femmes qui ont pleuré toute leur vie redevenue petite et infantile dès qu'avait retenti la voix du Seigneur" (Pt. II, Ch. vi; p. 125).
>
> ["Crouched in a corner, my mother was crying without sobbing, without shedding tears in the way that only women who have cried all their life know how. She had become small and childlike again as soon as 'the seigneur's' voice had made itself heard."]

Her plight does not end with the death of her husband: he has arranged for her to stay dependent on him even in death, going against laws and customs in order to accomplish this. Driss Chraïbi must have been aware that he was providing the social critic with a perfect example of the discrepancy between theory and practice, showing how mores can be even more archaic than religious laws, which are themselves often used according to people's preferences and priorities.[8]

The mother placidly performs her duties at the funeral, probably not caring about anything anymore: "Elle leur répond au hasard, par mono-syllables" ["She responds to them haphazardly uttering monosyllables only."] (Pt. II, Ch. v; pp. 92-93). As for Driss, his present feelings are summed up in an often quoted passage which has led many to think it was a final admission of defeat and impotent rage in a world where he finds himself left unprovided for.

> "Jamais, jamais plus je n'irai à la recherche de cerveaux, de vérités écrites, de vérités synthétiques, d'assemblages d'idées hybrides qui n'étaient rien que des idées" ["Never again shall I go looking for brains; for written truths; for synthetic truths; for assemblies of hybrid ideas that were nothing but ideas . . . "]

The contrasted behaviors of the mother and her son converge to create a whole where she takes the passive part, reduced to simply reflecting her son's emotions. Strong impressions of malaise and confusion accumulate. The hero is too preoccupied with his own feelings to focus on those of his mother.

Madini, (another brother), asks: "Je voudrais savoir pourquoi ils deviennent des animaux" ["I would like to know why they become animals."] (Pt. I, Ch. iv; p. 85). The revolting, unacceptable answer readily springs from the Koran and seems to leave no alternatives: "That is God's will" (Pt. II, Ch. vi; p. 119). This invitation and justification of fatalism, determinism, and stagnation can of course also be applied to underdevelopment. There is then no need to blame the way women, the weak, and the poor are treated. Nagib has the last word however: "Plus on a le ventre plein et plus on est croyant" ["The fuller one's stomach, the more one believes in God."] (Pt. II, Ch. vi; p. 120). He is clearly implying that faith is only a matter of convenience and expediency.

The "Seigneur" knows that desiring freedom (as Chraïbi does for women in a highly idealistic manner) is an entirely different matter from actually acquiring it. His synthesis only seems simple: "L'aide aux pays éternellement sous-developpés" ["Assistance to the eternally under-developed countries"]. (Pt. II, Ch. vi; p. 135). This theme of underdevelopment, which is closely linked to that of the oppression of women, clearly spells lack of balance, therefore unease, malaise: a complete loss of direction as in the case of Nagib; a resentful resignation close to a desertion for Driss while at the same time spitting on his "pariah's" life, always feeling the big split in his personality. Chraïbi did progress from North Africa to more universal themes and concerns in subsequent books but he did not desert his native culture having incorporated it into his work.

La "féminitude" is given the appearance of a convenient complement to "l'arabité," an abstracted but timely vehicle for the hero's "mal de vivre" and remaining dependence. How else can the "Seigneur's" words about his wife (left helpless in the midst of her restless sons) be explained except as a substitute for the male's own sense of failure?

> "A son âge, l'émancipation, le sentiment d'une liberté souveraine ne signifieraient rien pour elle, sinon un déséquilibre" ["At her age, liberation, the feeling of a sovereign freedom within herself, meant nothing to her, except perhaps a destabilization."] (Pt. II, Ch. vi; p. 132).

The hero should be aware that the "Seigneur's" argument is the oppressor's standard weapon: giving the illusion that the status quo is permanent and that it is the only sensible way of being. These are insidious means to keep the status quo, to discourage reaction in advance, to nip it in the bud: to speak in the name of those who might want change (denying them freedom of expression) and to say that they really could not handle, or profit from, any change. The author does not make it clear that this is the ultimate form of paternalism and demagoguery combined. Indirectly the feeling for the sons' dependence is reinforced; technically speaking, Chraïbi is using the mother to emphasize it. Both the mother and her sons lack an identity upon which to base freedom and responsibility. Here, the search for identity extends into an exploration of the two cultures that have failed to provide one.

The father's criticism is to the point when he blames them for making freedom just another possession. As Madini assumes the functions of the "Seigneur" and their by-products (responsibility, dignity, power, paternalism and stagnation) he gradually will come to represent, almost in spite of himself, everything that he distrusted and disavowed in the past. His option is worse since, unlike the "Seigneur," he had a real choice. He will keep "le souvenir lancinant d'un idéal révolutionnaire, d'année en année." [the painful rememberance of a revolutionary ideal, year after year.] He will also carry the dead past with him, thus becoming one with it, "une dépouille mortelle" ["mortal remains"] (Pt. II, Ch. xi; p. 183). He will be the unwelcome symbol of a dying civilization. Tellingly enough, he is specifically put in charge of his child-mother who will not receive any money. The "Seigneur's" will regarding her takes precedence over God's laws. Hence the "Seigneur" betrays himself. He admits that, at least for her, "nous voulons espérer que nous ne sommes pas encore mort" ["we would like to think that we are not dead yet."] (Pt. II, Ch. vi; p. 132). He cannot release his hold on her even when only his spirit remains.

What this amounts to is protracted dependence for the mother since it is in his father's name that her son will take care of her. She will be the only one who will not acquire more freedom as a result of the "lord's" death. She represents the predicament that a family (the nucleus of a whole society) finds itself in when it refuses to look forward to the future and takes refuge in the past instead.

The chapter "Ma Mère" would by itself furnish ample material for a study of the everyday reality of Moroccan women.[9] Characteristically, when the mother is finally allowed a monologue, she makes an uninterrupted speech, a plea for understanding. The only answer she gets is a desperate request on the part of her son that she stop her long litany. He too has no answer to the dilemma turned sour.

When the mother says: "J'ai trop de bile dans le ventre," ["I have too much bile in my belly"] we are reminded that bile (choler) used to be considered the reason for anger, irritability and bitterness in the Middle Ages (Pt. II, Ch. ix; p. 166). Her physical and mental health must be seen as a result of a life of abuse and indifference. Two other imaginary cardinal humors (blood and phlegm) were respectively attributed by the author to Driss (for his restrained passion followed by violent outbursts) and to the "Seigneur" for his calm and composure.

Chraïbi coins a perfect appellation for Driss' character: "la violence de la sensibilité . . . ;; ["The violence of sensitivity"] (Pt. II, Ch. iii; p. 33). He means that Driss' callousness comes from sensitivity.

The mother's principal complaint is a habitual one. She invokes the isolation, silence, and ignorance that surround her and sap her strength.

> "Et j'étais là, moi, à perpétuité, entre un homme qui ne disait pas un mot et des démons qui ne me disaient rien, jamais" ["There I was, perpetually caught between a man who did not say a word to me, and demons who never ever told me anything."] (Pt. II, Ch. ix; p. 167).

Chraïbi could be credited with objective and efficient reporting at this point, if he had made the mother specify that she strongly resented the shroud of silence around her since it was a permanent situation, mostly engineered by her closest relatives.

From the otherwise realistic account, we are left with a painful reminder: the Seigneur knew his sons well (and how they would act) yet he still chose to entrust his wife to them. In doing so, he is denying her all feeling and humanity. Chraïbi seems to support such conduct when he makes her say apologetically that she grew to actually like her prison. She outlives her husband but she can only be a "vestige" of the dying past in the patriarch's own words (Pt. II, C. vi; p. 133). When his illness made him leave, her husband didn't even tell her his destination or if he would return. He removed himself from his family for his last five years, and became a recluse while awaiting death. The old woman explains that childbearing was the only thing that comforted her and gave her a sense of identity and fulfillment since her children could at least understand her for a few years. They then became precocious little "men" in a society that demands it of boys (Pt. II,

Ch. ix; p. 169). She begs Driss to understand that she is trying hard to figure out the world with her limited means of knowledge.[10] The echoes of the son's own fears of lack of creativity and of loneliness and loss are loudest where they tell of their mutual suffering.

> "Je voulais bien qu'on me protège, qu'on me colonise, me civilise, me donne un brevet d'existence, mais ça?" ["I went along willingly, seeking the protection, colonization, civilization, mere acknowledgement of my presence on earth that were promised me but what was I left with in the end?"] (Pt. I, Ch. ii; p. 34).

They also represent the national feeling towards colonization at the start of the French infiltration into Morocco.

The chapter "Ma Mère" remains a sincere attempt—and a most compelling one—to portray a woman trying to express herself and to make a case for herself. Chraïbi could not ignore any further the crucial difference between the son's mental prison and the mother's, whose entrapment is grounded in reality. Chraïbi luckily lets her say in plain words that she has been living in a real prison:

> "Une prison, petite ou grande, est toujours une prison" ["A jail, whether it is large or small is still a jail."] (Pt. II, Ch. ix; p. 171).

This lifts her torture above that of her son and temporarily makes her stand for herself, apart from her son's malaise. The urgency of that malaise renders him temporarily unable to bear the unveiled, unobstructed pain that finally overflows and spills from his mother's innermost self.

The father ultimately had to put an end to his life: the cancer in his body took residence within his mind and brought down the seemingly unimpeachable fortress he was. Driss, although thus far he has received no part of the inheritance, is in charge of solving the puzzle that his father concocted. The astute father knew his son would be present, and the feelings that he would harbor.[11] In the same manner that he had found a way to directly reach his successors through the grave, the Seigneur will now guide Driss in his dispirited wanderings. Driss' continuing dialogue with the old man might breathe some new life into him. He is worn out by the adversities and contradictions of his ethnic background and his aspirations, and simply yearns to returns to his "tribe" suggesting the way the body of a dead soldier would be returned to be buried in his native land. Driss' own admission of defeat leads him to exclaim in a passage mentioned before in this chapter that truth belongs inside the voice of religion, Islam, "en dépit de l'immense héritage d'incrédulité que j'avais reçu de l'Occident" ["Despite the immense incredulity I had inherited from the West"] (Pt. I, Ch. iv; p. 81).

One is tempted to interpret this brief confession of faith as a mere coincidence. Such an effusive and hasty decision and feverish outpouring coming at the time when the hero is weakened by his grief over his father's death is not convincing. Driss is at the burial site during a soothing, merciful chant promising forgiveness and oblivion; the temptation is great therefore to see the entire nagging puzzle as but one of this life's petty preoccupations. The end of all evil is what appeals most to this abused audience. Driss is well aware of that fact. His denial of all idealism outside of religion is thus tainted: no other ideology wins him over, and like a prisoner subjected to torture, he gives in under duress.

His mother took no part in this event (although D. Chraïbi mentions that "hommes, femmes et enfants" were in attendance) at the funeral (Pt. I, Ch. iv; p. 81). As a woman relative, tradition forbids her to attend burials. She does not even appear to provide the background and complement of her son's lack of peace of mind. Once again, she is completely excluded. She cannot share in public functions. This observation leads to the next question: is there ever a true connection between a man and a woman in this book, or are their mental and physical beings forever separate and unequal?

It must be acknowledged, in Chraïbi's defense, that one woman is portrayed relatively favorably in such a situation of communion. It is Safia, Jaad's wife, the shack dweller who goes so far as to speak up for her husband—but not for herself. The female image she projects is typically one of complete self-denial and sacrifice for her husband's sake.[12] Such love by a Moroccan woman for a man is not only unusual and significant in its unabashed avowal, it is downright rash and adventurous. She says she loves him "plus que mes yeux" ["more than my own eyes"] and "plus que mes enfants" [more than my own children] breaking with a long-established tradition for women to see future security and salvation in their children, not in their husbands (Pt. II, Ch. viii; p. 161).[13]

The merging of Jaad and Safia in the destitute lifestyle he opted to share with her is not free of unconscious double standards. His trials take precedence and justify her seven unwanted pregnancies.[14] This hint by the author aiming at the lack of availability of contraceptive information and methods, shows that he does not condone a state of affairs which is unfortunately the norm. No mention is made of the woman's sexuality and her physical appearance is dispatched in three or four sentences (Pt. II, Ch. iii; p. 160). A lively but distancing use of dialogue sets in.

The description of "l'étrangère" [the female stranger] had been more erotic and tantalizing: "une longue chevelure couleur de bronze soulevée et tordue par le vent . . . " ["long heavy locks of hair the color of bronze, picked up and twisted by the wind"] (Pt. II, Ch. ii; p. 46). At first, the author had led us to think that she might be "frigid" (thus casting the all-powerful male curse upon her) but he finally lets her "passionate" feelings show through. J. Déjeux did not seem to have fully realized how much truth there

is to his statement that "les problèmes sexuels sont passés sous silence . . . "
["sexual problems are brushed aside . . . "] (Pt. I, Ch. i; p. 19). He
precludes its application to those authors of "la contestation," however.
Even Khair-Eddine who is one of them manifests very little positive interest
for women; hence one cannot easily generalize in this area.[15]

"L'étrangère" is seen as being shameless but sexier. She has more
freedom of action. Indeed, she can free the Arab male of his own inhibition
and sexual superiority complexes. She is often older and "knows better."
She has usually not grown accustomed to throwing opprobrium on her own
sex such as routinely qualifying any bad event as being "like the day she was
born a girl," a female expression. She has not, brainwashed by her society,
idolized the male sex in practice and in theory. Many Arab women, although
they might know what an orgasm is, have never had the courage to claim and
enjoy one in male-female intercourse.[16] They sometimes openly resort to
other women in exclusively female circles.

Chraïbi only whets our appetite with his feminist thirst for justice. He
seduces us instead with his consummate literary art. One small example is
his handling of the wind blowing the hair of 'l'étrangère': "Elle essayait de la
maîtriser, mais ses mains tremblaient et le vent était plus fort que n'importe
quel sentiment humain" ["She tried to control it but her hands were
trembling, and the wind was stronger than any human feeling"] (Pt. I, Ch. ii;
p. 46). His desire for change has yet to produce a novel able to withstand
clearheaded criticism that the heroine would make a poor role model for
readers, for a better society.[17]

Many conservative North African writers think that the time is not right
for women's liberation in their countries. Their reasoning is that if there are
no grounds to build a man's life on, how can there be any for a woman's?
They argue that women need to keep sacrificing themselves to the cause of
progress and wait for a better tomorrow. That is unfortunately the overall
message one gets from Succession Ouverte. La Civilisation, ma mère! . . .
differs in this respect showing the author's heightened consciousness.

However, in Succession Ouverte no attempt is made to seriously discuss
"une vie de femme" ["a woman's life"] although descriptions of women
contributed largely to establishing the atmosphere of uneasiness and dread,
and the hero's malaise.

Driss' mother had looked radiant at the time of her husband's funeral.
Watching her and her female counterparts, Driss had felt compelled to
attest that: "S'il y avait un mort dans cette demeure, il était mort depuis
longtemps" ["If there was indeed a dead person in this dwelling, he was long
since dead"] (Pt. I, Ch. iii; pp. 73-74). Another question which occurred to
me at this point was whether the dead man's disappearance heralded that of
the culture the characters had known and been distressed by. It was left
unanswered by the author. The mother never progressed from a childish
sense of relief to asserting herself. The pace had been set early for female

representation in the novel when Driss dispatched romantic involvements with French women in this manner: "J'ai connu nombre de femmes et ça s'est toujours limité là." ["I have intimately known a great number of women, and it never went beyond that."] He makes things worse by adding that he was only a "sauvage" [savage] un "étalon" [stud] for them, and they never meant anything to him as a result: he is conveniently laying all the blame on them (Pt. I, Ch. ii; p. 36).

There was also the first experience Driss had on landing, one that made the persona ask: "Mais où était donc l'humain?" ["But where was the human element hiding?"] The foreign woman (the typical "étrangère," whose physical appearance alone is depicted at first) with a cold invisible laughter has a chest "tendue par la vie qu'elle s'acharnait à tuer en elle à tout moment" ["made more compact by the life within that she was rabidly bent on suppressing at all times"] (Pt. I, Ch. ii; p. 32). Not only is this woman described without her participation to compound the effect, she is in addition, made to reflect Driss' feelings and not her own.

A first journey to a foreign country such as Morocco for her, as the bride of one of its nationals, ought to have plentifully excused the rigidity and apprehension on her face. As for her husband, the old "malaise" is written on his face since he is another person Driss can closely identify with. As it turns out the "educated" man will slight and neglect his poor old primitive father who came to take him home on his donkey, preferring to tell his new wife that the party concerned is only a "domestique" (Pt. I, Ch. ii; p. 50). Suspecting the truth, she makes an attempt at gaining control of the heart-breaking events around her. Her efforts are doomed however. She is the outsider unable to reach out to others. This episode is further altered to artfully suggest that Driss' self-assigned mission might fail also. The foreign woman eventually manages to let her true personality come out. She becomes a refreshing, thinking and feeling person, human if perhaps not quite a man's equal: "elle n'avait plus rien d'une phobo-obsessionnelle" ["She had now shed all remains of her obsessional phobia"] (Pt. I, Ch. ii; p. 50). After the clash, the two cultures temporarily seem to merge in a show of common humanity.

Unfortunately, East and West did not meet for the female characters of the book who in reverse to what Driss had been undergoing, were saturated with the older, more stagnant culture which always denied them an identity. Inside their traditional background, revolt itself does not mean anything. All they can feel, numbed as they are by their early training for submissiveness (as in the extreme case of Jaad's wife) is impotent rage, the rage of those who have been discarded from life, but do not want to lose their minds (Pt. II, Ch. viii; p. 160). Misery-laden women are definitely not allowed into respectable families, hence Safia's raging efforts can at best be channeled into a fervent desire to help her husband. He was rejected for having dared to marry outside and below his social class.

This revolves back to my main objection to Chraïbi's work. Women's plight is often indirectly and sometimes ambiguously stated and takes the form of one man's search for his own liberation in the reader's mind, as well as in the author's mind, even as he is dealing with a topic as close to his heart as the Moroccan mother, his mother.

Chraïbi did not seem to have any bright alternatives to offer the three female characters in the book. They stand powerless and disoriented when confronted with life. The French woman is not of course informed of the critical situation at hand. She might however be better off to learn on her own and wage her own fight. The mother and Safia, Jaad's wife, must lower themselves to the ground and beg, the first still hoping for a chance to assist her distant dying husband, and the second to be granted forgiveness, acceptance and help for her sick and exhausted but proud spouse (Pt. II, Ch. viii; p. 162). This work betrays on the whole, a traditionally moderate to conservative, belittling treatment of women. *La Civilisation, ma mère!* . . . gives Chraïbi a more legitimate claim to being a feminist writer as it illustrates better, but on whimsical terms, his growing support for women's liberation.

Except on a brief occasion in the chapter "Ma Mère," women never speak for themselves or for their own interests separate from those of their men, at least not in the course of *Succession Ouverte*. They never accede to an identity of their own. Further, the interaction between East and West is made to seem certain to fail where women are concerned.[18] I believe this is a bad omen since that interaction will be the decisive factor as to whether or not women will succeed in emancipating themselves in literature as well as in reality and become more able to help a country experiencing a dire need of improvement. More optimistic books are needed, if only to show women more favorable choices at work.[19]

NOTES

1. M. A. Alaoui attests: "Driss Chraibi et Rachid Boujedra, deux écrivains maghrebins, deux générations différentes, mais une preoccupation commune: la femme. Le héros, au sens litteraire de La Civilisation, ma Mère!. . . est précisement la mère." [Driss Chraibi and Rachid Boujedra are North African writers from two different generations but who have a common preoccupation: woman. The hero in *La Civilisation, ma Mère!*. . . is precisely the mother." *Afrique Littéraire et Artistique*, No. 34, 1974, p. 34.

2. Driss Chraibi, *Le Passé Simple*, Paris: Editions Denoël, 1954.
   _____, *La Civilisation, ma Mère. . .* , Paris, Denoël, 1954.
   _____, *Succession Ouverte*, Paris, Denoël, 1962.

3. Bouhdiba, *La Sexualite en Islam*, p. 66.

4. In one of his articles on the literature of the Maghreb, the mother is likened to a "caverne" inside a vicious circle in the authors' minds (Déjeux, La Littérature Maghrébine," pp. 17-19). J. F. A. Clément prefers to see this phenomenon as a "polygonisation" to use his own neologism (J. F. A. Clément, "Panorama de la Littérature Marocaine," *Esprit*, No. 34, 1974, p. 1059). I assume, for lack of further clarification and available information, and basing myself on J. Déjeux' explanation of *Le Polygone Etoilé* that J.F.A. Clément refers to "polygonisation" as the expression of personal and national alientation and fixation on the past. Déjeux' interpretation is needless to say, the one which resembles most the theory behind this work (Déjeux, *Littérature Maghrébine*, p. 217.)

5. "Son visage n'avait pas une seule ride. Elle le levait vers moi et, s'il m'avait été donné de voir à cet instant-là une scène de torture, je l'eusse supporteé sans faiblir, probablement" (Pt. I, Ch. iii; p. 68.)
   ["There wasn't a single line on her face which she raised towards me. Had I suddenly been exposed, at that instant, to a scene of torture, I would have probably withstood it without blinking."]

6. Even Chraïbi's childhood paralleled his mother's life. If one can judge from *Le Passé Simple*; his family life was empty and entirely dominated by his father: "Les affamés et moi nous nous ressemblons: nous sommes fonction, eux de treizes siècles d'Islam, moi du Seigneur, cristallisation de l'Islam"
   ["The hungry and I are alike: while they are descended from thirteen years of Islam, I am descended from 'the seigneur' (lord) who is a crystallization of Islam."] (Chraïbi, *Le Passè*, p. 12). J. F. A. Clément sees this "tendre haine" hovering over family relationships in Morocco and permeating everyone's consciousness" (Clément, p. 1059).

7. "Ils l'ont vidé de son sang et tué" (Pt. II, Ch. v; p. 106). [They emptied him of his life-sustaining blood"]

8. See A. Tillion's description of the practice called "Habous": "Afin de 'violer légalement la loi' dès qu'il achetait un terrain, le père de famille de Petite Kabylie ou de l'Aurès s'empressait de faire établir un acte par le qadi, stipulant qu'il avait choisi Dieu comme Héritier Final; toutefois en attendant que le 'Grand Héritier' prenne posssession de son bien, la jouissance en devait être exclusivement réservée à sa descendance masculine" Tillion, p. 177).
   ["As soon as he had bought a parcel of land, in order to 'legally violate the law', the father of a farming family in La Petite Kabilye or in L'Aurès hastened to have a testament drawn up by a justice of the peace stipulating that he had elected God as his Final Heir; however, until the 'Great Heir' had taken possession of His inheritance, the enjoyment and use of the land had to be exclusively reserved for his male progeny."]
   In other words: ". . . les paysans maghrébins—tous musulmans dévòts cela va sans dire,—ont opté pour les grandes flammes de l'enfer plutôt que de sacrifier l'appropriation de leur terre par leur lignée" (Tillion, p. 173).
   ["North African peasants—all devout Muslims of course—have opted for hell's inferno rather than sacrifice the appropriation of the land by their male lineage."

9. Mothers do share, theoretically, in the prestige of "la soeur-cousine" ["the sister/cousin"] mentioned by J. Déjeux (Déjeux, *Littérature Maghrébine*, p.

228). They too represent "la pureté inviolable du groupe" ["the inviolate purity of the group"] as J. Déjeux said of his sisters (Déjeux, "La Littérature Maghrébine," p. 34). However, during the independence war, the alleged "unassailability" and "veneration" granted to women were exposed. These false claims conceal harsh confinement and desertion. Evasion, mental illness, and suicide (rebellion and exile being available to only a few) are seen as being the only outlets available. A modern alternative (in an Arab context) is, increasingly, prostitution. *Harrouda* skillfully suggests this. M. N'Aït Attik had discovered its comparative advantages as early as the 1930s (M. N'Aït Attik, p. 15). J. F. A. Clément notes that it is mostly among women—and in their midst, peasant women—especially in land promotion areas that suicide rates are the highest. Economic progress does not go hand in hand with better conditions for women. The reverse is happening. In the cities, women are phased out and deprived of their traditional livelihood in favor of a few better trained men. He adds: "Au Maroc, le suicide semble surtout choisi par les femmes mais celles-ci ne font guère de littérature. Autant en Français qu'en Arabe, elles restent les grandes muettes" ["In Morocco, suicide seems to be an option that is taken mostly by women but Moroccan women do not express themselves through literature. In French as well as in Arabic, they remain mute."] (Clément, p. 1066).

In the countryside, where emigration has drained the available manpower, V. Maher tells us that "Agricultural tasks have been redistributed in such a way as to increase the workload of women" but that "it is commercial exchange, the value of commodities and their desirability—and the possibility of undertaking paid work in order to buy them that women must not discover" (L. Beck and N. Keddie, eds., *Women in the Muslim World*, England: Harvard University Press, 1978, p. 110). The same debilitating lifestyle is still dictated to the majority of Moroccan women, according to her. The dilemma resides in having to choose between subjection and physical ease or, a degree of independence marred by poverty and exploitation. Various forms of rebellion are more and more widespread: "high divorce rate, casual prostitution, intrigue, solidarity among women, ritual ridicule, ecstatic religion's validating nonsexual roles. . ." (Beck and Keddie, eds., pp. 121-122).

If in reality their outlook is bleak, in fiction, on the whole, it appears even somber. E. Accad, for instance is of the opinion that the main solution to women's problems in fiction is "victimization" when the books are written by men; and, more rarely for lack of more female authors, "la fuite, l'existentialisme dans le sens saganien du terme et l'engagement politique. . . " ["escape, existentialism in the context of Françoise Sagan's novels, and political engagement and action"] when they are written by women (Evelyne Accad, "La Longue Marche," *Présence Francophone*, No. 12, 1976, p. 4). Full feminist awareness remains to be acquired.

10. She is groping in the dark, half-aware that in her society as V. Maher said: Women must be kept from "understanding" their relation to the world, or realizing their real capacities or opportunities. The emphasis on trammeled perception of which the Tassaout woman. . .complains—"I have always been kept blindfolded, blinded"—is a recurrent theme. (Beck and Keddie, eds., p. 118)

It is not surprising that continuous years of childbearing, raising and domestic activities from age 16 (to the exclusion of any other occupation) amounted to total annihilation of many mental capacities.

11. "Au bout de seize ans, je n'avais pas encore trouvé un seul petit lopin de terre où enterrer mon arbre mort depuis longtemps" ["After sixteen years, I still had not found a single plot of ground where to bury my long-dead tree."] (Pt. II, Ch. xi; p. 180).

12. In his book *La Sexualité en Islam*, A. Bouhdiba, who sees through the lack of love in Arabo-Muslim societies where divorce is too common and too easy to obtain, makes a good analysis of the possessive mother. Having been denied any inherent value, women, frustrated and stripped of significant inheritance rights on their own, have to have as many children as possible for comfort and security. In a related article he explains that children constitute "un véritable système d'assurance vieillesse, d'assurance maladie, une garantie contre le destin . . . " ["a veritable insurance system against aging and illness, and a guarantee against the blows of destiny. . ."] However, the destiny their society—and their men—impose on them is not so easily deflected: the security acquired is a negative and illusory one. It is only through "total" emancipation that women can better their lives (Bouhdiba, "Le Royaume," p. 68).

13. From a literary standpoint, female inhibition can be evidenced in the complete lack of romans-poèmes by women. Those require the free flow of consciousness that women, risking violent censure and retribution, cannot afford. The exception, Mririda N'Aït Attik can be seen as a feminist "avant la lettre" expressing as early as 1946 the poetic inspiration of a free woman refusing to live by men's rules. Therefore, women seldom write, especially in Morocco. As can be guessed, they share equally the problem of censorship with men. The authors who dare touch taboo topics are either "unknown" in their countries of origin or read by a small number of people. They often attack the new nationalism and regression to traditional values that they blame for their country's backwardness. In *Le Passé Simple* Chraïbi threw into full view the dark corners of everyday life and caused much embarrassement. Here is one sarcastic quote he made of the Koran, concerning those "créatures de Dieu que le Koran a parquées" ["creatures of God that the Koran had fenced in. . ."]:

"Baisez-les et les rebaisez; par le vagin, c'est plus utile; ensuite ignorez-les jusqu'à la jouissance prochaine" ["Copulate with them a few times; inside their vagina since that is more useful. Then ignore them until your next pleasure-seeking."] (Chraïbi, *Le Passé*, pp. 40-41).

Chraïbi was made to disown this book which he now regrets having done (see Déjeux, *Littérature*, pp. 280-281).

14. In North African literature however, even Assia Djebar the author who champions "le couple," has seriously asked herself if she were not too far ahead of her times (Déjeux, *Littérature*, p. 255).

15. See his novel *Agadir* (Mohamed Khair Eddine, *Agadir*, Paris: Editions du Seuil, 1967, pp. 119-120). Jean Déjeux notices that in his work as can be expected from the author's background: "la femme est dégradée et inférioriseé..." ["woman is degraded and given an inferior status"] (Déjeux, *Littérature*, p. 415). Of Arabo-Muslim cultures, A. Bouhdiba writes: "on limite l'amour au

ludique et on ravale l'épouse au rang de femme-objet, dont l'unique fonction est la satisfaction du plaisir sexuel du mari" ["Love is limited to lust and the wife is relegated to the low ranking of a sex-object whose sole function is to insure the husband's sexual enjoyment."] (Bouhdiba, "Le Royaume," p. 66.).

There is no need therefore, to speak of any sexual problems since simple coital ejaculation is all that the husband owes to his wife. Even that right is limited by polygamy for instance. Taking into account their preordained relationship, one must admit that that is all he learns how to give her. The rest is entirely left to the woman alone who has no sexual education whatsoever and many socially induced inhibitions filling that function. Some of these inhibitions are derived from knowing that for her lover, embracing her means embracing evil and irreligion.

16. E. Accad transposes that into mores in fiction when she asserts that: "Nowhere is sex seen as an act of enjoyment, an act fulfilling in itself, a rapport of mutuality of feeling, a sharing and giving. It is a role-playing in a contractual sense, and it is the many evils of the contractual sex that the novels emphasize" (Beck and Keddie, p. 626). E. Accad lists a few related examples in fiction: "inevitably tragic endings to adulterous love affairs, the isolation of women from society. . .the fear old women have of being parasites because they can no longer procreate; the sadness with which the birth of girls is greeted. . .the punishment of sexual dishonor by death; the general acceptance of such practices as polygamy, prostitution, slavery, and arranged marriages. . .and the enforced seclusion and veiling of women, all of which demonstrate the refusal of society to grant women the right to seek sexual fulfillment" (Beck and Keddie, pp. 617-618).

Other examples of equal importance in novels as well as in real life need to be added to the endless catalog:—the hatred between the parents, and between them and their children, which make the family live in an atmosphere of "tendre haine" to quote again an ingenious apposition of Chraïbi's;

—the prevention of the formation of normal affectionate brother-sister relationships due to the brother's role as the sister's guardian even if he is much younger;

—the constant fear where a woman lives that she might find herself repudiated and without support and have to either return to her reluctant family or become a "huriya" (or "prostitutée");

—the exploitation of school-age girls from the countryside as twenty-four-hour-a-day maids and drudges in urban households.

—the all-inclusive suspicion which leaves no room for any kind of trust or real friendship between anyone for fear that one's "honor" will be besmirched in any of the hundred possible ways related to women;

—the early marrying off of daughters by possessive and dejected mothers hoping to saddle them down with children and a husband in close proximity, to help relieve their loneliness.

17. Female circumcision is a related area that no North African author has mentioned to my knowledge (with the exception of the highly dedicated novelist Nawał el Saadawi who is Egyptian). Perhaps things will change now that articles have appeared focusing on this tragic and demeaning custom of the Third World (Claire Brisset, "Excisées, jusqu'à quand?" *Le Monde*, 3 Apr.

1980, Sec. 1, p. 1, col. 2); and *Ms. Magazine*'s March issue covering Nawal el Saadawi's own retelling of her childhood clitoridectomy by Robin Morgan and Gloria Steinem, "The International Crime," (*Ms.*, March 1980, pp. 65-69). [*Editors' Note*: See Evelyen Accad's *L'Excisée* (Paris, L'Harmattan, 1982) and Tobe Levin's paper in this collection for further discussion of female genital mutilation.]

18. "Toute entreprise humaine vaut qu'on la commence. Et commencer, c'est faire la moitié du chemin" [Any human enterprise, deserves an attempt, a beginning which is half the amount of work it requires"] (Pt. II, Ch. vi, p. 131). The key word is "bilan," appraisal. The idea of "faire un bilan," taking inventory is one common denominator of many of Chraïbi's works. This theme betrays, in my opinion, an obsession with production, le "rendement," which is more indicative of the western influence in the author's psychological make-up. He keeps making his characters ask what the tangible results are of the struggle waged but there is no satisfactory response. Comparatively, when the mother leaves at the end of *La Civilisation ma Mère!...* she does not merely do so "pour constater" as M. A. Alaoui contends but in order to appraise and ascertain what has been done and what can be done in the future (Alaoui, p. 38). In that respect D. Chraïbi is very positive and shows that he is abreast of realities. The characters must accomplish something, in our social context, to make the reader care, and D. Chraïbi knows that.

19. As J. F. A. Clément has said, we need a work from a North African writer who will not opt for expediency: "Il n'y a aucune oeuvre de longue haleine, bien travaillée" ["There is no well crafted, long-term, all-encompassing work"] (Clément, p. 1068).

Women and Alienation: Analysis of the Works of Two Francophone African Novelists

Karen Smyley Wallace

Currently, there is a burgeoning emphasis on the Black female Francophone writer and her portrayal of the female character in the novel. African female novelists Mariama Bâ (*Une Si Longue Lettre*, 1980, *Un Chant Ecarlate*, 1984); Aminata Sow Fall (*Le Revenant*, 1976, *La Grève des Battu*, 1979, *L'Appel des Arènes*, 1982) and Nafissatou Diallo (*De Tilène Au Plateau: Une Enfance Dakaroise*, 1975) are among those noted for their accurate and penetrating portrayals of the woman. It is undeniable that the contributions of these African female novelists have been crucial in the meaningful evolution and revelation of the Black female character, particularly with regard to themes involving her search for identity.

Detailed examination of the powerful new presence of this Black female perspective is being carried out by this writer. But, it is nevertheless significant to reflect upon the image of the woman, as she was initially presented by male Francophone novelists. From this vantage point, one may better analyze the patterns of development and their success or failure in the characterizations of the Black female in Francophone African literature.

The inclusion of the female character within the scope of Francophone African literature, is certainly not a novel idea, for she has always occupied a position of some merit. Although poetry has provided a useful mode of expression for the depiction of the Black woman, (see David Diop's "A Une Danseuse Noire," *Coups de Pilon* (1957) and Léopold Senghor's "Femme Noire," *Chants d'Ombre* (1956), it was the novel which encouraged the broadest investigation of the female image. From the appearance of what is known as the first Francophone Black novel, (René Maran's *Batouala*, 1928) to the late 1950s, male Francophone novelists projected the images of the woman in her traditional setting, where the matters of home and family were her singular concern. Some of the more well-known examples are the depiction of the mother in Camara Laye's *L'Enfant Noir* (1953); the grandmother, wife, and other village women in Ousmane Sembène's *Les Bouts de Bois de Dieu* (1960); the mother and the old woman in Aboulaye Sadji's *Maïmouna* (1958); or Ousmane Socé's heroine in *Karim: Roman Sénégalais* (1948). Characterized as the symbol of the earth mother, the dutiful and obedient wife, or the nubile love goddess, the female character was often portrayed as a one dimensional figure, lacking any great literary palpability. The most characteristic and noteworthy feature of these earlier works, however, was the consistent representation of the African woman as a symbol of strength.

While the larger body of African literature has focused primarily upon the male protagonist and his conflict with western assimilation (see Ferdinand Oyono's *Le Vieux Nègre et la Médaille*, 1956; Bernard Dadié's *Un Nègre à Paris*, 1959; Cheikh Hamidou Kane's *L'Adventure Ambiguë*, 1961), the female character has consistently occupied a significant role in the works of Senegalese novelists Aboulaye Sadji and Ousmane Sembène. Sadji (1910-1960), a lesser known literary figure, whose style was greatly imitative of the late nineteenth century novel, is noted for two major works which highlight the impact of acculturation upon the African woman: *Nini: Mulâtresse de Sénégal*, 1947 and *Maïmouna*, 1958. (He also wrote a short fictional piece entitled *Tounka: une nouvelle*, 1946). Despite minor stylistic limitations, the heroines in Sadji's works have become classic in African literature. Due to his artful portrayals of African women frought with cultural ambivalence, he is acknowledged for having made a singular contribution to earlier colonial Francophone African literature, and has been acclaimed an "excellent portraitist of the Senegalese woman."[1]

Ousmane Sembène, a contemporary Senegalese novelist and filmmaker, is noted for his finely chiseled portraits of females as real, palpable individuals.[2] By creating women figures who do not merely represent shadows of the male figure, nor echoes of the male voice, Sembène's works reflect the complexities of a changing Africa. He departs measurably from the rather static images carved by Sadji, and renders the female character a dynamic being, who must constantly struggle to redefine her perception of self in the developing African continent and in the world.[3]

In their respective works, yet, often contrasting literary styles, Sadji and Sembène attempt to delve beyond the superficial portraits of the woman as mere exotic accompaniment to the male, in order to reveal her own psychic universe. Although in different degrees, both writers have spoken out against the effects of Western assimilation upon African culture, by focusing upon the woman and her reaction to this phenomenon. While Sadji paints a Senegal of 1947, and Sembene, one of 1960, the long range effects of colonization and cultural ambivalence are nevertheless startlingly visible in the female characters of both authors.

Thus, through their vast and colorful tableaux of women figures (market women, wives, mothers, daughters, political leaders, prostitutes, teachers, secretaries, etc.) Sadji and Sembène illustrate the tormenting world of the double self, anxiety and alienation. Although the notion of duality is expressed differently by each character, they are all linked by two factors: their intense struggle for survival in the colonial world, and the disintegration of their sense of "africanité." Thus, this article will provide a comparative analysis of each author's works, and of their compelling female characters, who have embarked upon a labyrinthine search for self.

Ironically, it was the colonial system, itself, which provided the impetus for the development of more intricate and subtle literary treatment of the Black female persona. From the period of the late 1950s and into the early years of independence from colonial rule, Francophone literature witnessed the emergence of a new and problematic female character. The goal of these new characters was "to redefine the position of the African individual in a changing and developing society."[4] Forced to struggle with social, political, philosophical or sentimental problems, the Black female character often found herself cut off from her past, and trapped within the confines of a system of alienation. In her work, *L'Angoisse chez les romanciers africains*, Monique Battestini comments upon this phenomenon of alienation and its impact upon African literature:

> In this rapidly developing universe, a new concern emerged: that of no longer being oneself. The West had overturned traditional Africa, and the African had sought in Negritude, a refuge, a triumph, and finally a new anxiety. This sense of uprooting, which resulted from the influx of foreign values, was experienced by all of the writers: thus, from this came the birth of a new generation of "dual souls."[5]

In the novel, *Nini: Mulâtresse du Sénégal*, Sadji created the unforgettable female character, Nini. As the embodiment of "things French" and "things Black," she remains an intriguing example of the alienated being. Nini's character may be analyzed from two perspectives. As an individual, her story reveals the psychological discord of one woman's search for racial identity.

On a larger plane, she becomes a part of a collective drama and the prototype of a people whose very existence is determined by the conflicting duality of an African soul trapped within a white skin:

> Nini is the eternal portrait of the mulatto female, whether she is from Senegal, the Caribbean or the Americas. It is the portrait of the physically and morally hybrid being, who . . .constantly seeks to elevate herself above a level of humanity she considers inferior, but to which destiny has inexorably linked her.[6]

Nini is both a product and a victim of the French colonial system in Senegal. Since the island of Saint Louis (original capital of Senegal and the setting for the story) was one of the most thriving centers for trade and banking in West Africa, it offers a clear picture of French assimilative policies in microcosm. In the early days of settlement, during the first half of the seventeenth century, close contact between Europeans and Africans in commerce was inevitable. As there were few, if any, French women among the first arrivals, "French companies often encouraged marriage with local African women."[7] These women became known as "*signaras*;" an adaptation of the Portuguese term *sinhora* (a title of respect, like *madame*, accorded a married woman). Although sanctioned by the government, these marriages were not legally binding so these women were technically concubines. History records, however, that some of the French settlers gave their names, some property, or a European education to the children of these unions. Having received privileges and benefits unknown to their darker skinned brothers, the "assimilés" became the first class of Africans eager to assimilate with France. Yet, the irony of their world was one of refuge behind the ivory tower of their "almost whiteness."

The story of Mademoiselle Virginia de Maerle is essentially simple. Nini, 22, unmarried, lives with her two older relatives, Tante Hortense and Grand'mère Hélène. Employed as a "perfectly stupid little secretary,"[8] at the Department of Rivers, she spends the majority of her time in pursuit of white men. Her list of previous suitors is long, although unsuccessful. Currently, her interest is focused upon a certain Monsieur Martineau, a middle management functionary, recently arrived from France. Nini's happiness, as well as the good name of her family, depends upon the ensnarement of the unsuspecting Frenchman. In her eyes, she has had the misfortune of becoming the love interest of an African co-worker, who, although far superior to her in education and in character, is nonetheless, representative of the Blackness she so loathes. The African is duly rejected; the Frenchman, actively pursued; Nini is seduced and abandoned; her ultimate escape is sought in France, in the arms of new white men.

As Nini gazes into the looking glass, the reflections she beholds provide either a false image of self and reality, or no image whatsoever. This symbolic mirror, as Nini's life itself, reflects a world of illusion and fantasy. These are poignantly brought to life by the dream-like atmosphere into which Sadji draws his readers. The descriptive passages artfully capture the old de Maerle house, with its southern French architecture, common to Saint Louis. The dilapidated exterior and faded, cluttered interior are the only remaining souvenirs of the family, and of a glory that is decidedly past.

The two old ladies, both "signaras" in their time, live in a faded world of memories. Having failed at the illusory search for whiteness, they have resigned themselves to the more comforting world of religion. Nini's search for white identity is a natural consequence of that "dream deferred." Sadji has created a demi-world of soft lights, playful shadows, half-closed venetian blinds, through which the symbol of the brilliant African sun is never allowed to penetrate.

The softly muted tones of the fading world of the old mulatto ladies is sharply contrasted with Nini's own agressive behavior. No matter how fixedly she stares into her looking glass, she is unable to see what she so desperately craves: the image of "a real white lady." Instead, she uses her skill and artistry to mold a reality more to her liking. Structuring her own behavior to accommodate her perception of whiteness, Nini embraces a world of controlled artificiality. She rises early, becomes exceedingly punctual, quickens her pace, sharpens her gestures, and raises the level and tone of her voice. Using language to further widen the gap between herself and "the Niggers," Nini exemplifies the impact of colonial bilingualism, as described by Fanon: "To speak a language is to take on a world, a culture . . .The colonized person is elevated above his jungle status in proportion to his adoption of the mother country's cultural standards. He becomes whiter as he renounces his blackness."[9] The adoption of the colonized language as a means of cultural acceptance, has also been poignantly captured by the poet Léon Damas, in the biting lines:

> Be quiet
> Did I not tell you to speak French
> French from France
> French of the Frenchman
> French French[10]

The robot-like gestures and the structured language, however, do little to camouflage traces of Nini's African past. It is not the reflection in the mirror that lies; rather it is Nini who refuses to see evidence of her African blood. What little she does see, she attempts to mask, in the same way as she uses face powder to cover her full lips and flattened nose and in the same way as she tightly disciplines the sway of somewhat generous hips. Despite these attempts, the African heritage Nini has long despised and tried to escape, is readily discernible. We see it in the depth of her passions and sensual nature, for it is she who encourages the erotic adventures with her white admirers. We sense it as she sways invitingly to the sound of the "rumbas and beguines" on the dance floor. We see it in her belief in the forces of traditional African magic. Although outwardly rebuking the use of fetishes and *gris-gris* (charms or amulets), Nini obediently swallows the magic love potion, prescribed by the old African marabout. It is only when the effects are negative that self-hatred motivates her to declare her hatred of "things black."

The irony of Sadji's story is bitter, for Nini is rejected by the Frenchman, Martineau, who returns to France and eventually marries "a real white lady." What is startlingly clear is that for him, Nini is after all, only several shades lighter of "café au lait": ". . .a Negress is a Negress. There's no way she could ever become white." (*Nini*, p. 303) Martineau's brutal departure provides the ultimate crack in Nini's distorted looking glass. Having rejected all avenues leading to her African heritage, and compelled by the twisted self-images from within, Nini's only means to escape lies in departure from the island: a consequence depicting the Stendhalien "search for happiness." The alienated Nini has condemned herself to an endless pursuit of whiteness.

Sadji's novel is neither a defense, an apology, nor a polemical discussion of the role of the mulatto female: "one can neither condemn nor blame these beings. I believe it is more charitable . . . to show them, as in a mirror, the reality of who they really are." (*Nini*, p. 315) As a prisoner of his time, and of his islamic beliefs in fatalism, Sadji could not envisage a rebellious mulatto character (as in Simone Schwarz-Bart's *La Mulâtresse Solitude*). While Sadji's novel provides a vivid portrayal of this particular tormented soul, it reveals aspects of the broader drama of racial and cultural alienation known to other Blacks. In this respect, Nini has achieved the dimension of a classic, although alienated, persona.

Ousmane Sembène has also produced several works in which the dominant motif is the alienation of the African woman. While none share the burden of the double heredity of French and African parentage, as had Nini, their sense of anxiety is nonetheless pronounced. For each, there is an intense emotional and psychological desire for assimilation into European-like society. N'Deye Touti, from the classic nevel, *God's Bits of Wood (Les Bouts de Bois de Dieu)*, provides a fine example of this inner conflict. This 1960 work tells the story of the Senegalese struggle for unionization along the Dakar-Niger railroad line, and for ultimate independence from French rule.

N'Deye, a young Wolof girl, lives in a humble compound outside of Dakar. One might say that she lives among the people, yet, not of them, for she has succeeded in creating an imaginary shield that protects her from what she views as an undesirable life. N'Deye's sense of duality is not caused by her desire to whiten herself or her race; rather to whiten her style of living. The torment she experiences, however, is as profound as that of her counterpart, Nini. The first step in the process of assimilation is to feel shame for one's own heritage. Nini had successfully removed herself from any close contact with her African roots, while N'Deye still lives among them. We note an intense sense of ambivalence, as she contemplates her childhood surroundings with shame, and withdraws more and more into a world peopled by school books and fantasies. Her very demeanor reveals a sense of superiority over those around her: what the author describes as "a great distance from those who were a part of her daily world."[11] The contrast is particularly notable in those passages which refer to *their* lack of civilization and to *her* acculturation.

Sembène, as Sadji, uses the image of the dream and imagination to portray N'Deye's existence. Amidst her daily activities, fantasies provide a temporary escape from what she refers to as "a living graveyard." The author has not created an insensitive character, so much as he has produced a woman who is prey to the same pangs of envy as are all colonized people. The fact that N'Deye wishes to avoid the issues of the railroad strike and seeks refuge in "the European sector, where the houses are bordered by gardens, and not the metal and wooden huts that are enclosed behind a wall of bamboo," (*GBW*, p. 107) does not make her a shallow individual. According to Fanon's observations in *The Wretched of the Earth*, she is merely paying one of the prices of the assimilative process. "The gaze of the colonized person upon the villa of the colonizer is a look of envy."[12]

Although the authors' styles differ, several factors unite Nini and N'Deye, as alienated beings. Both women conveniently ignore the opinions of the European, in their regard. Both must be shocked into the reality of their double existence. Having accepted all forms of ridicule on the part of white men, Nini had acquired the facility to soon forget the pain of their rejection and to proceed to newer prey. N'Deye, expressly created by Sembène to reveal African reality to Africans, must also suffer the pangs of humiliation. Having closely patterned her life after European standards, she is devasted upon overhearing two gendarmes crudely discuss her body, her people, her human worth: ". . .Say! Have one of your guards find her and offer two kilos of rice. Right now, they'll sleep with you for less than that!" (*GBW*, p. 186) The impact of this incident was considerable. It, along with the encouragement of Bakayoko, the leader of the strike, propels N'Deye into a type of self-redefinition. In this way, Sembene provides the once-alienated character with an opportunity for emotional and political growth through self-realization.

In many respects, Oumi N'Doye, the second wife of El Hadji, in the 1974 novel *Xala*, has achieved the material success so longed for by N'Deye Touti. As the wife of a prominent businessman, she benefits from her husband's high standing in the community. Oumi lives in a European sector of Dakar; she has her own villa; her children attend private schools in a chauffeured car; and there is even talk of buying a new Fiat for her daughter, Mariem. Oumi's is a world of prestige and acquisition.

Through her portrait, the author reveals the transition of Senegal from the days of colonialism to those of independence. As the story is set in the 1970s, one is able to see the long range effects of Western influence. Oumi speaks casually of such things as "black wig;" "Evian water;" "discotheques;" "Afro-American soul music." She prides herself on her knowledge of the latest European styles and is an avid reader of photo-magazines. She listens to radio broadcasts in French, refers to her husband in the third person, as "Monsieur," and bases her culinary skills upon ideas gleaned exclusively from French magazines.

Although unaware of the socio-political influences of neo-colonialism upon her world and her thinking, Oumi represents still another form of the alienated female character. Depicted as shallow and artificial individuals, Oumi and her husband, El Hadji, are unfortunate victims of the temporary *xala* (Wolof, for impotence) of an African struggling with its newly won independence.

Sembène's story, "La Noire de . . . ," from the collection *Voltaïque*, focuses upon one of the most psychologically intricate of his alienated female characters. Rather than become absorbed into European culture, Diouana, a young girl from Dakar, merely wishes to taste of its novelties. Initially employed as a babysitter for a French family in one of the finer sections of Dakar, her duties are shared with three other domestics, thereby rendering work conditions favorable. Seasoned with occasional leftovers from the family table and some used clothing, Madame, has little difficulty sparking Diouana's interest in returning to France with them. To Diouana, the family represents "great white folks." She is easily seduced by the dreams which metropolitan France offers; yet, once the ocean is crossed, the initial excitement subsides and Diouana's view of France, of the French, and of herself are catapulted into a bitter and painful world of reality.

Emanating from a culture of communal living, Diouana finds it difficult to adjust to this new world of isolation. The changes in the girl's personality, which result from the sharp thrusts of racism, are depicted with dramatic impact: torment, ridicule, humiliation and embarrassment. The French children call her "Savage" and "Négresse". Madame parades her from place to place, from house to house, as if on exhibit. She is touched, fondled, teased. Her household duties multiply until she is eventually forced to serve as babysitter-maid-cook-nurse-laundress.

While the process of depersonalization is intensified and reaches its apex, Diouana withdraws slowly into herself. Her color, now objectified, becomes something exterior to herself, while she regards it with the same distant aversion as the white family; a process which Aimé Césaire describes as "thingification"[13] of the human being: "Slowly, she began to drown into the color of her skin. Suddenly she was overcome with an unshakeable terror. Her blackness. Fearfully, she sought refuge within herself."[14] Realizing that she has become a mere object, an African curio, so to speak, Diouana's sense of isolation is painfully heightened. No longer referred to by her rightful name (always mispronounced), but as "the black girl," she can no longer be Black for herself. Diouana is thus deprived of color, race, heritage and existence.

In painting Diouana's portrait, Sembène has shown the schism separating the girl from her employers; the African from the French; the colonizer from the colonized; the black from the white. Unable to either grow or survive in this stagnating situation, Diouana opts for a simple, yet final alternative. Sembène's talent as a novelist, fused with his ability as a filmmaker have produced a powerfully dramatic, yet sensitive final scene. When questioned by the inspector. Madame remarks politely, yet cooly: "I don't know why she committed suicide. She was well treated here, ate the same food and even shared a bedroom with my children." (Noire, p. 161).

In the works of both authors, therefore, each of these female characters faces a moment of realization in which she must reflect upon her identity. Each is presented with alternatives and consequently must make choices: for Nini the hopeless escape into the illusory world of whiteness; for N'Deye eventual self-recognition and a rekindling of African pride; for Oumi imprisonment in the unfortunate xala of a newly independent Africa; and for Diouana death by her own hand.

Although each author stamps the novel with his particular mark of individuality, both Sadji and Sembene have chiseled characters who highlight the painfulness associated with the emergence of a sense of duality in the African female persona, and the exorbitant cost of their alienation from self.

Greatly reflecting the early Negritude period, Aboulaye Sadji writes as a moralist; thus, his portrait of Nini is a depiction of the ill-effects of the colonial system. On the surface, Sadji's narrative seems only to describe a somewhat synthetic figure. Certainly, Sadji's work does not approach the more accurate portrayals of this dilemma, as seen from the female perspective of several well-known Francophone Caribbean female novelists. On the same topic of race and the female identity, (see Mayotte Capecia's Je Suis Martiniquaise, 1950; Michèle Lacrosil's Cajou, 1961; or Marie Chauvet's Fonds des Nègres, 1960). Sadji's success lies in his attempt, as an African author, to penetrate this rather lightly sketched female character, and thus, shed some necessary light upon this particular aspect of the broader and more complex drama of alienation and the African woman.

As a more biting critique and keen observer of African culture, Sembène has raised a mirror of social realism and has placed it before the eyes of the African. Through the characterizations of N'Deye, Oumi, and Diouana, he has revealed a distortion in these reflections: a distortion brought about by westernization, colonialism and neo-colonialism. These characters, by no means represent the complete protrayal of the female in Sembène's work. While he is notably perceptive in his treatment of the effects of cultural ambivalence upon the woman, his strongest characters are those who endure less inner emotional conflict than N'Deye, Oumi, or Diouana, and who emerge as politically committed women: "la femme engagée." (See, Tioumbé, in *Harmattan*; Penda, in *God's Bits of Wood*; or Rama, in *Xala*.)

Although Sadji has provided rather vivid and colorful female characterizations, he seems to focus primarily upon the woman as a victim in the developing African society of that period. While Sadji seems content to merely describe the situation which promotes anxiety in his characters, Sembène both describes it and goes on to suggest change: change, invested principally in the hands of the woman. It is the very concept of participation which most readily differentiates Sadji and Sembène's interpretation of the female character. Much of Sembene's philosophy regarding the active participation of the woman in Africa's political development, reflects his espousement of the Marxist view of the female in society.[15] By encharging the female figure with a sense of responsibility, Sembène paints his characters in optimistic tones and shows that the female, (as her male counterpart) is able to transcend the burdens of cultural alienation in order to forge newer paths for Africa, and for herself.

Within the total body of African literature, Sadji and Sembène have been among the few male novelists to focus so intensely upon the female: her life, her concerns, her conflicts, her feelings. By expanding upon some of these original views of Black women by male writers, and by articulating the feelings of the Black woman, contemporary Francophone African female novelists are adding newer insights and greater depth to these original portrayals. Nevertheless, while they are clearly providing the necessary flesh and blood, writers such as Sadji and Sembène, are to be recognized for having presented some of the initial literary framework of the African female, as a principal figure in the novel.

NOTES

1. Robert Pageard, *Littérature négro-africaine* (Paris: Le livre africain, 1966, p. 79.
2. Ousmane Sembene's literary works include: *Le Docker Noir*, 1956; *O pays, mon beau peuple*, 1957; *Les Bouts de Bois de Dieu*, 1960; *Voltaïque*, 1962; *L'Harmattan*, 1964; *Xala*, 1974.
   His major films include: *Borom Sarret*, 1963; *Niaye*, 1966; *La Noire de. . .* , 1966; *Le Mandat*, 1968; *Taw*, 1970; *Emitai*, 1971;   *Xala*, 1975; *Ceddo*, 1976.

3. For further discussion of this point, see Karen Smyley, "Ousmane Sembène: Portraitist of the African Woman in the Novel," *New England Journal of Black Studies*, 1, no. 1, (June 1981), 23-27.

4. Sunday Anonzie, *Sociologie du Roman Africain: Réalisme, Structure et Détermination dans le Roman Moderne Ouest-Africain* (Paris: Tiers-Monde et Développement, 1970), p. 27.

5. Monique Battestini, *L'Angoisse chez les Romanciers Africains* (Dakar: Actes du Colloque, 1963), p. 162. Quotes have been translated by the author.

6. Aboulaye Sadij, *Nini: Mulâtresse du Sénégal* (Paris: Présence Africaine, 1947), p. 1. All subsequent references to this edition will be indicated by *Nini* and the page. All quotes have been translated by the author.

7. See Rita O'Brien, *White Society in Black Africa: The French of Senegal* (Illinois: Northwestern University Press, 1972), p. 31, for further discussion.

8. Frantz Fanon, *Black Skins, White Masks* (New York: Grove Press, Inc., 1967), p.55.

9. Ibid., p. 38.

10. Léon Damas, *Pigments et Névralgies* (Paris: Présence Africaine, 1972), p. 38. All quotes have been translated by the author.

11. Ousmane Sembène, *God's Bits of Wood* (New York: Doubleday & Co., 1962), p. 106. All subsequent references to this edition will be indicated by *GBW* and the page.

12. Frantz Fanon, *The Wretched of the Earth* (New York: Grove Press, Inc., 1963), p. 39.

13. Aimé Césaire, *Discourse on Colonialism* (New York: Monthly Review Press, 1972), p. 21.

14. Ousmane Sembène, *Voltaïque* (Paris: Présence Africaine 1962), p. 180. All subsequent references to this edition will be indicated by *Noire* and the page. All quotes have been translated by the author.

15. Sonia Lee develops this point in her article, "The Awakening of Self in the heroines of Sembène Ousmane," *Critique*, 17 (1975), 17-25.

Maidens, Mistresses and Matrons: Feminine Images in Selected Soyinka Works

Carole Boyce Davies

Literature, because it mirrors and/or recreates social, historical and economic realities, is one of the channels through which negative attitudes and stereotypes of women are perpetuated, even created. Modern African literature too, because it has adopted many of the Western patriarchal modes of thought and expression, often conveys some of these biased attitudes to which we refer. Revisionist criticism of African literature then has as one of its tasks the truthful assessment of the literary image of women. It must therefore approach already well criticized texts/authors from a critical posture which seeks to reveal and thereby correct some of these attitudes and in so doing challenge authors to project a complete picture of African social reality. Sonia Lee has already found in African literature of French expression that

> the feminine protagonist throughout the African novel presents a certain homogeneity of character which can be attributed to a basic similarity in the man's view of the woman . . . Through the role of the woman the writer may be re-examining man's role in his changing society. Consequently, the heroine often has a didactic function which deters her from psychological development.

75

Furthermore, the feminine character often plays a secondary role in the novel, frequently being placed in the fixed context of the village where she illustrates traditional life. In the changing contemporary society she seems to remain the constant factor because the social changes imposed upon traditional life by modern times are seen almost exclusively in the life drama of the male protagonist.[1]

My study of female portraiture in the Soyinka works reveals no significant departure from the above findings. In fact, a feminist reading of Soyinka reveals enough female stereotypes to suggest a definite sexist bias against women. Additionally, an examination of the characteristics of these women produces the distinct impression that the author is conjuring up the image of the same, ideal woman over and over again.

Studies which deal in any depth or detail with Soyinka's women are definitely in the minority in the canon of Soyinka criticism.[2] For the most part, discussion of women in the drama and fiction of Wole Soyinka has been peripheral to, or embraced within, more conventional literary criticism.[3] It is as if these female characters have been relegated to their "place" within this literary universe. This critical attitude, I would submit, harmonizes with the author's overwhelming treatment of women as objects of quest rather than as subjects in their own right. Soyinka's strong, Ogunnian[4] sense of the African hero has so far militated against his portrayal of women in any heroic sense.

A distinction can, however, be made between works which are set in a traditional, rural community and those in which the action takes place in an urban environment. In the traditional, rural setting, the stereotype is that of the submissive virgin, as portrayed by Sidi of *The Lion and the Jewel* (1963) and the unnamed virgin bride of Elesin in *Death and The King's Horseman* (1975). In the urban setting, the *femme fatale* or bitch-goddess dominates and here, particularly, the same woman seems to appear repeatedly. Simi of *The Interpreters* (1965) has almost identical physical features as Segi of *Kongi's Harvest* (1967), features and characteristics which are climaxed in Iriyise of *Season of Anomy* (1973). In these works which this study will limit itself to, the author creates a fantasized version of a woman, colored by a combination of Yoruba mythology and his own ideal of the feminine.

The Foolish Virgins

The most prominent physical characteristic of the Soyinka female character is exceptional beauty; a beauty which exists, however, to be possessed by the male. As early as *The Lion and the Jewel*, we find the image of the village belle with her natural, virginal, goddess-like beauty. In this play, particularly, the importance of male dominance is communicated. As the title, folkloric as it may be, connotes, the male is given the qualities of strength and prowess which the name lion suggests, while the female is endowed with the virtues of the ornament or prized *possession*.

The play can be read as a power struggle between male and female. Sidi is innocent of her beauty until she views photographs of herself in a Lagos magazine which is brought to the village by the photographer. Baroka, like the rest of the village community, becomes aware of her exceptional beauty and the fact that she is now famous while he has been symbolically relegated to a position of little importance in the magazine. Sidi says: "He shares the corner of the leaf with the lowest of the low—/With the dug-out village latrine!"[5] It becomes obvious that the *Bale*, (traditional ruler) whom Lakunle describes as a devil among women, cannot allow himself to be outstripped by a "mere woman". So Baroka immediately decides that he has to conquer this woman. Sidi has, by this time, assimilated some of Lakunle's (the village teacher) views of "modern womanhood" misguided though they are. Even before her appearance in the magazine she had exhibited an acute awareness of her self-worth, for when Lakunle tried to convince her that women had smaller brains than men she had called his thoughts "manly conceit" and when he tried to point out that women were the weaker sex, she had articulated the strength of the traditional African woman: "The weaker sex is it?/Is it the weaker breed who pounds yam/Or bends all day to plant the millet/With a child strapped to her back?" (p.5).

Clearly, Sidi becomes aware that the appearance of her photographs has kindled a power struggle between herself and Baroka. Thus when Sadiku, the Bale's senior wife who by tradition initiates the procurement of junior wives, comes with talk of marriage and the Bale's invitation to supper, Sidi, conscious of Baroka's strategy counters with,

> He seeks to have me as his property
> Where I must fade beneath his jealous hold
> Ah, Sadiku,
> The schoolman has taught me certain things
> And my images have taught me all the rest.
> Baroka merely seeks to *raise his manhood*
> Above my beauty
> . . . .(p.21) (emphasis mine)

The denouement of this play provides a good example of Soyinka's treatment and disposal of the female character. It seems unlikely that a girl who is so aware of herself, of the positive aspects of womanhood and of the outcome of Baroka's suppers would become so gullible when confronted with his trickery. Significantly Baroka's plan involves his pretending that his manhood has failed him because with Sadiku's dance of women's triumph, Sidi's delight at being on the side of the victor: "Hurray for womankind!" (p. 33), the play has an overt feminist focus. But the extreme opposite—masculine triumph—is the author's purpose instead. So Sidi is made to succumb to the Bale and Sadiku to function simply as a tool in Baroka' machinations.

As soon as Sidi enters the Baroka's chambers, with its masculine aura of wrestling, a different passive Sidi surfaces. She is in awe of the Lion's strength and skill in wrestling, of his use of language and eventually of his "stamp machine".[6] True, Soyinka is obviously making a statement on human vanity and, as others suggest, representing the symbolic merger of tradition with youth, the triumph of measured progress over hasty Westernization, life over empty rhetoric.[7] Yet fiery Sidi, with all her potential, loses her brilliance and slowly deflates in the estimation of the reader/viewer. Thus ends the promising career of Sidi, relegated, one would speculate, to pulling out the hairs of Baroka's armpits. Ogunba rightly says that at the end of the play one is left with "the feeling that we have experienced a distressing waste . . .Baroka regards women as commodities that must be used, squeezed dry and then thrown into the garbage can".[8] Never simple, Soyinka has created a situation in which the heroine has to choose between the lesser of two evils, since neither Lakunle nor Baroka is the ideal of African manhood. We are, of course, in the realm of comedy here, but obviously Soyinka, in his creation of Lakunle, the caricature of a semi-educated village teacher, was criticizing the empty, borrowed, Western concepts and attitudes which produce a soft masculinity which is totally undesirable in an Africa struggling with self-determination. So although Baroka is a comic grotesque, a terrible caricature of the traditional chieftain, his eventual triumph represents an implicit defense of the mystery and strength of the past. Yet, in his portrayal of Sidi, the classical stereotypical image of the foolish virgin reinforces a negative perception of self to the female viewer/reader and, concomitantly, a condescencion in the appraisal of women on the part of the male.

The image of the beautiful submissive virgin recurs in *Death and King's Horseman* and although more than a decade separates these works, and the latter is a tragedy based on an actual historical event, similar stereotyped definitions of the maiden reappear. Here, however, the young virgin becomes the symbol for all that detracts man from his seriousness of purpose. The beauty/danger dichotomy is clearly present in the contradictory Eve/Virgin Mary archetypes which inform the character. The virgin, a nameless, voiceless votary, like the virgin Egbo takes in *The Interpreters*, is perceived as object not subject. Her only expressions are sobs at her contribution to Elesin's demise.

Elesin is involved in the preparation for his ritual of following the dead *Oba* (king) to the spiritual region when, as the stage directions explicitly state: "The earlier distraction, a beautiful young girl comes along the passage through which Elesin first had his entry".[9] We discover from the Praise Singer and Elesin's own admissions that he has a deep affection for

beautiful women and although he is challenged to maintain his sense of
purpose in face of his grand task, Elesin, like Baroka, sees only the physical
beauty which he is somehow obliged to possess. He describes her in words
of extreme adulation: ". . .Tell me who was the goddess through whose lips
I saw the ivory pebbles of Oya's river-bed. Iyaloja, who is she?" (p. 19).
When he fails in his ritual suicide, Elesin tries to explain himself to the
young bride who sobs near the cell in which he has been incarcerated by the
British official who had intervened to stop the ritual:

> My young bride . . .
> now I feel I want to blame you
> for the mystery of the sapping of my will . . .
> Oh little mother, I have taken countless
> women in my life, but you were more than
> a desire of the flesh. I needed you
> as the abyss across which my body
> must be drawn . . .(p. 65)

Izevbaye contends that Soyinka "detests all forms of womb yearning" and
what we see from Elesin is pure lust, his inability to transcend the
material/physical plane.[10] Elesin's fall from grace becomes a tragedy of his
own making. But another minor tragedy, a personal tragedy (though not in
the Aristotelian sense) has occurred. The young bride whose life was so
totally fractured by Elesin's rapaciousness is virtually ignored in the grand
scheme of Elesin's demise. Her experience, like Sidi's, is the tragic loss of
self-worth, which she hides in sobs. Moreover, it provides another example
of the author's disposal of the female character.

Soyinka's dramatic technique had reached its height by the time of the
writing of this play. Yet there are many similarities in characterization in the
two plays. The older lustful man, the young maid, the young man, the
"mother of brides" are the same four major actors. The peripheral
characters attain more prominence here, but the main difference lies, of
course, in the fact that one is a comedy, the other a tragedy. So the major
characters, except the virgin bride, are more closely drawn and developed.
Olunde, Elesin's son, who takes his father's place in the ritual, is the truly
educated hero who is committed to the point of self-sacrifice to his people, a
character which Soyinka had been developing throughout his literary
career. Elesin, for his part, becomes a much more pathetic figure than
Baroka.

Mothers of Brides

Before going on to a discussion of Soyinka's *femme fatale*, it is pertinent
to consider his portrayal of older women, for here his characterization loses
much of its subjectivity and he succeeds in creating more rounded, less

stereotypical characters. Whereas in Western society middle-aged women are subject to severe depression at the loss of family, African women, as Iyaloja and Sadiku illustrate, gain, with age, additional status and power which, in some cases, equals and/or exceeds that of males.

In both plays, however, the older women bring about the capitulation of otherwise promising maidens. Sadiku of *The Lion and the Jewel* is procurer of brides for Baroka. On the surface she plays the role of the faithful senior wife but Soyinka hints that Baroka does not trust her completely. Her hidden resentment of male dominance is exhibited when she performs her wildly sexual dance of victory over Baroka's "impotence". Her ditty "Take Warning my masters/We'll scotch you in the end" becomes an anthem to the strength and endurance of women. Words like the following come from Sadiku:

> This is the world of women. At this
> moment our star sits in the centre
> of the sky. We are supreme. (p. 34)

Sadiku is talking here of sexual triumph, and if we follow her line of thought we can conclude that even though Baroka wins the minor skirmishes, the eventual victory of the battle will be the woman's, for there will eventually be one who will "scotch" the men of Baroka's type just as she "scotched" his father, Okike. Thus Sadiku's performance upsets the stereotype of the submissive wife in the polygamous household. She obviously rejects the system in which the male constantly re-enacts his dominance over the female.[11]

Sadiku's treatment in the resolution of the play is also worthy of consideration. Her triumph is cut short when she realizes that Baroka had feigned impotence, as Sidi revealed. So she mouths the resigned: "It happens to the best of us." (p. 59). But, although Sadiku has not achieved obvious triumph, every new bride that Baroka takes does indeed weaken him while it increases her status as senior wife. Ogunba has suggested that Soyinka probaly made a mistake in giving Sadiku a name which is normally a man's name.[12] One may as easily argue that her masculine name follows the general portrayal of the character as an extension of the male dominance system, for in the end Sadiku has achieved her original purpose, albeit indirectly. Again she becomes "Mother of Brides" and is in a position to bless Sidi with fertility and prosperity as she joins her household. Sadiku, from this point of view, may not be a "mere tool to be manipulated at will by the ingenious Baroka . . .";[13] her status as senior wife is assured.

This position is taken a step further in the characterization of Iyaloja in *Death and the King's Horseman*. Elesin suffers dearly, and as he descends in prominence, she ascends in stature and eventually ends the play on a note of dominance. Throughout the action, she wields tremendous power as the

"Mother of the Market", a woman who in Yoruba society is a well known social and political entity.[14] Although Iyaloja, like Sadiku, functions as the procurer of brides, in Elesin's case, she knows his desire for sexual dominance will be to his detriment. So in the end, as true earth-mother, she is in a position to castigate him for his weakness: "I wish I could pity you" (p. 68); "Oh Elesin, see what you've become" (p. 70). Indeed, she expresses much of the play's message and thus fulfills the didactic function to which Lee referred (as cited above). Iyaloja even triumphs over the colonial officer whom she constantly addresses as "Child" and, as the play closes, she charges the young bride to "forget the dead, forget even the living. Turn your mind only to the unborn" (p. 76). Sadiku had, of course, offered a similar charge to Sidi. It is important to reiterate here that in his portraiture of the mature woman, Soyinka is able to achieve greater objectivity and to capture the true position of the female elder in his society. Yet, there is no depth to the character. Instead she mouths the author's attack on the dissipation of energy on the acquisition of the material, man's inability to transcend the mundane and achieve spiritual excellence.

In this play, Sadiku's "Take warning my masters/We'll scotch you in the end" reverberates.

The Queen Bees

As early as *A Dance of the Forests* (1960) Soyinka had created Rola, who we learn had callously sent a stream of lovers to their deaths. It is here that the image of the *femme fatale* is set, and she reappears with amazing frequency in succeeding works. For the purposes of our discussion, Simi of *The Interpreters* is the first of these mysterious, quasi-mythical courtesans. Simi is a woman living and moving in the real world but she is imbued with the charcteristics of the river goddess. Simi is excessively beautiful, the "goddess of serenity" with the "skin of light pastel earth, Kano soil in the air."[15] But there is a quality of danger and hypnotism in this beauty, for she is the "Queen Bee" who destroys the drones who are nevertheless attracted to her. Because of Simi "of the slow eyelids"

> men lost hope of salvation, their homes
> and children became ghosts of past
> illusion, learning from Simi a new view
> of life, and, love immersed in a
> cannibal's reality, Simi broke men
> and friendships.   (pp. 50-51)

Soyinka does not leave Simi as the Queen Bee but juxtaposes that with another image of danger, for Simi is also the "Mammy Watta"—the mythological siren who lures men to their deaths with her alluring beauty. Egbo's relationship with Simi is a haunting one in which he seems to be under a magic spell. Already "notorious for his fear of women" (p. 51) his sexual desire for her is like being immersed in a flood:

> Egbo watched her while she walked
> towards him eyes ocean clams with
> her peculiar sadness . . . like a
> man drowning he was saying . . .
> only like a choice of drowning.(p. 251)

It has been pointed out that the Egbo-Simi attraction has deep roots in a certain mystical contact which the true creekman has with a water spirit and suggested that the mammy water figure also often functions as the African author's muse, or the link between death as loss and the ultimate transformation it represents.[16] Thus Egbo's "death" to Simi is only symbolic of his own self-sacrifice and fuller acceptance of himself. Yet one still must question the validity of the repeated use of the female character in this way, as throughout the novel the deadliness of Simi is pervasive. As well as the sensation of drowning, Egbo felt her impact as the "wanton strike of a snake and welcomed the poison through his veins" (p. 53). More animal imagery dominates the characterization as she becomes "the beast that lay in wait to swallow him" (p. 54) and even from the plant world "the thornbush at night". (p. 56)

Similarly, Segi of *Kongi's Harvest* is so beautiful, so alluring that she is, like Simi, the subject of praise songs. She too has hypnotic eyes (a physical feature which seems to fascinate the author) to which praises are sung, and nipples as "violent as thorns". She too is the "Mammy Watta" who "frolics by the sea at night". But this quality of danger is heightened in the description of Segi, for there is a beauty with viciousness expressed in the image of the *agbadu* "the coiled black glistening snake".[17]

Segi, Kongi's sometime mistress, is by far Soyinka's most dangerous woman, but at least, in this play, her venom has a practical use. As the play climaxes and Daodu is unable to carry through with the overthrow of Kongi, Segi resourcefully seizes the time and valorously sends the head of her executed father to Kongi.

As a character, Segi embodies the role of women in revolutionary struggle. This is so because Soyinka was able to effect a balance in the projection of Segi and to direct her quality of danger into a positive channel. There is a tremendous amount of energy in the Segi character. Although colored by myth, she endangers not the man she loves but the deserving agents of oppression. This positive portrayal of Segi is effected because the author does not limit the character to attributes of the mythical *femme fatale* but draws on actual Yoruba history of heroic women.[18] By making Segi a courtesan and an organizer of prostitutes and Daodu a farmer and an organizer of farmers, in *Kongi* Soyinka toys with the notion of class struggle and suggests a revolutionary potential for both groups. However, the author avoids any commitment to this ideal in the resolution of the play. While there is energy and potential, bound by the limits of actual history, the play never moves beyond the level of protest.[19]

The depiction of Iriyise in *Season of Anomy* seems to take the positive woman's image created in Segi several steps backwards, as the characterization moves from woman as subject to woman as object of quest. Iriyise again has the characteristics of the goddess, the image of the exceptional beauty that defines the Soyinka woman. She is "Celestial", "Iridiscent", "the Cocoa Princess". But she can be moody and "bitchy" (pp. 38-39) and one never knows if she is going to prepare breakfast for him or chase him with a stick (p. 78). Iriyise is also the "Queen Bee" who actually lives in what the author explicity describes as "a cell in a deep hive" (p. 58). Animal imagery again surrounds her portrayal. "Once in a while she unleashed the caged tigress in her at some trivial or imagined provocation . . ." (p.62)

Iriyise is mysterious too. She disappears and reappears at will without giving plausibe explanations for her absence. Indeed her act as the Cocoa Princess involves her disappearance into the pod and reappearance as the new shoot. In this context, there is a definite positive quality about her as expressed in her immersion into the life of Aiyero, a context in which Ofeyi felt he knew little of her (p. 7). Yet this quality of Iriyise is never developed by the author. Instead, her sexual attributes dominate as Ofeyi is caught in a trance admiring her beauty:

> Ofeyi folded his hands behind his
> head marvelling at the apparition
> of a goddess bathed in purple
> curtain-filtered light. It seemed
> to him that the room was mysteriously
> still, that the moment was
> frozen and replete. (p. 81)

But Soyinka admits, in an apparent authorial intrusion, that "vision is eternally of man's own creating. The woman's acceptance, her collaboration in man's vision of life results in such periodic embodiments of earth and ideal. Iriyise would reveal within her person a harrowing vision of the unattainable." (p. 82) Thus Iriyise, following the lines of the Orpheus myth disappears, and the rest of the novel involves Ofeyi's abandonment of any involvement in the struggle all around him, a struggle which the Dentist and the people of Aiyero are committed to, and begins his quest for Iriyise.[20]

In describing this mysterious "phantom lady" as one of the most frequent creations of male writers, Barbara Warren says

> As the man's supreme ideal, his
> ultimate desire, an image with which
> he compares all living women, this
> "phantom lady" is a barrier between
> himself and actual experience. He
> can only waste away in a fantasy
> world if he seeks her as a real woman
> for he will never find her in the flesh. . .[21]

Thus Ofeyi blindly continues to search for Iriyise, and Tailia, whom he constantly measures against Iriyise, can never become his woman. Although she exhibits kindness and tenderness in caring for the victims of war, she is still for him wrought in the image of the nun she once wanted to become. When Ofeyi, after much searching, finally finds Iriyise, she has become merely a shell of her former self, a rag doll, for she was only a dream anyway.

In disposing of Iriyise this way, one hopes Soyinka is discarding this type of mythical creature he has a penchant for creating. Just as Ofeyi cannot find the real Iriyise, so the author will not evolve credible female characters if they are continuously shrouded in myth. The Queen Bee stereotype is not only a negative portrayal of women but stylistically it affects the quality of the work. Moreover, Soyinka is unable to make these women plausible or interesting. For it is mainly in his descriptions of these "superwomen", that one sees a shortcoming in his usually fluid style.

Several conclusions can be drawn from our analyses of Soyinka's portrayal of women. First of all, the "dearth of negative images" of women which Rushing[22] finds in modern African poetry does not hold true in the drama and fiction of Wole Soyinka. To the contrary, the author exhibits a patriarchal attitude to women which reveals itself in several stereotypes, the *femme fatale* having primacy.

Additionally, a definite ambivalence in the author's characterization of women is communicated. One constantly gets images of women that are dichotomized and contradictory. Women are beautiful/deadly, pure/sensual, submissive/assertive, wise/foolish, life/death. This ambivalent treatment of women necessarily extends itself into male-female relations. For, along with male dominance, one gets a sense of the woman as indirect victor; as prize of the quest yet simultaneously causing the destruction of the male who initiates the quest. Hence the sex-as-death theme persists in all the Soyinka works, and death is more often loss than it is transformation. Elesin, for example, dies on two levels, the obvious one in which he commits an untimely suicide, and the other in which he loses his sense of purpose in his possession of the young virgin. Ofeyi similarly loses his sense of direction in his quest for Iriyise, and implicit in the resolution of the plot is

Soyinka's condemnation of Ofeyi's avoidance of commitment, like Elesin's, to serious endeavor.[23]

According to one critic, "the more successful characters, invested with the life force and strong personality traits, tend to be women."[24] This is clearly a conclusion that the literature does not support. This study has looked at the major works and cursory examination of his most recent works reveals the same tendencies. Indeed the only other noteworthy type not discussed here is the shrew as revealed in Amope in the Jero plays and Madame Batoki in *Season of Anomy*, for example, for in *Madmen and Specialists* and *The Strong Breed*[25] the female characters are also used as symbols in the male's struggle to conquer the life-threatening forces invading his world. The point is that although there are a few female characters who are more fully realized, the outstanding Soyinka female characters fit into one of the three categories we describe. The penchant towards consistently using women primarily as symbols is at issue here. Symbolic structuring does not shield a writer from negative or limiting portrayals. Pearse for his part is very cavalier about the way in which women are disposed. For example, I disagree strongly with his arguments that Sidi is made an "ordinary woman" and hence a better person when she is successfully seduced by the Bale, or that Simi's move from her mystical aloofness to subservience enriches her and makes her a rounded character.

This is not to detract from Soyinka's substantial literary achievement but to make the point that often for male writers there is a liberty to use women for various ends and in some cases to openly relegate them to derogatory roles and descriptions. Thus, throughout Soyinka's works one finds the kernel of positive portrayal of the female image which is never fully realized. The energy of Sadiku's victory song/dance and Sidi's fire, Segi's organization of the prostitutes, the challenges of the chorus of women and the young girls in *Death and the King's Horseman*, and Iriyise's brief involvement in Aiyero provide the basis for a balanced image of women in this literature. But the author continuously abandons these potentially positive female characters or characteristics. Dehinwa, a realistic, modern African woman is never developed in *The Interpreters* for example. Instead, we find the idealization of physical attributes of women or the quest for the ideal, which limits the author's development of plausible female characters.

Legend and actual history seem to provide Soyinka with material for more positively drawn characters than does mythology. While traditional mythology becomes a viable creative force in some stages of literary development, as Soyinka's brilliant career has demonstrated, it eventually becomes a limiting factor for it circumscribes the action, themes and development of character. This is amply demonstrated in his over-use of the *La Belle Dame Sans Mercie* motif. Iyaloja, modelled on the Yoruba *Iyalode*, becomes the giant among Soyinka's female characters. Segi, also modelled on the courageous female warrior of Yoruba history, is a much more stimulating character than Simi or Iriyise. One also gets a glimpse of the real power of senior wives in Sadiku, but this again is not clearly developed.

It can be argued that the writer is merely reflecting socio-cultural realities. But we already recognize that the artist has the power to create new realities; to represent male-female relationships and the role of women as they have been in the past and might be in the future: women as neither victors nor victims but partners in struggle. Ngugi wa Thiong'o in *Petals of Blood, Devil on the Cross*, and Ousmane Sembène in *God's Bits of Wood* have already begun this process.[26] Soyinka himself has demonstrated this possibility in Segi. Skill at female portraiture is not automatic but requires sensitivity and insight in all writers, and especially in male writers. The writer must also recognize when he is creating negative images and stereotypes and seek alternative images and symbols if he is to develop positive female characters.

NOTES

1. Sonia Lee, "The Awakening of Self in the Heroines of Ousmane Sembène," in *Sturdy Black Bridges*, ed. Roseann P. Bell et al, (New York: Anchor Press/Doubleday, 1979), pp. 52-60.
2. Kathleen Staudt, "The Characterization of Women by Soyinka and Armah," *Ba Shiru* 8.2 (1977):63-69; Adetokunbo Pearse, "Symbolic Characterization of Women in the Plays and Prose of Wole Soyinka," *Ba Shiru* 9.1&2 (1978): 39-46; C. Purisch, "Soyinka's Superwomen," a paper presented at the first Ibadan Annual African Literature Conference, July, 1976, has not been available in published form. Sylvia Bryan's paper on the changing Role of Women in Soyinka will be published in the forthcoming issue of *African Literature Today* (v. 15). A few studies of women in African Literature include some discussion of women in Soyinka's works: G.C.M.M. Mutiso, "Women in African Literature," *East African Journal*, 3:No. 3 (March, 1971) 4-14; Anne Lippert, "Women Characters in African Literature," *Afriscope*, 3, No. 10 (October, 1972) 44-46, 49; Kenneth Little, *The Sociology of Urban Women's Image in African Literature* (New Jersey; Rowman, 1980).
3. Gerald Moore, *Wole Soyinka* (London: Evans, 1971); Oyin Ogunba, *The Movement of Transition* (Ibadan Univ. Press, 1975) and Eldred Durosimi Jones, *The Writings of Wole Soyinka* (London: Heinemann, 1973) make reference to women in Soyinka as part of general discussions of the author's works. James Gibbs, ed., *Critical Perspectives on Wole Soyinka* (Washington, D.C.: Three Continents Press, Inc., 1980) contains no essay on this subject.
4. See Wole Soyinka, "The Writer in a Modern African State." *Transition* 6: No. 3 (1967), 11-13 and "The Fourth Stage: Through the Mysteries of Ogun to the Origin of Yoruba Tragedy," appendixed in his *Myth, Literature and the African World* (London: Cambridge University Press, 1976). Abiodun Jeyifo,

"Soyinka Demythologized Notes on a Materialistic Reading of *A Dance of the Forests, The Road* and *Kongi's Harvest.*" Ibadan, March 1975, explores Soyinka's expropriation of Yoruba mythology.

5. Wole Soyinka, *The Lion and the Jewel* (London: OUP, 1963), p. 12. Subsequent references are to this edition and appear in the text.

6. This writer viewed a Theatre Arts production of this play at the University of Ibadan in which the "stamp machine" appeared as a giant phallus which Baroka plunged up and down into a hole at the base of the contraption. The explicit sexual reference of this scene provided considerable response from the male members of the audience which was sustained up until the final triumph over Sidi.

7. See for example discussions of *The Lion and the Jewel* by Moore, Jones and Ogunba in their works cited above.

8. Ogunba, p. 40.

9. Wole Soyinka, *Death and the King's Horseman* (London: Eyre, Methuen, Ltd., 1975), p. 18. Subsequent references are to this edition and appear in the text.

10. D. S. Izevbaye, "Mediation in Soyinka: The Case of the King's Horseman," in Gibbs, pp. 121. 124.

11. Jones, p. 30, contains a further discussion of this point. Enoch T. Mvula's "Tumbuka Pounding Songs in the Management of Familiar Conflicts," *Cross Rhythms* (2) ed. by Daniel Avorgbedor and Kwesi Yankah (Indiana University, African Folklore Publications, 1985), pp. 93-113, discusses how women use pounding songs, as Sadiku does, to comment on male-female conflicts, struggles between co-wives and to castigate their men for any failings.

12. Ogunba, p. 49.

13. Ibid.

14. Bolanle Awe, "The Iyalode in the Traditional Yoruba Political System," in *Sexual Stratification*, ed., Alice Schlegel (New York: Columbia University Press, 1977), pp. 144-159.

15. Wole Soyinka, *The Interpreters* (London: Heinemann, 1974), p. 51. Subsequent references are to this edition and appear in the text.

16. Emmanuel Obiechina, *Culture, Tradition and Society in the West African Novel* (London: Cambridge Univ. Press, 1975), p. 115; also Peter Thomas, "The Watermaid and the Dancer: Figures of the Nigerian Muse," *Literature East and West* 12: No. 1 (March, 1968), 83-93.

17. Wole Soyinka, *Kongi's Harvest* (London: OUP, 1967) pp. 32-3. Subsequent references are to this edition and appear in the text.

18. Ogunba suggests that Segi is depicted like some of the famous Yoruba or Bini women of antiquity—Moremi, Emotan, Sungbo. See *Movement of Transition*, p. 197.

19. Omafume F. Onoge contends in "The Crisis of Consciousness in Modern African Literature: A Survey," *Canadian Journal of African Studies*, 8 (1974), 387-410, that Soyinka has failed to move beyond the critical realist stage into the socialist realist stage. Soyinka's position on this issue appears in the foreword to his play *Opera Wonyosi* (Bloomington: Indiana University Press, 1981) in which he takes issue with the Nigerian New Left Critics and their prescriptions.

20. Izevbaye shows how the novel structurally follows the Orpheus myth, even to the naming of the characters, in his "Soyinka's Black Orpheus," in Gibbs, pp. 243-252.

21. *The Feminine Image in Literature* (New Jersey: Hayden Book Company, Inc., 1973), p. 8.

22. "Images of Black Women in Modern African Poetry: An Overview, " in *Sturdy Black Bridges*, pp. 18-24.

23. One reading of the novel sees The Dentist and Iriyise as *alter egos* of the hero Ofeyi; aspects of his divided self which he is trying to reintegrate.

24. Pearse, p. 39.

25. Wole Soyinka, *Three Short Plays* ("The Swamp Dwellers", "The Trials of Brother Jero", "The Strong Breed"). London, Oxford University Press, 1969; *Madmen and Specialists* (Ibadan, Oxford University Press, 1971).

26. See Marie Linton Umeh, "The African Heroine," in *Sturdy Black Bridges*, pp. 39-51 and Sonia Lee's article cited above for further discussion of this issue.

Parasites and Prophets: The Use of Women in Ayi Kwei Armah's Novels

Abena P.A. Busia

The Ghanaian writer Ayi Kwei Armah has written five novels to date: *The Beautyful Ones Are Not Yet Born* (1968), *Fragments* (1970), *Why Are We So Blest* (1972), *Two Thousand Seasons* (1973), and *The Healers* (1978). All but the third are set literally, or symbolically, in Ghana and in them Armah seems to shift between two central perceptions of women— woman as parasite, and woman as liberating prophet. Importantly, as we move through Armah's works sequentially the prophets eclipse the parasites. The major transition in this vision of women throughout the five novels is the concern of this paper.

It must first be stated that but for the qualified exception of the female figures in *Two Thousand Seasons*, women in Armah's novels never have roles independent of the novel's hero or protagonist—always a man in a male dominated society. Women are always the lovers, wives, or blood relatives of the central male characters, and have significance in the texts only in so far as they affect those characters. Furthermore, another problem shared by prophets and parasites alike, is that these women, scattered throughout Armah's texts, are frequently unsexed or choose to deny their sexuality. As we shall see, Armah never truly finds a resolution for the difficulty he has balancing the different forces of sex, love, and power, when

89

exercised by women. Nonetheless, bearing these conflicts in mind, and taking the essentially secondary nature of their roles as given, we shall argue here that the roles played by women in Armah's novels have undergone, if not a revolution, then at least a positive reformation throughout the texts. That is, Armah's novels reveal two parallel motions concerning women, which operate in tension: on the one hand, the movement which liberates them from being predominantly symbols of opression to being symbols of liberation; and on the other, that for the most part *symbols* of womanhood, perverse or idealized, are essentially *all* they are.

Looking at the portraits of the women and the roles they play is one way of tracing the measure of resolution Armah finds in each text as he moves towards a greater understanding, or a more articulate explication, of the central problems he is exploring in all his works. For Armah, all oppression (whether social, political or cultural) is a form of disease, and the source of all division among mankind. In each of his texts the same two fundamental problems are explored—the conflict between the private and social worlds in modern Africa and the crisis of divided loyalties this creates, as well as the difficulty, for the sensitive individual, of ordering the oppression and chaos of contemporary life into a comprehensible framework which takes account of the past as well as the present.

So far as the portraits of women are concerned, in all five novels the division between parasites and prophets is stark. True to Armah's equation of things white with evil, and black with spirituality, the parasites are either Westernized African women, or, as in the case of Amy Reitsch in *Why Are We So Blest?*, both Western and white. The prophets are those women who are seen as being true to the aspirations of Black African people, true to the ancient 'way' that has long since been forgotten. In the two earliest novels, the female parasites are the mothers, wives and sisters of the heroes. That is, they are always attached to the hearth. Is is these 'loved ones', as they are called, who are portrayed as the burden on the soul of the struggling and suffering hero. They are, whether intentionally or not, seen as the oppressors. They make demands, generally material ones concerned with keeping up social appearances, which always provoke a storm of conflict in their men. Pitted against them are the liberating prophets. This conception of them springs primarily from the literal role they play in the fourth novel *Two Thousand Seasons*, the only work in which women ever initiate any action. In that novel, the voices of the prophets are female, and, at several crucial moments in the history being recounted, it is the women who save the nation, often in battle against the men. Yet, though their roles are not always so prominent, the other novels do contain women who are, in great and small ways, contending with oppression—their role being to understand their men in adverse circumstances, and, wherever possible, guard them and give them solace. They are liberating prophets in the sense that, even when powerless, they have a vision which can protect their men and at least steer them in the direction of some kind of salvation.

The stress in *The Beautyful Ones Are Not Yet Born*, Armah's first novel, is on the pervasive corrosive effect of a corrupt society whose essential decay is symbolized by Armah's much discussed imagery of filth and dung. The central problem for the hero, simply called 'the man' is to try to reconcile his vision of a whole, healthy and honest society with the need of his 'loved ones' which can only be satisfied, it seems, through compromise of those very aspirations. His relationship to his loved ones then comes to represent the fundamental illness of a society based on an unacceptable conflict between loyalty to the family and loyalty to the community at large. The representatives of the family in the first two books are strongly female characters, and in *The Beautyful Ones Are Not Yet Born* it is the wife and her mother who are seen as opposed to the service to the community that the man would like to be free to perform. They do not appreciate the sacrifice to *their* lives his refusal to be corrupt entails. They live in a world which is obsessed by the gleam of money, and the attendant glitter of prosperity, power, and success that it brings in its wake, no matter how the money is acquired. For example, the women see what they think will be a chance to share in this new and uncommon wealth by taking part in a fraudulent scheme, concerning the ownership of a fishing boat devised by the man's ignorant former classmate, Koomson, now an influential Party dignitary and 'Minister Plenipotentiary'. The women are to agree to the legal ownership of the boat on his behalf, in return for a share of the profits, for in the socialist republic in which the novel is set, a minister cannot own a profitable fishing boat operating under the rules of private capitalist enterprise. The women agree and are deceived. However, the man, while resisting this onslaught on his integrity, suffers nonetheless. His acute despair springs from his ability to understand and in some way sympathize with the needs and demands of his wife and family. His dilemma lies therefore in his sense of failure: he is the victim of their reproaches, which, when voiced, make him feel all the more guilty and responsible for the hopelessness of their situation. The family, not only the wife and mother-in-law, but the children as well, are dependent upon him, and remain a constant burden to him. They are paradoxically passive, but oppressively prominent characters. Every aspect of daily life becomes a form of criticism of the man, and even their silence in their suffering becomes a reproach to him. His situation is not improved by the fact that his wife is not averse to undermining his position by voicing her criticism. In her philosophy, life is like a series of busy roads of all descriptions, and those who go far are those who, ignoring the possibility of accidents, learn to drive fast. It matters not to her that to 'drive' means to learn to cheat the public and ride roughshod over those fellow travellers who are less capable citizens. She states in no uncertain terms that she considers her husband quite ineffectual and stupid. These unpalatable truths matter a great deal to the man, and he feels trapped. He remains trapped by his limited perception, and his feeling that it is the society, and not he, which is fundamentally wrong, remains instinctive. His spirit remains troubled and questioning, because he has no organized system of understanding. Living in his poverty, his sense of moral obligation intact, he has no faith or ideology to guide him.

In this novel the only representative of the 'prophets' is the engimatic, once beautiful and hopeful Maanan, who goes mad. She is a shadowy figure said to be beautiful in body and in spirit, who haunts the painful reminiscences of the text. She is not a prominent figure, but as a friend to the man she stands in opposition to the kind of behaviour displayed by his wife and her mother. Neither one of the troublesome 'loved ones' nor one of those who has compromised with the corrupt power structure, she represents all those Ghanaian people at the time of Independence who followed the 'leader,' were inspired by his ideals, and believed wholeheartedly that he was indeed a redeemer come to usher in a new and glorious age. It is her hopes, and through her those peoples' hopes, which are recognized as the most betrayed.

In the book it is Maanan who tries to teach the meaning of loving and communal unity, an endeavour which is to perplex all Armah's central characters until he finds a way for them to express it in the social and political analysis which gives form to *The Healers*, the last of his novels so far. In this early work, it is best expressed in a scene by the waterside in which Maanan first teaches the man to smoke 'pot' or 'wee' as it is called. The experience is a liberating one for our frustrated hero, and he learns to see many things for the first time, including Maanan's true beauty, which becomes symbolic of the suffering of all women:

> It was as if Maanan's face was all I would ever need to look at to know that this was a woman being pushed towards destruction and there was nothing she or I could do about it. She was smiling at me, but in myself I felt accused by a silence that belonged to millions and ages of women all bearing the face and the form of Maanan, and needing no voice at all to tell me I had failed them, I and all the others who have been content to do nothing and to be nothing at all all our lives and through all the ages of their suffering. So much of the past had now been pushed into the present moment at the edge of the salt water. I would have said something to Maanan if the things to say had not been so heavy, but even then I was sure she understood, that she had understood long before I had ever seen enough to ask her forgiveness, and that she had forgiven me as much as it was possible for the suffering to forgive those who only remain to suffer with them and to

> see their distress . . . Forgive me, Maanan, forgive us all if that is
> possible these days. (pp. 71-2)[1]

Maanan, far more a symbol than a woman, prefigures the prophetic women of *Two Thousand Seasons*. It is she who teaches the men to try to reach out, and overcome the seemingly constricting putrefying surroundings, to see, physically and spiritually, the pure salt water away from the stagnant pools. But in the end Maanan goes mad, and is last seen wandering around the beach sifting the fine sand through her fingers in search of something inexpressibly lost. In her madness, Maanan sees most clearly that the hopes of her generation have been irretrievably lost, but the man realizes neither she nor anyone else can give him the answers, for they must come from within. He finds nothing to bridge the distances between the members of the community because he has no true understanding of the reasons for the dislocation. Only Maanan knows it is possible for the breach to be healed, but the moment to reach out was lost not only historically, but spiritually. There is a recognition that something more substantial needs to be found to bring the desired peace and enlightenment. The hopeful vision which ends the novel occurs when the man, having been cleansed by the sea, sees a legend painted on a mammy wagon which gives the title to the novel, 'The Beautyful Ones Are Not Yet Born'.

As in *The Beautyful Ones Are Not Yet Born*, in *Fragments* the problem of the family being in conflict, rather than in concert with the community, remains to be resolved. We have again a similar division between those women who impose burdens, and those who wish to bring salvation. And once again it is the two women of the household who have pinned all their hopes for the future on the return of the hero, Baako, to such an extent that their expectations become a weight upon his soul. He is required to share in all their aspirations: to make the dream of a large and comfortable home come true, and to enjoy the status of being someone who, by virtue of a western education, is potentially a personage of much distinction. Their aspirations seem simple enough, but are therefore far more entrapping. They are presented as being based on an old and accepted tradition of the returning hero, the conquering son home from his travels bringing with him the fruits of his learning which produce miracles to bless the family. But there is a difference now:

> Now it's taken this modern form. The voyage abroad, everything that follows; it's very much a colonial thing. But the hero idea itself is something very old. It's the myth of the extraordinary man who brings about a complete turnabout in terrible circumstances. We have the old heroes who turned defeat into victory for the whole community. But these days the community has disappeared from the story.

Instead, there is the family, and the hero comes and turns its poverty into sudden wealth. And the external enemy isn't the one at whose expense the hero gets his victory; he's supposed to get rich, mainly at the expense of the community. (p. 147)[2]

The 'loved ones' are not simply corrupt, but are rather presented as unknowingly seduced by the society in which they live. The values of this society remain firmly materialistic and pretentious. Typically the returning traveller not only generates a show of glory, but he must also enjoy the false elevation this gives him in the eyes of his family and the community at large. What matters is how ostentatious a show can be put on, no matter the impotence it hides. As is brought out most forcefully by the attitudes of his mother and sister, in the eyes of Baako's family, the terrible failure of his foreign experience is dramatised by the fact that he returns home in shirt-sleeves rather than a suit, and carrying a guitar rather than bringing a new car, or some other status object such as a refrigerator. Neither his sister nor his mother initially questions these values, although in the end the mother does change. One of the burdens she had placed on the back of her son was her hope that he would return to finish the grand house she had started to build for herself, in his honour. Although by her standards this would seem a reasonable expectation, she manages to understand her son and recognize that he views the world from a different perspective. She finally takes him to her half-built mansion to explain her dream, and apologize to him for having expected him to fulfill it. Thus she shows a humility and a capacity for growth which eludes her son. As the portrais of other characters indicate, her initial expectations represent the societal norm. Once again our hero, by regarding her as perverse, is demonstrably out of touch with the times.

That it is the society at large, rather than the hero Baako, which is to be regarded as centrally at fault is re-enforced by the crucial scene which describes the name-day ceremony of his baby nephew, the child born to his sister and her ineffectual husband. This incident is central to an understanding of the work because it dramatizes the profound spiritual dislocation of the family and the society of which it is a part, and for which it stands. This traditional ceremony, to welcome the newly arrived child, and to thank the spirits of the ancestors for ensuring his safe arrival, has become perverted. In its new form it is a festive gathering during which the host family, in its quest for material goods, forces the guests to vie with each other to make the most outrageous contributions. The whole event is inauspicious; to begin with, the baby is born premature. Then, to make matters worse, the mother and the sister move the ceremony forward three days to the fifth day after birth in order to capitalize on a pay day, instead of waiting until the eighth day, the day by which traditionally the newly arrived spirit will have decided whether he is staying, or whether he prefers to return to the world of the ancestors from which he had just arrived.

The important aspect of these changes is the failure on the part of the rest of the family to learn from Naana, the grandmother, the original value of the ceremony. It is a measure of the social breakdown that even while she lives under the same roof, neither her daughter nor her granddaughter takes the trouble to consult or even to inform her of their plans. While she worries about the meaning of such a hastily called and secular gathering, on the pretext of a spiritual occasion, her daughter's paramount concern is that the son upon whom she had such high hopes is refusing to wear a suit or tuxedo for the occasion. While Baako's protest here is based on the rejection of the new forms, Naana is the one concerned with the *spiritual* perversion of customs. On the day itself Naana is the only one disturbed that libations are not poured for the child whose celebration it is supposed to be. For her this underscores the terrible reality that her children have forgotten the ancestors themselves. They no longer look to those gone before, and they no longer even celebrate the newly arrived soul. Even Baako, in his frustration and contempt, does not speak to Naana and so fails to learn from her that he cannot change the selfishness and sham of the new ways which so anger him if he does not first understand the spiritual significance of the changes.

Baako himself is a man in conflict. Having brought a sense of panic and frustration home with him from abroad, he spends much of his time and energy in flight. Like Naana, he can see the disease in contemporary society, but unlike her, he is unable to articulate clearly the nature of the disease in terms which have relevance to the community. A writer, he returns home with high hopes of using the media as a means for community education, to agitate for change and social equality for the benefit of the country. However, the directors of the television and film industry seem, to him, far more interested in exploiting the broadcasting corporation's resources for their own private needs. Baako finds the experience of being unable to do any of the creative, constructive work he had hoped to do quite traumatic. He must acknowledge first that the society has become essentially soul destroying, and, more vitally, that the desire both to please the family, and to work for the larger social good, have become oppressively unreconcilable aims. Both these verities give rise to a conflict within him that he must try to resolve. In order to do this, he has a series of therapeutic conversations and love scenes with his lover, Juana, and all his constructive insights and revelations, both personal and social, come to him through her.

Juana, a psychiatrist introduced to him by his mother, has come to Ghana in search of her 'roots'. She is herself a women in flight, from the United States and from her native Puerto Rico. Like Naana, she too knows that the real crime of human history is the ignorance of past crimes. She had found that the burden of her youth, and had come to Ghana to find some kind of peace, only to discover there was none to be found there. However, being stronger than Maanan, she at least manages to save herself by making a necessary accommodation. She learns to know by what visions people led their lives, or by what visions life led them, and for her, survival becomes a matter of "adopting a narrower vision every time the full vision threaten[d] danger to the visionary self." (p. 46) Like all prophets, Juana does recognize this visionary self even if, rather than playing a leading role in the community, it is fighting a rearguard action. She may not be able to save society, but she does what she can to save Baako. "Like some forest woman whose gods were in all the trees and hills and people around her, the meaning of her life remained in her defeated attempts to purify her environment, right down to the final, futile decision to try to salvage discrete individuals in the general carnage." (p. 177) Like all prophets, Juana is primarily concerned with salvation and the need to purify the environment; for all prophets salvation, and above all the salvation of the group, is of the utmost importance.

Because of the dislocation between the body and the spirit which occurs in the powerful prophets of *Two Thousand Seasons*, it is notable that Juana's role as saviour seems to take precedence over her role as mate. Even at their first meeting, though her response to Baako's overwhelming presence was as physical as it was spiritual, she spends much of her time trying to forget his physical body, thinking of him instead as "a kind of interior dome floating somewhere in her head." But they both have bodies and he will not permit her to forget this. He controls the movements of their friendship as he is later to control the movements of her body in love-making. For Baako she is not only a psychiatrist, but a friend and lover, and her strength is the source of his strength. She is a sympathetic listener for him, because she understands his yearning to perform crative acts in union rather than alone. In the end, after his breakdown, it is she who is preparing a home for him to come back to after his discharge from hospital.

Juana and the grandmother Naana stand in opposition to the mother and sister. They are the two women who understand him, and who, without his obvious personal limitations, share his vision. Naana's observations are fundamental to an understanding of this work. Her role in this novel is very much that of the blind and impotent seer. She cannot see with her physical eyes, but her spirit comprehends a great deal which she cannot or is not permitted to communicate, except in her own private thoughts. She is the closest to the protecting ancestral spirits, not only because of her age, but more especially because of her understanding, her sympathy, and her memories. Naana represents the communal memory which links the past with the future. Her powerlessness is thus a commentary on the breakdown of the society. She is not simply another old woman, she is the mother of the family, and a prophet rendered helpless.

The novel opens and closes with Naana's reflections. At the start, while awaiting the return of Baako, she establishes firmly the cycle of life—the exits and entrances, departures and returns, of which he is a part. But the journeys are not only physical but also spiritual, and the old beliefs establish a continuity between birth and death, with the movements of earthly life in between. For Naana the perversion of customs, such as the failure to pour sincere libations at life's thresholds, augurs ill, for it represents a lack of respect for the soul. She finds this attitude spiritually and physically destructive, and sinful. In those opening reflections, she forsees that the dreams of the family were no longer justified because "woven of such heavy earth" would so crush Baako's spirit he would never 'fly' again. But she is unable to prevent the inevitable, and in her reflections which close the novel she again pin-points the symbolic meaning of these changes:

> The return of this one traveler had held out so much of good hope. But there were those left behind who had their dreams and put them on the shoulders of the traveler returned, heavy dreams and hopes filled with the mass of things here and of this time. And another spirit has already found its death in the hot embrace of people who have forgotten that fruit is not a gathered gift of the instant but seed hidden in the earth and tended and waited for and allowed to grow—so busy have they become in their reaching after new things and newer ways to consume them . . .they have smothered another human soul in all their heavy dreams of things . . . I was powerless before the knowledge that I had come upon strangers worshipping something new and powerful beyond my understanding, which made all the old wisdom small in people's minds, and twisted all things natural to the service of some newly created god . . . The baby was a sacrifice they killed, to satisfy perhaps a new god they have found much like the one that began the same long destruction of our people when the elders first— may their souls never find forgiveness on this head—split their own seed and raised half against half, part selling part to hard-eyed buyers from beyond the horizon, breaking, buying, selling, gaining, spending, till the last of our men sells the last woman to any passing white buyer and himself waits to be destroyed by this great haste to consume things we have taken no care or trouble to produce. (pp.283-4)

In this reflection Naana, contemplating the madness of Baako and the death of the new born child, waits for death. She has seen the problems extant in the society at large internalized and destroying her own family, and has been helpless. The central problems remain; the 'seer' remains fundamentally alienated from the group because an oppressed people have lost themselves in chasing after 'strange gods'. Her reverence for the role of the ancestors and the old ways should not however be regarded as a reactionary vision. Her last reflection shows her awareness that understanding the link with the past in the end leads to progress.

Why Are We So Blest? can be consdidered as a pivotal text. In this novel
the hero, dominated by his experiences with white women, reaches the nadir
of destructive experiences. His death is brought about directly as a
consequence of his sexual relationship with his white girlfriend, and in this
novel the gulf between devotion to a 'loved one' and devotion to a cause is
dramatised to the irreconcilable extreme. All relationships with women in
this text are sexual ones, and nothing good comes out of any of them. The
two most destructive relationships are with white women, and they both
prove dangerous, and finally fatal.

There are two white women of importance, and to both of them Modin,
the Ghanaian hero, is ultimately the sex object *Black* men tend to be in
relationships of imperial and cultural domination. The first is Mrs.
Jefferson, the wife of one of the wealthy 'philanthropists' who fund the
scholarship on which Modin comes to America to study. The second is
Aimee Reitsch, Modin's American girl-friend of German descent. It is with
Aimee that Modin finally travels to North Africa in search of a revolution to
purge his soul, a journey which, for her, is just another radical exercise to
find an escape from boredom. The relationship between them destroys
Modin spiritually and he loses his sense of individual identity. The journey
they jointly undertake leads only to his death in vengeance for his
association with her. Although sexually the two women play diametrically
opposed roles, they both use Modin to the same end. Mrs. Jefferson proves
as insatiable as Aimee proves frigid, but they both represent his slide to
degradation and destruction. Though the dramatization of this degradation
is explicit sexual, the relationships with these two women are to be seen as
yet another consequence of the spiritually destructive nature of the impact
with the western world, a problem addressed in all Armah's novels. The
women do not just torture him spiritually, they kill him physically as well;
and Modin, uncomprehending, participates in his own destruction. It is the
tragedy of this hero that even Naita, the woman he regards as his 'prophet',
though Black, is a thoroughly westernized Black American, and even she
most of the time is absent and cannot save him.

The relationship with Mrs Jefferson is based solely on her desire to fulfill
what is presented as a white American woman's fantasy of sleeping with a
Black man, and with Modin it is all the more rewarding as he is the genuine
article, an African man. Mrs Jefferson, in her desire to live out the
American racial fantasy of the Black man as stud initiates all the sexual
contact between them. We are subjected to explicit scenes of mutual
masturbation between them, (sitting covered in a blanket in the back seat of
the car with her husband and daughter in the front), and graphic episodes in
which she wears him out trying to make him fulfill his role as sex object.
That relationship finally ends when Mrs Jefferson, who had claimed she
could not reach an orgasm with her own husband, takes Modin out into her
garden for sex in the middle of a party, and makes so much noise reaching

her climax that her husband, to whom she had earlier confessed the affair, comes raging into the garden after them and repeatedly stabs Modin in an attempt to kill him in revenge. Mrs Jefferson is the beginning of his descent into degradation. Aimee Reitsch completes his fall.

There is nothing good about Aimee. The portrait of her is the only extended one we have of a white woman in this or any other text, and she is a frigid, voracious destroyer. She is made to carry the burden of guilt for the whole of western civilization in all its destructive energy. As with all other information in this novel, what we learn of her we learn from her own journals, from Modin's references to her in his notes, and from the observations of Solo the failed revolutionary who inherits both sources. The misnamed Aimee is revealed as a woman totally incapable of loving. Although portrayed as being completely unattractive, for some curious reason all men who know her desire her. The feeling is never reciprocated however, and she abuses sexual relationships as an ineffectual antidote for boredom. Furthermore, despite her absolute obsession with sex, she is frigidly incapable of sexual satisfaction. In the sex scenes with Modin, she is even made to indulge in the grotesque fantasy of being the wife of a distant uncle in East Africa, who has successfully seduced her 'boy' into copulating with her in the absence of her jealous husband, in order to sustain the energy required to reach her climax. The pivot of the relationship between herself and Modin is his desire to make it possible for her to have this orgasm. We are subjected to the explicit details of this odyssey, and in its progress, as Modin's initial disgust turns to tenderness, he becomes ensnared in the trap loving her is made to represent. For her, the measure of a man lies in his ability to arouse her body, and she is shown to be pathologically incapable of physical sensation. This physical numbness is paralleled by her spiritual insensitivity. She is shown to be ego-centric, narcissistic, and cruel; the incarnation of all that is aggressively individualistic and destructive about the West, as well as all that is oppressive about private relationships which do not take the larger community into account. The presentation of her is so manipulated as to preclude the generation of any sympathy for her within the limits of the discourse. She never becomes human, but remains the voraciously female entrance to Modin's private hell. The association with her ultimately leads Modin, appropriately enough, to a horrifying death by castration in the deserts of North Africa.

The representation of Naita, though slight, is most important. She is the only figure that comes close to being a means of salvation, but she offers a most ambiguous solace, and this can be taken as a measure of the desolation of the book. Unlike Juana, Naita is absent when the real trials come, and as the two women play identical roles, the depth of Modin's spiritual isolation can be seen in the difference between them.

The parallels between Juana and Naita are strong; they are both Black women of the diaspora, but whereas Juana comes 'home' in search of her roots, Modin travels to Naita in search of enlightenment in the new world. Furthermore, where Juana was fleeing that new world in search of an older salvation, Naita is herself fully aculturated into that world and attempting to become a master of that space. Both Juana and Naita act as confessor figures to their respective men, and they both become lovers whose love-making scenes we share in explicit detail, but the differences between those scenes are significant. In Armah's novels, important spiritual scenes, like the one with Maanan or the man's last walk from *The Beautyful Ones Are Not Yet Born*, or the scenes of love and friendship in *The Healers*, always take place by moving water. It is a notable contrast therefore that the love-scenes with Juana take place by the sea, whereas that with Naita takes place indoors. However, in those with Juana, Baako is always the dominant teacher, drawing the woman out and controlling her responses whereas, in the one scene between Naita and Modin, she is the one in complete control. It cannot go unnoticed that Naita, the only woman so far in complete control of her own sexuality, disappears from the scene very quickly.

Naita in this text becomes a confessional figure, and a positive force for Modin, but only after she has left. While she was with him, it was her sexuality which became for him a means of salvation. She offered him, through her body, withdrawal, peace, and release from loneliness. He desires her most when he wishes to forget completely all the circumstances that are troubling him, and she has the power and control to make him do so. Making love to her he feels as though she encompasses his universe and makes him all knowing, and under such circumstances he feels he cannot be lonely anymore. She represents a means of self-forgetting, as if resting in her all his problems could be solved.

Unlike Juana, Naita does not believe in salvation, her approach is far more earthy and pragmatic, and could be called an instinct for self-preservation. Shortly after the start of their relationship, unable to tolerate any longer the hypocrisy of the white administrators for whom she works, and even more frustrated by Modin's initial blind acceptance of their racist attitude towards him, she departs, leaving no forwarding address. Her philosophy for salvation is one of distrust and suspicion. She tries to warn Modin that no people, and in particular no white people, are worth trusting. One of her major sources of frustration is that she sees so clearly that he is being used and abused. Her knowledge of the subleties of race relations in the United States is seen as the sources of her strength. Her experience of being Black in America has taught her who are the manipulators and who the victims of the terrible social games they must play. She knows how to protect herself, and leaves, but this is no positive resolution, for she fails to teach Modin even to understand why such protection may be necessary. He does not comprehend enough to accept her wisdom for survival, until it is too late. Her social role is rendered ineffectual, and the gulf between personal knowledge and social wisdom remains.

Naita offers only a partial private solace. This factor is emphasized by the fact that after her disappearance, when he has only her memory left, Modin talks to her, and confesses to her in his journal:

> I would have come to you; I would have asked you again had you not put a limitless distance between us. *I would not have needed to ask you—I would have come to you, and these fears would have remained unknown to me.* (emphasis mine) (p. 168)[3]

It is her spirit after she has left which becomes for him a source of wisdom and salvation. Modin is not having healing conversations with a visible, tangible presence; what comfort Naita brings comes only through the memory of her. He makes his confessions to her in his journal and tries to think of what advice she would give him if she were still present. Such is the role of women seen completely as functions of the man's development, that he even writes to her about the destructive Aimee, the incarnation of all the terrible women she tried to warn him against. The most intimate scenes between himself and Aimee are presented as recorded by him in his reminiscences to Naita—as if she would want to know. In the end there is no lasting understanding between them, and no saving vision shared.

Two Thousand Seasons is a significant explication of Armah's thesis on the origins of social malaise. The title of the novel refers to the length of time,—one thousand years, each with one wet and one dry season—, covered by the prophecy narrated in the book. This is a 'monochromatic' work, with the line between black and white starkly drawn. In this novel everything white is equated with decadence and terror, and Black people essentially have virtue on their side. The two groups of white people, the Muslim, Arab, "predators" of the first invasion who swoop down southwards from the desert, and the Christian, European "destroyers" who strike northwards up from the sea, both have the same devastating effect on the Africans with whom they initially come into contact. The Africans get caught between two waves of invasion and are destroyed. *Two Thousand Seasons* is a mythical chronicle written as a record so that the people may understand the history of their continent over the last one thousand years, and, as is the function of myth, to point the way to their salvation.

The most important aspect of his thesis is an understanding of "the way". This "way" is never fully explained, because when the history begins, it is already long lost, and only a few "remembers", "seers" and "hearers" are left trying to recollect and revive a way of life almost disappeared over the many generations. According to "the way", in the beginning all Black Africans were a single united people. Their initial migrations were motivated simply by the desire to make the most of the sheer abundance of water and fertile land bounteously alloted them. Though they scattered, they remembered their original kinship, and only later forgot their essential "connectedness".

The later migrations were attempts to escape the invasion of the Arab 'predators' from the north who sought to oppress them. However, their movement south and eastwards was stopped by the European 'destroyers' at that time moving north and westwards.

Throughout *Two Thousand Seasons* we see at crucial moments that it is the women upon whom salvation depends. In this text all the liberating actions are initiated by women. Only in this novel do we see women who initiate action and who have the power to perform deeds to save the community. The two most powerful groups of women in Armah's works are found in this work. But as we have stated, the problem here is that these female figures are more often than not simply female *voices*, and, as women, are unsexed. The one exception is the first group of women who early in the history act in concert to save the community from their debauched and tyrannical Arab masters. In this case the women, in a truly disgusting episode, prey on the perverted lusts of their masters and use their sex to slaughter them. Their sexuality, divorced from any sentiment of either love or individual worth, is seen and used as a powerful political weapon. The women willingly offer themselves up to be thoroughly debased in the service of the state, for the purpose of righteous vengeance. But once successful, their matriarchy when established, fails to hold. The sexual strength which drives them and empowers them to resurrect their homeland, in the end thoroughly emasculates their own men; when, in desperation, strong sexual women take control of affairs, the men are rendered impotent.

At the other extreme, the host of prophets who guide their people out of a succession of 'Egypts' in this work seem to be simply female voices detached from their bodies and without sexuality. The only one who fleshes out into a real character is the beautiful and much desired Abena who, despite her much vaunted charm, is the most insistent on denying her individual sexuality. Abena, like the prophetic Anoa before her, spurns taking a husband. She, like all the other brave and virtuous women, performs all her deeds and channels all her desires on behalf of the group, and this exclusion of any individual sexual expression is always presented as a positive and communal act.

In *Two Thousand Seasons* the opposition is not between good women and bad women as such, but between visionary women, and those who cannot see. All the prophetic voices are female, and most of the liberators, particularly the early ones, are women. The role of women as bringers of unity and healing, always present in the earlier texts, flourishes in this novel. After the carnage of the harsh and jealous rule of men, the restoration of peace is left to women. But having restored unity, the women become overgenerous and take over all the responsibilities once shared with the men. The comfort and fertility of the life they established make the men lazy and unwary, and therefore easy prey for the first group of incoming invaders, the 'predator' Arabs, masquerading as beggars needing shelter and succor. This succor received, the strangers preyed on the readily visible weaknesses of the society and gained power.

The people are delivered from the slavery which ensues after this first invasion once again by the action of the women, on 'the night of slaughter' already alluded to. Described in all the fullness of a seemingly perverse imagination, their liberation is bought at the price of a series of gruesome and brutal sexual acts in which they use the degradation to which they have become subject, to ensnare and slaughter those who have enslaved them. Those who had been debased, become the debasers, but it is a false liberation. The people have been corrupted from within; the years of slavery have created a hierarchical social structure and a host of leeches,— indigenous "cripples" "predators" and "destroyers"—upon whom the outsiders can rely to bring about the effective destruction of the societies from within, in return for material gain and undeserved social status.

It is to this group of people in danger that the first strong prophecy comes, from Anoa, the female with two voices:

> The first, a harassed voice shrieking itself to hoarseness, uttered a terrifying catalog of deaths—deaths of the body, deaths of the spirit; deaths of single, lost ones, deaths of groups snared in some killing pursuit; deaths of nations, the threatened death of our people . . . From the same prophetic throat came a second voice. It was calmer, so calm it sounded to be talking not of matters of our life and death . . . For every shrieking horror the first voice had given sound to, this other gave calm causes, indicated effects, and never tired of iterating the hope of the issue of all disasters: the rediscovery and the following again of our way, the way. (p. 24)[4]

The actual prophecy of Anoa declares that, seduced by "the whiteness of destruction's slope", the people are willingly rushing towards the period of two thousand seasons of pain and disaster terrible to comtemplate, and that painful as the descent of one thousand seasons of bondage will be, the struggle out of bondage will be harder still until finally they regain the ancient way of life.

The people migrate southwards again, in search of freedom, and on this second migration also the women come to the rescue. Depressed by doubts and insecurities, the people despair of ever finding a new and free homeland. Agitated by just one man, they turn on their advance guard and kill them before it dawns on them that in doing so they have killed the only guides who knew the terrain. Only two women, Ningome and Noliwe, had tried to help the guards, and were beaten unconscious for their pains. On reviving they repeat the ancient prophecy of Anoa, with a vengeance, then find the wisdom and the heroic courage to walk their people out of the wilderness to their unknown 'promised land'. On arrival, responding directly to the failure of courage and the absence of any communal spirit in the face of adversity, it is the women again who remind their people that their time—two thousand seasons—has not elapsed, and that the original prophecy had spoken of an invasion of destroyers coming north from the sea, who would be abetted by their own failure to remember their true "way" and keep to the path of "reciprocity".

The concept of "reciprocity" is an important one in this work. The tribulations begin when the people forget that for everything given, something must be received in return; "the way" teaches that those who give without receiving are the victims of their recipients, and their generosity is a form of self-hatred. This is the central concept which informs the opening words of the novel; the image of springwater flowing into the desert, without hope of regeneration, is an essentially self-destructive one. "The desert takes. The desert knows no giving", so the future of that springwater is one of extinction. When the people settle in their new found lands, the men behave like the desertflowing springwater. Under the influence of the newly arrived Europeans, they forget completely all the principles of the 'way' and do not hear the voices of the female prophets who remember, and remind them of their doom. The men accept the new division of people into parasites and producers, masters and slaves.

The most important consequence of this acceptance is that women, hitherto unquestionably social equals, have a subordinate role forced upon them by the men. To the men, it seems plain that the hazardous migration having cost so many lives, the obvious plan was "to make of every female a childbearer as soon as her body showed it was ready, and for as long as her body continued to turn manseed to harvest" (p. 94). It followed naturally, childrearing and housekeeping being such arduous tasks, that the women should and would be exclusively occupied. The men therefore abrogate to themselves all other powers in the community and, schooled by Europeans, begin to establish hierarchies in states where there had previously been none. The ploy succeeds because resistance would have meant further division, so the astonished women "accepted the place of childbearing bodies, in their soul wondering why the ability to do such necessary work should bring as its reward such vindictive slavery at the hands of men" (p. 94). The subjugation of women is seen as a specifically alien form of oppression which should have been resisted. Those few women who tried to do so were either annihilated, or had their sexuality denied by being 'elevated' to the status of honorary males. However, as during the wanderings in the wilderness, so too when settled in their new land, it is women who remain at the vanguard of the forces of resistance and revolution. When the institution of kingship is still newly established it is a woman who realizes that its trappings and ceremonies are a sham to hide an inferior being and first resists its callow authority. When the Europeans first come bearing gifts and seeking friendship with their king, it is a woman who first finds her voice and speaks for the people in protest—and her words remind them of the vital need to discourage the Europeans from settling amongst them. But in the end, as the prophecy works itself out, these women are defeated by the league of treachery formed between the Europeans and their king.

As this novel is a historical saga, it is not until the closing years of the "two thousand seasons" that we have extended portraits of any of the protagonists. But the last part of the novel deals with the last two hundred seasons including the years lived through by the griot reciting the history. The most important woman in this section, whose spirit dominates the end of the story, is the woman Abena, the last in the long line of liberators. Like the other women, she sees more clearly than most people of her time, yet despite this, she has hopes for most of the human spirit. Like Anoa, Idawa, and others before her, she is physically and spiritually a beautiful person. Yet we do not actually know what she looks like. As has been mentioned, Armah's strong, prophetic women in this text are somehow always divorced from their physical bodies. Either, like Noliwe and Ningome, the pair who lead them out of the desolation in the wilderness, they remain forever *voices*, or when they are said to be beautiful, we get no true sense of their physical presence. They are all Black beauties whose dominant characteristic is grace of movement; they are all in their age the most desired; and to a woman all have better things to do than marry, in readiness for other more grand communal purposes. Only on one occasion does this desire to eschew "the need for pairing" extend itself to the men as well. The group of twenty of Abena's age group, when doing "the dance of love" which ends their initiation rites, refuse to leap into mating pairs, which is the object of the ritual. Instead they leap together as a group, and escape to the forest together in search of a better way of life. This insistence on collective action is most fully developed in Abena, to the point that she is prepared to risk the possibility of being forced into slavery with her less perceptive friends, rather than take any action which would spare her alone, but leave her friends forsaken. She realizes, as do all Armah's central characters, that individual salvation is of no consequence, without the redemption of the group. This theme becomes prominent and is the reason why they manage to escape 'the middle passage' and help each other to free themselves from slavery. In this text, the spirit of survival is a female spirit, and that of repression, is male. So it is a measure of the spiritual health of this group that in the end the women not only fight, they help lead in the fighting. This dramatizes a return to the universality of roles under the old 'way'; fighting for freedom is neither kept nor regarded as a predominantly male prerogative.

This one factor dramatizes the fact that Armah, in his later novels, is demonstrably slowly liberating himself from some of the literary conventions followed by other male writers, whether Western or African, in their

representations of women in the novel. There are basically two traditions of
oppositions governing the portrayal of women in the novel which concern us
here: women as wholesome whores or victimized or virtuous virgins, and
women as nurturing earth mothers or destructive Jezebels. Armah has
broken away from one tradition altogether—he does not subscribe to the
convention of the free-spirited harlot; there are no whores in any of his texts,
heroic or otherwise. In this he breaks away from a tradition which has
existed for several centuries in the West (represented by such well-known
characters as Defoe's Moll Flanders, and Dickens' Nancy), and which has
also been recreated in the contemporary African novel by such writers as
Ekwensi and Ngugi.

As we have noted, Armah's women are conventionally women of the
household whose role is intended to be that of supporting their men, whether
or not they succeed. And just as in its very form and scope *Two Thousand
Seasons* breaks away from the conventions of the modern realistic novel, its
liberating, powerful prophets are strong, public characters, who carry their
societies with them, rather than being carried by them. This breaks the
mould of the second convention of woman as savior or woman as destroyer
which Armah incorporated into his earlier novels, in which all the women
either fed on the life blood of the hero, or were there to try to protect him. But
this dramatic break is in a sense a reaction, not a resolution, for it still
restricts the women to a *choice* between only these two modes of being.
Furthermore, in these prophets, like Naana, who are guardians of the
collective history and prophetic memory, Armah has managed to create a
body of socially active, powerful women who willingly divorce themselves
from the expression of their sexuality in relationships with men. This is most
curious as the novel contains a very powerful argument against the
discrimination of women on the grounds of their necessary childbearing
abilities. Yet it seems that the price of power and social commitment must
be the individual sexuality of the woman concerned. The power of sex is
rarely creative, and when it is, it is either not fully expressed, or it is not
sustained; the women must be nurturing without actually being mothers—
finally, there are no creative mothers who are politically or socially
powerful in any of these texts. There is a strange inability to reconcile virtue
and any sexuality in an active, viable, and socially influential relationship.
Thus the true significance of Armah's latest novel *The Healers*, so far as the
role of women is concerned, is Armah's attempt to work towards some kind
of resolution in the conflicted representation of his nurturing women.

By the time we reach *The Healers* one side of the equation, woman as
parasite, has completely disappeared. In this novel all the women but one
are positive factors, and their positiveness is rendered in conventional
terms. They are gentle, consistent, and people of beauty rather than force;
certainly although the central Healer, the principal initiate, and the most

influential patient are all three of them male, to become a "healer" is to take on these quintessentially 'female' characteristics. Though this may be regarded as positive, what it means is that Armah's women remain on the whole one-dimensional; we never find, in the same person, a true complex of both virtues and faults. However, in spite of this, the tremendous achievement of *The Healers* is that in this novel women, represented by Ajoa and Araba Jesiwa, are at last becoming more complete—including sexually complete—private *and* public persons.

The Healers, is a historical novel set in the closing years of the ninteenth century, and recounts the history of the British imperial wars of conquest on the Gold Coast, from the point of view of the defeated Ashanti. The larger social and political concerns Armah wishes to present are woven around a domestic story of local intrigue and murder which blights the lives of a male youth, the initiate Densu, and his group of visionary medical, spiritual and social "healers" who give their name to the novel.

The pattern of women as creative beings established in *Two Thousand Seasons*, is continued in this history. Even when minor characters, women in this novel are significant because they find a kind of resolution between being women of the household and women of history, which is lacking in the earlier works. Although still associated with domesticity, they are no longer outside history, and the resolution of the home is not divorced from that of the political marketplace. Women in this novel are learning, or have learned, to occupy both private and public spaces. Their predominant function is still domestic, and they are still in the text because they are related to, or provide this service for, the important male characters. But there are important differences. In the first place even the minor characters are presented more as persons than symbols; people with joy and tears and human frailties viewed from outside the limited perceptions of the men to whom they are attached. Furthermore, like the unfamilial prophets of *Two Thousand Seasons*, they have a knowledge which addresses, in some cases quite literally, the larger arena.

In an elaboration of a theme also established in *Two Thousand Seasons*, the royal courts are in this text the center of dissension. As the catalyst for destruction, through her association with the invading British, we have Efua Kobri, the powerful queen mother who, in using her influence and the subtle force of persuasive language to protect solely her privilege and the status of her group, ensures the destruction of the kingdom she affects to save. It is important that this sole politically powerful woman is also a dominating mother who acts to keep herself and her son in power. This is the preference for the "loved ones" carried relentlessly to its logical conclusion. The queen mother, in this case the mother of the chief, is a woman with the reins of power firmly in her hands. Totally seduced by power, it is she who reminds her son it were better to be king in a violated nation than nothing in a virgin land, and sabotages the plan to defeat the British because it would have made the heroic general more powerful than her son in the united and victorious kingdom. In the royal court it is the king who is weak and hesitant and the queen who is strong and sure. Her voice, with all the authority of history, in an international political arena, rules the day. But this same voice, speaking against the domestic community, is in the end self-destructive; ultimately the individual has no potential for survival outside the group, however desperately she may try.[5] Mercifully, however, though none has as much political power as she, there are many more creative than destructive women in this novel.

Although most of the women in this novel are associated with the sacred work of the healers, Armah gives us one other woman who can serve as a remarkable contrast to the queen mother even in her own secular world. Though she is a woman of lesser political significance, and though we see her acting in a private capacity only, the portrait of the royal grandmother of the young prince Appia is a forceful one. We see Nana Esi Amanyiwa only once, in the scene in which she buries her grandson Appia, whose murder occasions the narrative which is the novel. In the scene at the graveside, in the prince's mother's room, the quiet, dignified humility with which the grandmother expresses her grief over the loss of her favorite grandchild, is contrasted dramatically with the noisy, bombastic show of mourning put on by the uncle Ababio. The old woman performs in tragic silence all the loving rituals for the burial of the dead, yielding her treasured possessions for the spirit of her child, and throwing first into the grave the customary handful of that earth which would bury his dead body. But her desire to have a speedy, yet dignified and proper burial is interrupted by the display being put on by the uncle (a performance confirmed as pure sham at the end of the novel when it is revealed that it was he himself who was responsible for having had the prince murdered):

> Ababio rushed into the burial room. He came energetic, like a hurricane . . .[his] entry was not merely stormy. It was loud.
> "Let me go with my prince!" he shouted. "I shall not let him go alone!" So saying, he rushed past the silent Esi Amanyiwa. . . .
> The grave-diggers were baffled. They had been on their way out when Ababio hurled himself into the grave. Now Ababio had moved towards the corpse and, clasping its feet, had begun an incantation to the spirit of the dead prince. Uncertain about what to do, unable to force the tearful, grovelling Ababio out yet unwilling to leave him in the grave, the grave-diggers stood undecided beside him in the hole.
> Then Nana Esi Amanyiwa's voice was heard.
> "Let him go with him", the voice said, "since that is his wish." (pp. 58-9)[6]

The power of the grandmother in this scene lies in her ability to recapture language, and quite simply to render it literal. The question of utterance is itself crucial to this novel, both with respect to its very structure, and as integral theme. The ability to speak, and to speak truly, should be a prized quality in a whole, healthy society. Nana Esi Amaniywa's words therefore expose the hollowness of Ababio's by turning a glare on the distance between his words and his meanings; therein lies their power. As we shall see, though her words are enclosed within a domestic tragedy and do not have much impact on the course of events, it is her daughter Araba Jesiwa who is the only other woman in this novel whose public words have consequences as far reaching as those of the queen mother. But by the time she speaks, she is no longer either a wife or a mother; the one woman who, with the help of the healers, finds some sort of resolution between love and power in her own private life, has, by the time her words make public impact, lost both the man and the child who blessed that resolution.

In addition to Araba Jesiwa, the group of "healers", whose search for a private and public health is the central quest of this novel, are surrounded by a number of inspired women who support and encourage them in their work, give practical aid and succor, and sustain the hope that they will eventually win through. One of the most significant of them is the healer Damfo's daughter, Ajoa, because she is herself an apprentice healer.

Ajoa is instrumental in the healing of two of the most central characters in the novel, Araba Jesiwa, the mother of the murdered prince, and Densu, the apprentice healer whose history the narrative traces. When her son is murdered, Araba Jesiwa, also left for dead by the roadside, is mercifully rescued by the healers, and sheltered in their secluded communal village. She is not only physically broken, but so spiritually distraught she loses the power of speech. She has to be carefully nursed so that her broken bones can mend, and so that her spirit and therefore her voice may be restored. Throughout all the long months that this takes, it is Ajoa who faithfully cares for her, and notices her slow return to life. It is Ajoa also who nurses Densu to recovery when this becomes necessary. Densu suffers the trauma of being falsely charged, and almost executed by burning, for the murder of the prince. He is only rescued from this ritual murder by the sacrifice of his closest friend, Anan, who dies in his attempt to secure Densu's escape. Throughout his convalescence Ajoa remains first his friend, then finally consummates this childhood friendship by becoming his lover.

The portrait of Ajoa emphasizes the fact that, even amongst an enlightened group such as the healers, the sexual division of roles remains fixed. Until the closing chapters of the novel, these strong and supportive prophets never *initiate* any action. Ajoa remains a handmaid to her father, existing solely to follow his instructions by ministering to others. Yet though her role is practical and domestic, the first sight of her is that of an ideally beautiful, mystical being:

> She was a small, fragile-looking child, but already her skin had that
> darkness that was a promise of inexhaustible depth, and her eyes were
> even then liquid, clear windows into the soul within.
> She was beautiful.
> Her eyes, those eyes, were restless, full of a nervous energy. Even
> when they came to a momentary rest, they did not rest on Densu. They
> looked far away. Still, those eyes did not reject him. It was just that
> they seemed drawn to sights far beyond the present moment. And
> Densu himself, drawn to those eyes, felt no need to resist the power in
> them, or to resent the desire that turned them away from him.
>   It was this power of Ajoa's over his spirit, this attraction against
> which he neither needed nor wanted to struggle, that had first brought
> Densu close to Ajoa's father, Damfo. (pp. 63-6)

We are reminded of Maanan revealing the woes of womankind on her face,
only in this case the 'woman' is yet six years old, and Densu, on whom her
eyes have this power, is eight. Ajoa's knowledge is based on the instinct
which enables her to distinguish people who operate on the basis of love and
inspiration, from those who use manipulation and worldly authority. This
knowledge at a very early age, enables her to choose her humble father the
healer, over her step-father, the court physician. Years later, when Densu
starts his apprenticeship with her father, it is she who first suggests, in her
quiet unheard manner, the truth which will eventually solve the central
mystery of the young prince Appia's murder. It is this spiritual power of
Ajoa's which inspires Densu, and she becomes inextricably linked to the
search for understanding and knowledge which drives him to become a
healer.
    Yet, unusually in a novel by Armah, for all this spirituality Ajoa, though
initially coy, is a young woman at ease with her sexuality, a sexuality not
entirely divorced from her soul. Like all good women, she moves with ease
and grace, yet though beautiful, unlike the prophets of *Two Thousand
Seasons*, she does not disparage her body. Furthermore, she needs neither
to be dominant, like Naita, or, like Juana, dominated, before she learns to
appreciate the wonder of love-making. The love-making scenes in this novel
are presented as a mutually joyous experience for the young couple, and it is
noteable that in each of them Armah makes Densu deliberately place her so
they lie side by side, a significant shift from the love scenes of *Fragments*
and *Why Are We So Blest?*. Ajoa has learnt the lesson it took Araba Jesiwa
the better part of her life to learn, but she is not given a role that is as
dramatically public as Jesiwa's, or even as powerful as that of her own
impressive but socially and politically circumscribed father. Outside the
personal relationships in her limited community, Ajoa is a powerless
woman. We are left with the feeling that perhaps she can blossom; the
potential is there, but not the act, and it seems a peculiar factor of Armah's

novels that, even in the case of men, creative sexuality and social or political power appear forever divorced from each other.

The character of Araba Jesiwa, the mother of the murdered prince, manifests the tensions surrounding the question of powerful, sexual women having the freedom to act wisely, in a larger social context. In keeping with the traditional male and female roles retained in this novel, Araba Jesiwa must find a resolution between being a spiritually whole woman and being a mother; and motherhood represents not simply her private but also her *public* self, as she initially perceives it. Similarly, in a story which parallels Jesiwa's, there is an Ashanti general whose central role it is to find a resolution between his private and public selves; he must learn to reconcile being a bereaved uncle with being a national warrior. He too must find that balance between the public and the private which does not threaten the spirit. Both characters dramatize the necessity for that unity between private and public sanity which has so perplexed all Armah's earlier leading figures; but whereas the *man's* story disturbs the political unity of the *state*, the woman's story is initially dramatized with respect to a private, *domestic* happiness.

The story of Araba Jesiwa is centered around her coming to terms with her sexuality. At the request of her family she had married a man solely for the purpose of consolidating dynastic political power, and then found she could not conceive. This would be a burden intolerable enough for a private woman in a traditional society, but it is unacceptable in the woman who must bear the child who will ensure the continuation of her royal line. This burden nearly destroys her life, but she overcomes it because she finally learns that no demands, even those of "loved ones", can be met if it costs your soul. With the help of the healers, she learns to identify her 'true self', and the creative aspect of her story is her recognition of the links between self-health and social health. She learns to recapture the true meaning of conception in both personal and social terms, and therefore finds happiness by returning to her soul mate, the true love of her life. When her sense of social health is no longer divorced from her own sense of sexual well-being, conception becomes truly liberating. She then conceives in love and successfully delivers the child Appia, born of love rather than convention. Yet Araba Jesiwa is a woman with social status, and the point of her story is that she must choose between a man with social status whom she does not love, and a humble carpenter whom she loves with all her soul. She chooses the carpenter, but both the husband and the child, who represent her cure, die tragically young. That is, not only is she initially punished for choosing 'society' against her true self, she is also punished for choosing her sexually creative self in contravention of societal norms: apart from its literal veracity, the murdered prince is symbolically thrust back into her womb by being buried in her room, first because she cannot be allowed a private happiness in communion with a man, and retain both her power and her virtue, and secondly because she must learn a greater lesson and pass her wisdom to another, spiritual heir.

This dilemma is partially resolved by the powerful scene at the end of the novel, orchestrated around Araba Jesiwa's first public reappearance. Jesiwa, long believed dead herself, survives the attack which took the life of her biological son. She became dumb at the loss of that one son who symbolized her access to private power and sexuality, and *also*, by virtue of her social status, to public authority. He dies because she has to be re-born into a new family where princes have no sway, in order to 'give birth' again to another son, this time her *spiritual* heir, Densu. Densu is her spiritual son by virtue of their shared conversations, his experience of her life and her sufferings, and his initiation into her cause. Speechless and paralysed for many months, she appears unexpectedly in the public courtroom, where Densu is wrongfully on trial for the murder of her dead son, to speak the words which identify Ababio as the guilty power, and bring liberty to Densu. Those words, symbolic of her restoration to health and sanity, also represent a triumph for the healers. Ultimately, Araba Jesiwa's personal decisions *do* have group consequences, and her private experiences have force as public testimony. Symbolically at least, the influence of women is finally seen beyond the hearth, in a fashion in which the private and the public are not disparate but wedded.

So far as the representation of women is concerned, the story cannot be considered complete, for we leave the women at the threshold of action. However, the triumph of *The Healers* is that it is a truly creative book when considered in the light of the history it is trying to restore, and the social and political health it attempts to bring. In that aspect it succeeds. The use of women is only a small part in the overall thesis of the text, and even this use, when seen in contrast to Armah's earlier works, as well as in a larger context, is of itself reformative. Armah himself has travelled a long journey in creating the women of *The Healers*, who, although they pay a price to perform this function, do in the end point the way towards a society in which women themselves are healthy, fully empowered beings, in reflection of a people who are at last free, whole, and joyously united.

NOTES

1. Ayi Kwei Armah, *The Beautyful Ones Are Not Yet Born*, (New York, Macmillan-Collier Books, 1974), all subsequent page references are to this edition.
2. Ayi Kwei Armah, *Fragments*, (London, Heinemann Educational Books, 1974), all subsequent page references are to this edition.

3. Ayi Kwei Armah, *Why Are We So Blest?*, (London, Heinemann Educational Books, 1974), all subsequent page references are to this edition.

4. Ayi Kwei Armah, *Two Thousand Seasons*, (Nairobi, Kenya, East African Publishing House, 1973), all subsequent page references are to this edition.

5. For a radically different interpretation of the role of the queen mother see Virginia Ola, "The Feminine Principle and the Search for Wholeness in *The Healers*", (African Literature Association Conference Papaer, University of Maryland Baltimore County, April 1984). Although I share Ms. Ola's enthusiasm for Armah's achievement, and, like her, appreciate the overall positive and transforming roles that women have come to play in these later novels, I take issue with her over specific interpretations. Most particularly in her interpretation of the role of the queen mother, I feel she ignores very crucial scenes included in the text, and yet in her praise of the grandmother Nana Esi Amanyiwa, in which I share, she attributes much to her that is not supported by the text.

6. Ayi Kwei Armah, *The Healers*, (London, Heinemann Educational Books, 1978), all subsequent page references are to this edition.

PART TWO
Towards A Critical Self-Definition of The African Woman: Writers and African Woman's Reality

The papers in Part II "Towards a Critical Self-Definition of the African Woman: Writers and African Woman's Reality" introduce her functioning as her own spokesperson and agent. These characterizations, from the pens of both male and female authors, bring women to the foreground as protagonists, character study subjects, and as actors, thinkers, writers, and commentators. In these papers we see analyzed the motivations of political activists and community leaders, university students, mothers and women without children, widows, mistresses, entrepreneurs, women in the vanguard of the changing African social order and those entrenched in the traditional order. Naana Banyiwa-Horne's paper comparing Flora Nwapa's Efuru *and Elechi Amadi's* Concubine *actually straddles this section and the preceding one, similar to Abena Busia's article on Armah located in Part I. Banyiwa-Horne finds that Amadi, like many other male writers, presents*

*"images of African womanhood [that] tend to be from an idealized
and romanticized rather than from a realistic perspective. There
is little or no psychological growth in such portraitures which
often reflect male fantasies of womanhood and not meaningful,
in-depth, depictions."* By contrast, Banyiwa-Horne says, the protag-
ist in the work of the female writer Nwapa is the center around
which everything revolves; her presence is the causal agent for all
that occurs. Nwapa's Efuru, according to Banyiwa-Horne, shows *"a
determination to lead a fulfilling life. . . .control her own life rather
than blindly submit to tradition,"* a characterization that will
appear again in Irene d'Almeida's discussion below of Mariama
Bà's work.

   While Banyiwa-Horne's cogent and well-founded one-on-one
contrast between the feminine presentations by a male and a
female author reveal the male writer's handling as unrealistic and
unsympathetic, his example need not be generalized to all his
brother novelists. The two men writers discussed in the papers
by Anne Graves and Charles Nama are outstanding examples
to prove the point. If Elechi Amadi, as read by Banyiwa-Horne,
shows *"little or no psychological growth"* no *"meaningful, in-depth
depicitions"* of his women characters, Henri Lopès depicts women,
according to Graves, who make decisions based on their consciousness of their own growth. But their self-awareness extends even
beyond them as individuals, Graves points out, for a number of
Lopès' women characters view the advancement or progress of
their people as identical with progress for themselves as people. In
this paper Graves lays out her evidence for the position, articulated
earlier in the preface, calling for the re-defining of women's
roles in African literature, based on women-centered, rather than
man-centered criteria.

   As another example, broached above, of a sensitive presentation
of the feminine by a male writer we have Charles Nama's paper
*"Daughters of Moombi: Ngugi's Heroines and Traditional Gikuyu
Aesthetics."* Nama's consideration of the characters Mumbi from A
Grain of Wheat, Nyakinyua from Petals of Blood, and Wariinga
from Devil on the Cross asserts that the active roles these women
play as leaders and as guardians/protectors of the heritage, have
a long history, being indeed part of the Gikuyu tradition, extending
back to Moombi, female co-progenitor of the tribe. In demonstrating
the characteristics that make each of the examined characters
heroines in the Gikuyu tradition, Nama is combining two subjects
of supreme importance in Ngugi's thought (as repeated in his
theoretical as well as creative writing): "the concept that the
unequivocal liberation of Africans lies not in Westernization but

in the resuscitation of traditional cultural values that have been an intrinsic part of the people's lives from ancient times" and "the contribution of Kenyan women in the liberation struggle." Reference to Ngugi's work is also made by Chimalum Nwankwo in his study of Ama Ata Aidoo's No Sweetness Here *and* Our Sister Killjoy. *Drawing a positive comparison between her "successful treatment of feminist issues" and such treatment by Ngugi and Sembène, Nwankwo bases his analysis of Aidoo's work on his theory that "the African woman [must] accommodate that [subjective] individual experience within the stream of history—rapidly changing cultural and socioeconomic circumstances and consequently altered social relations." His discussion consists of a methodical analysis of the dilemmas that beset women in the various situations that Aidoo draws in her short stories and novel, showing, for example, in the title story of* No Sweetness Here *that "everything is, as usual, wrong with women," a picture he goes on to put into the full context of Aidoo's "controlled" presentation. One partial conclusion Nwankwo draws about the short stories is that they "successfully reveal that no choice is a good choice for the African woman." The significance of having a choice at all, however, is the focus of Irene d'Almeida's piece on the novels of Mariama Bâ. For d'Almeida (who approaches Ba's work from a different angle than does Edris Makward in Part III), Bâ breaks new ground in presenting the phenomenon of choice for the African woman. In the two novels produced in the brief career of this writer d'Almeida identifies several different types of choices, i.e. two risk-laden, costly alternatives to one situation, and choices for the individual woman that affect other people in her life. The essayist here contends that the African woman with education and a profession is doubly encumbered, or bears a "double yoke" that reduces, rather than increases, her choices in life's unforeseeable but consequential situations. The* Double Yoke *of Buchi Emecheta is discussed in Marie Linton Umeh's article analyzing Emecheta's treatment of the educated African woman. According to Umeh, Emecheta demonstrates not only African society's unconscious hypocrisy toward women, but also what she sees as a conservative fear among Nigerians of socially corruptive consequences of education for women.*

A different but related arena of intellectual activity among women in a sector of the Nigerian populace is the writing of poetry by Hausa women, as presented in Beverly Mack's paper. Although Hausa women who perform oral poetry already have attained some reputation, the women poets who are writing and publishing are indeed pioneers. While consciously keeping within the prescribed bounds of the traditional society, the two poets discussed here, whose work is the first to be published by Hausa women, feel that women have an important role to play in the success of their country, and do, therefore, bring a tone of nationalism to their verse. For Mack "...the very fact that these two women have produced a volume of verse is the most revolutionary aspect of their work."

A.A.G.

African Womanhood: The Contrasting Perspectives of Flora Nwapa's Efuru and Elechi Amadi's The Concubine

Naana Banyiwa-Horne

The question of African womanhood, though not given much consideration in critical evaluations of African literature until recent years, is one of
the subjects that often finds its way into the writings of both male and female
authors from the continent. Images of African womanhood abound in the
literature, with some male authors giving as much exposure to the subject as
female ones. In fact, some of the most fascinating and exotic women in
fiction have been created by male writers. Cyprian Ekwensi's Jagua Nana
is a novel by that name, and Wole Soyinka's Simi in *The Interpreters*
readily come to mind.

A close look at the various images of African womanhood provided in the
literature reveals that, to a considerable extent, depictions of African
women in the literature by African woman writers differ from the images
presented by their male counterparts. By virtue of their shared gender

experiences, women writers are inclined to depict female characters in more realistic terms, with a great deal of insight, and in meaningful interaction with their environment. Also women writers tend to create a woman's world in which women characters exist in their own right, and not as mere appendages to a male world. There are exceptions, of course,[1] but in the main, women authors explore alternate possibilities for self-actualization outside the sexual roles that are open to their women characters.

On the other hand, male depictions of female characters are often from a fiercely male perspective, reflecting male conceptions, or rather misconceptions, of female sexuality. Men writers tend to overplay the sexuality of their female characters, creating the impression that women have no identity outside their sexual roles. Their women are seen primarily in relation to male protagonists and in secondary roles. These characters usually serve to enhance the images of the male protagonists who occupy the central positions in the works. Furthermore, male images of African womanhood tend to be idealized and romanticized. There is little or no psychological growth in such portraitures which seems to suggest they are largely male fantasies of womanhood. The above does not suggest that every African male writer dabbles in stereotypes of African womanhood. There are brilliant exceptions. But generally, male depictions of African womanhood conform to the above stated observations.

These contentions are brought home forcefully when one examines two works that share a lot of superficial similarities—Flora Nwapa's *Efuru* and Elechi Amadi's *The Concubine*.[2] The term superficial is employed here to qualify the similarities between the two novels, because they are apparent mainly in the surface structure of the two works but cannot be sustained in any in-depth analysis of the themes, particularly as they reveal Nwapa's and Amadi's perspectives of African womanhood.

The titles of both novels suggest that a female character is central to each work. Nwapa's novel revolves around Efuru, whose name provides the title for the work. In Amadi's novel too, Ihuoma, a woman, plays a central role. Efuru and Ihuoma have a lot in common; they are exceptional in many respects. Moreover, both works are set in rural Igbo villages, and in both, the supernatural plays a dominant role in the lives of the women. The similarities, however, only apply to the raw materials the two authors employ in their works. Nwapa and Amadi utilize their materials in very distinct ways resulting in contrasting portrayals of their main female characters.

The following exploration of the attitudes of the two authors to the worlds they create, to their characters, and to their use of the supernatural reveals the two very different perspectives: Nwapa's *Efuru* provides a feminine perspective of African womanhood and gives a more complex treatment of the female character, while Amadi's *The Concubine* provides a perspective that is male and limiting.

In rural Ibgoland, where *Efuru* and *The Concubine* are set, close-knit family structures predominate, and everyone knows and is related to everyone else either by blood or by marriage. Each person's business is that of the entire community. No occurrence is sacrosanct. Both Amadi and Nwapa excel in creating the fabric and texture of their rural communities, bringing their characters and their worlds vividly to life for the reader. One leaves both novels with the feeling of having intimate knowledge of the fictional worlds and their inhabitants. The attitudes, beliefs, fears, loves, strengths and weaknesses of both individuals and the community at large are made apparent through the descriptions and the dialogue employed. There is very little authorial commentary in either work, though Amadi utilizes this technique a little more than Nwapa.

Nwapa depends almost exclusively on dialogue to reveal Efuru's world, and she proves very successful at it. Her novel is filled with the daily conversation mainly of women, a technique that captures most effectively the oral-aural nature of the world she unfolds. The constant banter of women reveals character as much as it paints a comprehensive, credible, social canvas against which Efuru's life can be assessed. The total world view is brought to life through dialogue. In commenting on this technique Maryse Condé observes that

> . . . by making her heroine unique among her fellow-villagers and by reporting the unanimously hostile and adverse comments of the other women on every one of Efuru's decisions and actions, Flora Nwapa gives, in fact, a disturbing picture of narrow-mindedness, superstition, malevolence, and greed and fear in traditional Africa and might go contrary to what she has thought to defend. In depicting her minor characters, she conveys a very poor impression of her society. Her men are weak, dissolute and irrational. Her women, a formidable gallery of malicious gossipers.[3]

Condé, apparently disturbed by Nwapa's frankness in bringing to life her women characters with their idiosyncrasies and their entire baggage of attitudes, concludes that the result of Nwapa's technique goes contrary to her objectives. She is of the impression that Nwapa is not a conscious craftsperson. But on the contrary, what she interprets as Nwapa's weakness is one of her fortes—a conscious manipulation of dialogue in the revelation not so much of individual personality as in the creation of a tableau against which social values and attitudes can be evaluated.

The "formidable gallery of malicious gossipers" as Condé sees Nwapa's women, is definitely more than just that. They enable Nwapa to portray her world from the perspective of women. She brings out quite clearly the ways her women view the world in which they live, and their reactions not only to the other womenfolk, but to those aspects of life that touch directly on their lives as women. The thought patterns of the individual personalities as they comment on and react to Efuru are revealed. Of course, the comments of the women on Efuru's life reveal their envy, their own shortcomings, and their aspirations; but that is human nature, and Nwapa does a good job of revealing character. After all, who among the village gossips would not want to be beautiful and prosperous? Which of the married women would not bask in the attention Efuru's husband lavishes on her? Above all, which woman would not wish to be appreciated for herself rather than for her childbearing ability? Even as the women decry Efuru's beauty, her leaving her child with a maid in order to pursue her profession as a trader, or her going to the stream with her husband, their reactions reveal the restricted, limited sense of accomplishment in their own lives.

Efuru's infertility is a source of concern, yes, and the constant lamenting of her condition, more by other women than by herself, reveals the importance her society attaches to childbearing. But, at the same time, Efuru's undaunted effort to live her life as fully as possible, regardless of this shortcoming, is striking. Her misfortune does not diminish the awe in which the other women hold her, and this is equally reflected in the envious comments they pass on her. What Nwapa achieves through her setting, therefore, is a life-like recreation of the world of women in her rural Igbo community.

Elechi Amadi also employs similar tools in depicting his world and its attitudes. The world he projects, however, is a male world, and the voices heard are mainly male voices. The statements made by these voices and even by the authorial voice reflect not just a masculine attitude to women but a chauvinistic one. When friends and relatives assemble to celebrate the second burial of Ihuoma's husband, Amadi portrays his men as a dignified group while his women are bunched together as a cantankerous lot—"The old men were served. As they crunched their kola nuts slowly they talked to each other with a dignified buzz, an octave lower than the high-pitched, piping, market-chatter of the women" (p. 43).

His male characters consistently pass disparaging comments about their women. Madume dismisses his wife with the statement, "Women argue forwards and backwards" (p. 70). Wakiri confides in his friend Ekwueme, "when it comes to nagging I treat all women as children" (p. 20). Wigwe, a dignified elder, advises his son to regard his wife as "a baby needing constant correction" (p. 181). Ekwueme, the major male protagonist, sees all women as stupid and horrible and dismisses them as unworthy of him (p. 182). Even Ihuoma, who is acknowledged as being superior to other women, does not escape Ekwueme's deprecations. He perceives her as "just a simpleton with as much heart as a chicken" (p. 117). Furthermore, the exemplary behavior of Amadi's heroine is acknowledged in highly chauvinistic terms. Wigwe admits reluctantly: "True, you are only a woman but your good behaviour has placed you a little above many other women in the village" (p. 144).

What emerges from the world Amadi creates, then, is a reinforcement of stereotypical male chauvinistic impressions about African womanhood. All of his women characters are depicted as inferior and subordinate to men with even Ihuoma portrayed in subordination to the dominant male characters. The story begins, in characteristic male fashion, with a fight between two men, Emenike and Madume. Ihuoma's introduction into the story is tied to her position as Emenike's wife and as a woman on whom Madume has designs with these factors aggravating the conflict between the two men. Amadi informs the reader: "Perhaps Madume's hatred of Emenike might not have been so great if only the latter had not snatched Ihuoma from him" (p. 6).

Amadi's depiction of Ihuoma is dehumanizing. She is not portrayed as a human being with a will of her own. She is more like a piece of land, or a house, or some form of property that is there to be grabbed. Clearly, the only significance that women have in Amadi's novel is sexual. All exist in a man's world, to be used by the men as sexual vehicles. Amadi's sexism circumscribes his heroine's entire existence, and the very title of his novel, *The Concubine*, reveals the rigidly sexual mold in which Ihuoma is cast. Whether in the spirit world or in her life on earth, Ihuoma's relevance is thus limited by the machinations of a man: "in the spirit world she was the wife of the Sea King, the ruling spirit of the sea" (p. 253). Though reincarnated, her life on earth is still governed by her status as the wife of the Sea King. Before this information is disclosed at the end of the novel, we already know that Ihuoma is being manipulated by the author to reveal only her circumscribed role. She is always either the devoted wife and mother, the pitiable widow of highly commendable behavior, or the prospective wife to be wooed. The plot of *The Concubine* revolves around her successive attempts to seek fulfillment in marriage and on the attempts made by three successive men to woo and marry or bed her. After the death of her first husband, her mother continuously advises her to think of remarrying because a woman needs a man to survive. The impression one gets is that Ihuoma can have no independent life; she must always be attached to a man, as she has little or no relevance beyond her role as a sexual object.

At the same time, Amadi spares no effort in idealizing his heroine. Most of the novel concentrates on her physical and moral superiority to the other women in her world and on her relentless efforts to be an ideal wife and mother. Amadi's main preoccupation in *The Concubine* seems to be to portray a character who will epitomize female perfection from a sexist perspective, and he is highly successful in that respect. His heroine is all that such a man would wish a woman to be. She is endowed with the kind of physical attractiveness that makes a man proud to possess her.

> She was a pretty woman: perhaps that is why she married so early. Her three children looked more like her brothers and sisters. She was young . . . she was just about twenty-two.

> Ihuoma's complexion was that of the ant-hill. Her features were
> smoothly rounded and looking at her no one could doubt that she was
> 'enjoying her husband's wealth.' Nothing did a husband greater credit
> than the well-fed look of his wife (p. 14).

Ihuoma's attractiveness is emphasized over and over again She seems
impressed by her own beauty, gazing at herself in the mirror every little
chance she gets. Calamity, the most notorious agent of premature aging,
adds only an ameliorating quality to her beauty. It gives her a "softly
alluring, deeply enchanting . . . bewitching subtlety that only deep sorrow
can give . . . young men and even the old gazed at her . . . irresistibly" (p.
45). The matured Ihuoma is even more fascinating; she is "confident without
being brazen, self-respecting yet approachable, sweet but sensible" (p.
249).

Ihuoma is, above all, a model traditional wife; she shows "her great
devotion to her husband in every way she could think of" (p. 9). She is
always polite and never gives offense. She is submissive and very
understanding. In short, she has none of those qualities that make a woman
threatening to a man. She's no good at invectives and other women talk
much faster than she does. She does not talk in parables; therefore, she
cannot infringe on the male prerogative of verbal excellence. She is a
staunch upholder of her society's values, and her high sense of morality
matches her high physical endowments. She is so preoccupied with
maintaining her good name as a woman that she readily sacrifices her
happiness to her good name. For example, she declines to marry Ekwueme,
a man she is in love with, because such behavior would be considered
improper in her society. She takes it upon herself to remind him that
tradition requires him to marry a young maiden who would obey him and
give him the first fruits of her womb.

Elechi Amadi's portrayal of Ihuoma fits five of seven stereotypes
catalogued by Roseann Bell. Ihuoma is the "Earth-mother, the concubine,
the loyal doormat of a wife, the sacrificial lamb, [and] the willing
mechanism in a polygamous drama."[4]

Compare Flora Nwapa's approach to her heroine, Efuru. She is at the
center of the world Nwapa creates. There is no event or situation in the
novel that does not stem from her. The novel is Efuru's story, and her life
provides the materials for plotting it. Other characters are brought in only
as what they do and say leads to revealing or clarifying aspects of Efuru's
life. Her presence controls the action, unlike Ihuoma whose actions are
reactions to male-initiated actions. While Ihuoma becomes prominent in
Amadi's novel only when her presence is required to complete the story of
one of Amadi's male protagonists, Efuru is always present in Nwapa's
novel in her own right. And this is significant because Amadi's work
purports to deal principally with a female character.

Efuru is exceptional in many respects. She is beautiful, the daughter of one of the last survivors of a vanishing age of traditional valor and grandeur, and a highly successful businesswoman. She is prosperous; it is as though anything she touches literally transforms into riches. She is also very compassionate and unassuming, qualities that couple with her beauty to give her a striking resemblance to Ihuoma, Amadi's heroine.

However, Nwapa's Efuru is no paragon of female submissiveness. She demonstrates a marked sense of independence and a determination to lead a fulfilling life. From an early age she reveals a resolve to control her own life rather than to submit blindly to tradition. She is by no means a revolutionary because she does not completely abrogate tradition, but neither is she enslaved by it. Whenever traditional stipulations stifle her individualty, she steps out of them to adopt alternative means that best enable her to express her personality. For example, she contravenes the mores governing male-female relationships and declares herself married by moving in with her lover who is of low social status and too poor at the time to afford her dowry. But later, through her enterprising nature, she makes enough money with her husband to pay her dowry. Also when her first husband deserts her, she continues to live in his house for a considerable length of time—two years. She even goes in search of him. But after waiting long enough to avoid accusations of impropriety, she returns to her father's house, an indication that she is ready, among other things, to consider other possible suitors. She marries again, shortly after moving back to her father's house and enjoys a period of near total marital bliss with her new husband. Not only do they work together, they do everything together. She acts as his counselor, advising him on what projects are ripe for pursuit. In addition, they enjoy a closeness that is not quite usual in the rural setting within which they live. They even go to the stream together to swim and thereby attract a lot of gossip from envious women bound by unexciting lives and the values of their rural world.

Nwapa, like Amadi, highlights her heroine's physical attributes—the village gossips always comment on her beauty. Both women are exceptional in their communities. But Nwapa emphasizes Efuru's other characteristics as well, some of them not totally complimentary, and by so doing, prevents the idealization of her heroine's image. Nwapa's approach to Efuru's beauty in no way reduces the heroine to being a sex object. In fact, the manner in which her beauty is depicted often plays down its positive nature. While there is no question about Efuru's great beauty, the village gossips always juxtapose it, her wealth, and her closeness with her husband to her childlessness, thereby attempting to diminish her endowments.

Above all, Nwapa's portrayal of her heroine presents an in-depth study of womanhood. Her novel is a study of the growth of Efuru, and both her physical and psychological development are brought to light as she searches for options for self-actualization. Efuru begins by accepting the traditional sexually-oriented prescriptions for defining a woman's identity, but she moves gradually towards a new definition of a sense of self, a better option for self-definition. Initially she attempts to find fulfillment both as a wife and a mother, hence her two marriages and her striving to make them work. Also in the early years of her married life she agonizes over her childlessness and goes to some length to remedy this anomaly. She goes to see a *dibia* who assures her she will bear a child. After this assurance, she is still alarmed by her tardiness and becomes overjoyed when she finally bears a child. She feels fulfilled, at last, as a woman.

> Efuru lay there thinking of it all, "Is this happening to me or someone I know. Is that baby mine or somebody else's? Is it really true that I have had a baby, that I am a woman after all. Perhaps I am dreaming. I shall soon wake up and discover that it is not real" (p. 31).

Her sense of fulfillment is threatened when her only daughter falls ill. ' "What will I do if I lose her?" she thought. "If she dies, that will mean the end of me" ' (p. 66).

The above image is that of the growing Efuru, still struggling to come to terms with her identity. The death of her child, however and the grief it brings, does not reduce her to a non-person; neither does the failure of her two marriages. She continues with her trade and proves herself a serious and successful businesswoman. Moreover she becomes a special wor-shipper of the woman of the lake when she is still married to her second husband. Thus even when she was still married, her other roles played down her sexual one, pointing her in alternative directions for self-realization.

Efuru's life is in some ways wryly ironic. With all her endowments, she fails miserably to find fulfillment within the sexual modes prescribed by her society. She fails both as a wife and a mother. She ends up each time, after two brief spells of marital bliss, back in her father's home. There is no question about her possessing qualities that make men proud to be her mate. Her beauty and the prosperity she brings to her husbands, in themselves, should enamor them to her. Her strong love for her mates and her unflinching devotion to them more than compensate for those qualities such as her strong will and determination that, when unrestrained, can threaten their masculinity. Still, her first husband deserts her for a woman who is Efuru's inferior physically and morally. Her second husband maintains an enviable relationship with her for two years, then becomes inattentive and mistrusting, believing a rumor about Efuru's infidelity. Appalled by her husband's lack of faith in her, Efuru, leaves him to return to her home of birth.

Efuru's matrimonial failures, in a superficial way, recall those of Ihuoma, who loses two husbands and ends up a widow at a relatively early age. However, Efuru's life is a failure only within a very limited sexual framework, on which unfortunately her society places so much importance. Her life is not a failure when seen through her own eyes and from a broader perspective. That she is a remarkable human being is communicated even more strongly than the sense of failure projected mainly through the comments of the village gossips. Her generosity, her wealth, and her general sense of worth to her community at large is as much a reality as her failed marriages and childlessness. The sense of accomplishment of Nwapa's heroine is no less strong because of her unsuccessful stint as wife and mother, a point which sets her off from Amadi's Ihuoma, whose life crumbles around her once she fails to lead a fulfilling sexual life.

The supernatural element plays a vital role in both novels. However, once more, Nwapa's use of the supernatural differs markedly from the way Amadi uses it. In Efuru's case, the supernatural becomes an extension of her sense of self while in the case of Ihuoma, it assumes a masculine form and hinders her development as a successful woman. In direct opposition, Uhamiri, the woman of the lake, the supernatural element in Nwapa's novel, is a symbolic representation of Nwapa's heroine, who is chosen as a special worshipper of this deity. Uhamiri becomes the alter ego of the matured Efuru who is invested with all of Uhamiri's qualities. Both of them are rich, beautiful and worshipped by those who appreciate their worth, but they have no children. Significantly, Uhamiri lavishes on her favorites wealth and not children, and she is worshipped even though she does not have children or give her worshippers children. Efuru's acceptance of her role as a special worshipper of the woman of the lake, therefore, becomes a symbolic representation of her acceptance of herself as a person in her own right. The novel's end supports this contention.

> Efuru slept soundly that night. She dreamt of the woman of the lake, her beauty, her long hair and her riches. She had lived for ages at the bottom of the lake. She was as old as the lake itself. She was happy, she was wealthy. She was beautiful. She gave women beauty and wealth but she had no child. She had never experienced the joy of motherhood. Why then did women worship her? (p. 221).

This passage is the crux of the story of Efuru, capturing well her final acceptance of herself, her coming to terms with her life, and her determination to live happily and reject those traditional prescriptions of the identity of women, which only diminish their sense of personal worth.

Maryse Condé is right in her observation that the closing lines of *Efuru* provide the clue to the whole book, but her interpretation of it reflects her limited understanding of Efuru's identification with the woman of the lake. Condé's interpretation of *Efuru* is that:

No happiness can be achieved for a woman unless in childbearing. . . . Efuru, for all her qualities and gifts, considers her life as valueless since she fails to have a child. She can deliberately and willfully decide to leave her husband and therefore live by herself, but she cannot follow the logical consequences. She cannot find in herself enough resources to counterbalance her sterility and never thinks of devoting her energies to something else.[5]

Ms. Condé's statements present a gross misreading of Nwapa's heroine. Nwapa makes it quite clear that, far from feeling that her life is valueless, Efuru seeks new alternatives through which to realize her life. There is no question that Efuru finds in herself enough resources to counterbalance her sterility and devotes her energies to the pursuit of other things, symbolically represented by her becoming a devoted worshipper of the woman of the lake, the spiritual embodiment of her own identity.

Nwapa's use of the supernatural is not dissimilar from Amadi's in so far as it bears directly on the life and identity of her heroine. But in this regard too, there is a marked difference. While Nwapa's supernatural being is a woman and functions to promote her heroine's search for identity, Amadi's supernatural being provides another means of confining his heroine to her sexual identity. It is a further projection of his male perspective of African womanhood. Ihuoma's chain of unsuccessful marriages, like Efuru's, stem from her special relationship to the supernatural. However, in her case, the supernatural thwarts her life rather than offers her alternatives for self-actualization. Being a human reincarnation of the spirit wife of the Sea King, a highly jealous male deity, who refuses to relinquish his hold on her, Ihuoma can at best be only a concubine to human men, but can never marry in her life on earth. So Ihumoa's relevance even in the spirit world is limited to a sexual one. She is bound body and soul to the Sea King.

This study therefore supports Lloyd Brown's[6] evaluations of these two works. The difference between Ihuoma's total sense of doom and despair at the end of *The Concubine*, and Efuru's ability to devote herself to something other than seeking fulfillment in the traditionally instituted female roles illustrates a basic difference between the perception of females from a strictly male perspective and from a female one.

While Amadi's character never becomes more than an instrument in someone else's scheme, Nwapa's Efura transcends those proscriptions, becoming an actor in her own, in woman's right.

NOTES

1. Buchi Emecheta is one of the exceptions. Her depiction of female characters, particularly in her early works, are limited to their sexual roles. Such titles as *The Bride Price, The Slave Girl,* and *The Joys of Motherhood* reflect the sexual emphasis she places on her characterization.
2. Elechi Amadi, *The Concubine* (London: Heinemann 1966), Flora Nwapa, *Efuru* (London: Heinemann, 1966). All references to these works are to this edition and will be referred to by page numbers only.
3. Maryse Condé, "Three Female Writers in Modern Africa: Flora Nwapa, Ama Ata Aidoo and Grace Ogot," in *Presence Africaine*, No. 82, 1972, p. 136.
4. Roseann P. Bell, "The Absence of the African Woman Writer," CLA Journal, Vol. 21, No. 4, 1978, p. 491. The other two are "The high-life floozy and the "been-to"."
5. Condé, p. 134, 136.
6. Lloyd W. Brown, *Women Writers in Black Africa* (Wesport, Conn.: Greenwood Press, 1981), p. 22.

The Work of Henri Lopès:
A Forum for African
Women's Consciousness

Anne Adams Graves

Henri Lopès is one of Congo-Brazzaville's most recognized prose writers. What has become his literary signature is a single-minded attention to—almost a pre-occupation with—the ideological parameters of the problems that affect the social, economic, and political progress of contemporary African society. His short-story collection, titled *Tribaliques*,[1] recipient, one year after its publication, of the Grand Prix Litteraire de l'Afrique Noire, includes stories such as "L'Honnête Homme," "La Fuite de la main habile," and "Monsieur le député," whose very titles imply an exposition of some of the self-acknowledged nemeses of African nations today. By effecting a tone of familial frankness Lopès engages the conscience of the members of his African family, warning, exhorting, nagging the family members to do some housecleaning.

In addition to the above-mentioned *Tribaliques*, consisting of eight short stories, published in 1971, Lopès' oeuvre includes three novels, *La nouvelle romance*, 1976, *Sans tam-tam*, 1977, and *Le pleurer-rire*, 1982. Depicting commonly found situations from all strata of contemporary African life, Lopès' works evoke such subjects as the pressures of tribal differences on individuals' lives in a now highly mobile society; the questions of management of a state's industrial resources; the means and ends of popular education; or the sociology and psychology of the changing

131

relations between men and women. In a significant portion of his work—
seven out of the ten total pieces—women and/or women-focused issues
take a central place in the narrative.

For an analysis of women's roles in African literature the model
furnished by Kenneth Little's *The Sociology of Urban Women's Image in
African Literature*[2] is of some utility, albeit limited. Arranging the
characters into six role categories, Little labels four of the six in terms of
varying levels of the women's associations with men. Those categories are
"girl-friends and good-time girls," "wives," "'free women,'" i.e. those who
"escape" the "trap" of "marriage under modern conditions" (p. 53), and
"courtesans and prostitutes." In addition to a category of "mothers"—
mostly of men characters—there is a final grouping called "'political'
women and workers," linked together apparently by virtue of their scarcity
in the literature. In drawing his conclusions Little grants that "most of the
characters are psychologically self-sufficient" and that "none of the. . .cate-
gories are mere appendages of the male sex" (p. 152). He concedes, though,
that "women have a definite place in the community as wives and sexual
partners. . .and in these terms women are, without any doubt, persons in
their own right. Political and economic affairs, however, are another matter;
and women's participation in them is usually a function of their relationship
with men". If Little finds his model to be the most functional for analyzing
the women's roles in the works of the thirty authors he takes on, that model
is not the most functional one for analyzing Hénri Lopès' women's roles.
However, some of Little's categories can serve in an analysis of our writer's
women characters, inasmuch as the situations in which they are presented
have recognizable correspondences with women's situations in other
African literature in aspects of the demographic, interpersonal, occupational
and other environmental parameters of the women's lives.

Indeed, practically every one of Lopès' female characters has a
relationship to a man, that contributes some material to the story. However,
the manner in which these characters execute their roles as wives,
girlfriends, mothers, sisters, lovers, working women, politically engaged
women, students, and teachers suggests a significant variation on a model
like Little's. Of course, there could be as many different arrangements of
such data proposed as there are individuals who care to make such a study.
Also, because of the amount of overlap or multiple membership that such
categorizations must allow for, the data become even less conclusive. But,
the Lopès technique in both the short stories and the novels draws
characterizations that present unmistakable evidence for identifying certain
other roles beyond those defined by the woman-man relationship. That
technique consists of limited action, the barest description of setting, and a
maximum of insight into characters' thoughts, reactions, motivations,
emotions. If his plots are thin, his characters are given great breadth,
Everything is conveyed through the perspective of a character, whether in

first- or third-person narrative, conversation, reportage, through indirect discourse, inner monolog, or epistolary form. (One entire novel, *Sans Tam-Tam*, is basically a series of five lengthy letters from a man fulfilled by his job as a teacher in a rural town, written to his closest friend, elucidating his refusal of a comfortable diplomatic post abroad.) In any case, owing to the limited action reflection in Lopès' works, any study of his characters must give at least equal attention to their psychological and intellectual characteristics—their consciousness—as is given to their actions or physical roles. This consciousness is given such depth of treatment through the inner monolog/conversation/epistolary form of the works, that it confers upon the characters additional roles of equal, if not greater, significance to the stories. Thus, in view of these considerations the characters examined in this study occupy multiple role categories.

The count of the female characters, covering the two novels and the five short stories in which females appear, is tallied at twenty-six. This accounts for each individual female adult (broadly construed) who appears or is introduced indirectly and receives meaningful attention, and includes also a few generalized groups of women treated as character types or collective characters. The inventory of the role categories follows here, reflecting the twenty-six characters' multiple roles, and proceeding in order from the categories denoting identification as individuals to those denoting identification in relationships with other people.

1) Working women and students. There are fourteen characters, who are either engaged in self-supporting employment or are attending some type of educational institution. In this latter sub-group we find one regular university student, one woman who at different times pursues further education, and four secondary school students. In the employed sub-group are two teachers, a seamstress, a nursemaid in an expatriate European family's household, two widows who own and operate night clubs that had been their husbands', and the prostitutes who entertain the patrons.

2) Politically engaged women and advocates of social change. There are six characters who play such roles, either through participation in formal political groups or through action or consciousness-raising on an individual, personal basis. These include two active political party workers who also do volunteer teaching in adult literacy programs; an aspiring writer; a freedom fighter in her country's war for independence; a collective character made up of the delegates at a convention of La Fédération nationale des femmes avant-gardistes; and, finally, a young betrothed woman who, during the course of a one-night stand with another man who is married, debates with him the issue of equality of sexual freedom.

3) Mothers and sisters. Of the eight characters in this category, only two, both single mothers of small children, function as parents per se. The remaining six function as emotional support and inspiration sources for other characters in their respective stories. Of the six individuals whose

lives are touched by these mothers and sisters, five are women. Thus, the role of mother and elder sister is not merely maternal here, but rather a spiritual source of strength for women. Some of the mother figures are indeed a single type: the traditional rural farmer mother whose lot, in Lopès' view, it is to till the fields while her husband sits in the sun drinking palm wine and engaging in debate with his cohorts. The sole male character whose mother is included in this category eulogizes her: "She. . .lived and died as a symbol of the country, of Africa herself. A symbol of our history, of our explication. She never knew."[3]

4) Wives, fiancèes, and girlfriends. To this group are assigned seventeen characters, all of whom are in relationships with men, based on a mutual commitment of assumed permanence, consistency, and fidelity. With seventeen of the total twenty-six women—more than two-thirds—involved in one of these committed relationships, Lopès is reflecting a situation lthat is quite normal. Even these numbers can be legitimately raised, if we include some women from other categories whose roles overlap with those in this group. For, while the two widowed entrepreneurs, who of course were once married, are numbered among the "wives" here, one single mother is also included, since she is repeatedly harrassed by family members and a traditional doctor for *refusing* to marry a certain man of the family's choice. Further, two other characters counted among these seventeen are actually one person. This is the title character in the short story "Ah, Apolline!" a university student, who, after having experienced a broken engagement dating back to her pre-university days, forms a satisfying and promising relationship with a fellow student, only to succumb finally to family and tribal pressures to return home and marry the former fiancé. But not counted in these seventeen are one or two others whose situations allow the reader to infer roles of wife, fiancée or girlfriend. One such case is that of the collective character of the women's federation convention delegates. And, finally, there are two characters, schoolgirls, who could not fit into this category by virtue of their young age.

5) Mistresses, casual lovers, and prostitutes. The seven characters in this final category have various levels of relationships or encounters with men, all of which are based on sex, and some of which involve some type of material compensation or support. Though this category encompasses women in steady associations such as three regular mistresses, two schoolgirl "pick-up" collective characters, and the prostitutes employed by the two night club owners, they account for a small number of the twenty-six women characters. Lopès does not fail to comment on the casual lovers and prostitutes. An example of such commentary is his description of one prostitute, a South African singer in one of the widows' night clubs who "entertains" the government dignitaries who frequent the club, "as her way of fighting against apartheid."[4]

Upon consideration of the last two role categories—wives/fiancées/girl-friends and mistresses/casual lovers/prostitutes—the data indicate that the majority of the characters in the seven works under discussion are indeed connected in some way with men. But this is not remarkable, nor is it unique to the work of Lopès. What does warrant more comment, however, is the fact that the great majority of the women characters who play roles as partners to men play the other roles given in this inventory, through which their consciousness of the social, political, and economic condition of their societies is projected.

Looking at the specifics of some of the works, it is immediately obvious that some characters and other elements found in the short stories, Lopès' first publication, are found in the novels in a more refined and developed form. It is as if, after creating the characters and presenting them in the confined framework of the short story, the writer had the need to let them open out in a large arena that could better accommodate their dimensions. A case in point is the young woman Mbâ, from the short story "La Fuite de la main habile," whose characteristics show up in the novel *La Nouvelle romance* primarily in its central character but shared partially with another. Mbâ, a dedicated primary school teacher and adult literacy volunteer teacher, waits faithfully for her beloved to do the welder's training in France, for which he has won a scholarship. After a few letters in the early months, his correspondence gradually drops off and then stops. Mbâ, immersed in her work, remains optimistic, until six years later she learns that he has settled down in France with his French wife and their child, earning a comfortable living in a factory. Mbâ's sustaining interests during the years of waiting are the children she teachers, their families, and the adults in the literacy class from whom she learns so much. She is also an enthusiastic participant in the local Party cell meetings. Her recollection of the difficult life of her mother and other village farm women inspires the desire to write a book on and work toward "'l'émancipation de la femme Africaine'".[5] Thus, the attention in this story is as much devoted to this depiction of Mbâ as to the lovers' story.

The personal characteristics of Mbâ outlined above are easily recognized in two prominent characters, Wali and her close friend Awa, of the novel *La Nouvelle romance*. From its title and foreword, borrowed from a novel by the French writer Louis Aragon, to its closing statement, this book speaks to "l'émancipation de la femme Africaine." Wali, the central figure, experiences much of the oppression that Lopès sees in the life of the African woman. But Wali also examines her situation and searches for viable alternatives. As the barren wife of an egotistic soccer star who manages to finagle himself a job in his government's embassy in Brussels, Wali must find a source of fulfillment and self-realization outside her marriage. Having been forced to give up her studies at the time of her marriage because her husband,

Bienvenu, believed that education took away a woman's femininity, Wali was at first occupied with caring for Bienvenu's sister's child. But later finding herself in a European capital in strange surroundings and among Europeans, who, as former colonialists, hold unconcealed prejudices against Africans, Wali feels very lonely since her husband provides no companionship for her and has long since lost sexual interest in her. Through her acquaintance with a Belgian neighbor couple Wali is introduced to and attends meetings of the communist party and is drawn to its doctrine regarding the status of women in the working class. She also enrolls in some courses in the People's University. These activities not only fill up Wali's time but also expand her consciousness of, and inform her perspective on, the developmental needs of her country.

In complement to these new acquantances and experiences, Wali maintains correspondence with her two closest friends from home, Awa and Elise. The former is a school teacher and eventually gets a scholarship to pursue the licence in Paris, the first female from her country to achieve this. Declining suggestions to study medicine or law, Awa chooses Liberal Arts to continue in her career in teaching because she believes that it is the teachers in her country who have the best opportunity to keep a vigilant eye on the direction in which the State is headed. She believes also that it is on the level of the intellect that women will achieve equality with men. Thus Awa zealously works to cultivate her own intellect, while deciding to postpone marriage. (Marriage is indeed available to the attractive Awa, as her friends Wali and Elise often tease her. Wali's husband Bienvenu says upon learning of Awa's receiving the first university scholarship awarded to a woman from their country: "Les femmes- là deviennent aussi des intellectuelles? . . . Mais elle, ça ne m'étonne pas. Ce n'est pas une femme. C'est un phénomène. Je me demande seulement comment elle fait pour être à la fois belle et intelligente?" (p. 139) ["Those women are turning into intellectuals, too?. . .But that doesn't surprise me about her. She's no woman; she's a phenomenon. I just wonder how she manages to be both beautiful and intelligent."]) Besides pursuing her own intellectual development Awa also pushes Wali to get her teaching certificate. This campaign is waged while they are still at home together before either goes to Europe as well as after they have separated and write letters to each other between Brussels and Paris.

Their other girlfriend is Elise, a seamstress and mother of a little girl, who enjoys her single life with her married lovers who give her enviable gifts. But in a conversation where the three friends analyze the situation of the married woman as compared with that of the single woman, several advantages and disadvantages are articulated for each. Elise, who at one point describes herself as "l'éternelle fiancée," also reasons that exclusivity in marriage leaves women like herself with no means of support. "Il est question de l'économie démographique!" (p. 67) ["It's a question of demographic economics!"]

That Henri Lopès the writer has a sustained commitment to using his works as a forum for the dialectics of African women's issues is evidenced by the proportion of his works that center around the status of women. Besides the novel *La Nouvelle romance* two of the *Tribaliques* stories, "Monsieur le député" and "L'Avance," are entirely concerned with women's issues, while three others, "Ancien Combattant," "Ah, Apolline," and La Fuite de la main habile" contain dominant themes involving women within stories whose focus is elsewhere. To look briefly at one of the women-focused short stories "Monsieur le député," we see an obvious conflict between theory and practice in the attitude of governments, and the men who run them, toward women. The fact that the central character here is a man, a member of parliament, in a story that features women from all five of our role categories allows the point to be made in the clearest light. Our Member of Parliament (M.P.), Ngouakou-Ngouakou addresses the convention of the Fédération nationale des femmes avant-gardistes, declaiming the immediate necessity for the effectuation of equality for women at every level of the nation's operation, including educational and employment opportunity and equalization of salaries. He closes by calling for the end of the tyranny of men over women, reminding his sisters there convened that women are the key to world peace. After receiving enthusiastic ovations he goes home, demands that his daughter get up from her mid-term math assignment to fix him a drink, turns on the TV and ogles the sexy Miriam Makeba singing and swaying, complains, when his small son brings him his slippers, that the boy is doing girl's work, and upbraids his wife, who is a little late with dinner, about having no understanding of the hardships of managing a family. After dinner he changes into casual clothers, goes out to a *rendezvous* with his mistress in the "Venez-Voir" night club, owned by an attractive widow. Later in bed with his mistress at a hotel, our MP is told by her that she is pregnant, to which he responds by suggesting that the paternity could lie with someone else. Thus Lopès sharply illustrates the discrepancy between theory and practice.

Conclusion

The presentation of the experience of the African woman is one of the qualities that makes Henri Lopès' work important in the literature of contemporary Africa. Factors such as the high frequency of women as narrators or focal characters, and topical content covering the broad spectrum of issues of the African woman's experience make the novels and short stories of this unfortunately little discussed writer a literary forum for African women's consciousness. By virtue of the quantity of attention Lopès devotes to women, the urgency for integration of women's issues into the African social process is made unequivocal. Lopès' women characters articulate their own self-consciousness. Even the fact that some of them are not able to articulate their self-consciousness is a part of their statement through the author as spokesperson. This situation is, however, representative of the contradictions surrounding women's relationships with all the other agents affecting their lives.

While the context of Lopès' creative practice is the family of African people, the context within which his works are set is quite frequently specifically Congolese but with situations drawn along broader African lines. The use of the homebased setting enables Lopès to be self-critical of Africa in general, with the attention directed at his own country. The problems, issues, contradictions which Lopès points to are presented unmistakably as African, not Congolese particularly. Thus from his own ideological stance Henri Lopès presents, in his work, the issues of social change in African society. The issues of women's status have a high place on his agenda for social change in Africa.

NOTES

1. Henri Lopès, *Tribaliques* (Yaounde: Editions CLE, 1971).
2. Kenneth Little, *The Sociology of Urban Women's Image in African Literature* (Totowa, NJ: Rowman and Littlefield, 1980).
3. Henri Lopès, *Sans Tam-Tam* (Yaounde: Editions CLE, 1977).
4. Henri Lopès, *La nouvelle romance* (Yaounde: Editions CLE, 1976).
5. Henri Lopès, "La fuite de la main habile," in *Tribaliques*, p. 5.

Daughters of Moombi;*
Ngugi's Heroines And
Traditional Gikuyu
Aesthetics

Charles A. Nama

The retrieval of the glorious, ancient age of African culture is a significant dimension of Ngugi wa Thiong'o's writings. All his works indict the importation of foreign cultures detrimental to African values. In this paper, I wish to articulate an important aspect of Ngugi's writings which has not received enough critical attention—his depiction of heroines who conform with specific conventions of traditional aesthetics, and who consequently play crucial roles as defenders of traditional cultural values.

In order to appreciate the relationship between Ngugi's heroines and his use of Gikuyu aesthetic convention it is necessary to understand the relevance of art in traditional societies. In "The Aesthetics of Old African Art," Isidore Okpweho observes:

> I have tried to identify the Old African Artist as a man with a very pressing sense of real and concrete presences, enjoying the closest intimacy with an environment that was both physical and metaphysical. By means of his dynamic sense of form he tried in all sorts of

*East African writer Charity Waciuma has an autobiographical work entitled *Daughter of Mumbi*, Nairobi: East African Publishing House, 1969.

combinations, with language and with material, to give tangible meaning to those visible and spiritual presences who gave context to his daily life and thought.[1]

The "physical and metaphysical" relationship implicit in many forms of African art was also evident in traditional Gikuyu society. In this conection, it is important to point out that, although Okpweho identifies the artist as male, the artists and artisans in traditional Gikuyu societies were both men and women. In *Facing Mount Kenya* Jomo Kenyatta informs us that certain artistic activities such as pottery and basket-making were the realm of the women. While building huts was the work of men, the women were charged with the responsibility of beautifying it by thatching. In their songs, the women poked fun at the artistic inadequacies of the men. As Kenyatta records it:

> You men, you lack the most important art in building, namely thatching. A wall and an empty roof cannot protect you from heavy rain, nor from burning sun. It is our careful thatching that makes a hut worth living in. . .[2]

This symbolic completion of a Gikuyu homestead underscores the artistic prowess of Gikuyu women in enhancing the "beauty" of Gikuyu art forms.

In *Homecoming* (1972), *Writers in Politics* (1981), and *Detained* (1981), Ngugi argues that the unequivocal liberation of Africans lies not in Westernization but in the resuscitation of traditional cultural values that have been an intrinsic part of the people's lives from ancient times. In *Detained*, he notes the special contribution of Kenyan women in the liberation struggle against British imperialism, remarking that:

> . . .the most remarkable of them all was Me Kitilili, the leader of the Giriama people's resistance to the British occupation of their country. She was already an old woman when she organized Giriama youth into a fighting force that took the British machine three years to subdue. Old as she was, she was very clearly the political character of the armed struggle. . .[3]

Like Me Kitilili, Ngugi's fictional heroines are active participants in the liberation struggles against foreign domination; Nyakinyua in *Petals of Blood* and Wariinga in *Devil on the Cross* are excellent examples.

In order to appreciate their role, it is imperative to understand certain salient aspects of Gikuyu traditional societies. The Gikuyus see life in mythic terms and believe that each person's existence is destined and controlled by *Ngai* the Supreme Being. Consequently, a sense of inevitability shapes the lives, actions, and aspirations of the average Gikuyu. The

Sartrean existential notion of man being responsible for and controlling his own destiny is alien to Gikuyu metaphysics. The creation myth which Ngugi recounts in *The River Between* clearly defines the sacred, religious and political responsibilities of women in the Gikuyu view of the cosmos. He observes:

> . . .and the Creator who is called Murungu took Gikuyu *and Mumbi* from the holy mountain. He took them to the country of the ridges near Siriana. . .But he showed them all the land. . .Yes children, God showed Gikuyu and Mumbi all the land and told them. . .This land I hand over to you. O man and *woman*, its yours to rule and till in serenity sacrificing only to me, your God under my sacred tree. . .[4]
>
> (my emphasis)

This religious, functional significance of women's role in the Creation Myth is also underscored in Jomo Kenyatta's *Facing Mount Kenya*, where he traces the matrilineal families of the daughters of Mumbi until the men revolted. In most of Ngugi's works, therefore, women play a major role analogous to that played by their counterparts in traditional Gikuyu societies.

Ngugi's heroines in his earlier writings, though not as overtly political as in his more recent writings, manifest strong traditional values. Muthoni in *The River Between* is an excellent example. She is torn by inevitable circumstances between two diametrically opposed religions—one foreign, one traditional. Her plight is an instance of a pattern which recurs for his other female characters. Although her father embraces Christianity, Muthoni still upholds the initiation rites of Gikuyu women. She finally succumbs to Christianity but her ultimate objective is "to be a woman made beautiful in the manner of the tribe" (p. 44). Even on her dying bed, she does not relent; she remarks to Waiyaki, ". . . Tell Nyambura I see Jesus. And I am a woman, beautiful in the tribe. . ." (p. 53). (Editors' note: See Levin's paper in this collection for a contrasting perspective on circumcision as a female initiation rite.)

Mumbi in *A Grain of Wheat* is another heroine who embraces traditional values in Gikuyu society. Even the major characters in the novel acknowledge her singular role as they glorify her with songs which evoke the origins of the Gikuyu clan. The chorus of Gikongo's song is indicative of their admiration for her unique role:

> Gikuyu *na* Mumbi,
> Gikuyu *na* Mumbi,
> Gikuyu *na* Mumbi,
> *Nikihiu ngwatiro.* . .[5]

When Karanja, Kihika and Gitongo encounter Mumbi at Gikonyo's workshop she is addressed in glowing terms by Karanga, "Mother of Men, we have come make us some tea" (p. 93). These tributes to Mumbi also illustrate her role in the world of the novel. At the height of the Emergency which Ngugi depicts eloquently in *A Grain of Wheat*, the people are betrayed by the enigmatic Mugo. Throughout the novel, Mugo is portrayed as an eccentric personality who is eventually ostracized. At the crux of his isolation and desperation he goes only to Mumbi to share his secrets and guilt. Although their encounter is merely a temporary palliative for the despised Mugo, it is an act of consolation for a rejected member of the family.

Mumbi's observations about her singular role are significant:

> ...Even when I got married, the dream did not die. I longed to make my husband happy, yes but I also prepared myself to stand by him when the time came. I could carry his sheath and as fast as he shot into the enemy, I would feed him with arrows. If danger came and he fell, he would fall into my arms and I would bring him safely to myself. . .[6]

Even the artist Gikonyo acknowledges her immense contribution to his self-esteem. Their early encounter is deeply engraved in his memory so that when he goes to jail, he draws upon it for emotional support. Speaking of Mumbi he notes:

> ...Before, I was nothing. Now I was a man. During our short period of married life, Mumbi made me feel it was all important. . .Every day I found a new Mumbi. Together we plunged into the forest. And I was not afraid of the darkness. . .[7]

She is eventually unfaithful to him, having an illegitimate child with his archrival Karanja. Killam's explanation in *An Introduction to the Writings of Ngugi* that the encounter "became the ultimate extension of her supreme joy in hearing her husband's release and Karanja merely becomes an agent in the process" (p. 67) seems appropriate if we consider Mumbi's explanation after the episode and Gikongo's reluctance to come to grips with his wife's unfaithfulness.

Like other powerful heroines in Gikuyu history and mythology such as Me Kitilili and Nyakinyua in *Petals of Blood*, Mumbi is an advocate of Gikuyu culture. She is fascinated by stories about brave women in Gikuyu culture and sees herself as a savior of her people. Although she does not fulfill the role of the Redeemer, the emotional support she gives to Mugo and Gikonyo in their moments of trial is an attempt to redeem the fallen though on a smaller scale.

The two most important women in *Petals of Blood*, Wanja and Nyakinyua are good examples of strong women in Gikuyu society although on different levels. Wanja means "stranger" or "outsider". Her behavior is similar to that of Cyprian Ekwensi's Jagua Nana and true to her name, she remains an outcast in her community. Her lackluster love affair with Kimeria, her dissolute life and her acceptance of brazen Western materialism are all anathema to the traditional values of Ilmorog. However, she is one of the most prominent members of the team who undertake the epic journey to confront their nonchalant Member of Parliament, M. P. Nderi Wa Riera, in Nairobi.

The other major woman character in *Petals of Blood*, Nyakinyua, is the embodiment of traditional values. She celebrates Gikuyu norms and the values of the ancient age especially in her singing. Ngugi uses her as a prototype of the woman with extraordinary prowess in Gikuyu traditional society. In *Facing Mount Kenya* Jomo Kenyatta illustrates the importance of such women in Gikuyu mythology:

> ...This large group was then formed and given the ancestral collective name of *Rorere rwa Mbari ya Moombi*, namely, children or people of Moombi or Moombi's tribe. In this women continued to be the heads of their family and clans for some generations...[8]

Kenyatta also remarks that "there was a great medicine man known as Mogo or Moro Wa Kibiro whose national duty was to foretell future events and to advise the nation to prepare for what was in store." Ngugi assigns Nyakinyua both of these roles: mother of the clan and prophet who foretells future events. She is Wanja's grandmother and more. She is also representative of other strong women in Ngugi's novels such as Nyambura, Mwihaki and Mumbi.

In a recent interview while answering questions on the writing of *Devil on the Cross* Ngugi remarked:

> Because women are the most exploited and oppressed section of the entire working class, I would create a picture of a strong determined woman with a will to resist and struggle against conditions of her present being. Wariinga will be the fictional representation of this heroine of Kenyan history. Wariinga, heroine of toil...[9]

These attributes also apply to Nyakinyua in *Petals of Blood*. However, Nyakinyua's overriding role in the novel recalls the legendary period in Gikuyu history when women ruled the land. She is cast in the mold of a man, the legendary seer, Moro Wa Kibiro. That is why she expends all her energies to inculcate traditional values into the young. Even her relationships with individuals such as that with her husband have a special significance to the entire clan.

A major function of Nyakinyua's role in the novel is related to her husband's gallant defence of Ilmorog. Both of them are staunch defenders of traditional Gikuyu greatness. We are told that "Nyakinyua's husband, Njamba Nene. . .that he was so old yet pointing a gun at a white man! He redeemed Ilmorog with his blood. . ." (p. 81). In addition, she articulates the conventions and norms of her people. She fulfills the role of the "griot" and the seer. Like Sundiata's griot in *Sundiata: The Epic of Old Mali*, she is presented in epic terms. Ngugi observes:

> . . .Thus Nyakinyua talked to them, kept up their spirits with stories of the past. . .Nyakinyua was the spirit that guided and held them together. And she talked as if she had been everywhere, as if she had actually participated in the war against the Germans, as if the rhythm of the historic rise and fall of Ilmorog flowed in her veins. . .Nyakinyua, mother of men; there was sad gaiety in her voice, she was celebrating rainbow memories of gain and loss, triumph and failure, but above all suffering and knowledge in struggle. . .[10]

Very few women in African literature have been portrayed in such glowing epic proportions, as the embodiment of the struggle. Nyakinyua's role as the essence of Gikuyu existence in *Petals of Blood* is exemplified by her participation in the *Theng'eta* and the sacred ritual dance, the *Giriro*. We are told that the *Theng'eta* is the plant "only the old will talk about." Nyakinyua says that they used to brew it before the Europeans came. And they would drink it only when work was finished, and especially after the ceremony of circumcision or marriage or *itwika* and after a harvest. It was when they were drinking *Theng'eta* that poets and singers composed words for a season of Gichandi and the seer voiced his prophecy" (p. 204). Nyakinyua's association with the *Theng'eta* underscores her significance as the embodiment of traditional values. She is the only one in the novel who by virtue of her age and wisdom knows the secret recipe for the preparation of the potent drug which is invaluable to society.

Nyakinyua's special role in the novel is also expressed in her singing. As the lead singer of the *Gitiro* her singular role as the bard of the community is confirmed. Ngugi informs us that "she was good at singing and she threw erotic abuse, compliments, or straight celebratory words with ease . . . Most of the dance songs had a refrain and everybody could join the chorus. It was Njuguna and Nyakinyua who provided the dramatic tension of the opera of eros" (p. 207). In *African Art in Motion*, Robert Farris Thompson reminds us that:

...the chorus forms a kind of melodic handclap, testing and supporting the soloist and his ingenuity. . .Unsurprisingly, the leader of the dancers is, often, the leader of the song. But it is not just the aesthetic impact that is at issue here, but also the moral condition of the singer or the dancer. . .The chorus as in ancient Attic tragedy, is therefore, a direct expression of public sanction and opinion. . .[11]

To illustrate Nyakinyua's special role in the clan as sanctioned by the community and the chorus, Ngugi notes that all "listened to Nyakinyua as she sang the *Gitiro*. She was singing their recent history. She sang of two years of failing rains; of the arrival of daughters and teachers; of the exodus to the city" (p. 209). Nyakinyua's role as the principal articulator and bard of the *Gitiro* justifies the acclaim bestowed on her by the chorus and eventually all the people of Ilmorog. It also typifies her function in the novel as the embodiment of Gikuyu values in accordance with the tribe's mythology. She is the essence of Gikuyu womanhood. Later on, after the sacred dance, she continues her pervasive roles of lending moral, intellectual and physical support to the travellers. In Nyakinyua, we see Ngugi's attempts to juxtapose the sacred, the mortal and the supernatural, all beautifully depicted in a multifaceted character.

In a novel of tradition such as *Petals of Blood*, Nyakinyua's death should not be interpreted as the death of the old ways as Killam has done.[12] Instead, it should be read within the cosmic context of Gikuyu thought. It is true that the *Theng'eta* has been commercialized and adulterated but Ngugi stresses that vestiges of traditional life still thrive in the new Kenya. Nyakinyua now attains a different status in the Gikuyu hierarchy—both living and dead. This special status accorded to her is seen in the climactic moment of the novel. When a series of strikes and revolutionary actions to overthrow the system are called for, Karega invokes her assistance. He has been thrown into jail for inciting the workers and Akinyi is sent to bring him up to date on the condition of the revolution. In the closing dialogue which ensues, Ngugi observes:

> "You'll come back," she said again in a quiet affirmation of faith in eventual triumph. He looked at her, then past her to Mukami of Manguo Marshes and again back to Nyakinyua his mother, and even beyond Akinyi to the future! And he smiled through his sorrow. Tomorrow . . . and he knew he was no longer alone . . . [13]

Hence, even in the forthcoming encounter Nyakinyua's prowess is invoked to continue unequivocal struggle for total liberation. Nyakinyua's death is not the end of the action; it is a transcendence into another realm of Gikuyu cosmology. Nyakinyua's death is analoguous to that of Samba Diallo in Cheikh Hamidou Kane's *L'Adventure Ambiguë*. Rather than the total destruction of traditional values, their deaths should be read as transcendence from one stage to another in the cosmic hierarchies of the respective traditional societies.

Ngugi's latest novel, *Devil on the Cross*, written in Gikuyu during the time of his detention, represents a significant milestone in his artistic development. The reasons are twofold. As he states in his earlier writings, he believes that literature must be a vehicle for the total emancipation of the masses whose dreams of *uhuru* have been betrayed by the Afro-Saxon elites. As a writer, his language or medium of expression is central to the resuscitation of African values which have been suppressed by imperialism. In *Writers in Politics*, Ngugi articulates the symbiotic relationship between literature and society and empasizes the cardinal function of language. He puts it this way:

> Kenyan national literature should mostly be produced in the languages of the various nationalities that make up modern Kenya. Kenyan national literature can only get its stamina and blood by utilizing the rich national traditions of culture and history carried by the languages of all the Kenyan nationalities. In other words, Kenyan national literature can only grow and thrive if it reaches for its roots in the rich languages, cultures and history of the Kenyan peasant masses who are the majority class in each of Kenya's several nationalities.[14]

By using artistic devices from Gikuyu lore in *Devil on the Cross* Ngugi has demonstrated his dedication to the linguistic revolution of Kenyan literature. His depiction of Wariinga as the proponent of traditional culture also enhances this concept.

As well, reflecting his concern for the suppression of women, he creates in Wariinga a very powerful heroine in *Devil on the Cross*. In *Detained: A Writer's Prison Diary*, Ngugi makes the following pertinent observations about Wariinga, language, plot, structure and characters in *Devil on the Cross*:

> ...I had resolved to use a language which did not have a modern novel, a challenge to myself, and a way of affirming my faith in the possibilities of the language of all the different Kenyan nationalities. ...But content—not language and technique—would determine the eventual form of the novel. And content? The Kenyan people's struggle against the neo-colonial form and stage of imperialism. ...[15]

Like Nyakiniyua in *Petals of Blood*, Wariinga is the embodiment of the struggle against corruption and adulteration of foreign cultures. Her fight is primarily against the neo-colonial elites which have subjugated women to secondary roles which are diametrically opposed to their revered status in traditional Gikuyu society. Wariinga's discussion with Gatuiria is illustrative: she attacks the condescending attitudes of men in the New Kenya, while Gatuiria attempts to exonerate the men by putting all the blame on foreign ideologies. Wariinga's response is poignant:

> The abilities and potential of our women are enslaved to the typewriter, the bars or the beds in those hotels we have put up in every corner of the country for the pleasure of the tourists. How insulting to our national dignity that our women have become mere flowers to decorate the beds of foreign tourists. . . . Even you, the Kenyan men, think that there is no job a woman can do other than cooking your food and massaging your bodies. . . Why have people forgotten how Kenyan women used to make guns during the Mau Mau war against the British? . . . . [16]

Devil on the Cross is dedicated "To all Kenyans struggling against the neo-colonial stage of imperialism." Wariinga is the chief architect of this struggle. The narrator of the story is the Gicaandi player who has been implored by Wariinga's mother to divulge the whole truth about the exploitation of her daughter. The narrator observes:

> . . . It was then that I heard the pleading cries of many voices; Gicaandi Player, Prophet of Justice, reveal what now lies concealed by darkness. [17]

The Gicaandi player's narration which ensues is a series of sporadic incidents which crystallize around Wariinga. She is ejected from her apartment by an unscrupulous landlord in Nairobi and fired by a lecherous employer, Boss Kihara, whose advances she had rejected. Unable to conprehend her chain of misfortunes, she concludes that her appearance is the sole cause. The narrator observes "what she hated most was her blackness, so she would disfigure her body with skin lightening creams like Ambi and Snowfire. . . " (p.11). Rescued from a suicide attempt, she decides to return to her family at Ilmorog by *matatu* (local mini-bus). In the course of this journey, she is invited to the Devil's Feast at Ilmorog, the central event of the novel. The participants at the Devil's Feast are domestic and foreign neo-colonial thieves who have stolen enormous wealth from the people. As Gatuiria and Wariinga listen to the testimonies of the exploiters, she is reminded of her own exploitation:

> She regretted having gone back to the cave for the afternoon session. The speeches, the thieves' attire, their hymns of self-praise, all these

things reminded her of the problems she had faced since she became pregnant by the rich old man from Ngorika and gave birth to a baby girl. . . . [18]

Wariinga is a victim of the educational, religious, political and social oppression by foreign and domestic exploiters. It is significant that as in the tradition of the strong Gikuyu women whom Kenyatta portrays in *Facing Mount Kenya*, Wariinga does not succumb to the stifling pressures of her oppressors. She encounters several obstacles and emerges victorious in the end. Although she is seduced by the rich old man and her original dreams of becoming an engineer are temporarily deferred, she fights gallantly and achieves her objectives in the end. Towards the end of the novel, it becomes apparent that she is unquestionably the leader of the new revolutionary movement composed of students, peasants and workers which sweeps through the country. The narrator informs us:

> . . . Wariinga was dressed the Gikuyu way. . . . Around her waist Wariinga had tied a knitted belt of white wool, the two long, loose ends of which fell the length of the cloth to her ankles. On her feet she wore leopard skin sandals. . . . She had Nyori-like earrings. [19]

Her otufit, in contrast to that of westernized Kenyans at the feast is a symbolic affirmation of Gikuyu culture. As the leader of the struggle, it is fitting that she kills the Rich Old Man, the symbol of the decadent, corrupt Kenya, even though he is her fiancé Gatuiria's father. Her active participation in the patriotic songs also underscores her dedication to Gikuyu lore. The following incantations with Gatuiria illustrate the point:

Wariinga:	Hail, the splendour of the land!
	Hail, the land ringed with deep lakes,
	Turkana to Naivasha,
	Nam-Lolwe to Mombasa!
	Hail, this necklace of blue waters!
Gatuiria:	Hail, hail, the shields of the land,
	From Kenya to the Mbiruiru mountains,
	From Kianjahi to the Nyandarua ridges,
	From Wairera to Mount Elgon!
	Hail, nature's defence to our land!
Wariinga:	And Hearken to the call of the land!
	The rivers flowing to the east,
	Ruiru, Cania, Sagana,
	Tana River, Athi River, Kerio River. . . . [20]

Ngugi's Nyakinyua in *Petals of Blood* and Wariinga in *Devil On the Cross* are two powerful heroines who possess the awesome responsibility of saving Kenya from complete foreign domination. It is significant that in attempting to retrieve the glorious age of Gikuyu greatness, Ngugi portrays his heroines in conformity with the traditional, original role assigned to them in Gikuyu mythology. Continuing the responsibilities assigned to them, such as the embodiment of traditional values, the unifying characters in their respective communities who assume epic roles and struggle for unequivocal liberation from foreign ideologies, Mumbi, Nyakinyua and Wariinga are true daughters of Moombi. Their pivotal roles in their respective communities are in conformity with their duties assigned by Murungu in the Gikuyu creation myth.

NOTES

1. Isidore Okpweho, "The Aesthetics of Old African Art," *Okike* 8 (1975), p. 10 See also Stanley Macebuh, "African Aesthetics in Traditional African Art," *Okike* 5 (1972), pp. 13-24.
2. Jomo Kenyatta, *Facing Mount Kenya* (New York: AMS Press, 1978), p. 80.
3. Ngugi Wa Thiong'o, *Detained: A Writer's Prison Diary* (London: Heinemann, 1981), p. 85.
4. James Ngugi, *The River Between* (London: Heinemann, 1965), p. 2.
5. James Ngugi, *A Grain of Wheat* (London: Heinemann, 1967), p. 41.
6. *Ibid.* p. 51.
7. *Ibid.* p. 60.
8. Kenyatta, *op. cit.*, p.6.
9. Jane Bryce, "Profile, Ngugi: My Novel of Blood, Sweat and Tears," *New African* (August, 1982), p. 36.
10. Ngugi Wa Thiong'o, *Petals of Blood* New York: E. P. Dutton, 1978), p. 123.
11. Robert Farris Thompson, *African Art in Motion*(Berkeley: University of California Press, 1974), p. 28.
12. G. D. Killam, *An Introduction to the Writings of Ngugi* (London: Heinemann, 1981), p. 117.
13. Ngugi Wa Thiong'o, *Petals of Blood*, p. 345.
14. Ngugi Wa Thiong'o, *Writers in Politics* (London: Heinemann, 1981), p. 59.
15. Ngugi Wa Thiong'o, *Detained: A Writer's Prison Diary op. cit.*, p. 8.
16. Ngugi Wa Thiong'o, *Devil on the Cross* (London: Heinemann, 1982), p. 14.
17. *Ibid.* p. 8.
18. *Ibid.* p. 182.
19. *Ibid*, p. 242.
20. *Ibid.* p. 128.

The Feminist Impulse and Social Realism in Ama Ata Aidoo's No Sweetness Here and Our Sister Killjoy

Chimalum Nwankwo

Feminism challenges, with justification, the secondary status of women in all societies. Some such challenges in African literature are suspisciously autobiographical and irredeemably subjective. Many are successful in presenting the universal dilemma of heterosexual relationships. Whether we are in the moribund traditional world of Flora Nwapa and Buchi Emecheta or wrapped in the earthy reminiscences of Charity Waciuma, certain crucial questions remain unavoidable. How does one translate individual subjective experience into legitimate questions for social redress? How does the African woman accommodate that individual experience within the stream of history—rapidly changing cultural and socioeconomic circumstances and consequently altered social relations?

If those questions are avoided, we can only read feminist literature in which suffering characters win only our empathy without our sympathy because there are no logical matrices to support the weight of feeling. It seems to me that no social issue successfully arrests attention without the kind of simultaneous involvement and detachment which one finds in this candid passage from Waciuma's *Daughter of Mumbi*:

> For myself, I have decided against polygamy but its rights and wrongs are still being argued furiously in our schools and colleges and debating clubs. There seems to have been a time in our society when there were many more women than men, possibly as a result of raidings. Under these circumstances polygamy may be socially good. Even today our women like to get someone to help them with the hard work of the farm and the house. Polygamy is clearly second nature to most Gikuyu men. I hate it because it hurts the position and dignity of women and exaggerates the selfishness of men.[1]

Here, Waciuma's indignation is subjective but historical and social circumstances are used in such a way that individual preference or predilection is validated.

Ama Ata Aidoo, Ghana's fine female writer perfects Waciuma's approach in her collection of short stories *No Sweetness Here* and novel, *Our Sister Killjoy*. In those works, the problems of the African woman are expressed as integral parts of the problems of colonial and post-colonial Africa. Aidoo's feminist concerns are not treated in isolation from Africa's political instability, the new master complex of the so-called elite, the atavistic problems of the rural African at the cross-roads of history, the fury and impotence of the radical African, the lure of the Western world, and so forth. Such problems are all neatly slotted into a cultural matrix often evoked successfully by the writer's rich personal experience.

There are eleven stories in the *No Sweetness Here* collection. Despite the diversity in themes, all the stories are products of an intense involvement not just in the problem of women but the problem of the Black race as a whole. Aidoo herself justifies her involvement in these words: "I cannot see myself as a writer writing about lovers in Accra because, you see, there are so many problems."[2]

Aidoo's plethora of problems is projected by various narrative voices in shifting perspectives. What this approach accomplishes is to make us accept the author as a detached and neutral observer advancing cases for all the underprivileged in society instead of being a solicitor for any special interests. Consequently we are compelled to suspend our own partisan prejudices and look at all the problems from a fresh and correspondingly neutral vantage point. We trust the "unseen" author and concentrate and rely on her created mouthpieces. The limitations of space will permit a few examples from a variety of impressively crafted situations in the short stories.

In "For Whom Things Did Not Change," the searing irony of independence comes alive in this exchange between a new African master and his African house servant:

'Massa, God knows I know my job.'
'Of course! As a man of the land and your wife's husband you are a man and therefore you do not cook. As a black man facing a white man, his servant, you are a black, not a man, therefore you can cook.'
'Massa, Massa. You call me woman? I swear, by God, Massa, this na tough. I no be woman. God forbid!
"Ah, Zirigu. I am only thinking something out. Ah. . . God is above, I no call you woman. Soon I go talk all for you.'
'But Massa, you no know. Don't call me woman.'
'No, I will not.'

When a black man is with his wife who cooks and chores for him, he is a man. When he is with white folks for whom he cooks and chores, he is a woman. Dear Lord, what then is a black man who cooks and chores for black men?[3]

Eloquently, the colonial and neo-colonial mentality in the minds of both big and small in society is intelligently tied up with the status of women in society. A strategic and apt authorial intrusion hones up the irony. Africans accept inferior status as a result of colonialism. That acceptance is a dangerous social habit like female passivity which lingers despite independence. This affects a national beauty contest in the first story, "Everything Counts," a contest won by a long-haired mulatto. That contest and its preference points at the same problem at the root of the exchange between master and servant in "For Whom Things Did Not Change."

"In the Cutting of a Drink" male chauvinism is illustrated in the city life of a girl called Mansa. Her brother is sent from the village to the city to bring her back. Shocked by the fast-paced and sensual city life, Mansa's brother is convinced that since the women of the city were smoking and drinking, they must all be 'bad' women. His own drinking habit is taken for granted. Such myopic vision of evil also ignores the sociological impetus behind the city lifestyles led by both men and women.

Several social attitudes in "The Message" leave women at the short end of the stick. They are blamed for being fat or thin, for being unable to have normal child deliveries, or for failing to arouse traditional support during emotional emergencies.

"Certain Winds from the South" counterpoints the situation in "In the Cutting of a Drink." This time, men are attracted to the Southern cities in Ghana. Even though no dreams are fulfilled, they keep on going. Their destruction passes blamelessly. M'ma Ansa, the seeing maternal eye of the story knows why. Tradition cannot be broken:

Is his family noted for men that rot? No. Certainly not. It is us who are noted for our unlucky females. There must be something wrong with them. . . (p. 51)

In the story "No Sweetness Here" from which Aidoo's collection takes its title, everything is, as usual, wrong with women. Circumspect traditional narrators play down the injustices in polygamy. So are the abuses and ill-usage which women suffer in marriage. Even women have been socialized into accepting their inferior status happily. An age old traditional value asserts that "a woman must sometimes be a fool" (p. 61). We are not shown instances where men must sometimes be fools to accommodate their female counterparts. Women are the witches nonetheless, and the tragedy is not mitigated by mandatory maternal responsibilities and the value placed on the accidental ability to have male issues. Death strikes the only son of a lonely woman in "No Sweetness Here" and threatens another child of another lonely woman in "A Gift From Somewhere" to accent the enormity of the problems which women have to grapple with in their daily lives.

Collectively, what these stories successfully reveal is that neither choice is a good choice for the African woman. Neither the woman who espouses traditional and conservative wifely values nor the woman who pursues her social pleasures liberally find life rewarding. "Two Sisters" especially confirms that dilemma. No matter how the characters turn out in these stories, Aidoo always succeeds in remaining reasonably detached. When an innocent girl is unfairly punished by her mother in "The Late Bud," we see how this relates to the author's nonjudgmental posture. Individuals always suffer when their worth is based on whether their behaviors fit or do not fit conventional behavior patterns that are by no means permanent. "The Late Bud" is therefore an indirect reference to the way women are socialized into traditional lifestyles and expectations which ultimately contribute to their inferior status in many societies.

The penultimate story in the collection is one of the most circumspect in its method of addressing the underprivileged status of women. "Something to Talk About on the Way to the Funeral" sums up one unspoken contention, that is, whichever way we look at society women cannot escape the vicious cycle of oppression. There are good men and good women, bad women and bad men, but eventually the bad men appear to escape socially unscathed. Not the women. Twice in that story women become premaritally pregnant and twice the men neither accept responsibility nor any punishment. The unfair assumption is that it is 'normal' for a 'bad girl' to become pregnant in that way. Of course, the profligate male is also meant to be just that.

"Other Versions," the final story in the collection depicts other versions of oppression. Capitalism, racism and sexism are shown to be identical in their *modus operandi*. The scenes shift from Africa to America but the human drama is enacted in the same way. In Africa, man and woman, husband and wife labor together to raise a child. The mother is shown to have a selfless interest in the progress of the child while the father expects material compensation. At dinner even in America, the woman is busy serving and the men eat enthusiastically.

This story suggests implicitly that any kind of power is dangerous because the wielder is without the human feeling necessary for good fellowship. The Merrows, who host Kofi, are so condescending to him that he feels, not without justification, that he is being devoured like a dinner.

The final lesson is that feeling, or intuition, a distinctive attribute of women will always triumph over that kind of power which makes men able to oppress women or the rich oppress the poor. Hence the lone woman Kofi meets in the subway ride awakens in Kofi the same kind of love he reserved for his mother.

All of Aidoo's stories share one thing in common. Even though they appear to touch many problems, their focus is the concern for women in society, but the feminist impulse is balanced in such a way that "Aidoo does not allow her criticism of this to become obsessive."[4]

Our Sister Killjoy, like Aidoo's short stories, deals with so many problems. Once again, its success depends largely on the ability of the author to lend all the problems equal spikes. In that regard Ngugi and Sembène come to mind—writers who are fully aware in their works that a campaign for social justice is meaningful only when all disadvantaged people in human society receive undiscriminating attention. It is that same principle which makes Aidoo's works feminist literature with a difference.

Our Sister Killjoy directs its opening barbs at a foe whose national origin or nature ceases to matter as soon as he/she is fully described:

> Nanabanyin Tandoh
> Who knows how to build
> people
> structures
> lives. . .[5]

We can guess immediately that the writer has no sympathy for any form of traditional structure when such structures are used for inhibiting people or artistic expression. Structurally, the work then proceeds to adopt a defiant artistic form in which prose and poetry freely blend with each other. That posture takes care of the feminist campaign for women's freedom but that is only part of the numerous problems in society, hence a quick shift to the doorsteps of the Black race.

We are brought face to face with an unfair social system within which *among other things* women are unnecessarily placed upon pedestals for sympathy which becomes irreverent because of the special attention involved. Consider, for instance, the opening vignette in *Our Sister Killjoy*. The 'heroine' is attending a send-off party or orientation session in Ghana before leaving for Europe on some form of Government sponsorship. The authorities "had pulled strings for her to obtain her passport in a week instead of three months" (p. 8). One of the men, Sammy, reflects a negative national image in his conduct at the party. Sammy "was very anxious to get her to realize one big fact. That she was unbelievably lucky to have been chosen for the trip. And that somehow, going to Europe was altogether more like a dress rehearsal for a journey to paradise" (p. 9). In Sammy, we are dealing with a situation in which an individual conceives an inferior spot for himself relative to others. We could blame or not blame Sammy depending on what we consider responsible for his diffidence and lack of self-worth. Sammy is a product of colonial intimidation and its conscious process of socialization.

In the relationship between men and women in society, identical power complexes emerge. Many women accept inferiority, many men accept mastery as the norm. Also, the distinction which Sammy makes between Africa and Europe is the same kind of distinction which enables one race to oppress the other, rich people to oppress poor people, and men to oppress women. Such relationships, no matter where they begin eventually undercut the supposedly egalitarian aspiration of all societies. This conclusion emerges easily from the end of the first part of *Our Sister Killjoy* where a reference to Sissie in German as a "black girl" (p. 12) activates a negative epiphany in which white people's skins are "the colour of pickled pig parts that used to come from foreign places" (p. 12).

Such deft linkages of feminist concerns with wider social issues opens the second section of *Our Sister Killjoy*. Here, impressions of Germany include the vision of castles superimposed on present realities indicating how long opression has been with human nature:

> And you wondered
> Looking at the river
> How many
> Virgins had
> Our sovereign Lord and Master
> Unvirgined on their nuptial nights
> For their
> Husbands in
> Red-eyed
> Teeth-gnashing
> Agony, their
> Manhoods
> Hurting. . .
> But *'all the days are not equal',* said the old village wall (p. 19)
> (my emphasis).

Of course, the major concern of the author is inequality, so there are discussions of the pitiful and peripatetic Black people from Africa to the diaspora. Their social and economic problems are fitted into the collage of oppression. A few 'Sammys' also reappear as pseudointellectuals who either dream of successful lives or pretend to live successful lives within the intimidating circumstances of Western technological society. Ironically, it is from the pediatric practice of one such medic that we find the root of sexism:

> '500 for a boy
> 400 for a girl'
> Why should it surprise
> That it costs a little more
> To make a boy?)p. 31)

Such measure of worth is universal as we find out from the discussions between Sissie and her lonely German friend, Marija.

Marija is a female prototype of Sammy in her meek acceptance of a subservient role in her society. She speaks of her only child with unconcealed delight. She "was very happy that he was a boy" (p. 51).

Throughout the rest of this second part, other sensitive issues weave in and out of feminist concerns: oppression in South Africa and Rhodesia (now Zimbabwe), cultural and socio-economic problems in Nigeria, Ghana, Upper Volta and so forth. The high point of this section is Marija's display of lesbian affection for Sissie from which the latter recoils with revulsion. Sissie's act is probably in keeping with Aidoo's. It symbolizes the gap between the European female and African female's response. Problems are not solved by running away from them, rather new ones are created as the depicted vagrant Africans in Europe and America may be aware.

Aidoo's "vision of the past and present is essentially tragic,"[6] observes Adelugba on Aidoo's short stories. That tragedy finds full expression when the writer's critical eyes show us Africans in Europe—male and female. In fact the females receive more criticism. Generally the problems of all are traced back to colonialism and its psychological aftermath. We find sarcastic references to Man in this section. There is intelligent linkage again. Man is the Christian Doctor of heart transplant fame but the feat hailed by a Nigerian psuedo-intellectual as scientific triumph is almost debunked as a product of the demonic alter ego of colonialism. Colonialism in turn is seen as Man's expression of an undying love to dehumanize his fellow man. Where Aidoo's logic appears to falter, verve is restored with poetic shots like this:

> to live in peace in man's world
> The virgin Birth
> Is not the only mystery
> One

Simply has to take
By faith. (p. 100)

However uncanny such reductionist approaches may sound, the implied relationship between Christianity, colonialism, capitalism, sexism and oppression appear to hold on well.

The three major sections of *Our Sister Killjoy* merge into each other in whorls. The concerns are the same and the examples used to support those concerns are similar as we shift from one geographical focus to the other. In the final major section, there is greater introspection because of the literary approach—a confrontational "love letter" from Sissie to an imaginary male partner. The letter suggests a way out of the morass—communication between man and woman. The same kind of self search and dialogue is endorsed for similar problems in Ngugi's *A Grain of Wheat*. Such dialogue based on a mutually comprehensible language would then form the secret springboard for the solution of *all* the spiritual and material problems bedeviling the Black world.

Aidoo has dealt with women's problems with arresting wisdom and grace. The conservative dissenter and the radical sympathiser will probably find her approach stimulating. Aidoo's forte is her tremendous *feeling* and honesty of sentiment in expressing those issues. Her works ring like the unimpugnable scold of a justly aggravated parent. "Although writers of both sexes have written about Mother" assesses McCaffrey "the woman writer naturally identifies with her female characters."[7] Aidoo's identification extends beyond "underprivileged womanhood and the arrogance of manhood"[8] to include a variety of social problems across geographical boundaries. Without doubt, like her feminist mouthpiece in her play, *Anowa*, Aidoo has learnt and heard that "in other lands a woman is nothing."[9] Despite that knowledge, "everything counts" in the way she assembles her materials in her short stories and novel, *Our Sister Killjoy*, to register a feminism reasonably in tune with social realities.

Certain problems remain apparent in spite of Aidoo's strengths. It is still difficult to avoid some degree of prejudice and presumption when dealing with issues concerning men and women especially in African societies. We still have to deal with psychological and cultural questions many of which do not appear within the scope of Aidoo's discourse. It is not enough to indicate that if human beings have values placed on their heads, 'boys' are always more 'costly' than girls. We must be willing to deal with certain root fears and desires. For instance, the predominantly African assumption that women eventually marry and leave their birth families to assist in building their husbands' families. That cultural attitude and the African love for large families still make polygamy possible in so-called modern African societies. We have to deal with the desocialization of traditional African males who still cling to the chauvinistic guns of the past despite changed and changing social relations. We must also extend our attention to certain rural circumstances where social relations remain affected by taxing agrarian occupations which restrict women to specific economic and social positions. Finally, the past is a valid reference point for understanding present reality and projecting future directions. The key to a means for resolving our problems is a reasonable degree of honesty in facing all of those problems. This is where Aidoo takes the lead among other African women in search for social justice through creative literature.

NOTES

1. Charity Waciuma. *Daughter of Mumbi* (Nairobi: East African Publishing House, 1962), p. 11
2. Dennis Duerden & Cosmo Pieterse ed. *African Writers Talking* (London: Heinemann Educational Books Ltd., 1972), p. 19.
3. Ama Ata Aidoo. *No Sweetness Here* (London: Longman Group Ltd., 1970), p. 17. All page references onward are to same text.
4. Dapo Adelugba. "Literature as Social Criticism." *Ba Shiru*, 6, 1 (1974), 16.
5. Ama Ata Aidoo. *Our Sister Killjoy* (New York: Nok Publishers International Ltd., 1979), Dedication. Further page references to same text.
6. Adelugba, p. 16.
7. Kathleen McCaffrey. "Images of the Mother in the Stories of Ama Ata Aidoo" *Africa Woman*, 23 (1979), 40.
8. Ezekiel Mphahlele's Introduction to *No Sweetness Here* (New York: Doubleday, 1972), p. x.
9. Ama Ata Aidoo. *Anowa* (London: Longman Group Ltd., 1970), p. 52.

The Concept of Choice
In Mariama Bâ's Fiction

Irène Assiba d'Almeida

One of the key concepts that emerges from Mariama Bâ's novels is that of choice. This is most striking in *Une si longue lettre* where the recurrence of words like *le choix, choisir, j'ai choisi, j'ai décidé, ma décision, j'ai voulu, je ni' ai pas voulu*, [the choice, to choose, I have chosen, I have decided, my decision, I wished, I did not wish to] is in itself indicative of the importance of choice for Mariama Bâ. In *Un chant écarlate*, even though words pertaining to choice are less recurrent, crucial choices are constantly being made throughout the novel. The act of choosing is shown as being pivotal in human experience. It is indeed a powerful act which gives shape and direction to human existence.

In *Une si longue lettre* the protagonist is Ramatoulaye, a Senegalese woman who has just been widowed. In a long flash-back she recounts her story through the medium of a letter written to Aïssatou, her best friend. The letter is essentially about how Ramatoulaye manages to survive socially, economically and above all emotionally after Modu, her husband, takes a second wife. Modu's second marriage is a double slap in Ramatoulaye's face. Indeed, in contracting this marriage without telling his first wife until the very day it happens Modu betrays their thirty years of marital life and the twelve children they had together. To make matters worse, Modu chooses as a second wife Binetou, a friend and schoolmate of their own daughter.

161

Ramatoulaye chooses Aïssatou as a confidante not only because they are friends from childhood but also because Aïssatou has gone through the same experience. The book then deals with the isolation of married women who refuse to accept polygamy in a society where it is sanctioned by Islam.

It is important to focus on the choices made by female characters in *Une si longue lettre* because women are definitely at the centre of the novel. Ramatoulaye is portrayed as a strong, dignified woman who is confronted with a number of options throughout her life; she is therefore called upon to make vital choices.

In a society where parents have a great influence on the choice of one's spouse, Ramatoulaye rejects her mother's preference for Daouda Dieng, a medical doctor who wants to marry her. Instead, her choice goes to Modu Fall who was then a high-school student like her and who will eventually become a lawyer. In explaining her choice Ramatoulaye gives credit to the liberating influence of school:

> Liberée donc des tabous qui frustrent, apte à l'analyse, pourquoi devrais-je suivre l'index de ma mère pointée sur Daouda Dieng, Célibataire encore, mais trop mûr pour mes dix-huit hivernages.[1]
> [Thus, free from fustrating taboos and capable now of discernment, why should I follow my mother's finger pointing at Daouda Dieng, still a bachelor but too mature for my eighteen years.]

When she finishes school Ramatoulaye chooses a profession that she likes. Even though she is aware that teaching is often unrewarding and unrewarded, she chooses to become a teacher. She is dedicated to the acquisition of knowledge for all and emphasizes the importance of education for women in particular.

When she is told that her husband has married a second wife, Ramatoulaye chooses to receive the news with great calm and dignity, keeping to herself the pain and despair she feels:

> Je m'appliquais à endiguer mon remous intérieur. Surtout ne pas donner à mes visiteurs la satisfaction de raconter mon désarroi. Sourire, prendre l'évènement à la légère. (p. 58)
> [I forced myself to check my inner agitation. Above all, I must not give my visitors the pleasure of relating my distress. Smile, take the matter lightly.]

Once the news is broken to her, Ramatoulaye spends a long time thinking about the next step to take. Now that she has a co-wife who could be her daughter, will she leave her husband's household to express her disapproval or will she stay? After a thorough analysis of her new situation and in a very lucid manner, she decides to stay. Her choice is made even more difficult because her children, her daughters in particular, cannot comprehend Ramatoulaye's choice. In the past, they had heard their mother rise up against the iniquities of polygamy. Indeed, when Mawdo, Aïssatou's husband took a second wife and wanted to justify himself and ask for understanding, Ramatoulaye was outraged:

> J'étais offusquée. Il me demandait compréhension. Mais comprendre quoi? La suprématie de l'instinct? Le droit à la trahison? La justification du désir de changement? Je ne pouvais être l'alliée des instincts polygamiques. . . (p. 62)
> [I was shocked. He was asking me for understanding. But understand what? The supremacy of 'natural' urges? The right of betrayal: Justification for the desire for change? I couldn't be the ally of polygamous urges.]

At that time, little does Ramatoulaye suspect that she also will have to go through the trauma of the numerous women who were "méprisées, reléguées ou échangées, dont on s'est séparé comme d'un boubou usé ou démodé" (p. 62). ["despised, relegated or exchanged, who were abandoned like a worn-out or out-dated boubou." (caftan worn by West African Muslim women especially)]

After Modu's death, Ramatoulaye chooses to remain single. She refuses to accept Tamsir's marriage proposal. Tamsir, who is her brother-in-law, could, according to custom, marry her, but he only wants to do so for economic reasons. Ramatoulaye, who knows this, expresses her total rejection with great indignation:

> Tu oublies que j'ai un coeur, une raison, que je ne suis pas un objet que l'on se passe de main en main. Tu ignores ce que se marier signifie pour moi: c'est un acte de foi et d'amour, un don total de soi à l'être que l'on a choisi et qui vous a choisi. (J'insistais sur le mot choisi). p. 85.
> [You forget that I have a heart, a mind, that I am not an object to be passed from hand to hand. You don't know what marriage means to me: it is an act of faith and of love, the total surrender of oneself to the person one has chosen and who has chosen you. (I emphasized the word 'chosen'.)]

In the same way, but for different reasons she turns down Daouda Dieng. She was Daouda's first love and he proposes to her again. Even though she knows that Daouda is loving and reliable, she likes him but is not in love with him. Another reason why she rejects him is that he is already married. She says: "Abandonnée hier par le fait d'une femme, je ne peux allégrement m'introduire entre toi et ta famille" (p. 100). [Abandoned yesterday because of a woman, I cannot lightly bring myself between you and your family.] By taking this stand Ramatoulaye implies that a greater solidarity among women is needed to alleviate the agony women go through in polygamous situations.

As far as her relationship with her children is concerned Ramatoulaye tries to give them a fairly liberal education. Her last choice consists in standing by her second daughter when she discovers her to be pregnant:

> Je ne pouvais pas l'abandonner, comme le dictait l'orgueil. . . La vie qui frémissait en elle m'interrogeait. Elle grouillait pour s'épanouir. Elle vibrait pour demander protection. . . Ma décision d'aider et de protéger émergeait du tumulte. Elle se fortifiait au fur et à mesure que j'essuyais [ses] larmes, au fur et à mesure que je caressais [son] front brûlant. (pp. 121-2)
> [I could not abandon her, as pride would have me do. . . The life that fluttered in her was questioning me. It was eager to blossom. It vibrated, demanding protection . . . My decision to help and protect emerged from the tumult. It gained strength as I wiped the tears, as I caressed the burning brow.]

The second main character in *Une si longue lettre*, Aïssatou also had to make significant choices. Her husband Mawdo married a second wife because Tante Nabou, his mother, had never approved of her son's first marriage. He, a prince, had married a goldsmith's daughter. Tante Nabou saw this marriage as a disgrace to the family's social status and decided to plan her son's second marriage in a thorough manner. When Mawdo gave in to his mother's pressures Aïssatou chose to leave with her four sons, and this she did with great dignity:

> Les princes dominent leurs sentiments pour honorer leurs devoirs. Les "autres" courbent leur nuque et acceptent en silence un sort qui les brime. . . Tu veux dissocier l'Amour tout court de l'amour physique. . . Si tu peux procréer sans aimer, rien que pour assouvir l'orgueil d'une mère déclinante, je te trouve vil. . . je me dépouille de ton amour, de ton nom. Vêtue du seul habit valable de la dignité, je poursuis ma route. (p. 50)
> [Princes master their feelings to fulfill their duties. 'Others' bend their heads and, in silence, accept a destiny that oppresses them. . . You want to draw a line between heartfelt love and physical love. . . If you can procreate without loving, merely to satisfy the pride of your declining mother, then I find you despicable . . . I am stripping myself of your love, your name. Clothed in my dignity, the only worthy garment, I go my way.]

Aïssatou then chooses to build a second life on her own. She finds that, in her society, class differences can be an obstacle to self-fulfillment. However, she knows that education is attainable by all and can serve as a levelling asset; therefore, she decides to go back to her studies. She then goes to France to train as an interpreter and eventually finds a job at the Senegalese Embassy in Washington, D.C.

What then is the significance of all these choices? In this novel Mariama Bâ affirms that "chaque femme fait de sa vie ce qu'elle souhaite" (p. 128) [Each woman makes of her life what she wishes"]. This affirmation is very reminiscent of Jean-Paul Sartre's pronouncements on choice. Indeed, in *L'être et le néant*[2] and, in more simple terms in *L'existentialisme est un humanisme*[3] Sartre posits that human beings are nothing else than what they make of themselves. They are the sum total of their choices and through the act of choosing, they create themselves. Sartre, then, views choice as essential for the creation of self. Even though Mariama Bâ does not go as far as to make choice a metaphysical concept like Sartre who thinks that human beings are condemned to choose, she does consider choice to be of vital importance, to be the ultimate affirmation of self. It is indeed through choice that Ramatoulaye and Aïssatou find the strength and courage to face problems that overburden women, to overcome what threatens to deny the self. It is also through choice that they arrive at self-realization. However, this is not achieved without pain, without conflict.

More than any other character, Ramatoulaye is the one who constantly battles with conflictual situations within and outside herself. No doubt her choices are informed by her unrelenting desire for change but they are also mediated by a strong streak of conservatism. What Ramatoulaye really wants is to be a modern woman, conscious of her rights as an individual and determined to fight for these rights. However, being a modern woman is at once seductive and threatening. Seductive because it opens up to the possibility for freedom and change, threatening because potentially, it has the power to destabilize the ground on which she stands. And so, Ramatoulaye is always torn between modernity and tradition. This *déchirement* ["tearing apart"] is characteristic of women and men of her generation as she rightly points out:

> Nous étions tous d'accord qu'il fallait bien des craquements pour asseoir la modernité dans les traditions. Ecartelés entre le passé et le présent, nous déplorions les "suintements" qui ne manqueraient pas. . . Nous dénombrions les pertes possibles. Mais nous sentions que plus rien ne serait comme avant. Nous étions pleins de nostalgie, mais résolument progressistes. (p. 32)
> [We all agreed that much dismantling was needed to introduce modernity within our traditions. Torn between the past and the

present, we deplored the 'hard sweat' that would be inevitable. We counted the possible losses. But we knew that nothing would be as before. We were full of nostalgia but were resolutely progressive.]

Indeed, Ramatoulaye is progressive but not radical and her choices bear this out. For instance, she is fiercely against polygamy; yet she accepts it implicitly by choosing to stay with Modu after he marries Binetou. In his "La polygamie et la révolte de la femme africaine moderne", Cyril Mokwenyé contrasts Aïssatou and Ramatoulaye's reactions to polygamy by saying:

A travers les deux femmes nous avons deux personnages symboliques. Aïssatou symbolise la jeune femme capricieuse et peu patiente qui réagit trop spontanément, alors que Ramatoulaye est le symbole de la femme qui ayant investi dans son mariage, est ouverte aux compromis. Elle ne veut pas agir sans une réflexion profonde. Sa révolte sera une révolte psychologique. . .[4]
[Through the two women we have two symbolic characters. Aïssatou symbolizes the capricious, impatient young woman who reacts too spontaneously, while Ramatoulaye is the symbol of the woman, who, having invested in her marriage, is open to compromise. She does not want to react without deep reflection. Her rebellion will be a psychological one.]

The truth of the matter, however, is that Aïssatou is in no way whimsical or overly impatient. If she wastes no time in making her decision, it is not because she has not pondered the situation; it is because she goes *all the way* in her protest. For her, and this is her choice, divorcing her husband is the only acceptable solution to the problem she is confronted with.

Mokwenyé also praises Ramatoulaye for choosing to abide by the dictates of her religion and for staging what he calls a "passive resistance", which according to him produces positive results. He contends that by staying in the household Ramatoulaye forces Modu into an "exil conjugal". The point to be made here is that if Modu is ill at ease in his own home, his exile is indeed a rosy one. After all, all he really wants is to be with his new bride and learn how to be young again! And so, by a curious reversal of situation, it is Modu who decides to leave the household. Thus, Ramatoulaye ends up being on her own even though she has not had the courage to make the necessary choice.

Another conflict that affects choice is the one which emerges from her relationship with her children and with her daughters in particular. She wishes to give them a liberal education; yet she has problems letting them wear pants, seeing them smoke. She is lost in disbelief because her daughter who is well brought up, efficient and considerate has allowed herself to get pregnant, as if these things were mutually exclusive. She uses this incident, however, to show how unfair it is to throw pregnant girls out of school while their male counterparts are left to continue with their studies.

An area which shows the split in Ramatoulaye's behavior is that of her ideas on women issues. On the one hand, she stresses the importance of education for women and the necessity to take a more significant part in politics so as to have a say in the decision-making process. Ramatoulaye describes the plight of working women who have a double yoke to bear and she also demands recognition for the interminable work done by women who stay at home. Yet, on the other hand, she has internalized a number of stereotypes about women and women's behavior. For instance she tells Aïssatou: "Je t'envie de n'avoir mis au monde que des garcons" [I envy you for having had only boys"] (p. 127). Also, while speaking of the responsibility embedded in being a mother as well as the exaltation that motherhood provides she says: "Passionante aventure que de faire d'un bébé *un homme* sain" ["A thrilling adventure, to make a whole *man* from a baby"] (p. 71. My emphasis).

If Ramatoulaye is the persona that represents the writer's point of view, then Mariama Bâ belongs to a generation of African female novelists whose writing is characterized by a certain malaise. This malaise emerges from the dilemma women face in wanting to keep traditions while, at the same time, wanting to reject what, in society, ties women down. To find an acceptable and viable *modus vivendi* between the forces of tradition and the realities of the present is almost a *tour de force*. That is why, a writer like Flora Nwapa, for instance, sets her novels *Idu* and *Efuru* in the traditional context and deals in both novels with the importance of bearing children in African society. Indeed she takes refuge in subject matters that are safe in that they do not demand that the order of things be challenged, let alone subverted.

From Flora Nwapa's early writings to Mariama Bâ, a lot of ground has been covered. However, Mariama Bâ does not go all the way in her protest and she is aware of it. Ramatoulaye, her mouthpiece, is acutely aware that men's power on the one hand and the weight of traditions on the other coalesce to slow down women's progress:

> Je sais mouvant le terrain des acquis, difficile la survie des conquêtes: les contraintes sociales bousculent toujours et l'égoisme mâle résiste. (p.129)
> [I know that the field of our gains is unstable, the retention of conquests difficult: social constraints are ever-present, and male egoism resists.]

Given this situation, it becomes easier to understand the motives that lead Ramatoulaye to make what could be called a forward-backward motion. Indeed, when she makes two steps forward, she almost immediately makes one step backward. It then becomes clear that, in *Une si longue lettre*, choice is not perceived as a given but as a long, painful and conflictual process which ultimately has the potency to upset established rules and internalized conditioning.

Un chant écarlate deals with choice in a very different way. Here all the characters are called upon to make choices and they are all affected by each other's choices. The story revolves round two young students in philosophy who are in love and want to be married. He is Ousmane Guèye whose father is an important figure in the Muslim community and whose mother is an ordinary woman, well grounded in the African traditions. His friend, Mireille de la Vallée is a young French girl who comes from a bourgeois family. Her father is a diplomat working at the French Embassy in Dakar. All his beautiful speeches about the necessity of breaking racial barriers are put to a test that reveals his true self the day he discovers that his daughter is having an affair with a Black man. His reaction is instantaneous: he sends his daughter back to France that very day, and Mireille's mother, who is a very submissive wife, has no say in this decision. However, this separation only succeeds in strengthening Ousmane and Mireille's relationship. At the end of their studies they get married in Paris, in the Muslim tradition.

It is when they go back to Dakar that they have to deal with serious cultural clashes that cause their relationship to deteriorate to such a point that Ousmane has to seek for his emotional as well as what he calls his cultural needs outside the home. He finds them in Ouleymatou, a childhood girlfriend whom he eventually marries unbeknown to his first wife. When Mireille discovers the marriage, she is first incredulous, she is then totally broken, turns hysterical and finally becomes stark mad. She kills her son Gorgui, whom she says will never fit in any society, be it white or Black. She then attempts to kill her husband as he comes back from his second wife's house in the wee hours. Eventually, the French Embassy sends Mireille back to France where she will end up in a lunatic asylum while the reader is left to imagine what will happen to Ousmane.

All the characters in *Un chant écarlate* make important choices. Ousmane chooses to marry Mireille, and to remain faithful to his culture. He also chooses to marry a second wife even though his father who is a staunch Muslim married only one wife. However, Ousmane feels justified in his action not only because Islam allows it but also because

> Ouleymatou était devenue sa vraie moitié, celle en qui il reconnaissait son prolongement. Elle était à la fois. . . sa racine, sa souche, son élan, sa floraison. . . Les liaient. . . leurs origines: les mêmes ancêtres, les mêmes cieux. La même terre! Les mêmes traditions! La même sève des moeurs imprégnait leur âme.[5]
> [Ouleymatou had become his true other half, the one in which he recognized his extension. She was at once. . . his root, his stock, his

spirit, his blossoming. . . They shared common origins: the same ancestors, the same heavens. The same earth! The same traditions! The same cultural sap courses through their souls.]

Mireille, on the other hand chooses to study in Dakar so she can see Ousmane; she also chooses to be converted to Islam without measuring the implications of such a conversion. She also chooses to remain faithful to her own culture. Her efforts of adaptation to Senegalese lifestyle are short-lived and frustrated by antagonistic forces.

Mr. and Mrs. de la Vallée choose to send their daughter to France and to reject her when they eventually learn that she married Ousmane without their consent. In fact, it is Mr. de la Vallée who makes these choices. His wife goes along with him even though, deep down, she does understand her daughter.

Yaye Khady, Ousmane's mother, chooses to reject Mireille even before she meets her, just because she is white, and she chooses to encourage and accept Ouleymatou as her son's true wife.

Soukeyna, Ousmane's sister and the only one who makes friends with Mireille, chooses to tell her sister-in-law that Ousmane married a second wife. Finally, Ouleymatou chooses to seduce Ousmane and even calls in the Griots who tell him how he went astray by marrying a Frenchwoman:

> Tu es prince Lébou.
> Une Blanche a renié sa patrie pour te suivre
> Mais mieux que la blanche,
> La fille noire te convient. (p. 180)
> [You are Prince Lebou
> A White has renounced her country to follow you
> But better than the White girl
> The Black girl is suited to you.]

After an elaborate seduction, Ouleymatou chooses to marry Ousmane.

Even though the concept of choice underlies both novels, there is an essential difference in the way it is treated. In *Une si longue lettre* there is no doubt that Modu, Binetou, Tante Nabou and Mawdo make choices that affect others. However, the emphasis is clearly on the two main protagonists, Ramatoulaye and Aïssatou. Here, choice is essentially seen as it affects the individual lives of these two women, as it allows for growth, as it activates the development of consciousness. In *Un chant écarlate* on the other hand choices affect not only the individuals who make them but also the people who are close to them.

In choosing to marry Mireille, Ousmane also chooses to sever her from her cultural milieu and to create a cleavage between his family and him. In choosing to remain faithful to his culture, Ousmane pays little attention to the fact that Mireille also has a culture. He brings the discussion to a close by peremptorily saying: "En épousant un homme, on épouse aussi sa manière de vivre." ["In choosing a husband, one is also choosing a way of life."] (p. 133). In choosing to marry a second wife, Ousmane also chooses to deny Mireille his love and attention and ultimately to shatter her life. On the other hand Mireille cannot stand Ousmane's ways. She thinks that communal life is a form of parasitism and resents her mother-in-law's violation of her privacy. After a few attempts at adaptation, Mireille also chooses to remain faithful to her Western culture. By doing so she widens the gap between Ousmane and her and antagonizes Ousmane's friends and mother.

The choices made by Ousmane and Mireille's parents affect the couple. In choosing to reject their daughter, Mr. and Mrs. de la Vallée deny her a chance to turn to them in periods of crisis. In choosing to reject Mireille, Yaye Khady makes Mireille's integration into Senegalese society more arduous and sows the seeds of discord within the couple. In choosing to encourage Ouleymatou, Yaye Khady also chooses to affect Mireille's emotional balance. Djibril Guèye, Ousmane's father, makes no choice because he sees all that happens as being ordained by God. In making no choice, he still chooses to follow the course of events.

In choosing to seduce and marry Ousmane, Ouleymatou deeply affects Mireille's life. Finally Soukeyna's decision to inform Mireille of Ousmane's second marriage is made out of friendship but it is nonetheless responsible for Mireille's tragic end.

It is important to note that all the choices made in *Un chant écarlate* converge to bring about Mireille's destruction. Ironically, and even though this is only implicit in the novel, Mireille's destruction will affect all the people who have made these choices. It then becomes clear that the concept of choice in this novel is closely related to the concept of responsibility. Here again Sartre comes to mind for he feels that it is impossible to dissociate choice from responsibility:

> . . .Man is responsible for what he is. . .When we say that man is responsible for himself, we do not mean that he is responsible only for his own individuality, but that he is responsible for all men.[6]

In *Un chant écarlate* the link between choice and responsibility is strongly made. It is responsibility toward others because choices, even if they are made by individuals, in isolation, can have an impact on other people's lives. It is also responsibility toward self for there is no doubt that Mireille and Ousmane are both weak, self-centered individuals who lack what it takes to meet each other half-way. And so, as main characters they are not only responsible for what happens to others as a result of their choices but they are also responsible for what happens to them as individuals, as a couple, as members of the larger society.

In conclusion it is possible to say that in *Une si longue lettre* Aïssatou and Ramatoulaye have made different choices in similar situations. However, what is important is that the choices have been made. For too long a time women have been denied to choose the course of their lives, even though choice is at the center of what gives significance to human existence. In this novel Mariama Bâ shows clearly that women do have a deep consciousness of the options opened to them and that they are willing to make the choices that will make their lives more wholesome, no matter what the consequences might be. There is also a strong intimation that the generation of Daba (Ramatoulaye's daughter) will go even further in their choices and will deal with that concept in a more radical way.

In *Un chant écarlate* Mariama Bâ widens the scope of the concept of choice by showing how all human beings, female and male, Black and white deal with that concept and the consequences that choice can have on the self and on the human community.

After a long silence, women like Mariama Bâ have chosen to talk. Their voices have sprung up to revive the role that women have traditionally played as story tellers. They now tell their "modern stories" through the medium of the written word. Using their female sensibility, they approach womens' issues from within, offering a female way of looking at the world. This is indeed a choice that needed to be made.

NOTES

1. Mariama Bâ. *Une si longue lettre*. Dakar, Abidjan: Les Nouvelles Editions Africaines, 1980, p. 28. All subsequent quotations from this work will be indicated by the page number within the text.
2. Jean-Paul Sartre. *L'être et le néant*. Paris: Gallimard, 1949.
3. _____. *L'existentialisme est un humanisme*. Paris: Editions Naget, 1946. Translated into english by Philip Mairet under the title of *Existentialism and Humanism*, London: Methuen & Co. Ltd., 1948.
4. Cyril Mokwenyé. "La polygamie et la révolte de la femme africaine moderne: une lecture d'*Une si longue lettre* de Mariama Bâ" in *Peuples Noirs, Peuples Africains*, no. 31, (janvier-fevrier 1983) p. 91.
5. Mariama Bâ. *Un chant écarlate*. Dakar, Abidjan: Les Nouvelles Editions Africaines, 1981, p. 183. All subsequent quotations from this work will be indicated by the page number within the text.
6. Jean-Paul Sartre. *Existentialism and Humanism*. Op. cit. p. 30.

Reintegration With The Lost Self: A Study of Buchi Emecheta's Double Yoke

Marie Linton Umeh

Double Yoke is a love story told in the blues mode. The story laments a loss; yet it sings a love song. Its theme of the perilous journey of love, is a major preoccupation in author Buchi Emecheta's dramatic work. On an equally fundamental level, *Double Yoke* describes the tragic limitations of Nigerian women in pursuit of academic excellence and the anxiety of assimilation. Similar to her earlier novels, *Double Yoke* assesses the predicament of women in Africa. By describing the sexual and cultural politics in Nigerian society, Emecheta again campaigns against female subjugation and champions her case for female emancipation. Nko, the author's intellectually oriented heroine, provides some insight into the psyche of modern African women who are encumbered by traditional African misconceptions attached to the university-educated female.

Firstly, *Double Yoke* is a love story but with tragic implications. Buchi Emecheta is at her best in describing the anxiety lovers often experience because of mutual distrust at one time or another and the inability to reconcile their difficulties. According to the author, love, if betrayed, is directly responsible for the misery that afflicts the human soul. The tale of the terrifying journey of the possibilities and failures of love is then at the dramatic center of *Double Yoke*.

This theme of romantic conflict is not entirely new in African literature. The principle characters in Chinua Achebe's *No Longer At Ease*, Chukwuemeka Ike's *Toads For Supper*, Okot p'Bitek's *Song of Lawino*, and Flora Nwapa's *One Is Enough*, similarly narrate their personal traumas over lost loves. Diverging from her theme that Igbo women are enslaved to Igbo traditions which subjugate them to certain customs, Emecheta extends her metaphor by stating that Nigerian men are similarly enslaved. Ete Kamba, a central character in the story, is described as a traditional African man who is sorely disappointed when he falls in love with Nko, a modern African girl. Because Nko gives herself to Ete Kamba who has just gained admission into the university she is faced with untold hardships. Ete Kamba's love for Nko turns to distrust. He begins to question her virginity. This develops into a kind of neurosis, forcing him to lose sleep and cease concentration on his studies. He tells Nko, "You are not a virgin are you? Were you a virgin? There was not a drop of blood. You are a prostitute, a whore and you keep putting on this air of innocence as if you were something else."[1] Their problems are magnified when Ete Kamba consults a spiritual advisor, the Reverend Professor Ikot, who dissuades him from the love affair with ulterior motives:

Nko is from my part. She is a true Efik from Duke Town, and women from our part have always brought great honour to their families. She will be in this university in a year or two. So what do you want a graduate wife for? Why don't you get a trained teacher or a nurse or something. Let us pray my boy, so that God will give you the wisdom to learn to sew your coat according to your measurement. (p. 90).

It is not long before Ikot succeeds in seducing and impregnating Nko. Ete Kamba, unnerved by Nko's air of independence and self-assertiveness, had set the stage for this fall. He therefore expresses his grief and the pain he feels about what has happened to him to Miss Bulewao, a character in the novel apparently speaking the mind of author Emecheta.[2]

The significant tragic implication here is that Ete Kamba is not the modern African man. Despite his pursuit of western ideals, i.e., a university education and a university-educated wife, his reliance on traditional African mores stands out. His quest for a humble, chaste wife signifies one of Nigerian society's myopic perceptions of the making of the perfect African woman. Emecheta's dominant realization of women is that of a being limited by the dictates of men in a patriarchal society. Nko, with a feminist orientation, probes the root of things, questions where she is going and attempts to control her fate. Ete Kamba cannot cope with Nko's heightened sensibilities. He is unable to love and live with Nko on a plane of equality and mutual respect. Herein lies the tragedy. Although Ete Kamba wants a beautiful, educated and sophisticated wife to grace his home, his ideal seems to be the quiet, submissive, innocent female who looks after the children and the house, cooks, earns money and puts his interests before her own.[3] For the African woman, the implications are more devastating. The African woman more so than the African man, is caught in a bind. In order to be liberated and fulfilled as a woman she must renounce her African identity because of the inherent sexism of many traditional African societies. Or, if she wishes to cherish and affirm her 'Africanness' she must renounce her claims to feminine independence and self-determination. Either way she stands to lose; either way she finds herself diminished, impoverished. It is Emecheta's growing awareness of the futility of attempting to resolve this dilemma that accounts for the growing bitterness that engulfs Nko.[4] Emecheta, a sensitive artist and student of society, distinguishes between the idealization of womanhood and the realities of a woman's place in the African community. Ete Kamba's ambivalence towards Nko mirrors African society's unconscious hypocrisy towards women. It never occurs to Ete Kamba that it was Nko's innocence and purity of spirit that attracted her to him. It never occurs to him that he practically raped Nko the night she lost her virginity to him and that any resistance against his desperate advances would have been futile. He deflowers Nko, only to turn around and search for another virgin queen: someone he feels he can respect, someone his children can call mother. Ete Kamba's double standards are simply co-existent realities in his environment. The conflicting standards in Ete Kamba's perception of women is shared by his roommates. Their collective image of females is an idealized rather than a realistic portrait of the African woman's situation.[5] The African man's perception of the educated African woman often ignores some of the realities of her sex.

Emecheta in another episode, illustrates how innocent young females are often turned into prostitutes at places one would least expect: academic institutions. When approached by the Reverend Professor Ikot, Nko retorts:

> Most girls here come to read for their degrees. If they become what you think, which is 'prostitues Nigerian style', it is because people like you made them so. But with me sir, you are not going to be let off lightly. My reward is a good degree. I did not believe in bottom power until today sir. (p. 141).

One then asks, why does Nko submit to Reverend Ikot's advances? Why does she stray away from those goals she so clearly defined for herself? What is peculiar in all of Emecheta's novels up to the present time is a consistent female view that sometimes mars her art by its emphasis on the all-suffering, victimized female. However, author Emecheta generally attains a balance in that she looks at women not in the narrow advocacy of feminine rights but in a wider context of a concern for the female and by implication the species they represent. In describing some of the injustices that have been transcended, she captures the quintessential core of female discrimination in a male dominated society as it has remained among the Nigerian ethnic groups and most other patriarchal social organizations. The answer also lies here. Nko is about to fully participate in Nigerian elitist society to a level much greater than most women. Perhaps the thought of this participation places too great a psychological strain on her. She lives with the fear of disappointing her parents and community by not suceeding in earning a good degree and helping her parents to train her younger sisters and brothers. She is obsessed with succeeding. It can also be said that she has internalized a narrow and limiting role pattern which casts her as a woman into subservient behaviour. Nko's inconsistent behaviour stems from her being brought up both formally and informally to believe that this is a man's world and that she is merely a woman, a second-class citizen. Feelings of anxiety about a degree, indoctrination into acceptable female roles and Ete Kamba's ambivalent and troubled feelings towards her, pressure Nko into surrendering herself to Reverend Professor Ikot. One needs courageous determination and encouragement to stir oneself out of being programmed into passivity and psychological servitude. A related problem is the questioning and disavowal of a woman's genuine, individual merit. It is almost a common assumption that a woman's merit resides in her sexuality. This of course is a threat to the concept of female merit in institutions of higher learning. Thus Nko's reliance on stereotyped female wiles at this point is out of character. Additionally, it conflicts with Nko's inclination towards feminism, vividly portrayed in earlier parts of the novel in her struggles for equality and self-respect with Ete Kamba.

This idea which Emecheta explores introduces the elements of women's liberation and the correct role for women in Africa. The right path for them is not clear as Mrs. Nwaizu, a character in the novel, puts it: "We are still a long way from that yet. Here feminism means everything the society says is bad in women. Independence, outspokenness, immorality, all the ills you can think of. . ." (p. 104). The feminine protest in this novel is not as subtle as in Flora Nwapa's *Idu* and *Efuru* or Efua Sutherland's *Edufa*. Nko vehemently protests against female victimization which brings her psychological strains. Similarly, university women today in Nigeria find themselves at the crossroads of losing their identity in male-female relationships (marriage) or attaining self realization by earning a degree thus forfeiting family life. In any event, in the novel the basic illustration is that Emecheta attacks certain masculine preserves such as having children out of wedlock and expectations of humility in women especially in the traditional sense. Miss Bulewao asks Ete Kamba, "Are you strong enough to be a modern African man? Nko is already a modern African lady, but you are still lagging . . . oh so far, far behind." (p. 162). Nko's characterization of a modern African lady though is not totally impressive. Moral laxity need not be equated with the New African woman. Ironically, Emecheta in her plot does not promote female liberation in Africa. Instead, she strengthens the belief of conservative Nigerians who fear that female education leads women to all sorts of corruption.

This leads us to another issue raised in *Double Yoke*, namely, the limitations of females in pursuit of self-realization in Nigerian society. This subjugation of women consistently emerges as one explores Nigerian society's history of raising women to perform the narrow, unidimensional, traditional role of wife/mother, while at the same time encouraging the male to expand and explore his capabilities to the fullest. Hence, society's division of sex roles limits woman's human capacity for the pursuit of self-realization thus destroying any attempt at fulfillment outside the family.[6] In *Double Yoke* Emecheta unmasks areas of human experience so far subsumed under the myth of the decorous stable institution of marriage as witnessed in the social organization of Okonkwo's household in *Things Fall Apart* and Ezeulu's most equitable household in *Arrow of God*. Through Emecheta's characters we learn that this norm, prescribed by traditional African society is in fact abnormal. In *Double Yoke*, the female psyche emerges as an important quarry for concern. From multiple female voices such as Nko's, Mrs. Nwaizu's, Miss Bulewao, and Nko's roommates, emerge pertinent questions that put the nature of the female's well being at the heart of traditional African social organization.

Emecheta then surpasses Flora Nwapa, another Igbo writer, with her consistent unbiased exploration of the opressed female psyche, although Flora Nwapa in *One Is Enough* is more decidedly feminist. Emecheta points out artistically, as have other feminist writers such as Simone de Beauvoir and Germaine Greer, that the very structure of patriarchal social organizations creates a suppressed individual by making an existential being an object for male subjectivity. Author Emecheta is not in a class of her own. She shows, like Kate Millet, that patriarchy is a power structured relationship that in most cases exploits women through a system of assigned and devalued roles.[7] Through her characters she challenges some of the assumptions of traditional Igbo society which frustrate the gifted woman from the realization of herself as an entity. Through her heroine we realize with Catherine Mackinnon that gender is a learned quality not essentially a biological fact.[8]

A sub-theme in *Double Yoke* is the exploration of the dilemma of men and women positioned between modernization and traditionalism in this instance on university campuses in Nigeria. Young adults become disoriented by conflicting standards of morality and the role of men and women in a changing society. Ete Kamba and Nko quarrel about whether or not the latter should attend the Reverend Elder Ikot's Revivalist meeting. They are trapped by conflicting standards in religious obligations and patriotism. Emecheta writes:

> How he [Ete Kamba] wished his girlfriend had been just a simple village girl to whom he could simply say, 'you must not go to the Revivalist meetings again, because I don't trust the head of the movement.' He could never say a thing like that to Nko. She would like to know all the reasons behind his orders. (p. 124).

At another time Ete Kamba demands Nko confess whether or not she is a virgin. He is trapped by conflicting standards in morality. What kind of woman makes the 'ideal wife'? One of his roommates rationalizes: 'Give me a fourteen-year-old village girl with uncomplicated background any time.' (p. 163).

Apart from Ete Kamba's inability to throw off the precepts of traditional African society which give certain prerogatives to men and deny them to women, author Emecheta points out that today's modern female is also torn between two worlds and unable to function properly in either. Nko is confused about the actual role the educated female should play in Nigerian society. The title of the book, *Double Yoke*, then is symbolic. According to the author, because educated Nigerian women are expected to play both the role of the submissive, gentle, docile female and the modern, sophisticated individual, there is confusion about which values to adopt: those of traditional African society or those of the west. Both African men and women are therefore in bondage. Living in two different cultures brings too much tension. Hence, they must live with a 'double yoke' for daring to walk where angels fear to tread.

There is satire too in *Double Yoke*. As well as the clash between the old and the new, there is a clash between the genuine and the false. In the character of Reverend Professor Ikot, pretentious and immoral university professors in Nigeria are attacked. Ikot, like the true trickster figure is shrewd, cunning and loquacious. Posing as a religious leader and educator, he dupes others but is rarely duped himself. His strong archetypal appeal, ability to outwit others and articulate his ideas enable him to exercise power and control over people. Even when caught in the act, he exploits the situation and emerges a winner. Note how he handles his confrontation with Ete Kamba in one of the most dramatic scenes in the book. Playing on the intelligence of his people, he fabricates a story knowing full well what the policemen want to hear. Emecheta, pointing to the exploitation of students on university campuses and the abuse of Christian teachings, protests against the corrupt, opportunistic nature of contemporary Nigerians. Rather than working towards the acquisition of souls or imparting knowledge to students, Ikot preoccupies himself with "getting a piece of the cake."

Almost risking his chances of being the next Vice-Chancellor at Unical, he shamelessly destroys the lives of both Nko and Ete Kamba.

Finally, Ete Kamba exemplifies primacy of the group ethic over individual self-interests, which is so embedded in traditional African society, by sympathizing with Nko upon hearing of her father's death. Ete Kamba begins to realize that despite their inexperience they have to resolve their problems for no other reason than because they love each other. Ete Kamba and Nko choose to grow from their blunders and bear their double burden together. Ete Kamba's deep feeling of affection for Nko, despite a certain myopia which blinds him to manifest ambiguities within himself, helps him to understand that no one knows very much about the life of another. This ignorance becomes vivid, if you love another.

This ending is not altogether convincing even in these modern times. It then becomes obvious that author Emecheta is ascribing her personal modes of thought even though they may be way ahead of her audience. Most of us are still very conservative. In the fusing of the old and the new traditional African society's intolerance of one's right to choose one's destiny rather than consider the common good seems to be strengthened. In spite of this, *Double Yoke* is quite entertaining while it explores several political and social issues common in African literature. Emecheta's simplicity of style covers her exploration of these important issues in strikingly new and provocative twists.

NOTES

1. Buchi Emecheta, *Double Yoke*. London: Ogwugwu Afor Company, 1982, p. 57 (All subsequent references to this text will be referred to by page numbers).
2. See Ezenwa-Ohaeto, "The Texture and Variation of Commitment To Protest and Violence in Recent Nigerian Fiction." Paper presented at the *Fourth Annual Conference of The Literary Society of Nigeria*, 22-25, February, 1984, University of Benin, Benin City, p. 15.
3. Kenneth Little and Anne Price, "Some Trends In Modern Marriage Among West Africans. *Africa Journal of the International African Institute*. XXXVII, October, 1967, pp. 413, 421 raise this issue in their work.
4. Katherine Frank, "African Womanhood in the Novels of Buchi Emecheta." *World Literature Written in English*. Vol. 21, No. 3, 1982, p. 478, provides interesting angles on Emecheta's works.
5. See Lloyd W. Brown, "The African Woman as Writer," *Canadian Journal of African Studies*, Vol, 9, No. 3, 1975, p. 495, for discussion of Emecheta's early work.

6. This position is validated in Chinua Achebe, "The Social Limitations of the
    Academic Woman to the Pursuit of Excellence." *Nigerian Journal of
    Education*, Vol, 2, No. 1, p. 107.
7. Simone de Beauvoir, *The Second Sex*. Translated and edited by H. M.
    Parshley. Harmondsworth: Penguin, 1976, p. 483.
8. Catherine Mackinnon, "Feminism, Marxism and the State: An Agenda for
    Theory." *SIGNS*, Spring, 1982, Vol. 7, No. 3, p. 529.

Songs from Silence: Hausa Women's Poetry

Beverly B. Mack

A significant portion of Northern Nigeria's oral and written poetry remains unknown to the world and unrecognized in its own cultural setting because it is created by women. Women's extemporaneous oral verse is not regarded as serious artistry because it is created by those who are not considered respectable; the written works remain hidden with their authors, traditional Hausa women who are secluded in their homes in urban areas. It was not always this way: female praisesingers have in earlier times been highly regarded as the guardians of social mores and historical traditions, and Nana Asma's, who lived in northern Nigeria in the nineteenth century, is still known for her contributions to the Islamic cause through her inspirational written religious verse.[1] She is remembered as an exemplary traditional Muslim woman.

The reasons that Hausa women are not now recognized as creators of oral and written poetry are based on social and religious precepts which have evolved in recent history; since the *jihad* of the early nineteenth century, local interpretation of Islam has deemed that Muslim Hausa women remain secluded in their husbands' homes. In such circumstances it is no surprise that women—who are expected to be invisible elements in Hausa society—rarely have the opportunity to flourish as popular entertainers, unless they are willing to forfeit their respectability as private secluded women. Rarely instructed in Koranic verse, or able to complete primary level secular education, Hausa women often are illiterate, and thus ill-equipped to compose written verse.

181

Despite such odds Hausa women of northern Nigeria do, however, create both oral and written literature that is reflective of their situations, attitudes, aspirations, and perspectives on their community. The creative artists discussed here are indeed exceptions in Hausa society; nevertheless their material constitutes a significant expression of the attitudes of their silent sisters—the Hausa women for whom they perform and of whom they speak. This study offers a brief survey of varieties of poetry produced by contemporary Hausa women in northern Nigeria.

Hausa Wakoki—Written and Oral Verse

Northern Nigeria has for centuries enjoyed a rich Arab/Islamic literary tradition, beginning with religious verse composed by Muslim scholars and extending to secular verse modeled on the orthodox pattern. Created in the literary form that is a legacy of Islam, these verses contain the standard opening and closing doxologies, as well as strict rhyme and meter common to Islamic religious verse. Such traditional verse was transmitted through chanting, and preserved in print by Islamic scholars. Thus Hausa literature has long been expressed in both oral and written forms.

Among the Hausa the term *waka, s.* (*wakoki,* p.) includes in its definition a range of compositions from the extemporaneous oral declamation to the written verse.[2] *Wakoki* may be expressed orally, for the term itself implies the concept of "song" as well as "poem." Scholars do, however, distinguish between the oral and the written *waka*, which are as diverse in style and theme as the circumstances in which they are delivered. Indeed there are situations for which one type may not be substituted for another.

The oral *waka* is appropriate to praise song for prestigious individuals, naming and wedding celebrations, spirit-possession cult ritual, pacing domestic tasks, etc. It is suited to the non-religious—the ritual, entertainment, and quotidian situation. These extemporaneously delivered *wakoki* are basic to Hausa entertainment in both private and in public settings. Although they are not preserved in print, oral *wakoki* do have form, for they follow established patterns of the genre which may be studied as readily as those of written works.[3] Repeated performances of extemporaneous, orally composed *wakoki* reveal an entertainer's own repertoire of interchangeable phrase patterns. An entertainer may be known for a particular style of phrasing, and thus may influence other entertainers who listen to his or her performance. As a genre, the oral *waka* also has been influenced by the standards of the written *waka* to the extent that the oral work often contains doxologies and repeated phrases invoking God's blessings.

The standard form of the written *waka* reflects its function, for the written verse is appropriate to religious education. Following the verse patterns of the Koran, Islamic scholars traditionally have produced religious tracts which contain opening and closing doxologies to God, and follow strict patterns of rhyme and meter. Since the 1930's these have been published in chapbook form by a northern Hausa press.[4] These *wakoki* may also appear in Hausa newspapers or be broadcast on local radio stations. In contrast to extemporaneous *wakoki*, the written works are of a private nature—they are written by individual authors who have the time to rethink and revise the work, and the subjects are usually serious, contemplative concerns. The function of the written *waka* is to inspire and instruct more than to entertain.

Oral Poetic Artistry

Despite the wealth a successful entertainer may accumulate, these Hausa creative artists have rarely enjoyed respectable social status.[5] Whether a praisesinger in a royal court, or an entertainer for celebrations around town, the *mawaka* (praisesinger or oral poet) is considered to be of a separate class with which most Hausa people do not care to be associated.

The northern Nigerian women who perform extemporaneously forfeit for their profession even more respectability than do their male counterparts because they are neither secluded nor subject to a husband's demands. Thus they do not represent the typical, traditional Hausa woman; but neither are they typical of one another. One very successful performer of bawdy songs is married to a man who farms and tends the children while his wife travels around the North taping television and radio shows and performing in public. Another entertainer is an older woman who sings at political rallies for her favorite candidate; by virtue of her age and seniority over her younger husband, she is free to be autonomous. Among the Emir of Kano's courtiers is an older, widowed woman who has for twenty years been the Emir's official *zabiya*, or female praisesinger. When her husband was alive he approved of her profession since he himself was a musician for the Emir. Yet another older woman extemporizes bawdy verse to entertain groups of secluded women at celebrations in private settings as well as mixed public audiences throughout the North. In none of these cases does the woman subordinate herself to her husband's demands, but pursues her career at the expense of her status as a respectable Hausa woman.

Typical of the bawdy verse performed by the first woman, Maimuna Coge, cited here is a song delivered to a mixed public audience of students at a university in Kano.[6] Performing extemporaneously with a chorus of women beating on upturned calabashes, the singer shapes her material to the interests of the audience. She points out that respectability and success are two distinct attributes; comparing her own profession with the higher status profession of the educated bureaucrat, she observes that both have been successful economically:

> . . .And for a long time he has held the pen; and for a long time I have been well-off[7]

The bureaucrat enjoys a high social status, and a position of affluence, the two of which are often related. But this entertainer reminds her status-conscious audience that wealth brings comforts, regardless of how it is acquired. Money earned by the prostitute buys the same comforts as a bureaucrat's money; between the well-respected bureaucrat and the prostitute there is a difference of social status only. In fact, the prostitute may be the more affluent of the two:

> I beg the forgiveness of the married women
> For I will do the movement of the European-style prostitutes
> For you know, in Funtuwa, in that city,
> There are European-style prostitutes
> Prostitutes in a European-style house,
> Drink beer and smoke cigarettes
> They wear white gowns and thrive[8]

The prostitutes *thrive*, even though their profession is not respectable. Who, the entertainer asks, can judge an individual by their income, or deny affluence to one whose profession is not "appropriate"?

For a man, respectability is related in large part to his income; for a woman, respectability has everything to do with being "proper." Implicit in this woman's song is the understanding that role-playing is central to social order, and those who deviate from the system may not enjoy the social rewards, but that does not prevent their reaping other benefits. In the ultimate irony, this entertainer is paid well for reminding her pretentious audience of the gap between their social status and her own.

A less controversial version of this genre of oral praise is performed by the Kano Emir's female praise singer, Maizargadi. She strides before the Emir shouting extemporaneously rearranged sets of epithets that warn his subjects of his proximity. Typical of her repertoire are phrases that commemorate his royal line, confirm his position of authority in Hausa culture, and express thanks for his generosity in providing gifts for her:

> Emir of Kano, Alhaji Ado Bayero, rest easy, son of Abdu,
> From today until the end of the world, thanks be to God or the
>   generosity he has shown
> Bull Elephant, ancestor of Dabo,
> Our righteous one, who is here and is well
> Greetings to the master of thousands, master of Abdu's horse,
>   Bull Elephant, ancestor of Dabo,
> I give thanks, I multiply the blessings on the Emir of Kano,
>   Alhaji Ado,
> I give thanks for his wealth, the giver of blouses . . .

> Emir of Kano, Alhaji Ado Bayero
> Grandson of Alu Mai Sango. . .[9]

This type of oral poet is closest to the griot of other cultures, the oral historian who preserves, in verse, genealogies, historical events, and meetings between a patron and other dignitaries. Although she does not enjoy royal status, she nonetheless is considered to play an important role in expressing high regard for the monarch, and reflecting such positive public opinion of him.

Yet another Hausa woman, Binta Katsina, has become known for her song advocating women's participation in the Nigerian work force. In it the entertainer encourages Nigerian women to participate in "every kind of work," thus rejecting the northern traditional injunction against women's active public roles:

> You should do every kind of work, you should know every kind of work
> You can write papers, you can pound the typewriter,
> You can fly airplanes,
> You know how to be in the office,
> You could do the government work,
> And you could be the police workers,
> You could do the customs work,
> Let's give you the chance
> Women of Nigeria
> Women of Nigeria, you know every kind of work[10]

With the exception of praise songs for royalty, oral performance by Hausa women artists represents the irreverent, the revolutionary in Hausa society. It is performed by women whose own lifestyles deviate from traditional and conservative women's roles, and represents convention only as it departs from it. Like the court jester, these women say and do what other Hausa women cannot, criticizing the status quo, and encouraging behavior that is not normally condoned. Despite their negligible social status, they play an important role in a stratified society, expressing what others dare not say.

The Written Works

In contrast to the oral poet, the writer of verse is usually respected as a scholar and is known as an author rather than as an entertainer. These are usually Hausa men, who are trained as religious scholars and writers of Islamic verse from their youth. It is rare to find a woman who is comparably trained. There are, of course, exceptions to this. Sometimes a young girl whose father is a religious scholar will learn the Koran from him. Such study requires the rote memorization of Koranic verses—a mode of learning that provides the educational tools for the creation of one's own verses. Representative of this are the works of two Hausa/Fulani women in their late forties, Hauwa Gwaram and Hajiya 'Yar Shelu. Their recently published volume of collected verse is the first of such works by women ever published in the North, where Hausa men's poetry has been published in both Hausa and English for fifty years.[11] These works were chosen for publication because they fulfill the literary expectations of Hausa male editors; the poems are well crafted, with rhyme and meter that rival those of traditional Arab/Islamic verse. The contents of these works is conservative, advocating the deferential behavior expected of traditional Hausa women and praising national heroes or political figures. These poems deviate most expressly in their consistently secular nature; this often distinguishes women's written *wakoki* from men's.

Several of the published works are *wakoki* that were composed for use as teaching aids for adult education courses taught by women to other Hausa women. These advocate methods of hygiene, child care and nutrition, explain the aims of national census-takers or changes in public practices, such as the transition from left to right-hand drive. Some works describe local monuments, such as one which catalogues the animals in the Kano zoo. Some are nationalistic or commemorative, such as the verses eulogizing Nigerian soldiers, and recounting the events of the Biafran civil war. Through the oral recitation of these verses the authors inform secluded women of current events in northern Nigeria.

At the same time, though, these informative verses had to be couched in conservative terms in order to be chosen for publication by editors who were not sympathetic to women writers. *The Song for Modern Times* is a prime example of the attitude that male publishers felt should be exhibited by female writers. In it Hajiya 'Yar Shehu describes the rabble in the streets, affirming that they bear no respect for married women, shouting at them, grabbing them:

> If they see married women they will shout,
> Hey, Binta, Hey Hajiya—and they'll even pull at your dress.[12]

The only remedy for this is an aloofness that exhibits one's superiority—convivial repartee is not an appropriate response. Composure is an outward sign of the character of a proper Hausa woman; silence in such a situation is by far the most respectable response.

In another verse the author emphasizes the low moral character of those women who refuse the traditional woman's role—prostitutes, she warns, are rejected even by their own children:

> See the prostitutes whose own children don't love them.
> They follow that big friend of theirs, Satan. . .[13]

Here two assumptions are reinforced: that one must love and respect one's parents and that the respect due a mother—especially in Islam—is forfeited by a prostitute. The role of domestic guardian, wife, and mother, is the role that a Hausa woman must fill.

The author elaborates on other dangers of "modern times", such as the chaos that is common in contemporary urban streets. In that setting, she notes, one finds people of questionable character:

> Then you see them, they are shouting and rushing about,
> These are Satan's advocates.[14]

The public scene, she reiterates, is no place for a proper woman. Those who hurry and shout are Satan's advocates, therefore it is not appropriate for a woman to involve herself in the threatening bustle of the urban scene lest she be caught up in modern conflicts like the following:

> If you tell them that God forbids adultery,
> And that relations with a married woman are worst of all,
>
> They'll reply to you, "Well, we must be progressive,
> It is God who has brought about these modern times."
>
> But listen to the words of our praise singer,
> When he responded to this talk about religion.
>
> He said, "As for the world, if there were no religion,
> The world itslef would not exist, much less modern times."[15]

This poem advocates devotion to one's domestic role, proper deportment whenever one must appear in public, and the desirability of keeping oneself apart from the public sphere with all its temptations and bad influences. These "modern" types she warns, are devoid of shame, fear, and respect; they are advocates of Satan—including even television programs with their cowboys and spaceships, which divert one's attention from God:

> Let us refuse to watch spaceships and cowboys
> They and shows like them are the works of Satan.[16]

In her work on the census Hauwa Gwaram moralizes in a comparable way, this time advocating active support for one's country. She insists that to omit reporting any person, however newborn an infant may be, is to do an injustice to the nation, since knowing the right population can help to improve the economic situation of the country. She emphasizes the individual's civic duty to cooperate with census officials and—most important—she insists that the census is for the benefit of Nigeria, *not* another colonial imposition.

Other verses are more informative than didactic. *The Song for Self-Sufficiency* describes the vegetable gardens that fed Nigerian families, the effort toward public hygiene, the work of expert tailors that has become known world-wide. In this work the author boasts that everyone gets along well in Nigeria, without jealousy or presumptuousness, and emphasizes the role she feels women may play in Nigeria's welfare:

> May God help us to achieve our goals,
> The women of Kano have been diligent in their work.

> May God help us to achieve our hearts desires
> The women of Kano persevere in their farming.

> I will end here, lest you say I have overdone it,
> The song on women, who will make our country successful.[17]

It is the contention of these authors that women have an important role to play in the success of their country, but in contrast to the creators of oral *wakoki*, they feel women's behavior must remain within the constraints imposed by tradition. They maintain a respectable attitude in their works; the political tone is nationalistic, the social perspective conservative.

But because women do not normally write verse, the very fact that these two women have produced a volume of verse is the most revolutionary aspect of their work. They have accomplished a great deal with this volume, not only communicating historical facts and current events to those who would not otherwise be exposed to such news, but also acting as role models for prospective women authors who might earlier have subscribed to the assumption that "women do not write poetry."

Conclusion

For Hausa women, too long presumed to be the anonymous guardians of the domestic sphere—illiterate, nonpolitical, unconcerned with public events—these oral and written poems are proof of their eagerness to know about social and political change as well as proof of their ability to participate in their society beyond the limits of the compound walls. In addition, they accomplish such participation in the public sphere without violating their religious and social mores. When their works are broadcast on local radio stations, they reach their audiences without requiring secluded women to leave their homes. Such broadcasts also mean that these works have an impact that novels cannot hope to have among the illiterate. Hausa women's poetry is no less significant than the literary works of other Nigerian women—it is only less well known because it is rarely published, and when it is, it is published in Hausa rather than in English. For the woman of northern Nigeria, however, these artists of oral and written works are more than newscasters and entertainers. Their works are representative of concerns and attitudes common among Hausa women of northern Nigeria. As artists they have forged the way for a wider variety of Hausa women's literary expression; perhaps more importantly, however, they have raised the issue of the woman's changing role in modern Nigeria.

NOTES

1. "Daughter of Usman Dan Fodio, leader of the 1804 *jihad* to promote Islam in northern Nigeria, Nana Asma'a wrote in Arabic, Fulfulde, and Hausa. One of the foremost authorities on Nana Asma'a is Jean Boyd, who lives in Sokoto, Nigeria. She has written a biography of Nana Asma'a, as well as having collected and translated Nana Asma'a's poetry.

2. These and all subsequent definitions of Hausa terms are from: R. C. Abraham, *Dictionary of the Hausa Language*, 2nd ed., London: University of London Press, 1962.

3. For an analysis of patterns in Hausa women's oral poetry see: Beverly B. Mack, *"Wakokin Mata*: Hausa Women's Oral Poetry" unpublished dissertation, University of Wisconsin-Madison, 1981.

4. The Northern Nigerian Publishing Company in Zaria, Nigeria also publishes volumes of secular poetry, educational texts, novels, etc. in Hausa and English.

5. For a full discussion of the Hausa praisesinger's social status see: M. G. Smith, "The Social Functions and Meaning of Hausa Praise Singing," *Ibadan*, 21, (October, 1965), 81-92.

6. The audience is comprised of both male and female university students as well as faculty members and their familites. This unusual circumstance of men and women sitting together in public further emphasizes the shocking nature of the risque material.

7. *Wakar Ta Yabon Kungiyar Hausa* (Praise Song for the Hausa Conference) by Maimuna Coge, 1980, 1.75. For this and all subsequent translations, this author takes responsibility. All selections cited in this study were recorded from the artists by this author in 1980 in Nigeria.

8. *Ibid*, l. 126-132.

9. *Wakar Alhaji Ado Bayero, Sarkin Kano* (Praise Song for Alhaji Ado Bayero, Emir of Kano) by Maizargadi, 1980, 1.11, 14-17, 45, 47, 61 and 62.

10. *Wakar Matan Nijeriya* (Song for the Women of Nigeria) by Binta Katsina, 1980, 1.70-79.

11. Hauwa Gwaram and Hajiya 'Yar Shehu, *Alkalami A Hannun Mata* (A Pen in the Hands of Women), Beverly B. Mack, ed. Zaria: The Northern Nigerian Publishing Company, 1983.

12. Hajiya 'Yar Shehu, *Wakar Zamani* in *Alkalami A Hannun Mata*, stanza 11. This and all subsequent citations are this author's translations of works contained in *Alkalami A Hannun Mata*, cited above.

13. *Ibid*, stanza 22.

14. *Ibid*, stanza 25.
15. *Ibid*, stanzas 26-29.
16. *Ibid*, stanza 36.
17. Hauwa Gwaram, *Wakar Mu Ci Da Kasarmu in Alkalami A Hannun Mata*, stanzas 31-33.

PART THREE
Social and Political Themes: Women's Issues in African Literary Criticism

In their treatment of African institutions the papers in Part III, "Social and Political Themes: Women's Issues in African Literary Criticism" adopt approaches that range in scope from the mythological and religious underpinnings of the institutions, to their material ramifications in daily life. In the purely fictional and the autobiographical novel, the short story, and poetry handled in these papers, the aspects of those institutions as they bear upon women—and therefore necessarily also on men—are analyzed on social scientific as well as literary criteria, bringing theories from those fields to bear on the studies, which set in relief the feminine facet of some fundamental structures in African life. The dialectics of Senegalese customs, particularly those based in Muslim tradition, as laid out by Ousmane Sembène, undergo cogent review in Brenda Berrian's paper "Through Her Prism of Social and Political Contexts: Sembène's Female Characters in Tribal Scars.*" Looking at four of the short stories in the Sembène anthology (*Voltaïque*), Berrian zeroes in on the compelling arguments made by the women in challenging laws and/or practices which not only ignore any rights of women but which also do not hold up under*

191

questioning. In her selection of the four stories she treats, Berrian finds the issues of divorce, child custody, arranged marriages, and tyrannical men, as these issues are seen by the women involved. She elucidates the politically controversial nature of the women's challenges in their potential to erode some firmly entrenched pillars of Sengalese institutions that have allowed men to hold unlimited and uncontested power over women. The explosive challenge to a similarly controversial tradition is the subject of Tobe Levin's paper "Scapegoats of Culture and Cult: An Activist's View of Circumcision in Ngugi's **The River Between,** *" As Berrian does for Sembène, Levin draws attention to Ngugi's dialectical presentation of the traditional practice of female circumcision. Using a perspective that combines elements of anthropology, psychology, theology, and comparative literature, Levin's analysis integrates Kenyatta, Freud, the Bible, and several African writers, to present the arguments and counter-arguments from the several positions represented in the narrative: the young girl who elects to undergo circumcision, her sister who does not; the Christian Church as reflected by the girls' father, the schoolteacher, and the mission hospital staff; and Gikuyu tradition as reflected by the village council opposed to the encroaching influence of Western culture. Acknowledging Ngugi's efforts to end circumcision on humanitarian grounds, Levin illustrates not only what she perceives to be the protection of a vested interest on the part of the Gikuyu men who insist on this ritual as the basis for moral and social education, but also the hypocrisy in the Christian Church's misogynous reasons against circumcision (and its basically incredible claim of virgin birth).*

The relation of sexuality to religion as well as the disorientation regarding the symbols of womanhood that has affected the Igbo man as a by-product of the conversion to Christianity, is likewise the subject of Elaine Savory Fido's paper on Christopher Okigbo's poetic work **Labyrinths.** *Fido's assertion that "Anxiety about the female principle is . . . a strong element in male Eastern Nigerian writers' work" forms the basis for her hypothesis that "a vital aspect of [Okigbo's] agony . . . is particular to modern post-colonial African man, and indeed to Igbo man." Grounded in the autobiographical content of the poem, this discussion offers an explication of the complexities of the poet's personal relationship with female deities vis-a-vis his own maleness, on the basis of a theory that "the feminine is closely intertwined with his idea of traditional religion, whereas the male-dominated Christian ethos is antitethetical to Igbo tradition." Another look at Igbo tradition, through the works of four other Igbo writers—here novelists—is* *the subject of Carole Davies' paper scrutinizing the presentation of motherhood. Davies' assessment of the differences between the presentations by women writers and by men writers reveals not only the absence of concencus on definitions of "mother" but, more significantly, divergences of view regarding the centrality of motherhood in the African woman's life, psychologically as well as physically. The comparison between male and female writers' presentations of the feminine is taken to another level in Naana Banyiwa-Horne's paper in Part II. Davies and Banyiwa-Horne both, though with different emphasis, take up the issue, in Flora Nwapa's* Efuru, *of the African woman who does not bear children, and the attitudes of the woman herself and of her community about this phenomenon. Motherhood is extended to the grandmother by Mildred Hill-Lubin, who discusses the continuities in grandmother depiction in different parts of the African diaspora. Basing her study on African fiction by Aidoo and Mphahlele, and African American autobiography by Maya Angelou and Frederick Douglass, Hill-Lubin sees the crucial role of the grandmother as threefold: preserver of the extended family, disseminator of family and community wisdom, and communicator of values and ideals of the family.*

That the influence exerted by the extended family can sometimes be detrimental, at least for a marriage, is the subject of Edris Makward's article "Marriage, Tradition and Women's Pursuit of Happiness in the Novels of Mariama Bâ." From his reading of Bâ's two novels Makward sees the author's position to be not a condemnation of polygamy as practiced in her country, Senegal, but as an argument in favor of the necessity in modern life for the egalitarian monogamous marriage. Of the traditional, polygamous marriage Makward finds that Bâ shows "with insistence, that the extended family's action could invariably make such relationships fizzle out in bitter failure." In viewing Bâ's novels as statements that the happiness of the whole society must be based on the happiness of the women and the men in marriages, i.e., a close association between two equals, Makward demonstrates the egalitarian, cooperative emphasis in the feminism that Bâ advocates for Senegalese society. This assessment of marriage, along with the other studies of social and political institutions in Part III, are ultimately re-assessments of the meanings these structures hold not only for the African woman but also for her family and larger community.

A.A.G.

Through Her Prism of Social and Political Contexts: Sembène's Female Characters in Tribal Scars

Brenda F. Berrian

If there is one enduring presentation in African literature it is the African mother. From the Soundiata epic to the epistolary novel, *Une si longue lettre* (1979) by the deceased Mariama Bâ, reverence for the African mother is expressed in various forms. In the past, the traditional African mother has been a Queen Mother, a trader, a soldier, an organizer of protest demonstrations, and the nurturer of future generations of children. Cognizant of the role that the mother plays in African societies is Ousmane Sembène, who prefers to set his female characters in their traditional settings as mothers and wives, in order to illustrate specific political and social points of view. Through the women, Sembène notes that in order for them to have new perceptions of themselves and to develop a more defined self-awareness, their men should no longer be the determining factor in their lives. Sembène is convinced that changes in social and political structures and attitudes in Africa are necessary if the African woman is to realize her full potential and importance in the future of her country.[1]

A self-taught man, writer, and filmmaker from Senegal, Sembène is devoted to writing about African people and their aspirations. Most importantly, he is one of the first African writers to move his female characters from a secondary role, in which they compliment their men, to a primary one in which they express their feelings, hurts, joys, and think and react to pressing situations. For instance, in four selected short stories from *Voltaïque. Nouvelles* (1962)[2] Sembène introduces his mother who demands custody of her children at a divorce hearing; the mother who defies a tyrannical king in defense of her daughter; the mother who confronts her neglectful husband with his callousness, and finally, the mother who comes to terms with her marriage to a much older man.

In the short story, "The Bilal's Fourth Wife," Sembène slips in modern ideas about marriage and divorce in a traditional village setting where he presents the couple, Suliman and Yacine. Suliman, a man past middle-age, takes great pains to present himself as a pious, devout Moslem and family man before the public whereas, in private, he berates and beats his three wives unmercifully. His appetite for women younger than his daughters has not waned, and he takes advantage of his position as the bilal of the village mosque to make lecherous remarks and to fondle them. Because of his carefully preserved public image as a humble man and a guardian of polygamy, the young victimized women dare not complain expecting that their cries of outrage would not be believed. As the story progresses, Suliman is so consumed with his lust for young women that he fails to keep the mosque clean. Sympathetic male villagers take it upon themselves to find a fourth wife for Suliman in the person of the young, Yacine N'Doye.

Yacine, a 20-year old former "tomboy," is deemed to be a good candidate for Suliman's fourth wife for she has frightened the young men in the village with her outspokenness. Presumably, an older man like Suliman will be able to tame and mold her into a submissive wife, since it is assumed that she is naive and ignorant of her rights and sexual desires as a woman. Although Yacine would have liked to raise some objections, she follows her father's wishes and marries Suliman. Later, after three years of marriage and a son, the bored Yacine takes Suliman's nephew as her lover, as Suliman's sexual drive is diminishing. Her decision to take a lover is justifiable, for, in her mind, she is in her physical prime and married to a man she does not love. However, this triangle—wife, husband, and lover—becomes the main topic of village gossip when Yacine bears a son for her lover. In an attempt to salvage his tarnished image and manhood, Suliman vents his rage and jealousy upon his three wives and demands a divorce from Yacine. To his surprise, his demand receives a rebuttal from Yacine.

In "The Bilal's Fourth Wife" Sembène, with great humor, pokes fun at Senegalese attitudes toward divorce. He attacks the practice of double moral standards, which place women at a disadvantage. Sembène uses the character of Yacine to question and to disagree with the patriarchal Moslem marriage rules drawn up by males centuries ago. In spite of the rumors and intense external pressures, Yacine reveals a tremendous self-confidence.

First, she refuses to be coerced by Suliman and her family into a divorce. Second, she is adamant about being treated on equal footing as a woman by the Cadi (special council of male elders called to review her case). Third, she questions why the woman is not free to take a lover when a man in a Moslem society can have four wives with the approval of the Koran and legal laws. These unyielding stances force the male elders to accept, with reluctance, the fact that there are two sides to every marital disagreement, and the woman's position is just as important as the man's.

As for Suliman, he has been made the laughing stock of the village by his inability to control his wife. His ego suffers a beating due to his physical limitations of not satisfying his young wife's sexual needs. What is at stake is Suliman's determination to humiliate Yacine publicly, for she has flaunted her relationship with his nephew with the birth of a child. Double standards, which govern the behavior of men and women in a Moslem polygamous marriage, are addressed again when Suliman asks for custody of his "son" and the return of the dowry.

Suliman does not regard Yacine as a human being who has feelings and rights, but as one of his possessions who is expected to boost his ego. A woman's place, he feels, is to obey her husband and to build her life around him. When his possession (Yacine) no longer brings him pleasure or bends to his needs, he must squash or beat it into submission as he has done with the other three wives. Since Yacine will not conform and retreat into the expected docility, Suliman tries to use psychological pressure and works within the traditional legal system to bring about her downfall. He becomes obsessed with the need to cause Yacine deep pain. Yacine's indiscretion must be exposed to draw attention away from his own inadequacies.

As mentioned before, through Yacine's protests and the divorce hearing, Sembène brings forth the argument that traditional Moslem marriage laws should be reevaluated and rewritten to protect the rights of women too. In support of Sembène's argument, Yacine demands that Suliman should return her virginity knowing full-well that virginity is highly prized and is linked to one's honor and esteem. With this brave announcement, she makes clear that something precious has been taken away from her—her honor and respectability.

Yacine's request to have her virginity returned is a clever tactic and approach in presenting her case in court. She knows that she was more valuable when she was chaste and that her value dropped with her affair with Suliman's nephew, making her second-hand merchandise. Suliman too cannot bear knowing that his wife has been handled by somebody else. His pride and respect have been challenged. He also fears Yacine's power over him—the power of informing the villagers of his sexual weakness.

Since Suliman cannot physically return Yacine's virginity and make her "pure as spring water" again, Yacine hopes that her request will enable the villagers to be more sympathetic toward her. The question then becomes why should women in Moslem marriages hand over the custody of their children to their former husbands. Fortunately, Froh-Toll, the head of the Cadi, is wise enough to debate the custody topic and rules in favor of Yacine with the statement:

> So by what right does Suliman demand custody of the child? There can always be doubt as to who is the father of a child. But never as to who is the mother.[3]

With this pronouncement, Froh-Toll supports women's child rearing rights, which is an admirable step.

In Moslem societies, attitudes toward adultery are one-sided. Traditional customs tend to endorse the fact that married men engaged in extra-marital affairs cannot commit adultery, only women. The Senegalese society is built upon a patriarchal system with a Moslem/Christian/Animist religious foundation. As a consequence, the person who passes judgement on men and women is a man; the society, in which men and women operate, is male dominated. In the eyes of traditional Moslem law, the man's word is accepted as being truthful and binding, but the woman's word does not have the status and legitimacy. So while Suliman is not chastised for engaging in a sexual act with a young woman in the village, the villagers agree that Yacine should be punished for her affair. Yacine's actions upset the value system, which supports the idea that women must be faithful to their husbands. Consequently, her conscious revolt becomes a social act against the antiquated Moslem divorce laws and ingrained value systems.

Sembène's short story, "The Mother" is another example of the application of double moral standards n a Moslem society in Africa. This point is presented through the personnage of the tyrannical king. The king, who has no intentions of cultivating the love and respect of his constituents, alienates himself and evokes the hatred and fear of his subjects to the point that they dream about seeing him burnt alive. Meanwhile, these same subjects are passive and obey the king's orders to murder men over fifty-years old. Thus, the king thinks that he owes no allegiance to anyone. He proceeds to pass a law that he will deflower every virgin before she is married. Over the years, only a few brave mothers succeed in saving their daughters from such a fate. When it is time for the king's daughter to marry, he repeals the law—separate rules for the poor and rich.

For the king, women represent danger, and he wishes to destroy them. By his actions, it appears that he harbours a deep hatred for women and cannot resist raping them. This psychological deviant is confused, insecure, and enjoys exerting his power through violent means. The king obviously likes inflicting pain upon women, because they are said to be the weaker sex.

Since nobody has the courage to defy the king's orders, the people's fears increase. It is only when the king travels that he encounters open resistance to his overtures from a young woman he fancies. In anger he has her locked up. The young woman's mother, a woman of "certain age," fights and pushes past the six feet tall servants to gain an audience with the king. The mother verbally battles and acuses him of outlandish and unfit behavior. Further, she courageously looks the king directly in his eyes and attacks him for not showing any respect for the mothers in the kingdom. She makes the point that without the love and tenderness of his mother he would not have been born. The king responds by slapping her face.

The subjects jump to the mother's defense after the king's display of anger and guilt. The mother's words had hit their target shaming the remaining males in the kingdom for their cowardice and failure to protect their women folk. The king's rule has been divisive and had led to the distrust of one another to the detriment of the society. This exhibition of internal strength and resilience by the mother topples the king's government. One conclusion is that anyone, male or female, who abuses power will not keep it.

Clearly, the king and the mother during their confrontation had struck each other in their most vulnerable spots, he on her face, and she at his ego. Yet a reversal of roles emerges for the so-called weak, defenseless mother becomes the stronger of the two. Without his bodyguards to shield him, the king, like most bullies, is defenseless. His deliberate attempt to limit the freedom of women ultimately results in the loss of his kingdom as a consequence of the words spoken by the African mother.

There is another interesting aspect in the Mother's depiction. One could say that Sembène has succumbed to one of the biased attitudes directed toward women when he describes the mother as ugly. However, it could also be said that Sembène deliberately calls the mother ugly, because of its common use in Senegalese society for strong-willed women. In African literature the good women, who stays in her place, is always gentle, kind, and beautiful, but the woman, who possesses the courage to debate male prerogatives, is frequently labeled or pictured as a physically ugly person. Thus Sembène ends this story by singing praises in honor of mothers who rise up to protect their children.

This particular story argues that one's biological origin and sex do not alleviate one's responsibility to the collective community. Making the female character in "The Mother" bigger than life is characteristic of Sembène in both his films and literary works to convince and draw attention to the African woman's special place in contemporary African society. The men, in the story "The Mother," were paralyzed with fear and failed to challenge the maniacal orders of the king. They also did nothing to overthrow the king-dictator. It was the woman, the mother, who came to the men's rescue. By magnifying the character of the mother Sembène scolds the men for their moral impotence and reproaches them for their lack of position action to oppose the king's oppressive policies.

The mother has done what is necessary to save and protect her daughter. She is, as Lippert would say, "super human in her love.[4]" The mother may be ugly on the outside, but she is beautiful inside with her concern for her child's misfortune. She possesses spiritual qualities which allow her to look directly into the king's evil heart. This special power permits the mother to weave a hypnotic spell on the male listeners, causes them to grab the king, and renders them half-conscious of the fact that they have aided the mother in her triumph over the king.

Mores of another kind are explored in the short story, "Her Three Days," where one meet Noumbé, the third wife of Mustapha. When the story opens Noumbé is preparing for her husband's visit during her allotted three days as dictated by the Koran. Drawing upon his filmmaking skills Sembène zooms in on Noumbé to show her haggard face, her weakened body after the bearing of five children in rapid succession, her anxieties and fears of being replaced by the fourth wife, and her fight to handle a heart condition. Although Noumbé is still young, she looks older because of her full financial duties of providing for her children.

In a sympathetic voice Sembène attacks the misuse of polygamy. If a man marries more than one wife, he is to treat them equally and not differentiate between them. This is a difficult task and even the best of men find that there is always one wife that he prefers among the group. For this reason, the remaining wives do not enjoy their husbands' companionship on an equal basis. In "Her Three Days" Mustapha prefers his fourth and youngest wife. It is his fourth wife's turn to be flattered and spoiled by him, and he casts aside his other three wives.

Relying upon a technique that worked successfuly in *Les Bouts de bois de Dieu* (1960), Sembène delays Mustapha's entrance until the last pages of the short story. In this way, Mustapha is seen through Noumbé's eyes and thoughts. Hence, Mustapha is known before he actually appears in the text. Leaving Mustapha's entrance until the end of "Her Three Days" creates the necessary suspense and enables the sensitive reader to feel the internal struggles and pains that Noumbé undergoes during her long wait for Mustapha. With this combination of sympathy for Noumbé and tension it is not impossible to understand why she lashes out at Mustapha on the eve of his arrival on the third day.

During these three days of waiting Noumbé has cooked Mustapha's favorite dishes, beautified herself, dressed with extreme care, saved the meat, and borrowed money from her next-door neighbor to ensure Mustapha's comfort. When Mustapha does not show after two days and fails to send a message, Noumbé's physical pain is almost as great as her mental pain. While dosing herself with medicine to prevent a heart attack, Noumbé wonders why she and her three co-wives allow themselves to be Mustapha's playmates and wives of one man. She contemplates divorce, the hypocrisy of the co-wives in their pretense of happiness, and ponders how to escape from such an unsatisfying and demeaning relationship.

Apparently, these thoughts frighten Noumbé somewhat because they are in contradiction with her upbringing. She has been raised to be a submissive wife dependent upon her husband's whims, just as Mustapha's personality and behavior have been formed by years of indoctrination that the male is the dominant person in a male/female relationship. As his "right" and with the support of Moslem doctrines the acquisition of four wives is linked with his virility and manliness. As for Noumbé she has achieved status and esteem with her marriage and the births of her five children. Companionship, mutual respect, and sharing are not part of the bargain.

Mustapha has an exaggerated sense of his ego and masculinity. With an air of impatience he comes to see Noumbé at the end of the third day demanding that she serve him and his two male companions. No words of comfort or apologies pass across his lips. In response, Noumbè displays a sarcastic side of her personality in an attempt to preserve some shred of dignity. This small rebellious act brings on a mild heart attack, and Mustapha calmly leaves Noumbé to fend for herself while announcing his horror and disbelief that the Malian government has just passed a resolution condemning polygamy.

The collectivity of female support in the compound is demonstrated when the women rush to Noumbé's aid. It is characteristic of Sembène to show how the women come together and lend each other their strength and advice. On the first day of Noumbé's three days of waiting the women sing to share Noumbé's happiness and unconcealed joy. When Mustapha fails to show up, Aida, the next-door neighbor, kindly helps Noumbé and offers to keep her company. For fear of hurting her feelings the women stay away from Noumbé and avoid meeting her eyes so that she can save "face." However, they all run to her defense when she collapses from the strain of asserting herself before Mustapha. In short, the women come together because they know that their turn to be the displaced wife is coming. Still, Noumbé is resolved to be a mother and resigned to joining ranks with her abandoned co-wives. She once loved Mustapha, but she now rejects him. Her sense of self-worth is linked with common sense and necessity; therefore, she will not leave Mustapha for she is entrenched in Moslem traditions.

Without a doubt, Sembène wants his readers to note that Noumbé is a victim of circumstances. At the same time, he wants his readers to know that African women are also guilty of accepting rules imposed upon them and are responsible for some of the social evils. Noumbé's physical pain ties in with her timid knowledge that she is not pleased with her marriage. She submerges the thought that she is a playmate, since it is uncharacteristic for a devoted wife to question her plight. All of her life Noumbé has been groomed to be a good wife and mother, but not at the expense of her dignity. The waiting and the slow disintegration of hope cause her to mock Mustapha, who throws around his authority. Sembène's silent suggestion is that it is up to African men and women to solve their difficulties and take the initiative to improve their lot.

By lingering over Noumbé's suffering, jealousy, loneliness, and anger Sembène pleads the case against the African male's misuse of polygamy: their failure to treat each wife equally in all ways, including their failure to provide each with adequate financial, temporal and emotional support.

Like Noumbé, Nafi in "Letters from France" has been raised in a patriarchal society where man rules over woman, and one class over another. Viewed as a second-class citizen by her society and father, she is tricked into marrying a 73-year old man, who lives in Marseilles, France. The topic of love is not entertained for marriage is based on loneliness, a wish to live in France, and an old man's desire to retain his lost youth. Nafi, the young wife, will serve Dembe, her husband, be an instrument for his pleasure, bear his children, greet his friends, and care for him in his old age. By selecting a young wife, like Suliman in "The Bilal's Fourth Wife," Demba hopes that she will be easier to control and thereby gain much from the unbalanced relationship. Unfortunately, the carefully laid plan backfires when Demba succumbs to cancer.

Alone in a damp room with four walls in Marseilles, Nafi has plenty of time to reflect upon her situation and to examine, in a proper perspective, the social and moral values that are imposed upon Senegalese women. What she sees and comes to terms with (as Yacine and Noumbé did) is that she has to bear some of the blame for her marriage. She also must admit that she was initially pleased with the possibility of living in France, and smitten with the picture of a handsome young Senegalese man. The adjustment and the astonishment occur when Nafi arrives in Marseilles to learn that the young man in the photo is actually seventy-three years old.

In isolation for the first time in her life, cut off from sunshine, gaiety, and human warmth, Nafi rebels through the medium of letters to her girl friend in Senegal. She implores her anonymous girl friend, who is her link with the happy past, to believe in her. Nafi feels that she has touched "rock bottom" with her marriage to Demba. She is furious that she has married an old, unemployed man without a pension, cannot bear for him to touch her, and even wishes to contract a mysterious disease. As the story develops, Nafi is reduced to begging for a job for her husband with a shipping company, when she learns that she is pregnant. Divorce is contemplated, but she has no independent means and no friends to turn to for aid in Marseilles. Nafi's future brightens, however, when Demba is given a short-term job on a ship, sends money to her, and asks a young dock worker, Arona, to watch over her. Closed in with a crying baby, sad to find that Demba has cancer upon his return, but miserable enough not to play the role of a grieving wife,

"Letters to France" reaches a melodramatic climax when Nafi tells Demba, on his death bed, that she is returning to Senegal.

Demba's elderly friends are greatly disappointed in Nafi for her failure to conform and exhibit some compassion for Demba. Nafi's explanation is that she is in an incompatible marriage locked in by loneliness. Her dreams to be independent and her own mistress haunt her. Nafi is not ashamed to confess to her girl friend that she had wished for Demba's death in order to be free. Nevertheless, her release does not come until the same elderly friends of Demba meet to decide her fate. Thanks to Arona's intervention she does not have to be hypocritical by mourning Demba for the required 40 days. The decision is that she will be sent back home.

With bitterness and relief, Nafi's past, present, and future have been monitored by male decisions. She is basically shy and innocent in Marseilles and finds it difficult to relate to the French and other Blacks. Nafi, who has some formal education, is a traditional young woman, who is not satisfied with her life. Although she protests loudly to her girl friend in her letters, she lacks the independence to rebel. Without recognizing it, Nafi is tied to her beliefs in the security of the clan and the extended family. There is an awareness that times are changing, but this does not lead her to disobey her father and husband. It is Demba's death that frees her from despair and makes it possible for her to return to Senegal.

Martin T. Bestman notes that: "Sembène paints the image of Africa that is convulsive, a world that questions its norms and values."[5] Indeed, Sembène does not hesitate to take to task such explosive topics as child paternity, adultery, arranged polygamous marriages, tyrannical men, divorce, child custody, and the imposition of double moral standards upon women. He identifies these issues and explores them in his fiction as a committed social critic. Sembène is committed to defending the rights of African women by insisting that they need to reclaim the economic, political, and social positions that they had held in the past. He is not afraid to expose the contradictions that control people's actions, and the collision with their menfolk that occurs when women assert themselves.

Sembène's female characters are not losers. In the four short stories each woman triumphs no matter how small the victory. By presenting such women Sembène opens up opportunities for African women to develop a more positive self-awareness and to draw upon capacities that have laid dormant within themselves. In order for Senegalese women to move forward, they must cast off outdated ideas and modes of behavior and view their plight realistically. In short, they must place themselves on the outside in order to look in. By doing so, they may begin to take steps to eliminate ignorance and mass illiteracy and improve their status in the twentieth-century. All four women—Yacine, the mother, Noumbé, and Nafi—challenge the traditional order, which condemned them to a secondary role. They, as mothers, are believable as characters. They, as mothers and women, through the prism of social and political contexts, will turn their faces to the future with hope for the future generation, their children.

NOTES

1. Martin T. Bestman, "Sembène Ousmane: Social Commitment and the Search for an African Identity," *A Celebration of Black and African Writing*, eds. Bruce King and Kolawole Ogungbesan (Oxford: Ahmadu Bello University Press and Oxford University Press, 1975), p. 142.
2. The original text was published in French entitled *Voltaïque. Nouvelles* (Paris: Nouvelles Editions Latines, 1962) by Ousmane Sembène. In this paper all quotations are from the English translation, *Tribal Scars and Other Stories* (Washington, D.C.: Inscape, 1975).
3. Sembène Ousmane, "The Bilal's Fourth Wife," *Tribal Scars and Other Stories*, p. 17.
4. Anne Lippert, "The Changing Role of Women as Viewed in the Literature of English-Speaking and French-Speaking West Africa," (Bloomington: Indiana University, Unpublished Ph. D. dissertation, 1972), p. 253.
5. Martin T. Bestman, p. 140.

Women as Scapegoats of Culture and Cult: An Activist's View of Female Circumcision in Ngugi's The River Between

Tobe Levin

I was six years old that night when I lay in my bed, warm and peaceful in that pleasurable state which lies half way between wakefulness and sleep, with the rosy dreams of childhood flitting by, like gentle fairies in quick succession. I felt something move under the blankets, something like a huge hand, cold and rough, fumbling over my body, as though looking for something. Almost simultaneously another hand, as cold and as rough and as big as the first one, was clapped over my mouth, to prevent me from screaming.

They carried me to the bathroom . . . I was frightened . . . something like an iron grasp caught hold of my hand and my arms and my thighs, so that I became unable to resist or even to move. I . . . remember the icy touch of the bathroom tiles under my naked body, and unknown voices . . . interrupted now and again by a rasping metallic sound which reminded me of the butcher when he used to sharpen his knife before slaughtering a sheep . . . My blood was frozen in my veins.[1]

The author of this passage, Egyptian physician and activist Nawal El
Saadawi, recalls fearing that the intruders were preparing to cut her throat,"
which was always what happened with disobedient girls like myself in the
stories that my old rural grandmother was so fond of telling me."[2] But it was
not the child's neck they were after. Instead they groped

> . . . somewhere below my belly, as though seeking something buried
> between my thighs. At that very moment I realized that my thighs had
> been pulled wide apart, and that each of my lower limbs was being
> held by steel fingers that never relinquished their pressure. . . Then
> suddenly the sharp metallic edge seemed to drop between my thighs
> and cut off a piece of flesh from my body.
> I screamed with pain despite the hand held over my mouth, for the
> pain was not just a pain, it was like a searing flame that went through
> my whole body. After a few moments, I saw a red pool of blood
> around my hips.
> I did not know what they had cut off from my body. . . I just wept, and
> called out to my mother for help. But the worst shock of all was when I
> looked around and found her standing by my side. . .
> The memory of circumcision continued to track me down like a
> nightmare.[3]

To ensure a shared understanding of the reality behind the euphemism
"female circumcision," I have begun with this quotation.[4] Circumcision of
the clitoral prepuce is indeed an anatomical possibility, given adequate
surgical instruments in a clinical setting. But such a delicate operation is
nearly impossible to perform on struggling little girls and women on the cold
floor of the bathroom or compound. Nor can it be properly carried out
during initiation rites, within a framework of 'sex education', festival and
joy. Instead, clitoridectomy and, in the Horn of Africa, labial excision and
infibulation are practiced. In the novel, *L'Excisée*, by Lebanese author
Evelyne Accad, the unmitigated horror of the latter custom is shared with
the reader as the narrator, E., a foreigner, is forced to witness the slaughter
in her home:

> Et les femmes ont saisi la première fillete. Elles la tiennent de tous les
> cotés. Elles lui soulèvent la robe et la font s'asseoir sur un tabouret qui
> surplombe un bol blanc. Elles lui écartent les jambes et exposent son
> sexe rasé. . . La sage-femme écarte les grandent lèvres et les petites
> lèvres. Elle fait jaillir le clitoris et le jette dans le bol. La fille hurle de
> douleur. Et le sang coule. Les femmes tiennent la fillette plus
> fermement. La sorcière continue son oeuvre de mutilation. Elle
> découpe les grandes lèvres, comme de grandes oreilles rouges de peur,

qui vont rejoindre le clitoris dans le bol. . . . les cris de la fillette
resemblent à ceux d'un chien qu'on égorge.[5]
[And the women siezed the first little girl and held her on all sides.
They raised her dress and made her sit on a stool that overhung a white
basin. They spread her legs apart and exposed her shaved pubic area.
The mid-wife separated the labia majora from the labia minora,
whacked off the clitoris and tossed it into the basin. The girl wailed
with pain, the blood running. The women held the girl tighter. The
sorceress continued her mutilation. She cut off the labia majora, like
large ears red with fright, that joined the clitoris in the basin. . . .The
little girl's cries sounded like those of a dog being slaughtered.]

(editor's translation)

E. is seized with compassion for the victims of what is frankly termed a
"massacre," but females are so powerless in this desert society that only
one solution seems viable: the younger, 'uncircumcised' sister of an initiate
is offered the opportunity to flee. E. herself accompanies young Nour
(meaning "light") to the seacoast where she transfers the girl to the care of
an Egyptian woman traveling to Switzerland. E., who has been threatened
with excision by the other women in her compound, chooses a different way
out. Having placed her hopes in Nour, who vows to return to "aid her
sisters,"[6] E. drowns herself. Although physically unscathed, the heroine's
knowledge of the circumcised woman's suffering seems to have irrevocably
altered her consciousness of women's oppression. Indeed, the clitoris
severed from the body is a telling symbol of female status in phallocratic
culture. For once amputation has occurred, no regeneration is possible. As
in Accad's novel, female solidarity in suffering results in the perpetuation of
that suffering, for the women present at the massacre scream and clap to
drown out the cries of the children, taking "their revenge."[7] Or, as El
Saadawi writes, she exchanged a glance with her sister after the event, a
look which "seemed to say: 'Now we know what it is. Now we know where
lies our tragedy. We were born of a special sex, the female sex. We are
destined in advance to taste of misery, and to have a part of our body torn
away by cold, unfeeling cruel hands.'"[8]

When sympathetic human beings are exposed to these devastating facts,
they can only share the authors' hopes of exploding the cycle of horror in
which mothers become, in Mary Daly's words, the "token torturers" of
their daughters who, in turn, accept a self-denying code imposed on them by
the 'dominant' sex. As in Accad's novel, the initiates, though trembling with
anxiety and terror, struggle to maintain their composure, knowing that to
become a woman, one must accept the knife: "they will not be able to
marry if they are not cut open and resewn."[9] Other than flight, there appears
to be no alternative, for custom is tenacious where women are concerned.

When Accad's heroine E. asks her husband how he can condone his compatriot's mutilation of the women's "most delicate, most precious and most important sexual organs," reminding him that they had originally come together to his country as social revolutionaries, he snickers and replies: "It's tradition."[10] "Tradition" has become a shibboleth in the mouths of men who themselves are quite willing to accept change, provided their own privileges remain intact.

Yet "tradition" can also be invoked with pride where the customs in question are innocuous. In the international struggle to extend human rights to women, the need to distinguish between beneficent and malicious practices has become more acute than ever, for if our aim is the eradication of dangerous 'rites', western activists must learn to enter the value system of the 'circumcised' to avoid the counter-productive approach based on ignorance and indignation alone. In this regard, the Association of African Women for Research and Development (AAWORD) in Dakar, Senegal, has warned feminists against viewing African societies exclusively in terms of female oppression and insists that "solidarity can only exist alongside self-affirmation and mutual respect."[11]

One avenue to increased understanding of African traditions, providing a basis for mutual respect, is literature, for in fiction we find revealing treatment of the female circumcision theme in a number of works by African authors. For example, in *From a Crooked Rib*, Somalian novelist Nuruddin Farah demonstrates a high degree of feminist awareness in approaching the problem of infibulation,[12] criticized also by Malian writer Yambo Ouologuem in *Le Devoir de Violence*. In this ironic novel, infibulation provides the means of reconstructing virginity after the ruler has "claimed for himself the right of the first night."[13] Ouologuem ridicules male complacency and self-deception for demanding that 'purity' be feigned at such inhuman cost. Similarly, Amadou Kourouma in *Les Soleils des Indépendances*[14] renders so sympathetically the initiate's state of mind during the experience of clitoridectomy that one can hardly doubt the author's indignation. Finally, Nawal El Saadawi, in *Woman at Point Zero*, uses excision as a leit-motif of loss: the heroine, with a man she loves, cannot feel pleasure. "It was as if I could no longer recall the exact spot from which it used to arise, or as though a part of me, of my being, was gone and would never return."[15] Mutilation is permanent—an extremely serious violation of integrity which cannot be condoned.

And yet, two additional African novels deal with the theme from a perspective of compromise: Flora Nwapa's *Efuru* and Ngugi wa Thiong'o's *The River Between*.[16] Flora Nwapa is a Nigerian author and publisher whom I interviewed on the subject of female circumcision at the 1980 Frankfurt Book Fair. She felt then that the western media tended to exaggerate the extent of the problem. However, in November, 1980, I received a letter from her in which she admitted the need to revise her point of view—the practice was indeed more prevalent (and the consequences graver) than she had imagined.

Nevertheless, her fiction represents the earlier attitude, accepting female circumcision as one integral part of a vital culture. In *Efuru*, for example, "having a bath" is a euphemism for clitoridectomy, and the ritual "purification" may follow marriage but must precede the birth of a child— one baby's death is attributed directly to the mother's fear of the razor. Since Nwapa presents traditional society in a realistic mode, her portrayal of attitudes favoring genital mutilation is, on one level, entirely appropriate. In fact, she scrupulously avoids over-simplification by showing how humanly (and even humanely) concerned the midwife herself and the neighbors are for the health and comfort of the initiate, denying neither that the operation can be dangerous (the operator refuses to proceed without absolute assurance that Efuru is not pregnant), nor that certain operators are inept—one is named who has caused numerous casualties. Yet one disturbing aspect of the narrative lies in the defeatism of the following exchange. When asked how she is feeling, having gone to be circumcised with as much trepidation as we might feel on visiting the dentist, Efuru replies: "'It is much better now. It was dreadful the first day'," which elicits the resigned response: "'It is what every woman undergoes. So don't worry'."[17] The author seems to share this essential conservatism as she highlights the compensatory festive context in which the operation is embedded. Feted and coddled for one to three months afterwards, the former patient, her relations and neighbors are shown to relish the special situation, one given to displays of happiness, culminating in the offer of gifts in the marketplace to a woman then at the apogee of beauty. Sadly, we are given to understand the attitudes of women themselves, a type of solidarity in adversity without any significant attempt to challenge or question the *raison d'être* of a practice which causes them pain.

Ngugi's narrative takes a similarly complex approach, disconcerting at first to hard-line opponents of genital mutilation. The only fictional work I have found which elevates female circumcision to a position of central thematic importance, *The River Between* has the issue serve as battleground in the clash between conservative tribal elements and the patriarchal Christian church, a plot based on events of the nineteen twenties and thirties marked by growing nationalist sentiment in Kenya. The era witnessed the founding of two oppositional groups, the Young Kikuyu Association led by Harry Thaku, and Kenyatta's Kikuyu Central Association. (KCA), "dedicated to removing British colonialism and restoring the traditional values eroded under white rule. In the midst of this nationalist revolutionary fervour, Jomo Kenyatta, who would later become Kenya's head of state gave the definitive male view on female circumcision which would be subsequently recorded in his book *Facing Mount Kenya* (1938). Kenyatta asserted that "not a single Gikuyu worthy of the name wants to marry a non-excised woman because that operation is the basis of all moral and religious instruction,"[18] an insight which inspired his first official act as chief executive: cancelling the ban on female circumcision. Similar opposition greeted attempts by the Presbyterian Mission to eliminate the practice in the nineteen twenties. In response to the ultimatum, issued in 1929—"they must now choose the church or the KCA"[19]—many male fraternity members opted for excommunication and expulsion from the schools rather than see 'their' women freed from the knife. In fact, resistance was so strong that during the carnage taking place on both sides, some African men used English women to make their point. For instance, " . . . to show people's wrath and hate for Irigu (uncircumcised females), on 2 January, 1930, Miss Hilda Stumpf of the A.I.M. Kajabe, died in Hospital, after some men broke into her house at night and forcibly circumcised her."[20] Again in the nineteen-fifties, during the Mau Mau revolution, similar scapegoating of women occurred within the context of freedom fighting. In a strange twist, circumcision of women came to be equated with the return to traditional Kikuyu values.

Yet, this reaffirmation of the tribal heritage was not without its redeeming dimension: the Christian community's exclusion of the circumcised led to the founding of independent institutions such as the Kenya Independence Schools Association on whose leadership Ngugi bases his portrait of "The Teacher," Waiyaki, a man dedicated to following a middle road between the tribal heritage and the white man's knowledge: hence his unwavering but illusory faith in education, education against, among other things, female circumcision.

Resistance to abolition of the rite is clearly, in part, an oppositional gesture against colonialism. Although the "climax of the rivalry between the two ridges (Makuyu and Kameno, Christian and traditionalist camps) was brought on by the missionaries' ban on female circumcision,"[21] the basis for this internecine hatred is to be sought elsewhere:

> . . . and all at once Waiyaki realized what the ridges wanted. All at once he felt more forcefully than he had ever felt before the shame of the people's land being taken away, the shame of being forced to work on those same lands, the humiliation of paying taxes for a government that you knew nothing about.[22]

Ngugi places the renewed insistence on initiation rites within the context of land expropriation, the imposition of taxes and de facto forced labor to pay them. By highlighting this explanation he is in harmony with other influential critics of female circumcision, including Nawal El Saadawi and Stella Efua Graham. The former attributes "the lower status of women in our societies," of which genital mutilation is a symptom, "to certain economic and political forces, namely those of foreign imperialism operating mainly from the outside, and of the reactionary classes operating from the inside."[23] Confirming this analysis based on class struggle, Stella Efua Graham of Ghana, president of the London-based Women's Action Group against Excision and Infibulation, adds that:

> . . . female circumcision is a very sensitive and political subject tied to complex sociocultural structures and to underdevelopment. It is directly related to the depressed political and socioeconomic position of women in these societies.[24]

Typical of many indigenous approaches to clitoridectomy,[25] El Saadawi, Graham and Ngugi understate the causal dimension accentuated by western feminists[26]—irrational male complicity in the continuance of mutilation, a complacency rooted in unconscious fears of the female and ambivalence vis-à-vis sexuality.[27] Still, whether an emphasis on sexual politics constitutes an appropriate strategy in the early stages of consciousness raising against the practice remains subject to debate.[28]

Ngugi's novel, in any case, deals with female circumcision not from a feminist, but from a humanist and progressive standpoint, leading its readers gently and ironically to understand that male insistence on female 'rites' is displaced impotence and is ultimately de-constructive. He shows, for example, how the brothers are mistaken in viewing circumcision as a still unsullied source of cultural integrity from which strength can be drawn in preparation for the battles ahead, to repossess the land. Ngugi further links this futile hope to renewal of the martial image, in turn tied to the vehement insistence on female mutilation. For without removal of the clitoris, without 'purity', it is assumed that female sexual energy would threaten the tribe with destruction, as Ngugi records:

> There was a new edge to the songs. Uncircumcised girls were the objects of cutting attacks. Everything dirty and impure was heaped on them. They were the impure things of the tribe and they would bring the wrath of the ancestral spirits on the ridges. A day would come when all these *Irigu* would be circumcised by force, to rid the land of impurities.[29]

Not the whites, but the deviant African women are to blame for the apocalypse.

Thus, in the wake of imperialism, women are assigned a new symbolic function. As critic Judith Cochrane benignly notes, they become the "guardians of the tribe," an ascribed status not necessarily of benefit to them as a group. On the contrary, excluded from the 'development' process by the importation of western-style sexism, pushed out of economic fields in which they had been sovereign, women have been systematically disempowered and abused, as illustrated by a figure from Waiyaki's nightmare, presaging the failure of his own attempts at reconciliation through marriage to an *Irigu*:

> They were all pulling her into pieces, as if she were a thing of sacrifice to the god of the river, which still flowed with life as they committed this ritual outrage on her.[30]1

It is doubtful, however, whether the 'river between' demands such sacrifice. Called *Honia*, meaning the cure or "bring-back-to-life," it separates but also potentially units the feuding hills, serving mainly as the backdrop for actors on the stage of significant events: political meetings, lovers' trysts and circumcision. The latter theme is in fact introduced on its banks, where Nyambura and Muthoni, children of the Christian convert Joshua, have come to fetch water. They discuss the rites, defying the injunction that "a daughter of God should never let a thought of circumcision come into her mind."[31] The thought, however, is clearly elicited by the river, as Nyambura notes:

> During the initiation ceremonies, boys and girls came to wet their bodies here on the morning of circumcision. It had long been discovered that very cold water numbed the skin, making it less painful during the operation. Nyambura thought of this and felt slightly guilty. She looked apprehensively at her sister, who was still drawing water. Nyambura wondered whether such thoughts ever came to Muthoni. She thought not and envied her. For Nyambura had learnt and knew that circumcision was sinful. It was a pagan rite.[32]

This passage fulfills two theoretical tasks, criticising both the critic and the rite. First, it undermines Christian teaching, for instead of opposing mutilation in order to preserve the wellspring of pleasure, the church takes the repressive puritan stance of forbidding any mention of sexuality (a position firmly rooted in misogynist tradition). Defined as "sinful" not because it destroys sexuality but recognizes it instead, the rite is dismissed, as though labeling were a sufficient deterrent.

Yet criticism of the church does not constitute approval of the custom. The passage also establishes an immediate link between the terms "circumcision," "numbness" and "pain," without attempting to revalue these states or redeem them in any way. In fact, Waiyaki ". . . thought that if he had been in (Muthoni's) position he would never have brought himself into such pain."[33] As for the male, his situation differs: first because he sees circumcision as a test of manly courage and, second, because, despite the identity in nomenclature, he is the only one actually circumcised. As we have seen, something else is done to women.

Marielouise Janssen-Jurreit, comparing female to male rites, notes the differing goals of the two interventions, the female designed mainly to produce docile wives.[34] Indeed, it is to become a wife that Muthoni undergoes the ceremony, wishing to be "made beautiful in the tribe" in order to acquire "a husband for (her) bed (and) children to play around the hearth."[35] The implication is that she must choose between chastity and mutilation, as Waiyaki's father ironically confirms:

> "Who ever heard of a girl that was not circumcised? Who would ever pay cows and goats for such a girl? Certainly it would never be his son."

The fact that it IS his son, the Teacher, who chooses to break the taboo and ally himself sexually with an Irigu accentuates the fundamental tendency of the novel—to oppose those customs which no longer fulfill a beneficent social function. Yet neither the traditionalists nor the Christians present viable alternatives for women. Indeed, the Christian model of the submissive wife, when conscientiously followed, achieves the same goal as mutilation. It is thus hypocritical to oppose circumcision in the name of the 'life-denying' creed.[37]

Miriamu represents western-style marital comportment, demonstrating a meekness so studied that the author seems compelled to contrast it with a more natural mode of being. He suggests that her Christian humility is superficial, her silence the result of instruction, not character. She has merely learned by rite "the value of Christian submission."[38] Concerned only to maintain peace in the household, her motto has become "'Obey your father'." Yet the more genuine paradigm is there, as the author notes: "Christianity was a religion learned and accepted: inside the true Kikuyu woman was sleeping."[39] For the cultural model of womanhood was not submissive but powerful, as an old Kikuyu legend shows: "Long ago women used to rule this land and its men," Chege tells Waiyaki. "They were harsh and . . . owned everything."[40] In revolt, the men took advantage of the women's pregnancies to overthrow their despotism, but traces of the (real or imagined) power relations were not erased from social memory.

Thus, it is in light of her foremothers' independence that Muthoni's controversial decision, to submit to clitoridectomy, has been judged. One is tempted to censure her, but disapproval may be softened if her gesture is seen as an act of rebellion against her father's rigid code. Eddah Gachukia, for example, goes so far as to credit her with heroism:

> Take Muthoni's unbelievable courage. . . She has great daring in deciding to do what she felt was the right thing, regardless of consequences.[41]

And Judith Cochrane agrees:

> ... (Muthoni's) act of rebellion in forsaking the home of her
> Christianized father in order to participate fully in the rites and
> ceremonies of the tribe is a personal act of courage.[42]

Certainly, this may be true, and yet Muthoni's desire to escape the
stultifying lovelessness of her father's faith serves better to expose Christian
sexual hypocrisy than it does to support initiation. After all, she dies as a
result of circumcision, her mission a failure.

The text informs us that other girls had previously died of the operation,
but Muthoni's demise differs from theirs in time and context, assuming an
amplified symbolic meaning for both camps, the traditionalists blaming the
victim and her father for impurity and neglect of the prescribed sacrifices
that would have ensured recovery, the Christians reacting with righteous
anger, finding confirmation of their belief in native barbarity. As for
Muthoni, faced with two equally untenable alternatives, she expresses the
hopelessness of her position in her last words to Nyambura: "'. . . I see
Jesus. And I am a woman, beautiful in the tribe. . . '" Doubly alienated, her
attempt to achieve wholeness through mutilation, to reconcile the tribe and
Christianity, cannot bear fruit.

Christianity's failure is perhaps of greater concern to the author than the
obviously reactionary stance of the Kiama. And certainly, nowhere does
the western church appear more ridiculous than in the dogma of the virgin
birth. Since the celebration of Christmas and the initiation season coincide,
Ngugi takes the opportunity to both introduce and undermine the Christian
alternative:

> (Joshua) renounced his tribe's magic, power and ritual. He turned to
> and felt the deep presence of the one God. Had he not given the white
> man power over all?
> He learned of Jesus -
>   Behold, a virgin shall conceive,
>   And bear a son . . .
> He realized the ignorance of his people.[44]

One needs little maturity to doubt the credibility of an organization
condemning clitoridectomy but espousing belief in a virgin birth. In fact,
concerning sexual matters, the tribe appears to be infinitely more sophisticated than the Christians. For example, the clitoris is at least acknowledged
by the former (being too powerful, it is removed), while the organ has been
treated by western ideology as though it didn't exist.

As a result, the Christian campaign for abolition of excision, concerned
neither with female health nor with women's integrity, but rather with

sexuality as sin, was seriously misguided. Furthermore, in failing to differentiate sufficiently between the mutilating aspects of initiation and the framework of festivities, it proved itself totally incapable of engaging in dialogue concerning the custom. Livingstone, for instance, once came to witness the rites but was so shocked at the partying the night before that he could not grasp the import of the following morning's events. In the evening he witnessed:

> Old and young, women and children, . . . Losing themselves in the magic motion of the dance. . . . Women, stripped to the waist, with their thin breasts flapping on their chests, went round and round the big fire, swinging their hips and contorting their bodies in all sorts of provocative ways, but always keeping the rhythm.

> They were free. Age and youth had become reconciled for this one night. And you could sing about anything and talk of the hidden parts of men and women without feeling that you had violated the otherwise strong social code that governed people's relationships, especially the relationship between young and old, man and woman.[45]

By failing to look below the surface of this behavior, the church cannot possibly recognize the safety-valve function of "the (illusory)chaos of locked emotions let loose," that is, sexual expression contained within prescribed limits of taboo and license. As Waiyaki points out, despite appearances, it was actually forbidden "to go with a woman on such an occasion."[46] The Christians are therefore judged incompetent to meddle with a custom whose real significance in the tribe the clerics are too "dense" to comprehend. Condemning the rite's practitioners as savages, with nothing more convincing than the celebration of a virgin birth to offer in exchange, the church is revealed as hypocritical, a judgment reinforced by the fact that Christian males are no freer from brutality than others, as the text shows. Joshua regrets having married a circumcised woman and even reproaches Miriamu for this. Yet the narrator adds:

> Not that Miriamu shared or cherished these sentiments. But she knew him. Joshua was such a staunch man of God and such a firm believer in the Old Testament, that he would never refrain from punishing a sin, even if this meant beating his wife.[47]

Christian and indigenous males alike are ultimately similar in one respect: their claim to power over the female. Both share a belief in the *femme fatale*: Like Eve, Nyambura is charged with Waiyaki's downfall: "'. . . it is the girl'," the Kiama claims. "'The girl has turned his mind the wrong way.'"[48] And the cure for such high treason? "'As we said earlier', one more (Kiama member) commented, 'all these Christians should be circumcised. By force.'"[49]

It is in light of this hostility toward women in the gynophobic *Weltanschauung* of Christian and traditional African males alike that the circumcison controversy in Ngugi's novel may be viewed. When theorizing about the conflict, the narrator himself concludes:

> Circumcision of women was not important as a physical operation. It was what it did inside a person. It could not be stopped overnight.[50]

On first reading, this seems unconscionably moderate. But what precisely is meant by "not important"? That clitoridectomy is trivial, like removing the tonsils or appendix? Or does it mean non-essential, unnecessary for effecting that transformation "inside a person" which the rite of passage is intended to accomplish; thus, "not important" to the goal of symbolizing maturity and group cohesion? The latter would seem to be the case, as the narrator goes on: "It could not be stopped overnight"—but it should be stopped! "Patience and, above all, education were needed. If the white man's religion made you abandon a custom and then did not give you something else of equal value, you became lost. An attempt at resolution of the conflict would only kill you, as it did Muthoni."[51] In fact, Muthoni's gesture illustrates this thesis: she intends to combine Christianity with custom. The isolation she would otherwise feel is suggested by her cry: "How could I be outside the tribe, when all the girls born with me at the same time have left me?"[52] Peer pressure is certainly one of the major reasons why the practice of clitoridectomy continues but, as Sigrid Peicke notes, Muthoni's act remains problematic: "We are not convinced by (her) enthusiasm in having herself initiated. Her decision has a clichéd ring to it, being too strongly charged with an untenable symbolic function."[53]

The difficulty with Ngugi's handling of the theme may be traced to his lack of feminist insight at that time (1965) into the unconscious motivation of males who support initiation for women. The text does seem to support an idealistic hope of purging the rites of their harmful dimension while maintaining the liberating, communal aspects. However, recent history shows a reverse trend. Fran Hosken's research reveals an accelerating neglect of the rite accompanied by the spread of excision performed in hospitals on girls at increasingly younger ages, for whom the amputation is totally divorced from any kind of moral, ethical or even sex-educational dimension. The death of 14 young girls resulting from this intervention in 1983 led to the passage of an edict against the operations in Kenya.[54] At the same time, law without the force of custom remains impotent, as the experiences of the Sudan and Egypt show. The practice has thus proven to be far more tenacious than a man of Ngugi's good will seems to have anticipated.

Why? Sociologist Carola Donner-Reichle sees one explanation in "gerontological African patriarchy," meaning that, where polygyny is prevalent, men fear being unable to satisfy too many non-excised women at once.[55] And psychoanalytic theory supports this view. Karen Horney's research on "the dread of women," Margaret Mead's suggestion of "womb-envy," the vast collection of vagina dentata myths—all are relevant as possible factors accounting for female excision. We even have a paper presented by Mohammed Shaalan at the 1979 U.N. Seminar in Khartoum on "Traditional Practices affecting the Health of Women" revealingly titled "Clitoris Envy: A Psychodynamic Construct Instrument in Female Circumcision." Ngugi's novel sheds little light on these aspects of initiation, though it does support the line of reasoning whereby colonialism, oppressive to both sexes, is recognized as significantly more detrimental to the welfare of women. The River Between, showing the connection between expropriation and repression of the indigenous male and his scapegoating of the female, reinforces the interpretation of numerous African activists engaged in fieldwork, and therein lies its relevance for the Western feminist reader.

One novel I have not yet mentioned dealing with the theme of female circumcision from both a moderate and a feminist standpoint, thus offering a constructive contrast with Ngugi, is Alice Walker's The Color Purple, which dramatizes an Afro-American woman's encounter with a tribe where genital mutilation takes place. In a series of letters to her sister, the missionary Nettie both evaluates Olinka tribal custom and objectively reports how she herself is evaluated. For her part, Nettie openly criticizes women's subordinate status under polygny, women's exclusion from educational opportunity, their occasional forced exile through sale "to the trader" should they refuse to marry the man chosen for them. Nettie patently applies egalitarian values to what she finds amiss in human relations. For instance, she is unable to approve of women's meekness in the presence of men, nor of the men's comandeering, supercilious attitude toward women which, she writes, "reminds me too much of Pa."[56] In fact, she retains her vision of unabridged human rights for females, including the right to self-determination and bodily inviolability.

Her hosts, however, judge her quite as harshly as she does them. She learns that they pity her for the very qualities of which she is most proud: her independence as a single woman and her professional dedication. The Olinka of both sexes regard her as a wretched creature—neither wife nor mother, she is seen as abandoned. In the opinion of Tashi's father:

Our women are respected here—We would never let them tramp the world as American women do. There is always someone to look after the Olinka woman. A father. An uncle. A brother or nephew. Do not be offended, Sister Nettie, but our people pity women such as you who

are cast out, we know not from where, into a world unknown to you,
where you must struggle all alone, for yourself.

So I am an object of pity and contempt, I thought, to men and
women alike.[57]

Closing her letter, "Good-bye until the next time, Dear Celie, from a pitiful
cast-out woman who may perish during the rainy season," Nettie tries to
dilute her bitterness with humor. But the sting remains. Apparently,
although "things are changing," views pertaining to women are not
modified apace. Rather one has the impression that women's subordination
is the pillar to which male tribesmen cling while everything else falls apart.
Like Ngugi, Walker sees excision fulfilling this purpose. Despite the
explicit "repugnance" of her American boyfriend, Tashi agrees to initiation
to demonstrate that the Olinka "still have their own ways. . . even though
the white man has taken everything else. Tashi didn't want to do it," Olivia
remarks, "but to make her people feel better, she's resigned."[58]

Women are indeed the scapegoats of tradition. As Audrey Wipper notes,
"urban African women (in western dress) are (being) used as targets of
agression (sic) to symbolize the source of strains" resulting from "rapid and
deep-rooted social change."[59] The returning of women to the "veil" in
Northern African Islamic societies is another example. In fact, she sees in
misogynistic media campaigns echoes of the European witchhunts, thus
confirming Ngugi's view that increasing disempowerment of males results
in intensified pressures of females. In his later works, too, Ngugi shows
women suffering the devastating effects of a misguided development policy
and, as Sigrid Peicke writes, "oppression becomes the central theme" in his
later portrayals of women.[60] He gives us, for example, in *Petals of Blood*
and *Devil on the Cross* two young heroines aware of the politics behind their
disadvantages and active in the struggle to change their societies. And
though both Wanja and Jacinta personally prosper, the author shows that
women *as a group* have been betrayed—having fought for independence,
they are denied its fruits.

Perhaps the value of Ngugi's work for feminists lies here, in his dialectic
vision of women in revolt. Often in the face of crushing odds, his heroines
survive. They are active, intelligent, courageous, defiant. Even Muthoni, in
The River Between, rebels; a rebellion misdirected but of great symbolic
import. For her choice is both right and wrong. It is right to defy the father's
law; it is wrong to choose clitoridectomy. Her act does not allow of
simplistic interpretations. Yet the activist is tempted to oversimplify.
Excision is a crime, mutilation an atrocity. These 'rites' should be stopped.
Yes. But how? Not merely by demanding that they cease, but also by
understanding why they happen. *The River Between* takes a step in this
direction, for understanding precedes change.

NOTES

1. Nawal El Saadawi, *The Hidden Face of Eve. Women in the Arab World.* Trans. Dr. Sherif Hetata (London: Zed Press, 1980), p. 7.
2. *Ibid.*
3. *Ibid.*, pp. 7-8.
4. In a letter to *Ms.* magazine, J. Knepp notes that "the term 'female circumcision' should (not) be used to mean clitoridectomy. . . The parallel mutilation of a male would be cutting off the *whole tip* of the penis, not the foreskin." *Ms.* August 1983, p. 12. Furthermore, one should be aware of the potentially devastating side and after-effects of these interventions (the more serious accompanying infibulation). These include bladder infections, tetanus and septic anemia, infrequent fatal hemorrhaging, cysts, vaginal fistula resulting in incontinence, keloid formations, infertility due to chronic pelvic infection, delay in the second stage of labor resulting from the inelasticity of scar tissue, sometimes leading to brain damage of the infant, etc.
5. Evelyne Accad, *L'Excisée* (Paris: L'Harmattan, 1982), p. 121-2.
6. *Ibid.*, 170.
7. *Ibid.*, 121.
8. Saadawi, 8.
9. Accad, 122.
10. Ibid., 140.
11. In "A Statement on Genital Mutilation," in Miranda Davies, editor, *Third World: Second Sex. Women's Struggles and National Liberation* (London: Zed Press, 1983), p. 217, AAWORD charges the western press with extreme insensitivity in the handling of this theme. A plethora of media tracts on the issue are guilty of "aggressiveness, ignorance or even contempt." Effect has been achieved through sensationalism, violating "the dignity of the very women (to be) save(d)." Finally, certain western campaigns have drawn on "the latent racism" present where "ethnocentric prejudice is so deep-rooted."
12. Nuruddin Farah, *From a Crooked Rib* (London: Heinemann, 1970).
13. Yambo Ouologuem, *Bound to Violence.* Trans. Ralph Mannheim (London: Heinemann, 1971), p. 47.
14. Amadou Kourouma, *Les Soleils des Indépendances* (Montréal: Presse de L'Université, 1968; 2nd edition Paris: Seuil, 1970).
15. Nawal El Saadawi, *Woman at Point Zero.* Trans. Dr. Sherif Hetata (London: Zed Press, 1983), p. 15.
16. As a matter of interest, influential Nigerian novelist Buchi Emecheta has also expressed moderate views on the subject, in particular expressing doubt about the efficacy of western feminist intervention (unpublished taped conversation with Sigrid Peicke, January, 1983).
17. Flora Nwapa, *Efuru* (London: Heinemann, 1966), p. 15.
18. Jomo Kenyatta cited in Benoîte Groult, *Ainsi soit-elle* (Paris: Grasset, 1975), p. 105, author's translation.
19. Carl Gustav Rosberg and John Nottingham, *The Myth of Mau Mau Nationalism in Kenya* (London: Pall Mall Press, 1966,) p. 120.

20. S. N. Ngubiah, "Ngugi's Early Writings: 'The River Between' and 'The Black Hermit'" in Chris Wanjala, editor, *Standpoints on African Literature* Nairobi: East African Literature Bureau, 1973), p. 70.

21. *Ibid.*, 66.

22. Ngugi wa Thiong'o, *The River Between* (London: Heinemann, 1965), p. 142.

23. Saadawi, *Eve*, p. 41.

24. Stella Efua Graham, "Female Sexual Mutilation," *Minority Rights Group Newsletter*, No. 15, April 1983 (London: 36 Craven Street, WC 3), p. 3.

25. A marked exception to this approach emphasizing class struggle is the view of Dr. Asma El Dareer in her book *Woman, Why Do You Weep? Circumcision and Its Consequences* (London: Zed Press, 1982). Dedicated "To All Women," her standpoint is feminist, not unlike that of Raqiya Haji Dualeh Abdalla in *Sisters in Affliction. Circumcision and Infibulation of Women in Africa* (London: Zed Press, 1982). Dealing with mutilation in the Sudan and Somalia respectively, both books are based on the authors' field research and include an account of current projects aimed at eradicating the practice.

26. Western feminists taking this approach include Mary Daly, Fran Hosken, Marielouise Janssen-Jurreit, Benoîte Groult, and Séverine Auffret.

27. For a review of 'reasons' and 'rationalizations' given for the practice, many pointing toward a psychoanalytic explanation, see Tobe Levin, "'Unspeakable Atrocities': The Psycho-sexual Etiology of Female Genital Mutilation," *The Journal of Mind and Behavior*, Autumn, 1980 (Vol. 1, No. 2), pp. 197-210.

28. For example, at a Paris meeting of European women's groups against genital mutilation, sponsored by the Commission pour l'Abolition des Mutilations Sexuelles (CAMS) on July 9 and 10, 1983, Stella Efua Graham expressed her belief that western feminist rhetoric frightens the majority of African women and that, to be effective, another tone must be used. In contrast, Awa Thiam of CAMS (with headquarters in Dakar) takes a more uncompromising view, linking clitoidectomy specifically to other forms of violence against women. Thiam goes so far as to introduce the radical lesbian alternative to dependence on men and marriage as a solution worth consideration.

29. Ngugi, 121.

30. *Ibid.*, 120.

31. *Ibid.*, 23.

32. *Ibid.*

33. *Ibid.*, 45-6.

34. Marielouise Janssen-Jurreit, *Sexismus/Über die Abtreibung der Frauenfrage* München: Carl Hanser Verlag, 1976), p. 542.

35. Ngugi, *ibid.*, 44.

36. *Ibid.*, 37-8.

37. Eddah Gachukia, *Notes on Ngugi wa Thiong'o's "The River Between"* (Nairobi: Heinemann, 1975), p. 8.

38. Ngugi, *ibid.*, 34.

39. *Ibid.*

40. *Ibid.*, 15.

41. Eddah Gachukia, "The Role of Women in Ngugi's Novels," *Busara* Vol, 3, No. 4 (1971), p. 30.

42. Judith Cochrane, "Women as the Guardians of the Tribe in Ngugi's Novels," ACLALS-Bulletin, Vol, 4, No. 5 (1977), p. 2.
43. Ngugi, *ibid.*, 53.
44. *Ibid.*, 29.
45. *Ibid.*, 41.
46. *Ibid.*, 42.
47. *Ibid.*, 129.
48. *Ibid.*, 129.
49. *Ibid.*
50. *Ibid.*, 142.
51. *Ibid.*
52. *Ibid.*, 44.
53. Sigrid Peicke, *In den Frauen liegt die Zukunft: Frauengestalten im Werk des kenianischen Schriftstellers Ngugi wa Thiong'o* (Frankfurt am Main: Nexus Verlag, 1981), p. 21-22. My translation.
54. "Kenya," *Courage* (July, 1983), p. 25.
55. Carola Donner-Reichle, *Die Last der Unterentwicklung: Frauen in Kenia* (Berlin: Dialogus Mundi, 1977), p. 41. My Translation.
56. Alice Walker, *The Color Purple* (New York: Harcourt, Brace, Jovanovich, 1982), p. 137.
57. *Ibid.*
58. *Ibid.*, 202.
59. Audrey Wipper, "African Women, Fashion, and Scapegoating," *Canadian Journal of African Studies*, VI, ii (1972), p. 329.
60. Peicke, *ibid.*, 78.

Okigbo's Labyrinths *and the Context of Igbo Attitudes to the Female Principle*

Elaine Savory Fido

Igbo culture is a complex entity, and the boundaries which define it áre diffuse. Igbo people have intermarried with peoples along their borders, and the colonial intrusion and its aftermath has so changed things that it is hard even for scholars bent on determining essential facts to find them. The process of disentangling colonial influences and non-Igbo influences from the core of traditional Igbo culture is ongoing, but debates persist as to whether one element or another is old Igbo or is the product of a continually changing and adapting cultural ambience. To be sure, there are deep-seated blendings of the traditional and the modern and the Igbo have become known for their capacity to accept and absorb change (Achebe: 1958, 1964). One major area of this debate concerns Igbo attitudes to women.

Christopher Okigbo was born at Ojoto, a town near Onitsha in which a local but powerful goddess, Idoto, had her shrine.[1] Many of the riverine areas of Igboland and of Eastern Nigeria in general have goddess cults of various kinds, including the Mammy Water[2] and the sea-goddess *Owu-Miri*,[3] who is worshipped around Oguta[4] and Egbema. This prevalence of female deities is in accordance with the theory that the Igbo traditional religion was based around the female principle, centrally around the Earth Goddess Ala,[4] described by Michael Echeruo as the most likely deity to be called supreme god of the Igbos.[5] This theory is not unchallenged since Chukwu, a male deity, is often described as having become more important than Ala. However, some theologians (Arazu: 1982) claim that this was only a response to Christian missionaries and Igbo Christian theologians need to find a supreme god amongst the Igbo pantheon (one is tempted to add a supreme *male* god). There is also a view that the Arochukwu people extended Chukwu's power in the service of their own aggressive expansionism.[6] Other Igbo theologians argue that "the supremacy of Chukwu has never been challenged by any divinity in the Ibgo religious pantheon" (Agwu: 4). Whatever the precise history of Chukwu and Ala may be, the fact is that female deities figure largely in the culture and literature of the Igbo people, right up to this day and even in literature written by men in the English language.

Eastern Nigeria has produced a number of significant writers, including the most well-known of all African writers at this date, Chinua Achebe. It is notable that Igbo women as a group are the most numerous and productive of African women writers. Whilst it is difficult to say for certain what factors predispose Igbo culture to encourage the development of women as creative writers, it is clear that they exist, and it is also apparent that male Igbo writers are particularly concerned with the balance of male and female values in society and write about the results of inequities in male and female principles as being dangerous to social health (Achebe: 1958, Amadi: 1969). Igbo culture is favorable to the development of relative individualism, and the variations in dialects and customs between villages reinforce an impression of social flexibility, a factor which played a part in Igbo attitudes to established colonial rule and education.[7] But beyond that circumstance which might give rise to female independence and development within cultural restraints, there are definite links made by Igbo people between strong women and specific social and cultural realities. For example, asking where the Igbo novelist Flora Nwapa was born, I was told that she comes from a place where the women are very strong (namely Oguta).

A few years after Okigbo was born, in 1932, a woman anthropologist[8] published a study of Igbo women in which she detailed their close bonding with one another and their sense of independence and identity, as well as their closeness to the female Earth Goddess, acknowledged by their men. Her comment on Igbo male attitudes to women is important:

> One hears it said that the Igbo man 'does not respect women'. He does: he even respects her in a way so original and so modern that Europeans have only just begun to think of it.
>
> (Leith-Ross: 1939, 231)

Leith-Ross' study covered both rural and urban Igbo communities and included Port Harcourt, Onitsha and the intervening area. Her findings importantly point to what amounts to a women's sub-culture amongst the Igbo, with councils which almost amount, she suggests, to the power of secret societies, belief in the fecundity of women being linked to that of the yam deity,[9] and a relation to the male world which was easy enough to permit men to say they would not mind being reincarnated as women, which could scarcely be the case in a really sexist society. Leith-Ross' position also supports the current arguments of the Bendel Igbo dramatist Zulu Sofola[10] who argues that tradition benefitted women more than the modern post-colonial situation. Furthermore, the research of the Yoruba historian J.F. Ade Ajayi[11] corroborates the idea that colonialism worsened the situation of the African woman. This is not surprising since the British colonialist period was marked in Britain itself by strong sexism.

There is some evidence that the traditional role of Igbo culture concerning gender might have been somewhat androgynous. Androgyny is defined in this sense as the capacity emotionally and intellectually to accept every human being as a mixture of male and female elements, with ideal human social relations permitting both sexes to utilize the 'other' in their nature freely and usefully.[12] Certainly there is much psychological evidence that adrogynous people are more mentally healthy than those who subject themselves to extremes of gender roles, and this may have an effect on creativity (Williams: 1979). Leith-Ross, at any rate, found that there was an androgynous flavour to Igbo culture: she describes "glimpses of some peculiar conception of sex or of a thread of bisexuality running through everything . . . or of a lack of differentiation between the sexes—or of an acceptance of the possibility of the transposition of sex." (p. 101) Chinua Achebe deals centrally with unbalanced maleness in *Things Fall Apart*, and Carole Boyce Davies argues that he seems to be saying that survival involves man in unifying male and female qualities (Davies: 1983). In one interview, Achebe said: "There is always some kind of war between the sexes, you know, but in the traditional society it was good-humored." (Evalds: 1977, 17.) This focus on male-female relations as the underpinning of society seems to characterize both female and male writers from Eastern Nigeria, such as Flora Nwapa, Buchi Emecheta, Zulu Sofola, Christopher Okigbo, Cyprian Ekwensi and Onuora Nzekwu, who are Igbo[13] and Elechi Amadi who is Ikwerre.

Yet for all the suggestions of possible advantages to women in traditional cultures, tradition was certainly not ideal, and modern influences such as British sexist colonialism further complicated gender relations. Some writers, like Amadi, have specifically written on women's issues, but only to reveal their own conflicts. Amadi's essay on the Nigerian civil war, *Sunset in Biafra*, reveals his adherence to British-style army training, not surprising since he undertook that himself. But perhaps it partly explains why, when he talks of women, he sounds very much like a Western man:

> Because man recognises instinctively that feminine powers are
> overwhelming, he is reluctant to concede any further powers and

privileges to woman . . . This is the feminine sexual power which men fear. The women who oppose the femininst movement are mostly those who recognise this power . . .

Amadi: 1982, 79, 80.

The same authoritarian, anti-emotional tradition which shapes soldiers in the Western style also makes men incapable of giving up their rigid surface controls to enjoy intimacies and equalities with women. Okigbo, whilst not a professional soldier, was killed in the Biafran war and his poetry clearly articulates the stress of determining identity amidst cultural crisis and gender crisis. In his work, fear of women can also be clearly perceived. Anxiety about the female principle is in fact a strong element in male Eastern Nigerian writers' work, whereas in writers such as Flora Nwapa, there is a profoundly different perception, an engagement with the reality of trying to be female and an individual in a society which constantly tries to mythologize about women to distance any danger they might pose. Nwapa's *Efuru* shows a woman trying to come to terms with loss of husband and child through her relation to a water-deity, a sort of divine role-model who helps her to decide that childlessness is not the end of the world. There is a great difference between using myth to make reality more workable and endurable and using myth to create fantasies which deny the reality. Much recent critical work by women has found the latter tendency strong in male creative literature, and of course the anger which women have begun to express can sometimes lead to intense hostility to men, itself a social divisive force. Buchi Emecheta's work, influenced as it is by her British experience, is characterised by a greater element of what one might call Western style feminism than is true of other African women writers in Nigeria. So it is possible to see that on both sides, male and female, there is a mixture of dissatisfaction with present male-female relations based on the central belief in Eastern Nigerian cultures that society is built on these relations and that something is presently wrong. A variety of solutions based not only on knowledge of tradition[14] but also on colonial and post-colonial cultural influences from Britain have further polarized the sexes.

Okigbo's poetry ought to be seen in this context, for his presentation of his own spiritual odyssey is framed by the developing images of a female principle which shapes and informs the adult male psyche. *Labyrinths* is a spiritual journey to rebirth as an adult consciousness and a creative voice. The creative artist who made the poetry was himself a collection of contradictory elements: poet and man of action who was killed in war; mystic with ambitions to be a financier; proud Igbo and yet lover of European poetry; a man ambivalent about *négritude* but extremely attracted to symbolism and committed to the rehabilitation of his race and culture after colonialism; and Christian trained yet an adherent of older religions. The creative process made it possible for him to find coherence in himself, and his poetry shows the stages of integration of the disparate elements of his vision.

In his life, Okigbo had problems in his relations with women. He tried to save his marriage by making one last trip to visit his wife at Yola, a trip described in his preface to *Labyrinths* as being "in pursuit of what turned out to be an illusion". Yet women or the concept of the feminine in various forms shape the major images in his poetry. People who were close to Okigbo believe that the poems are all or almost all based on real relations with women. Yet the emotional tone of the poems is often agonized, as if when faced with the physical and emotional reality of sexual love Okigbo found great pain and self-doubt tormented him. Ideals and abstractions are, in that case, a good deal easier. Sunday Anozie[15] has written that Okigbo adored his wife and daughter. But that surely is too simple a statement. When the poetry is closely examined, there seems to be running through all of its emotional textures a tension between love and fear, desire to submit to intensities of emotional and physical love and desire to remain separate, adoration of the mother and terror of the sexual partner. Also evidenced is a need to restore the ancient mother-ruled images of traditional religious cults and so rid his culture of colonialism, countered by a need to be an adult male, independent of needs for softness and protection given by a woman. In many ways, Okigbo's twists and turns of desire are those characteristic of man in many if not all cultures, where mother-domination in early childhood creates a fear of woman's power and a desire to dominate women in order to be adult and a man (Dinnerstein: 1976). But there is a vital aspect of his agony which is particular to modern post-colonial African man, and indeed to Igbo man, with his history, it seems, of close and relatively balanced relations with the feminine. That is, while the feminine is closely intertwined with his idea of traditional religion, the male-dominated Christian ethos shaped his public idea of himself as a man in colonial and post-colonial society, and that is antithetical to Igbo tradition. In addition, British culture portrays the male poet as an effeminate man, someone less than fully developed as a masculine figure.

Okigbo's commitment to poetry coincided with his conviction that he was the reincarnation of his maternal grandfather, who was a priest of the goddess Idoto. Thus his ethnic and spiritual identity was bound up in his poetic development. His return to tradition was a return to the 'Mother' Idoto and a rejection of the male god of patriarchial Christianity. The very androgynous quality which often characterises highly developed creative writers is arguably the result of imaginative effort to transcend gender in order to create a full human canvas: Okigbo makes no attempt to depict real woman in his poetry, but instead deals with the mythic and symbolic qualities which she can hold for a male imagination. Yet his poet-protagonist's strivings for self-creation seem to point to a desire for androgyny, a sensuous and emotive union with the 'other'. Chukwuma

Azuonye links Okigbo's woman symbols with Jungian psychology (Azuonye: 1981), but resists the idea that Okigbo expresses fear of the feminine. However, the masochistic quality noted in the poetry by Sunday Anozie (Anozie: 1972) derives its force from the painful dilemma of the sensitive man—whether to submit to sensuous experience and give up control of the woman or to risk the loss of self-possession which must come in surrender to sexual experience. The fear of woman which informs Okigbo's images of the Lioness is an ambivalent one, but nevertheless there is an anxiety within it that the man will be castrated by the act of surrender.

Let us examine the spiritual quest which shapes *Labyrinths*. Critics have discussed Okigbo's use of the Idoto cult and Christianity, and occasionally note has been made of Okigbo's references to ancient Middle Eastern cultures (Izevbaye: 1973).[16] But there is a major thread of meaning in the poems which relates to Okigbo's knowledge of ancient history and which ties Idoto to the cults of an ancient Egyptian goddess, Isis,[17] who was in her various incarnations Isis, Ishtar, Inanna and finally, much reduced, the Virgin Mary, the most widespread deity in the ancient world. There are in fact three religions intertwined in the poetry: Idoto-worship and traditional Igbo worship of the femine; Christianity and the worship of Isis-Ishtar.

The very title, *Labyrinths*, is best interpreted through the ancient Cretan culture which Okigbo himself refers to in his preface. The Cretan goddess is of course connected to the legends of the Labyrinth and Nor Hall has explained it well:

> A Minoan statue of the mother goddess from Crete embodies this message in archaic form . . . With a snake in one hand and a tool (her double-edged axe) in the other, the goddess connects the chthonian realm of matter (the Mother) and the upper world of the sky-god, who calculates, measures and perceives . . .
>
> The axe came to mean many things. It is called *labrys* and is related to *labyrinth*, the underground dwelling of the goddess. In order to pass through the labyrinth it was necessary to make a full 360-degree turn, to turn completely round on oneself to go out the way one came in. In the ancient world this action was meaningful on what we would call a psychological level, as evident in the conjecture that it was the crossing sweeper *Labys* who is credited with the maxim 'know thyself'.
>
> Nor Hall: 1971, 9-10

Okigbo links the double-edged axe of Crete with the Aro culture of the Igbo people in his preface, thus connecting the ancient Middle East/North Africa together with his own ethnic traditions. The labyrinth is of course the ancient symbol of the womb, and there is a strong theme of rebirth and initiation in Okigbo's poem cycle. But that initiation takes place in the world of the Mother, opposed to which, in *Labyrinths*, is the measuring, geometric world of Kepkanly, the primary school teacher of the colonial Mission school. Earth and sky, the water goddess and the Christian sky god, are the poles of spiritual existence at the beginning of *Labyrinths*.

Okigbo's poems are obscure, symbolical, full of personal allusions and unexplained references to foreign poets and to political events or Igbo cultural traditions. Nothing is clearer than Okigbo's intention not to be fully understood, even to himself. There has been complaint about this (Chinweizu, Onuchekwa Jemie and Ihechukwu Madubuike: 1980). But perhaps it is best to accept that when a writer is deliberately obscure, out of competence rather than out of failure to be clear, there is good reason. Then, perhaps, the most appropriate way to approach Okigbo's work is as if he was writing the kind of mystical, gnomic verses which characterize ritualistic poetry in African cultures, e.g. in Ifa worship amongst the Yoruba. Okigbo's relation to spiritually tormented poets like T.S. Eliot (who also uses the symbol of a powerful and threatening woman associated with myth in his poetry) has long been recognized. If the complexity of spiritual truths felt and explored by a finely tuned intelligence is added to the complexity of Okigbo's socio-political and historical context, then it is not particularly surprising that his work is difficult.

The relation of the three religions in *Labyrinth* is difficult to disentangle for Okigbo's method of composition is associational and he does not provide explanatory links. But much of the imagery has several layers of meaning which connect religious traditions at a deep symbolic level. For example, the Igbo folktale which tells of a monkey dazzled by the armpit of a lioness until he destroys himself[18] clearly accounts for the image of the 'armpit dazzle of the lioness' in *Labyrinths*. But it is also true that one of the titles of Isis, Queen of Heaven, was Lioness of the Sacred Assembly, and that Sakmet was the lioness-headed goddess of Ancient Egypt who was symbolic of war and pestilence and who annihilated her enemies. Similarly, eggs, which are important in the worship of Igbo water-goddess[19] and which figure largely in the ritually important symbolisms of the poetry, were one of the important symbols of Isis. White light, which surrounds the Watermaid in *Labyrinths* is not only the dazzle of the Lioness, but the moonlight which has always been associated with female deities, including Isis and her various forms. Other clusters of images have this syncretic overtone, including those of water, the sea, corn and associated golden objects (the gold crop, ears of the secret, amber, golden eggs, yellow memories), Nature, snakes and birds. Most of these are strongly associated both with Igbo traditions and with Isis and goddess worship in the ancient world.

It is important to place these connections in the context of Igbo legends that the Igbo people came originally from Egypt. These legends, which are said to explain the celebrated terra-cotta skin of many Igbos as well as their relatively small land area and their migratory tendency to resettle and intermarry with other peoples, as well as their sense of being different from other peoples in Nigeria, might well have been the original impetus behind Okigbo's fascination with ancient history.

In *Labyrinths*, Okigbo interweaves Christianity complexly with Igbo traditions. In the opening cycle of poems, the protagonist submits to Idoto as a 'prodigal' with all the Biblical overtones of that term. He thus points to the conflict within him which is again expressed strongly when he begs his dead, saintly mother, Anna Okigbo, to protect him from "them fucking angels" (p. 17). Anna is a particularly important name itself to carry ambivalences if one remembers, as Azuonye (p. 38), that Anna was not only Okigbo's mother's actual name but a major part of Jung's 'anima' term. Yet again, Christianity significantly appears as the colonialist eagles who rape Igbo culture, bringing with them their God who silences the longdrums and causes the forest gods to be forgotten and their shrines abandoned. Yet their violence is in the service of a religion which teaches love (and we know from Achebe the impact of a new faith which could release some Igbos who felt themselves persecuted by Igbo religious principles). Similarly the old cults of Isis could involve the sacrifice of males (Stone: 132-6). So men must have feared the power of women within that context. There is therefore a good deal of violence in *Labyrinths*, much of it linked to female cruelties to men via the dangerous experience of sexual attraction as well as to the Christianizing/colonising experience. Christianity first taught toleration and love, then suppressed women, of course, with increasing ferocity, waging a war on the remnants of pagan cults which often reflected the place of women in the ancient world and which seemed to give them greater power and freedom than Christianity was willing to permit. Instead of a sexually active ideal of women, Christianity created an ideal of virginity/chastity and motherhood and Okigbo's poetry communicates these images together with a great deal of ambivalence toward female beauty (linking it to power and cruelty to men). Sunday Anozie quotes a passage from Robert de Montesquieu which deals with the story of John the Baptist in a way very reminiscent of Okigbo's treatement of male fear of women:

> The secret is none other than that the mystery of her being is to be violated by John, who catches sight of her and pays for this single sacrifice with his life; for this free spirited virgin will only feel pure again, when she is holding the head of an executed man . . .
>
> Anozie: 1972, p. 99

This passage seems to be to capture Okigbo's spirit of fear in the poems which relate to sexual woman. But, Christianity, after all, suppressed women so much so that such violence against men was virtually impossible to conceive of, and the sexual strictures against women subdued their sexual nature to the service of their god. Celibacy replaced sexuality as the spiritual centre of physical devotion to God.

The relation of sexuality to religion is crucially important in *Labyrinths*. The poet-protagonist develops from his rebirth as Idoto's returned son to a sexual awakening with the Watermaid and afterwards as agonised adult experience with the Lioness, which culminates in his 'homecoming' as the bridegroom of this powerful and destructive female presence, seen paring her fingernails amidst the carnage of dismembered limbs and blood. Even small details in the poetry bring the reader to link violence, sex and religion. In the poem to Awolowo[20] 'Lament of the Drums', the reference to Celaeno and her harpy crew, the image of the sea as raped and the waters as sultry all conjure up a disturbed female sexuality, which is either threatening or violated and thus hurt. The language of the poetry abounds with images of the fruitfulness of the goddess, of her connection with water, and with powerful and threatening nature, as in 'Distances III' where she is associated with a molten centre of earth and her labyrinths are connected with violence. The androgynous forest gods are raped. There is a strong castration theme which runs through the poetry, and which links it with the old world of self-castration associated with the cult of Cymbele, a Greek version of Isis, and Attis, who was castrated and who gave rise to the custom of self-castration by priests of Cymbele.

The origins of this connection between sexuality, religion and violence was the necessary death and rebirth of vegetation along the Nile valley as the great river ebbed and flowed. The river was Isis, the vegatation Osiris, who died and was resurrected each year. The legend went that Osiris, Isis' brother-lover was torn to pieces and Isis put his body together again, but his penis was missing. She created him whole and blew life into him and he caused her to conceive her son, the god Horus. Afterwards, the goddess' husbands and lovers were always associated with death and rebirth. But the Babylonian goddess, Ishtar, had as her consort her son, Tammuz, whose death she did not cause but rather mourned. Okigbo includes in *Labyrinths* the lament of Ishtar for Tammuz, which was identified by Dan Izevbaye as a virtual translation of an ancient Sumerian song (Izevbaye: 1973, 140). In Biblical times, Hebrew women performed a ritual lament for Tammuz, showing how ancient traditions of goddess worship had permeated even their male-oriented religious culture. It is plain that historically, men gradually resisted the self-surrender and death-rebirth myths associated with the goddess' consort. The myth of Gilgamesh, often described as the first epic, tells how Gilgamesh refuses to become the goddess' lover, saying that Ishtar has hurt too many lovers before. He goes off to become the first patriarchal hero and Enkidu is sacrificed in his stead. Okigbo weaves mention of the Gilgamesh epic[21] into 'Fragments out of the Deluge'. Christianity was the triumph of male ascendency and also the triumph of a gentle, loving god-figure in Christ himself, yet of course it has been a bloody and oppressive religion to those ground down by colonialism and slavery and forced to accept the god of those who exploited them. Okigbo's sense of conflict in relation to his Mother Idoto and to the powerful goddess images is made very clear by his references to Christian violation of Igbo culture and even by references to the drowning nuns who represent womanhood totally submissive to a god who does not save them.

Fertility, associated of course with creativity and therefore with the poet, is associated with the female deity. In the lament for Tammuz, there is mention of special concern for the loss of various kinds of fruition: 'fields of crops', 'fields of men', children in reference to 'barren wedded ones' and 'perishing children'. The sinister 'potbellied watchers' who despoil 'her' in this poem suggest a male violation of the goddess' plenty. Here Okigbo's sympathy apears to be with a hurt maternal Nature, but he seems to have ambivalence towards the feminine in many other places. When the poet-protagonist finally achieves his 'birthday of earth', there is an overtone still of fear and adoration at the same time for the goddess who has been his inspiration and his mate. It is as if the poet risks his manhood and his existence to achieve his poetic vocation through union with the Lionness. In the sensuous passage of sexual encounter with the Watermaid, the poet is a submissive and loyal subject. Even the sea is 'spent', presumably from loving her. When he washes his feet in the 'maid's pure head' at the end of *Labyrinths*, he is afraid of her variegated teeth. These tensions are charac-teristic of the poetic journey of the protagonist, in which he becomes, for example, a skeletal oblong, (the oblong is associated with both his mother Anna through the church organ panels, and with the Lionness' head), a shape created by his attraction to the female deity he follows but reduced to a skeleton. For patriarchy depends on potency, on domination of women, in fact, and the poet stands between the matriarchal world of Idoto and the patriarchal colonial one of Christian education and culture: submission to woman risks potency, yet provides fusion with the Igbo traditions which the poet desires, and also promises a delicious and masochistic pleasure of domination by another and release from the responsibility of domination.

The geometric shapes which are a linked series of images in the poems are connected to notions of ridigity and excess, hypocrisy and exploitativeness found in both religious and secular leaders and men of responsibility. The cross itself functions as a complex symbol, and a huge fiery cross links itself with geometric shapes in the poet's mind as he dreams in 'Distances' IV. Initiation ordeals, including the knife (circumcision and also the old Igbo ritual of cutting the face to prove endurance on the part of the initiate) are linked with the idea of Christian ritual. Kepkanly, who presides over the initiation of the young poet into the Catholic catechism, is the god of the schoolroom, but the world he promises is one where precise thinking and rigid attitudes (symbolised by various geometric shapes) seem to Okigbo to betray the mysteries of the spirit and put pragmatisms, and therefore moral corruptions, to the forefront. The fiery cross of 'Distances' is reminiscent of the KKK, the racist American organization which more than any other has publicized the Christian involvement with prejudice and hatred, including killing innocent people because of their colour or ethnic identification. The young poet is scarred by Christianity in the way that the old Igbo ritual scarred its initiates to prove courage on their part. In 'Distances' IV there is a surreal vision of geometric shapes in a cosmic setting, and in V Okigbo links the 'kiss' which is so much associated with Christ to the scar, and to two swords. As in the Isis myths and in Igbo religion, Christianity is a mixture of violence, sexuality and spiritual purity, a dangerous environment for the unwary.

The image of the Mother is crucial to the poems. Idoto is the deity who is symbolic mother to the young poet returning to his culture and to his spiritual base. But also Anna, the poet's earthly mother, whose funeral is the theme of the lovely poem "SILENT FACES at crossroads", in "The Passage", becomes associated by the shape of the oblong with the Lioness herself. 'Distances' V brings together the idea of form as a cosmic and religious frame for the soul with the 'panel oblong', associated with the church organ and the coffin of Anna's burial and the Lioness' head, and the sanctuary at the centre of the earth where Mother Earth will receive her children, where water runs through tunnels (with the obvious suggestion of female sexual secretions), and this looks forward to 'Distances' VI. There is a constant interweaving of symbols and thus the sexual overtones of the Lionness are interwoven with the maternal aspects of Idoto/Anna. It is interesting that Isis cults, too, had this dualism, where the female diety was both protective and nurturing and destructive and threatening to man. Similarly also Isis worship was finally destroyed (her temples sacked) and her identity subsumed into the Virgin Mary by Christianized Rome in much the same way as Idoto and the forest gods[22] were destroyed by Christian British imperialism and its local Igbo adherents. In 'Fragments Out of the Deluge' Okigbo makes reference to the Flood, which was associated with the goddess before it was Biblical (she is supposed to have sailed on the waters in a crescent moon boat and her symbols included the dove). Also in this poem, Okigbo mentions the Lionness and in a footnote explains that she had killed the hero's second self, which is a clear reference to the epic of Gilgamesh and a clear identification of the poet with Gilgamesh himself (the sacrificed Enkidu being the second self of Gilgamesh). So there is here a dualism within one poem which is repeated over and over again in *Labyrinths*: the female principle becomes the creative-protective-destructive cosmic centre of the universe.

Fear plays a major role in Okigbo's poetry, whether it is fear of the void or the abyss, fear of woman, fear of becoming or of dying. (Egudu: 1978, 9-13). The fear is caused by the ambivalence which a person such as the poet-protagonist must feel, for his psyche is partly shaped by colonialism and

Christianity which he regards as "fireseed", i.e. destructive to him. Of course his attitude to woman must be equally ambivalent, for she is essential to his being as well as on an ongoing threat to his potency and domination. The fear motivates the poetry in creative and constructive ways, for courage, whether creative or physical is not the absence of fear but the capacity to act despite it. *Labyrinths* was a brave thing to do, just as Okigbo's involvement with Biafra was direct and cost him his life. He was never a coward. In his last poems "Path of Thunder", he returns to the image of the ram tethered for sacrifice as presenting his own situation in the War, and in a moving and prophetic statement, indicates knowledge of likely death:

> O mother mother Earth, unbind me; let this be my last testament; let this be
> The ram's hidden wish to the sword the sword's secret player to the scabbard—

—Okigbo: 1971, 72

Once again, the Mother image becomes instrumental in presenting the realities of the poet's psychic condition: he is victim again, and in need of the protection of "Earth", of becoming once more the 'prodigal', and the hints of parallels with Christ's Passion which are prevalent in *Labyrinths* seem relevant again here. The poet is one of the "stars" which come and go, as poets, prophets and leaders come, do their work and die. Okigbo's presentation of the religious vocation of poet brings him to perceive suffering and even death as a necessary offering of experience which has to be made by those who seek greater understanding and knowledge, and who seek to serve their culture in times of stress. His ambivalence about Christianity does not prevent him from seeing the isolation, self-discipline and suffering of Christ himself as a model for the fate of the poet-prophet in other conditions and times. In the syncretic world of Okigbo's poetry, however, the Christ figure is close to the male sacrificial victims of the old goddess cults, where the death and resurrection of a chosen man meant renewal of crops and life for the community, a necessary triumph for the life principle in defiance of seasonal changes. The effect of the power of the goddess in *Labyrinths* on the poet is like the relation of Isis and Osiris, so that the submission to her cruelty, her deathly aspect and her power is like a voluntary self-sacrifice in the service of greater knowledge and poetic experience. The poet becomes, as it were, the earthly servant of both Idoto and the other female deities who inhabit the poetry, and in this way becomes a kind of Christ-victim figure, serving a lone apprenticeship in preparation for his own Calvary, and being ultimately sacrificed, not, as in *Labyrinths*, in a psychic and sexual sense subsumed into the goddess' power in order to rise again, but in the final sense of his mission being completed, his star leaving the heavens, as a casualty in war.

Okigbo was self-consciously a mystic, fully accepting of the romantic ideal of the poet as seer. His own comment on the composition of his work, although perhaps misleading given the erudite texture of borrowings from European and American poets which characterizes his earlier work, suggests a reconfirmation of the spiritual core of his poetry:

> ... all I did was to create the drums and the message they deliver has nothing to do with me at all.
>
> Duerden and Pieterse: 1972, 147

It remains true that his work is essentially religious and mystical, but it should be recognised that the centre of that mysticism is the poet's complex relation with a series of female deities and with his own maleness in that context.

NOTES

1. Chukwuma Azuonye has identified a newspaper article recording the destruction of the shrine of Idoto by Christian converts at Ojoto in 1926. See Azuonye: 1981, n. 10, 47.
2. This generic name covers water deities of various sorts, including a mermaid-like creature. Cults spread all over the African diaspora, and the name is recognised in the Caribbean, South and North America and Africa. The deity is usually beautiful, seductive, powerful and can vary between malevolence and protective good nature. The relation of the nature of the cult and the social position of women in the community associated with it is an area which begs for research in the various parts of the African diaspora.
3. The word for 'sea' in Igbo varies according to dialectal differences: but may be "miri", "mini" or "mili". In Elechi Amadi's *The Concubine* 1966), there is a male stream god called "Mini Weku". Although Amadi claims the separateness of the Ikwerre, his people, from the Igbo, this has been to some extent a result of the stresses of land claims during and since the War, and in fact, their languages are close.
4. The birthplace of Flora Nwapa, the Igbo woman novelist.
5. Echeruo: 1979.
6. Aro chukwu means "sons of god". The fact that *chukwu* is *chi-ukwu* or the great *chi* means that it is odd that it has become a male entity, since *chi* is the Igbo concept of the divine essence and is not only in women as well as men but in all of nature. See Achebe: 1975, Aruzu: 1982).
7. See Isichei: 1973 for a discussion of Igbo attitudes to colonial education, and the way these changed from resistance to enthusiastic espousement.

8. Sylvia Leith-Ross' *African Women: A Study of the Ibo in Nigeria* (1939) has some crassly Eurocentric views but is on the whole an independent woman's view of women, sympathetic and original-minded.

9. The Igbo are the only people known to worship the yam as a god.

10. Sofola has written several plays on the theme of woman's role in Nigerian society and the relation of traditional to the modern. Her latest play, a television script, is on the subject of the massacre of young men in Asaba in the War, centred around a woman chief or *Omu*. (*Omu-Àkò of Isele-Oligbo*). The whole subject of women's councils and chieftaincy titles amongst the Igbo people is important and needs more research. I am grateful to my colleague Dr. Stella Ogunyemi for the information that a woman cannot become Omu until she is past the menopause since menstruating women are not allowed in the presence of men. When she assumes the title she leaves her husband's house and returns to live with her father's kin in his compound. It would be important to discover how long the taboo against menstruating women has been in operation.

11. The position of the Yoruba woman in her society is the subject of various recent studies but one most relevant to this paper is Judith Hoch-Smith's "Radical Yoruba Female Sexuality: The Witch and the Prostitute" (1978). In this she concludes that female independence amongst the Yorubas generated a vicious response on the part of men, producing witch-hunts etc. This contrasts with the findings of Leith-Ross, who observed that Igbo women had strong social roles, such as dibias, rainmakers and doctors, yet found few witches except in urban Onitsha. But the two studies certainly emphasize the ambivalence with which female power may be regarded by men.

12. See Kimbrough: 1981.

13. See Emenyonu: 1978.

14. Tradition, as exemplified in folk tale and custom, as well as historical material, reveals Igbo women possessing strength and determination, as well as organisation. For example, Chukwuma Azuonye, for whose advice on Igbo culture I am deeply indebted in the preparation of this paper, has discovered evidence that Chukwu was merely a minor trickster god in Igbo tradition, supporting the view that Ala (Ana, Ani or Ajaálá according to dialect area) was the major deity. In addition, there are epic tales of brave heroines (Azuonye: 1983) and in *Equiano's Travels*, the narrative of an Igbo slave on his culture and background, women figure importantly. Then in colonial times, the Aba Riots of Calabar and Opobo in December 1929, in which the Igbo women's stubborn resistence to colonial authority over a tax question finally provoked colonial violence killing and wounding a large number of people, proved Igbo women were a power to be reckoned with. See Leith-Ross: 1939, 23-39; Isichei: 1976, 121, 125, 151-5.

15. Anozie: 1972.

16. I am grateful to Professor Izevbaye for his comments on a draft of this paper.

17. See Witt: 1971; Stone: 1976; Hall: 1971; Frazier: 1958; Hooke: 1963; Wallis Budge: 1969; Frankfurt: 1948; Bratton: 1970; Wolkstein and Kramer: 1983.

18. I am grateful for this information to Dr. Chukwuma Azuonye.

19. Eggs and pieces of broken mirror, which also figure importantly in Okigbo's symbolism, figure in rituals associated with water goddess in the East of

Nigeria. Men who believe they have married a water spirit believe she will return to the sea or to water at will and to bring her back they must break eggs carefully in an unbroken trail back to the house. She will follow the egg-shells.

20. Chief Obafemi Awolowo was arrested for treason during the troubles in the Western Region in the period 1962-4 and was imprisoned. Okigbo's poems have definite political bias and comment embedded in them but he refused to acknowledge responsibility for this, saying that the poems had their own meaning and it was nothing to do with him.

21. See Moore: 1969, who comments on Okigbo's use of Egypt and Sumer. Izevbaye (1973) discusses the use made of Enki by Okigbo in an original line opening "Fragments out the the Deluge" section VII (see also Anozi: 1972). Enki, whose mention was cut out of the final version of the line, was the Sumerian god of wisdom and father of Inanna, the Sumerian version of Isis. He gave Inanna many powers whilst drunk and then regretted it and tried to get them back. Izevbaye offers an interpretation of the name Enki from Thomas Campbell *The Masks of God* Vol. II (Secker and Warburg London 1962) as being "The Lord *En* of the goddess Earth *ki*." It is therefore evident that Okigbo would have been attracted to Enki, although he turned from this reference in final draft.

22. Dan Izevbaye discusses the connection between Ishtar, and Irkalla, the Sumerian queen of the Underworld, to whose realm Ishtar descends in Sumerian legend and the gods of the forest in *Labyrinths* (Izevbaye: 1973). Here again there is an organic link between the female deities of the ancient world and the traditional deities of Igboland.

REFERENCES

ACHEBE, Chinua. *Arrow of God*. Heinemann London 1964; *Morning Yet On Creation Day*. Heinemann London 1975; *No Longer at Ease*. Heinemann London 1960; *Things Fall Apart*. Heinemann London 1958.

AGWU, Very Rev. Dr. A.O. Iwu. "The Supreme God in Igbo Traditional Religion: A Comment on Arazu's Thesis" 1982, published in *Uwa Ndi Igbo: Journal of Igbo Life and Culture* No. 1 April 1984.

AMADI, Elechi. *The Concubine*. Heinemann London 1966; *Ethics in Nigerian Culture*. Heinemann London 1982; *The Great Ponds*. Heinemann London 1969; *The Slave*. Heinemann London 1978; *Sunset in Biafra*. Heinemann London 1973.

ANOZIE, Sunday O. *Christopher Okigbo*. Evans London 1972.

ARAZU, Rev. Fr. Dr. Raymond C. Arazu, C.S.Sp. "The Supreme God in Igbo Traditional Religion" 1982 published in *Ùwà Ndi Igbò: Journal of Ibgo Life and Culture*. No. 1 April 1984.

AZUONYE, Chukwuma. "Okigbo and the Psychological Theories of Carl Gustav" in *Journal of African and Comparative Literature*. Vol. 1 no 1 (March 1981), 30-51; "Stability and Change in the Performance of Ohafia Igbo Singers of Tales" *Research in African Literatures* Vol. 14 no. 3 Fall 1983, 332-380.

BRATOON, F.G. *Myths and Legends of the Ancient Near-East*. Thomas Y. Crowell New York 1970.

CHINWEIZU *et al. Towards the Decolonisation of African Literature*. Vol. 1 Fourth Dimension Publishers Enugu 1980.

DAVIES, Carole Boyce. "Concepts of African Motherhood: A Comparative Assessment of Attitudes to Motherhood in Igbo Society in Selected Words by Male and Female Writers" First Draft 1983, made available by the author.

DINNERSTEIN, Dorothy. *The Mermaid and the Minotaur*. Harper New York 1976.

DUERDEN D. and PIETERSE C. *African Writers Talking*. Heinemann London 1972.

ECHERUO, Michael. "A Matter of Identity" 1979 Ahiajoku Lecture Imo Newspapers Ltd. Owerri 1979.

EMECHETA, Buchi. *The Bride Price*. Allison and Busby London 1976; *In the Ditch*. Allison and Busby London 1979; *The Joys of Motherhood*. Allison and Busby London 1979; *Second Class Citizen*. Allison and Busby London 1974; *The Slave Girl*. Allison and Busby 1977.

EMEYONU, Ernest. *The Rise of the Igbo Novel*. Oxford University Press, Ibadan 1978.

EQUIANO, Olaudah. *Equiano's Travels*. Heinemann London 1966.

EVALDS, Victoria. "An Interview with Chinua Achebe" *Studies in Black Literature*. Vol. 8 no 1 (Spring 1977).

FRAZER, Sir J.G. *The Golden Bough*. Macmillan New York 1958.

FRANKFURT, H. *Ancient Egyptian Religion*. Harper and Row New York 1948.

HALL, Nor. *The Moon and the Virgin*. Harper and Row New York 1971.

HOCH-SMITH, Judith. "Radical Yoruba Female Sexuality: The Witch and the Prostitute" in *Women in Ritual and Symbolic Roles*. ed. Hoch-Smith and Anita Spring, Plenium Press New York 1978, 245-267.

HOOKE, S.H. *Middle Eastern Mythology*. Pelican Baltimore 1953.

ISICHEI, Elizabeth. *A History of the Igbo People*. St. Martin's Press New York 1976; *The Ibo People and the Europeans*. Faber London 1973.

IZEVBAYE, Dan. "The Poetry of Christopher Okigbo" in *The Critical Evaluation of African Literature* ed. C. Heywood London 1973, 121-148.

KIMBROUGH, Robert. "Androgyny Old and New" *The Western Humanities Review* Vol. XXXV no 3 (Autumn 1981) 197-215.

LEITH-ROSS, Sylvia. *African Women: A Study of the Ibo in Nigeria*. Routledge and Kegan Paul London 1939.

MOORE, Gerald. *The Chosen Tongue*. Longmans London 1969.

NWAPA, Flora. *Efuru*. Heinemann London 1966.; *Idu*. Heinemann London 1969.

OKIGBO, Christopher. *Labyrinths*. Heinemann London 1971.

SOFOLA, Zulu. *Old Wines Are Tasty*. Ibadan U.P. Ibadan 1981; *Omu-Ako of Isele-Oligbo*. Unpublished television script; *Reveries in the Moonlight*. Unpublished playscript; *Song of a Maiden*. Unpublished playscript; *The Sweet Trap*. Oxford U.P. Ibadan 1977.

STONE, Merline. *When God Was a Woman*. Harvest New York 1976.

WALLIS BUDGE, E.A. *The Gods of the Egyptians*. Vol. 2 Dover Pub. New York 1969 (reprint from 1904).

WILLIAMS, Juanita H. *Psychology of Women*. W.W. Norton and Co. Ltd., 1979.

WITT, R.E. *Isis in the Graeco-Roman World*. Cornell University Press Ithaca New York 1971.

WOLKSTEIN, D. and KRAMER, S.N. *Inanna: Queen of Heaven and Earth Her Stories and Hymns from Sumer*. Harper and Row 1983.

Motherhood in the Works of Male and Female Igbo Writers: Achebe, Emecheta, Nwapa and Nzekwu

Carole Boyce Davies

The condition of women in African society is fraught with contradictions, tensions and oppositions, most arising out of the colonial domination of Africa, others intrinsic to the organizational structures of particular societies. A distinct African feminism therefore has already been defined by Filomina Chioma Steady in *The Black Woman Crossculturally*.[1] In her introduction, Steady delineates its features and concludes that,

> The birthplace of human life must also be the birthplace of human struggles, and feminist consciousness must in some way be related to the earliest divisions of labor according to sex on the continent. But even more significant is the fact that the forms of social organization which approach sexual equality, in addition to matrilineal societies where women are central, can be found on the African continent . . . True feminism is an abnegation of male protection and a determination to be resourceful and self-reliant. The majority of the black women in Africa and in the diaspora have developed these characteristics, though not always by choice.[2]

Yet the very features which make for her independence and control (for example, her economic freedoms, polygyny, motherhood), can also function for her repression and submission. A rigorous, feminist approach to African society would therefore reveal numerous examples of excesses in structures and situations which deny women equality. For example, genital mutilation, infertility as well as fertility, the lack of choice for young women, enforced silence, to cite only the most obvious, all contribute to woman's oppression.

So, the polarized discussions which claim either that African women were/are or were not/are not repressed, both fairly common in sociological and anthropological circles, neglect a host of contradictions involved in African women's reality.

Numerous stereotypes and misconceptions of African women were created during the colonial period and have been perpetuated up to the present time. According to one writer, "the personality and inner reality of African women have been hidden under . . . a heap of myths, so-called ethnological theories, rapid generalizations and patent untruths."[3]

The systematic destruction of these stereotypes and the exploration of the various facets of African womanhood is in process. First of all African male writers, on the heels of the various national movements (along with a number of African scholars) sought to present the truth of their cultures as a direct rebuttal to the distortions perpetuated by white/colonial missionaries, anthropologists and sociologists. In their writing, the image of women was in some ways and to an extent rehabilitated, but in many cases, new sexist stereotypes were created and older African ones went unchallenged. Now, African women writers are taking the process of *telling one's own story* oneself even further. One can chart a movement from a few tentative beginnings in which the woman's prescribed role was challenged from a quasi-feminist perspective or discussed from an apolitical posture to a more militant feminist position in which writers like Buchi Emecheta and Mariama Bâ question and overturn some of the more traditional attitudes to womanhood and woman's place. This paper contributes to the activity of exploring and defining African womanhood. Its concern is motherhood as portrayed by both male and female writers, but its focus is Igbo society.

I have limited my discussion to Igbo society for several reasons:

1. Igbo women have in their history a period of militancy and a documented instance of actual struggle and female assertiveness. The women's war of 1929, in Eastern Nigeria, which is described by Caroline Ifeka-Moller in "Female Militancy and Colonial Revolt,"[4] as "an African case of feminism," challenged white male domination.

2. Igbo women (like Igbo men), are proportionately the most prolific of African writers.

3. Ibgo writers, notably Chinua Achebe, were among the first writers in the post-colonial period to represent African cultural life in fiction.

4. Various studies of traditional Igbo society indicate a clearly expressed female principle in religion, politics, economics and the social sphere. Additionally there are several structures which make for female solidarity. Sylvia Leith Ross says about women's social status in Igbo society:

> ... among the women, there seems to be something—perhaps the bond of sex—that links them up over wide areas so that a woman's call to women would echo far beyond the boundaries of her own town. The fact that the men generally live in their own home town while their wives often come from other towns ... emphasizes the difference. The women are thus already members of two towns: their husbands' in which they live and their parents', which they visit. Their marketing takes them far afield, as do visits to their married daughters; but beyond these tangible factors there does seem to be an intangible communion, normally latent and without visible organization, but so profoundly felt that the slightest stir sets the whole body trembling.[5]

This Leith-Ross description is clearly borne out in the literature, especially in the works of Achebe, Elechi Amadi and Flora Nwapa.

Although a number of approaches to womanhood could be explored, my analyses center on motherhood because in many African societies *motherhood defines womanhood*. Motherhood, then, is crucial to woman's status in African society. To marry and mother a child [a son preferably], entitles a woman to more respect from her husband's kinsmen for she can now be addressed as "Mother of _____." Again, quoting Steady,

> The most important factor with regard to the woman in traditional society is her role as *mother* and the centrality of this role as a whole. Even in strictly patrilineal societies, women are important as wives and mothers since their reproductive capacity is crucial to the maintenance of the husband's lineage and it is because of women that men can have a patrilineage at all. The importance of motherhood and the evaluation of the childbearing capacity by African women is probably the most fundamental difference between the African woman and her Western counterpart in their common struggle to end discrimination against women.[6]

This preoccupation with motherhood is evident in almost all modern African fiction. At some point, almost every novel dramatizes a woman's struggle to conceive: her fear of being replaced, the consequent happiness at conception and delivery or agony at the denial of motherhood, various attempts to appease the Gods and hasten pregnancy, followed by the joys and/or pains of motherhood.

A survey of the literature written by men often reveals the mother character as the most truthfully realized character. All other women pale, in comparison, are pitied or are even treated contemptuously. Yet misconceptions about true motherhood are also evident and in fact there is often an idealization of motherhood and of suffering women who live solely for their children. This romanticizing of motherhood is furthered by its symbolic equation of mother with earth and Africa. While this is in some cases flattering and desirable, it masks the reality of motherhood. The Negritude poets, for example, luxuriated in metaphors of motherhood and land and Africa. Senghor, in his classic poem "Femme Noire" concretized this mystique of the transcendental mother. Andrea Benton Rushing sees African culture as containing several distinct images for women, including those related to motherhood, which differ from the European/American female images, but concludes, nevertheless, that almost all African poetry is written by men and that

> poems which distill the kaleidoscope of women's lives on the African continent and create images of black women with the vigor of those rooted in the religious and cultural matrix of precolonial days may not emerge until African women write the poetry . . .[7]

Preliminary surveys of African literature reveal that the novels of men, like the Negritude poetry, treat mothers more as symbols than as living, suffering individuals. This study will examine mothers and motherhood in the works of four writers: two male novelists (Achebe and Nzekwu) and two female novelists (Emecheta and Nwapa). Focusing mainly on major works, it will isolate individual author-specific portrayals and finally offer some comparisons and conclusions on the treatment of this theme.

In an important appraisal of Black American women's literature, as compared to Black men's literature, Paula Giddings says that the Black woman tended to look within while her male peers concentrated on the external forces that shaped their lives.[8] This question of differences in the literature of Black male and female writers is raised with fair frequency in the interviews by Claudia Tate, in *Black Women Writers at Work*.[9] The answer is still being sought and demands wide ranging analyses of many works.

My study does reveal some differences in the ways in which Igbo male and female writers perceive reality and supports the Giddings conclusion. The women writers deal with the conflicts of motherhood. Rather than presenting an idealized view of motherhood, they present both its joys and pains, the details of the woman's experiences of motherhood. The male writers present womanhood and motherhood but within the context of the larger societal problems. In all of the novels in this study, there is no single view of motherhood. Various types of mothers are projected. One point is clear, however, motherhood is crucial to the happiness of the woman and to her ability to control her life. From a Western perspective, this is seemingly a contradictory anti-feminist argument. But if we understand Steady's definition of African feminism and the centrality of children, it is not. Let us examine how motherhood is portrayed in the literature.

Chinua Achebe: "Mother is Supreme"

The most common name given to a child in Igbo society is Nneka— "Mother is Supreme" (p. 121). Why is this so? This is the rhetorical question which Uchendu, Okonkwo's kinsman, poses to him, and by extension to use the readers, in *Things Fall Apart* (1958).[10] Uchendu's response constitutes the novel's deliberation on the question of motherhood and femininity and nurturing as opposed to fatherhood, masculinity and aggression. This conflict becomes one of the novel's central concerns.

The question is particularly relevant to Okonkwo, who throughout his life had struggled not to be what his father was—a poor, effeminate man: a woman—in a society where masculinity is treasured. Okonkwo, a successful provider, leader of his clan, rules his compound with a heavy hand, beating wives, repressing all emotions except anger, refusing to show tenderness to his children. Because of his aggressive personality Okonkwo commits several crimes against the Earth Goddess including the accidental shooting of a man during a festival. Importantly, this accident is called a "female crime"—the equivalent of English manslaughter—as opposed to a "male crime", murder (an obvious comment on the male and female principle). It leads to Okonkwo's forced exile from his village and his having to seek refuge in his motherland. Okonkwo is depressed at this turn of events and at the fact that he has to live in Mbanta, although he is well entertained there. This is when he is chided by Uchendu, his uncle, who answers the question he had posed by saying,

> It's true that a child belongs to its father. But when a father beats his child, it seeks sympathy in its mother's hut. A man belongs to his fatherland when things are good and life is sweet. But when there is sorrow and bitterness he finds refuge in his motherland. Your mother is there to protect you. She is buried there. And that is why we say that mother is supreme (p. 122).

Further, he tells Okonkwo, "If you think you are the greatest sufferer in the world ask my daughter, Akueni, how many twins she has borne and thrown away" (p. 122). Again a deliberate distinction between male suffering and female suffering is made.

Okonkwo completes his seven-year exile and hastens to leave Mbanta. Upon return to Umuofia, he finds that the colonial government is in place, that people have lost their former dignity and have no solidarity. A series of events leads to his killing a messenger and his suicide at the novel's end.

If Okonkwo's rise and fall stands for the clan's and by extension African society's at that historical juncture, then Achebe is suggesting that for survival and transcendence and safe passage into the future one must learn to unite both male and female qualities, to fully respect both male and female and combine them into an ideal existence. If this is resisted then self-destruction follows. That this is an ideal is suggested in Ndulu and Ozoemena's (the old couple) togetherness in life and death.

> "It was always said that Ndulue and Ozeomena had one mind," said Obierika. "I remember when I was a young boy there was a song about them. He could not do anything without telling her." "I did not know that," said Okonkwo. "I thought he was a strong man in his youth." "He was indeed," said Ofoedu. (p. 62)

One must understand that Okonkwo had attained a position of leadership in the clan, but still failed to grasp the significance of uniting the male and female qualities. Okonkwo fails, additionally, because he ignores or cannot accept the wisdom of traditional respect for "Mother."

While the novel deals primarily with man's experience (and women are tangential) on the symbolic level, it clearly stresses the importance of female roles. Okonkwo's beating of his wives represents his heightened disregard for this female principle. It is well documented that in Igbo society, there is a definite female quality to religiosity. The most important Igbo deity is *Ala*, the Earth Goddess, who is characterized as a merciful mother who intercedes for her children, as the spirit of fertility who increases the productivity of the land. It is believed that women are closer to her than men and can obtain quicker hearing.[11]

In one of the most memorable scenes in African fiction, Achebe develops the significance of the priestess Chielo, whom we see, when possessed, transformed from an ordinary woman to a person of great strength and wisdom (pp. 90-7).

Achebe thus defines a separate world of women, which moves both within and beyond the purview of men. He conveys in Chielo a sense that the tragedy of Okonkwo expresses itself within the structural residues of a society which at one point had certain ideals of equality which exist now only in vestigial form.

Okonkwo's relationships with his sons and daughters also show his insensitivity. Okonkwo seeks to make his son a man, but Nwoye only puts on the veneer of manhood to please his father. Nwoye actually prefers his mother's stories to the masculine stories of wars and prowess (p. 42). The boy, who is described as having too much of his mother in him, begins to internalize those female values, and reflect on some of the excesses of his society and his own father's preoccupation with masculine achievements. In his search for an alternative, he becomes first in the family to join the Christian church.

Ironically, Okonkwo has better luck with his daughters, particularly Ezinma, although he constantly reminds her to "sit like a woman" (p. 40). Yet he repeats over and over again "she should have been a boy" (pp. 57, 58, 60, 156, 157). Again this points to Achebe's position that gender ought not to be a barrier to excellence or achievement. For Ezinma is bright and articulate, possessing all the credentials, except masculinity, for success and leadership. Another important motherhood-related structure is the mother-daughter relationship between Ekwefi and Ezinma. Ekwefi had lost many children soon after their births but, finally was able to keep Ezinma alive. Whereas Ezinma has a mother with whom she can develop closeness, Nwoye is unable to connect in the same way with his father.

Perhaps more important than the biological mother is the spiritual mother of Ezinma—Chielo. Symbolically Ezinma's journey with Chielo takes her out of Okonkwo's/society's defined role for her as a young woman and suggests larger possibilities for her life. The Chielo-Ezinma episode is one of those situations over which Okonkwo has no control (the other two are his expulsion from the clan and the colonial take-over). We see him here humbly and blindly following Chielo in the darkness. His machete, the symbol of male aggression, is of no use at all in this context.

The Chielo-Ezinma episode is an important sub-plot of the novel and actually reads like a suppressed larger story circumscribed by the exploration of Okonkwo's/man's struggle with and for his people.

In the troubled world of *Things Fall Apart*, motherhood and femininity are the unifying mitigating principles, the lessons for Okonkwo, the lessons for Africa and the world.

It is important to make a point about a second novel, *No Longer at Ease* (1960),[12] in which Achebe again deals with man's alienation and suffering but at intervals, juxtaposes that with the mother's suffering. Obi Okonkwo is Achebe's anti-hero. The women in his life are Clara, who gets pregnant with his baby but ends the pregnancy because of Obi's irresoluteness, and his mother who on the symbolic level of the book represents tradition or Africa. Again the abortion of the pregnancy comments on the abortion of the motherhood role as described above. In these two novels as well as in his subsequent two novels,[13] Achebe expresses, on literal and symbolic levels, the importance of women and motherhood. Yet his primary concern is woman's place within man's experience and man's lone struggle with larger social and political forces. While Achebe's works are obvious classics within the African literary tradition, a re-examination of his work from a feminist position reveals woman as peripheral to the larger exploration of man's experience.

Onuora Nzekwu—Motherhood as Control

Nzekwu's *Highlife for Lizards* (1965)[14] ends with a discussion of power as it relates to men and women in Igbo society which in actuality is the author's discourse on male/female relationships. The book deals with the experiences of a woman, Agom, from her teenage marriage to about age fifty. Agom has many experiences of womanhood. At first she is infertile and as a result her husband takes a second wife without her consent. She later becomes pregnant and successfully delivers three children. But much more than that, she has success in trading, participates in political struggle, takes titles and finally joins the ranks of the female elders.

Yet Agom, in her discourse in the epilogue seems to be commenting on the folly of modern young women who use education for competing with their husbands and claiming equality. The author has her saying,

> Instead of using her education to make herself more of an ideal wife, she becomes her husband's rival. She claims She is his equal (p. 191).

She continues to discuss the undesirable qualities in modern woman but her conclusions are only a litany of stereotypes of male/female relationships.

> It is natural for man to be direct in his ways with women and she to be devious, him to be plain; she to be subtle; him to roam the earth as he pleases, she always to be home; him to be strong, she weak . . . these laws are not man made, and anyone who honestly believes they can be reversed is a freak. (pp. 191-2)

These comments seem strange coming from Agom and jar against her reality. Agom had throughout her life struggled to attain a measure of equality in her marriage, had taken titles, become a priestess, and even joined the exclusive masquerade cult—the preserve of men—so that she would be beyond the harrassment that they mete out to women in public. Additionally she had achieved economic success and led a protest against colonial intrusion. What is more disturbing is that the author has Agom speaking this nonsense to a group of admiring women.

The facts of Agom's existence definitely conflict with her words in the epilogue. It can be inferred that Agom, who had been childless in the first years of her marriage and did not conceive until her husband had taken a second wife, is suggesting that she is the perfect woman who has achieved success *in all spheres*. Also, she may be mouthing certain words that would impress men but ironically hinting at "female control" for she does in the end smile and ask who wields the real power? The novel, at any rate, ends on an ambivalent note. Additionally the (male) author, Nzkewu, is obviously trying to redirect the reader from an otherwise logical conclusion for he has in the rest of the narrative created a very positive female character. Another point of consideration is that in Igbo society, as in many other African societies, women who have moved out of the vulnerable childbearing phase become technically "honorary men," and Agom could be playing out her new seniority role, as it relates to young women. Nzekwu, notwithstanding, communicates mixed messages on the status of women. But in the overall panorama of Agom's life, we see that having children, especially a son, marked a change in her fortunes and became an element of control.

It is instructive to make a passing comment about Nwadi, Agom's junior wife who is the stereotypical jealous wife (a character which reappears with amazing frequency in African literature), who attempts to conceive a son first, uses medicine from a traditional doctor on her husband and is eventually thrown out of the home. Nwadi's life is one of unhappiness, for she could not live with the competition among wives in her first husband's household and is thrown out of Udezue's compound in disgrace. Nwadi's demise is an interesting contrast to Agom's.

The fairytale ending of *Highlife for Lizards*, however, suggests a final peace and happiness for Agom, although Nzekwu implies that all women do not share this happiness. Whatever the ambiguities of this text, motherhood is clearly seen as crucial to that happiness and to the woman's ability to control her life.

In direct contrast to the glorified images of motherhood presented by their male counterparts, the Igbo women writers, considered here, challenge this fairytale ending of children, success and happiness. Both Emecheta and Nwapa categorically state that having children does not necessarily mean happiness or success. Instead, they present women who seek to define their lives over and beyond fecundity. In fact, one sees unhappiness, despair and death among mothers whose lives remain unfulfilled in other areas.

Flora Nwapa: The Male Woman or the Non-Mother

Flora Nwapa has written three novels, *Efuru* (1966)[15] and *Idu* (1970)[16] and *One is Enough* (1984)[17] which deal with motherhood. First of all, unlike Achebe and Nzekwu she often titles her works with the names of her heroines, indicating that she is telling strictly of the woman's experience. This is in striking contrast to the male writers who avoid names as titles altogether, even when telling essentially a woman's story as is the case of Nzekwu.

The first point to be made is that in *Efuru*, the author creates a world of women; men are shown to be intruders. Gossip, small talk, trading and selling, concern over each other's activities all have places in this women's world. In her first paragraph, Nwapa introduces her heroine simply as "the woman." It is only in subsequent paragraphs that she names Efuru.

Nwapa presents Efuru as a very assertive young woman who exercises her personal choice. She decides whom she wants to marry in defiance of the men of her family and goes to her husband without dowry . . . the first feminist statement of the book. Next she decides that she is not going to farm, contrary to her family's wishes, but will trade instead (p. 7). She refuses to stay in confinement the customary three months, but here we see she is made to submit to the cultural regulations regarding women. So she submits to the painful clitoredectomy (pp. 10-11) and is made, by her seniors, to kneel to her husband during the marriage ritual.

> Efuru was called. She was given the glass by her husband and when she was about to drink, the people shouted: "Kneel down, kneel down, *you are a woman*." Efuru quickly knelt down and drank . . .(p. 23) (Emphasis mine.)

This vacillation between independence and dependence, masculinity and feminity, characterizes Efuru's existence up until the end of the novel when she leaves her second husband. Much of her feeling of insecurity stems from her inability to conceive and be the "complete woman" her society respects. "I am still young, surely God cannot deny me the joy of motherhood," she often said to herself (p. 23). But childless "Efuru, was considered a man since she could not reproduce" (p. 23).

Efuru does eventually produce a daughter but this does not guarantee her happiness, for before the child is two, her husband leaves her for another woman. (We realize that his departure is not because of Efuru's personality but is the re-enactment of his father's desertion of his mother). Efuru's life at this point is so closely tied to her daughter's that she wails "What will I do if I lose her? If she dies, that will mean the end of me" (p. 79). The child dies but this is not the end of Efuru. She harnesses her grief and learns from the other women that woman's life is one of mastering suffering. Says one sympathizer,

> I conceived eight times. All died before they were six months old. The last one was a girl and when she did not die after six months, I killed a white fowl for my *chi*. I named her Ibiakwa—Have you come again? After a year and she did not die, I called her Nkem—My own. She was a beautiful girl . . .
> Then I returned from the market one day and saw that she was shivering with cold . . . In the night, she developed a convulsion and died . . .
> My only child died . . . The world was in darkness for me. I wept like a human being, I wept like an animal. I threatened to jump into the grave and be buried alive with my only child. but I am still alive today. I have not had another baby since then. Have a heart my daughter, you are still young. It is still morning for you . . .(pp.90-1)

Efuru recovers from her grief, makes her decision to return to her father's house. We are reminded over and over again that Efuru was a good woman. She helps the sick and acts independently until she is courted again. In her second marriage she has some happiness but the absence of children mars the relationship. Eventually the marriage ends as Efuru decides to return home again after her husband's accusations of adultery.

In the first portion of the novel a distinction is made between Efuru's handling of her husband's unfaithfulness and her mother-in-law's action in the same situation. Ossai is the long-suffering wife and mother who waits and who rears the same kind of son as her husband, both deserters of wife and mother. Ajanapu, her sister-in-law, tells her one day:

> You are the cause of your child's bad ways. You never scolded him because he was an only child. You delightfully spoilt him and failed to make him responsible . . . (p. 197)

Woman's responsibility for self is a central concern in *Efuru*. There is persistently the fear of being considered a 'male woman' (p. 129), but women seem to realize that men rarely have reins on their freedom and will oppress women if allowed. Ajanapu, for all her abrasiveness is a woman who controls her life and will not allow a younger woman to waste her life away. When Efuru is weakest, and being persecuted by her husband, Gilbert, and family, she calls on Ajanapu who comes with great haste (p. 275). Ajanapu lectures Gilbert on his betrayal of Efuru and he deals her a slap which makes her fall, but

> She got up quickly for she was a strong woman, got hold of a mortar pestle and broke it on Gilbert's head. Blood filled Gilbert's eyes (p. 276).

Before Efuru goes home to her father's compound she realizes that marriage was the beginning of her suffering (pp. 211-212), that you cannot buy happiness of children (p. 220), that living in a man's house means chores and subjugation to his whims. She wavers between helplessness and decisiveness.

In the end, Efuru finally achieves peace in her father's compound but it is a self-contained peace that is not controlled or directed by men.

> So here I am. I have ended where I began—in my father's house. The difference is that now *my father is dead*. (p. 280) (my emphasis)

There is a faint suggestion that she still considers this free and independent state to be misfortune for it suggests too much masculinity or control of one's life, a deviation from societal norms.

The novel does end on a positive note for we see Efuru realizing that her existence was not totally defined by motherhood. This confidence is given by the goddess of the lake to whom she becomes a priestess, and is the symbolic representation of the acceptance of self.[18]

> Efuru slept soundly that night. She dreamt of the woman of the lake, her beauty, her long hair and her riches. She had lived for ages at the bottom of the lake. She was as old as the lake itself. She was happy, she was wealthy. she was beautiful. She gave women beauty and wealth but she had no child. She had never experienced the joy of motherhood. Why then did the woman worship her? (p. 281)

The Woman of the Lake and Efuru's adherence to her reaffirm her belief in herself and her contributions to society and provide a societal alternative to motherhood for women "who are not so blest". Her novel *Idu* shows a woman fulfilled in a marital relationship at first without and later in spite of her children. Idu and her husband are so close that when he dies after a troubling illness, she decides that she is not going to be the wife of his brother according to tradition. Instead she wills herself to join her husband in death and does so leaving her children alive. *One is Enough* deals with themes similar to *Efuru*: the childless wife who is otherwise successful but rejected by her husband. Here, Amaka, after she has achieved her financial goals, conceives twin boys miraculously. In a sense then, the novel plays with the "immaculate conception" motif because the children's father is a man of God (a Catholic priest). Amaka disdains marriage now, hence the title, and is satisfied with her business success and her two sons. The ending of *Efuru* which deals with "the joy of motherhood" sets the theme for Emecheta's classic novel on motherhood which we will discuss next.

Buchi Emecheta: Mother as Slave

The message communicated in *Efuru* is echoed in Buchi Emecheta's *The Joys of Motherhood*.[19] The protagonist Nnu Ego, unlike Efuru had given all her life to producing and cultivating her children, had made no friends nor taken care of herself. She had followed all the traditional guidelines concerning motherhood and care of children but she realizes too late that she had all but wasted her life. As her children begin lives of their own, and she has, as yet, no grandchildren, she feels totally dislocated:

> I don't know how to be anything else but a mother. How will I talk to a woman with no children? Taking the children from me is like taking away the life I have always known, the life I am used to (p. 222).

The novel starts with Nnu Ego's agony at the loss of her four week old son. She is about to commit suicide because her life is already so tied to conception and motherhood. Emecheta ironically calls this chapter "The Mother" for we realize that Nnu Ego is no longer a mother. In fact we realize in Chapter Three that she was unable to conceive in her first marriage, that she was divorced for nursing her co-wife's child with her dry breasts. The symbolism of breasts for motherhood is evident here for when we first see Nnu Ego we feel the agony of her loss as we witness her breasts oozing milk which goes to waste for her child has died.

The story of a slave girl's death and rebirth informs the novel. Agunwa, the senior wife of Agbadi, Nnu Ego's father, had died. Her personal slave had been called to die with her but the young girl did not wish to die and begged for her life. This annoyed some of the men and she was dealt a blow and pushed into the grave. She still struggled to climb out of the hole but was given a final blow, and as she died she said to Agbadi, who had prevented any further mutilation of her:

> Thank you for this kindness, Nwokocha, the son of Agbadi. I shall come back to your household, but as a legitimate daughter. I shall come back (p. 23).

Ona, Nnu Ego's mother, had recently conceived and when the child Nnu Ego was born with a lump on her head, the *dibia* was consulted and he divined that:

> The child is the slave woman who died with your senior wife Agunwa. She promised to come back as a daughter. Now here she is. That is why this child has the fair skin of the water people and the painful lump on her head from the beating your men gave her before she fell into the grave (p. 27).

Emecheta therefore makes the slave's life and woman's life parallel and portrays Nnu Ego, the mother, as living the life of a slave, slave to her children, slave to tradition.

Ona, Nnu Ego's mother, is worthy of some discussion here. Ona provides another societal alternative to marriage but it is still male defined and therefore a limited alternative. Her father and her lover Agbadi strike a bargain over ownership of her unborn child based on its sex. Nnu Ego is female so she goes to her biological father Agbadi. Unfortunately the author lets Ona die during the birth of her second child and Agbadi ignores her dying wish that her daughter's life not be circumscribed by society's regulations on marriage and female roles. Ona would have been a dynamic character had she been developed by the author.

But the author's purpose is clearly to show the tragedy of woman's existence when it remains circumscribed by motherhood alone. The only reward for Nnu Ego is a good funeral and a shrine in her name. The latter is the only distinction between the slave woman and Nnu Ego.

Yet the lesson of her life and death remain misunderstood by the rest of her community:

> Stories afterwards, however, said that Nnu Ego was a wicked woman even in death because, however many people appealed to her to make women fertile, she never did. Poor Nnu Ego, even in death she had no peace. Still many agreed that she had given all to her children. The joy of being a mother was the joy of giving all to your children, they said. (p. 224)

For the reader, however, the irony of Nnu Ego's life and death is a forceful lesson in the pains of motherhood.

Emecheta has consistently dealt with those traditional attitudes to women, including those which the woman herself accepts, which tend to enslave her. For this reason, the slave woman is a fairly common Emecheta emblem. Motherhood, therefore, is just one of the routes to woman's potential enslavement. Her other novels, *The Bride Price* (1976) and *The Slave Girl* (1977)[20] play on this "slave to tradition" theme. Her two painful autobiographical novels *In The Ditch* (1972) and *Second Class Citizen* (1975)[21] deal with the personal race, class and sex oppression which came out of her experiences in Nigeria and London as girl-child and woman.

Conclusion

The novels in this study project no single view of motherhood. Various types of mothers are presented. Invariably the image of motherhood fits into the writer's larger political view and his/her purpose for writing. So for Achebe, perhaps the best representative of the African male writer, it is man's experience, colonial domination and the struggles of Afreican man, personal and political, within the traditional and contemporary situation. Motherhood is then a symbolic representation of tradition and Africa, within a larger frame.

In Nzekwu's work, largely a male interpretation of a woman's experience, we have a writer's commitment to the revelation of specific social and cultural information and the woman's place and possibilities within Igbo society. But we have an idealization of motherhood, the inability of the male writer to present the details of woman's experience. The writer's truthfulness gives us a positive female image in Agom but several stereotypical presentations of other women. His decision to include an epilogue which comments on male-female relationships and Agom's successes collides violently with the reality of Agom's life and her transcendence.

African women writers provide the other half of African people's story. They present reality from the woman's point of view and create distinct female worlds. They present the "great unwritten" stories of African literature. Importantly motherhood is not idealized but many of its pains detailed. Children are not the final and only happiness for their mothers but are elements in the acquisition of success in life as Nwapa demonstrates in all her works. But all women and men do not have children and they may not bring the happiness or success that is supposedly assured by their presence in the society. Alternative routes to success may be chosen by women. Indeed, African women have never been limited totally to childbearing but have consistently attained excellence in other spheres. This is why Nnu Ego's life is such a tragedy.

In the works of Nwapa, there is the conscious movement of women against restrictions of sex. In Emecheta, the true African feminist is revealed in the consciousness of political oppression of colonialism, Western domination and societal domination of a sexist nature. Women seek to liberate themselves from these various types of oppression and to exercise individual choice and are as Lloyd Brown suggests engaged in,

> striving to achieve a fulfilling sense of themselves, as distinctice human personalities while remaining loyal to all the encompassing community around them.[22]

African women writers in detailing the submerged realities of African women's lives are participating in the struggle to achieve the correct balance.

NOTES

1. Filomina Chioma Steady, *The Black Woman Crossculturally*, (Cambridge, Mass.: Schenkman, 1981), pp. 7-36.
2. Ibid., p. 35.
3. Maryse Condé, "Three Female Writers in Modern Africa: Flora Nwapa, Ama Ata Aidoo and Grace Ogot," *Presence Africaine* 82(2nd quarter, 1972), p. 132.
4. Caroline Ifeka-Moller, "Female Militancy and Colonial Revolt", in *Perceiving Women* ed. by Shirley Ardener (New York: John Wiley and Sons, Ltd., 1975), p. 127.
5. Sylvia Leith-Ross, *African Women* (New York: Praeger, 1965), pp. 21-22.
6. Steady, p. 29.
7. Andrea Benton Rushing, "Images of Black Women in Modern African Poetry: An Overview" in *Sturdy Black Bridges*, ed. by Bell, et al (New York: Anchor Press, 1979), p. 24.
8. Paula Giddings, "A Special Vision, A Common Goal," *Encore* (June 23, 1975), pp. 44, 46, 48.
9. Claudia Tate, *Black Women Writers at Work*, (New York: Continuum, 1983).
10. Chinua Achebe, *Things Fall Apart*, (London: Heinemann [African Writers Series], 1958).
11. Victor Uchendu, *The Igbo-Speaking People of South East Nigeria* (New York: Holt, Rinehart and Winston, 1965), p. 87.

12. Chinua Achebe, *No Longer at Ease*, (London, Heinemann [African Writer Series], 1960). Philip Rogers, "Achebe's 'Heart of Whiteness,'" *Research in African Literatures* 14:2 (Summer, 1983),pp. 165-183, explores Obi's growing alienation from his people and includes a discussion of the mother's place within Obi's distancing of himself from tradition.

13. Chinua Achebe, *Arrow of God* (London: Heinemann, 1960), AWS 16 and *A Man of the People* (London: Heinemann, 1970), AWS 31. Another writer, Elechi Amadi, is omitted from this study but his work is amply covered in this edition.

14. Onuora Nzekwu, *Highlife for Lizards*, (London: Hutchinson & Co., Ltd., 1965).

15. Flora Nwapa, *Efuru*, (London: Heinemann, 1966), AWS 26.

16. Flora Nwapa, *Idu*, (London: Heinemann, 1970), AWS 86.

17. Flora Nwapa, *One is Enough*, (Enugu, Nigeria: Tana Press, 1984).

18. See Lloyd Brown's incisive discussion of this point and several other important ones in his *Women Writers in Black Africa* (Westport, Conn.: Greenwood Press, 1981).

19. Buchi Emecheta, *The Joys of Motherhood*, (New York: George Braziller, 1979).

20. Buchi Emecheta, *The Bride Price* (New York, George Braziller, 1976); *The Slave Girl* (New York, George Braziller, 1977).

21. Buchi Emecheta, *In the Ditch* (London: Allison and Bushy, 1972); *Second Class Citizen* (New York: George Braziller, 1975).

22. Brown, pp. 182-3.

The Grandmother in African and African-American Literature: A Survivor of the African Extended Family

Mildred A. Hill-Lubin

The Black family in America has been the subject of considerable discussion. Earlier sociologists and theorists such as E. Franklin Frazier and Daniel Moynihan followed the traditional line of scholarship and argued that the distinguishing features represent weaknesses.[1] A new group of scholars led by Andrew Billingsley, Robert Hill, Demitri Shimkin, and Herbert Gutman, point out that many of these irregular features in the Black family may be termed strengths.[2] Furthermore, they assert that despite the upheaval and damage created as a result of slavery, Blacks in America have preserved many of the qualities associated with a strong family and community life which characterized the existence of their forebears in traditional Africa. One such strength has been the Black grandmother, who has been a significant force in the stability and the continuity of the Black family and the community. Her function, role, and importance can be traced to the revered status, position, and responsibilities which elders hold in West African society. The Black grandmother in America, then, represents the most tenacious survival of the African extended family.

257

In African-American literature, she re-appears as a central character in numerous novels, autobiographies, short stories, plays and poems; but unfortunately, as in real life, she has not received the scholarly and critical attention that she deserves. In like manner, though the grandmother has been important in most African societies,[3] she has not found a prominent place in the creative works of the major African writers. Surely, one reason for this omission is that the field has been dominated by male authors and their leading characters have been men. The grandmother does, however, occupy a noteworthy position in the imaginative works of some Ghanaian and South African writers. With more female voices entering the arena and more males willing to acknowledge and remember the contributions and the fundamental role women have played in Black societies and in history, I anticipate more images of the grandmother to be revealed.[4] Certainly, as teachers and critics become more aware of the need to clarify and define issues and to establish the fact that the hero need not always be a male, our critical and scholarly activities will inevitably lead us to this courageous, heroic, and giving figure.

Using examples from both African literature in English and African-American literature of the United States, this paper will explore the image of the Black grandmother. Through this comparative study, we shall be able to observe that, whether in Africa or in America, in traditional or colonial society, during and after slavery, post independence, she has been a pivotal figure in Black life and literature.

While the literature does not provide us with the grandmother of traditional Africa, we are able to reconstruct her image. With the assistance of materials from ethnographers, social historians, anthropologists, and folklorists and by looking at the Black grandmother as she has been depicted in other periods, we observe that both the African and the Black American grandmother stem from a common cultural background. As women who possess a common African heritage and who have participated in kindred subjugating experiences, we note that they, in turn, have responded in parallel fashion when confronted with foreign situations. To illustrate, this discussion will focus on four works, two by African-American authors and two by Africans. For the Black experience in the United States, we refer to the autobiographies of Frederick Douglass, *My Bondage and My Freedom* and Maya Angelou's *I Know Why the Caged Bird Sings*. For the African analogies, we turn to the excellent book of short stories by the Ghanaian author, Ama Ata Aidoo and the heart-warming autobiography, *Down Second Avenue* by the South African, Ezekiel Mphahlele. In these works, the grandmother functions in three major capacities: one, as the preserver of the African extended family; second, as the repository and distributor of family history, wisdom, and Black lore; and third, as the retainer and communicator of values and ideals which support and enhance her personhood, her family, and her community.

Of the many patterns undergirding the traditional African family and its American extension, one was the importance of the grandparents. In the motherland grandparents were honored because it was believed that they were the closest to the ancestors, and the ancestors were important because they could assume revered status. It was from the grandparents that children learned their family history, family wisdom, community lore, and traditional values. Among certain groups, the grandparents named their newborn grandchildren. With others, such as the Ashanti, grandmothers, both maternal and paternal, tremendously influenced the growth and development of their offspring. When Blacks were brought to the United States, they brought with them this ancient and honorable tradition of family. While slavery caused tremendous disruptions in these patterns of family life, it did not eliminate all of them. In some instances, it inadvertently reinforced many of these patterns, because it prevented the complete assimilation of Blacks into the new world cultures, and it also created situations which fostered many of the traditional customs and beliefs of Africa.

One of the earliest examples in literature of a household where the grandmother is a major force in the preservation of the family is in the narrative account *My Bondage and My Freedom* by Frederick Douglass. Here the author credits his grandmother with providing him with a positive self- concept and for creating a family for him. As a slave and the child of his master, Douglass was deprived of a normal family life. At an early age, he was separated from his mother, but he writes, "Living here, with my dear old grandmother and grandfather, it was a long time before I knew myself to be a slave."[5] These grandparents not only provided a home for Douglass, but for the children of all of their five daughters." The mothers had been sent elsewhere to work. While the author acknowledges that both of his grandparents shared in this endeavor, he relates most vividly throughout the autobiography that his grandmother was a central influence in his growth and development. As we will see later, he was most proud of her independence, resourcefulness, and skills.

In the literature which mirrors every period of Black life in the United States, we find examples of the grandmother who has assumed the role of heading an extended family. Most often her household includes some of her unmarried children, a married child and spouse, grandchildren and frequently non-related members whom she has taken in. In many of the works, especially those set in the early or middle twentieth century, the grandmother is a widow. Although the grandfather is dead, his presence is still a part of the family. He is kept alive through the stories of the grandmother, who usually describes him as having been a good man, a rigid disciplinarian who worked hard, loved his family and struggled to provide a decent home and livelihood for his family. Now that he is no longer alive, the grandmother is committed to keeping the home together and to making sure members will survive. Realizing that most often her financial resources are too meager to give extra money to her children and grandchildren, she permits them to return to the family dwelling where they all live together and pool their resources. In this manner, they are assured of the necessities of life or if not, they are able to support each other in their suffering and hard times. Langston Hughes' single novel, *Not Without Laughter* and Lorraine Hansberry's play, *A Raisin in the Sun* serve as two examples with such a figure and family. Maya Angelou's *I Know Why the Caged Bird Sings* offers a marvelous illustration; for in this magnificent autobiography, we have two grandmothers, one living in rural Arkansas and the other in urban St. Louis. In both instances, we have strong, independent, skillful women who are able to manage their families and to insure their survival in a segregated and hostile society. Both grandmothers take their grandchildren into their homes. In reflecting on her and her brother's return to her grandmother in Arkansas, Ms. Angelou writes: "Years later I discovered that the United States had been crossed thousands of times by frightened Black children traveling alone to their newly affluent parents in Northern cities or back to grandmothers in Southern towns when the urban North reneged on its economic promises."[6] As in this work, many Black children were sent or taken to their grandmothers while their parents remained in the North to work and to improve their situation. In many such homes, the grandmother fulfilled the role of the parents for a limited time and remained a major factor in the growing up process of the children. In other cases, the grandchildren were given to the grandmother when they were babies, and the older woman reared them to adulthood. Sometimes the mother lives in the home but works on a job that takes her away from the home. There are other pieces which reveal that during the summer, grandmothers received their grandchildren to help out the family so that the parents would not have to worry about child care or bear this expense while the children were out of school. By having them in the summer, it also meant that parents would not have to be concerned about their children's safety and well-being on the city streets. In works which describe urban life as in Langston Hughes and Roy De Carava's *The Sweet Flypaper of Life*, many of these grandmothers take their grandchildren in because they believe they will be able to save them from the streets. In all cases, the primary concern of these grandmothers as heads of their extended families has been to preserve their families at all costs.

Turning to African literature, we find literary models in parallel situations. Ama Ata Aidoo's *No Sweetness Here* contains short stories set in the period after independence. As in the Black American works, we witness a similar kind of uprootedness and devastation in the African family as a result of colonization. The roles of the male have become confused. In the pre-colonial family, women were most often associated with the preparation of food; but in colonial Africa, many Black males were trained to cook for their masters. To accept this change in family roles, it was agreed that African men could cook European foods, but African women would still be in charge of the African "chop" foods. With independence, problems erupted over this issue. "For Whom Things Did Not Change," one of the short stories in this volume details the trouble. The white master is replaced by a Black as "Big Man." He desires African foods, but the African cook does not know how to handle the situation when he is asked by his new master to prepare the indigenous dishes.[7] Other stories demonstrate the devastating impact of colonialism on the African families. They explore situations where the males had to leave their families to find work or as one of the characters reveals, be involved in "other people's wars." Consequently, women and specifically grandmothers, are forced to assume the role of heads of the extended family. "Certain Winds from the South" provides an example of a grandmother who is determined to preserve her family. This tale, as many of Aidoo's works, projects a sense of continuity and a feeling of repetitiveness; for it describes two generations, in which the life of the younger family appears to be a repeat of the experiences of the older family. Upon learning that her son-in-law is leaving on the night of her grandson's birth to go South to find work, the grandmother M'ma Asana recalls her own life. She relates that a few days after her daughter was born, her husband too had come to tell her that he was going South to join the army to help "the Anglis-people" fight their war against the Germans. Although the husband had promised that he would return and take her South with him, he never did. As we eavesdrop on the grandmother's revelation to her daughter, both about her son-in-law's plans to leave and her husband's going, we recognize that the grandmother is hurt and feels unlucky; nevertheless, we are impressed with her strength and determination. As she describes how she managed to survive and provide for her daughter, we know that she will keep her larger family going. The story ends on a positive, determined note: "I am going to market now. . .Today even if it takes all the money, I hope to get us some smoked fish, the biggest I can find, to make us a real sauce. . ." (p. 67).

M'ma Asana is not the only grandmother in this collection who is concerned with the well-being and care of her grandchild and with the perpetuation and survival of her family. In the story "The Message," we have a grandmother, Esi Amfoa, who has already buried all of her children, including her son who went "to sodja in the great war overseas." She has recently been informed that "her only pot," the one daughter of her son has been "opened up" in order to have her baby removed. Having never heard of a caesarean section, the grandmother is convinced that the big doctors up at Cape Coast have killed her granddaughter and will now use the body for instruction. We follow her as she boards the bus, anxious and heavy with sorrow, because she believes she has lost all. We also enjoy the communal spirit, the rivalry and jostling she takes on her trip. Finally, she arrives at the hospital and we are told, "The old woman somersaulted into the room and lay groaning, not screaming by the bed. For was not her last pot broken?" (p. 55). But to her surprise, she hears the voice of young, Esi Amfoa, her namesake. She looks up to discover that her "only pot" had refused to break. Her family remains alive.

Ezekiel Mphahlele's classic, *Down Second Avenue*, as Maya Angelou's *I Know Why the Caged Bird Sings*, portrays a Black youth growing up in a segregated society. This autobiography offers a picture of life in apartheid South Africa while Angelou describes life in the American South. Both works show grandmothers who serve as heads of their extended families and in both books, the grandchildren live with their paternal and maternal grandmothers. But, in each case, one grandmother plays a much more significant role in the life and development of the narrator. Similar to Angelou's work, *Down Second Avenue*, opens with the grandchildren's being sent from the city to the country to stay with the paternal grandmother. The young Eseki recounts that his Granny of Maupaneng was not the loving, kind person as his maternal grandmother, the one he later moves in with on Second Avenue. The rural grandmother is portrayed as "big as fate, as forbidding as a mountain, stern as a mimosa tree."[8] While she is not the warm grandmother, she does take her young grandchildren into her home to help ease the burden of the troubled younger family. In addition, the Granny of the country and the mountain is described as functioning like many Black American grandmothers. She has taken other relatives and non-relatives into her home. Besides the grandchildren, an uncle and a young woman named Sarah reside in the home. Sarah has been adopted by the older woman following the death of her mother in childbirth. Thus, this South African grandmother is fulfilling another one of the functions of the traditional African extended family, that of taking care of all the kin, including, at times, members of the larger community.

In Mphahlele's autobiography, we also find evidence of the family under severe stress. The dominance of the Black male no longer exists. Most of the men have already left the village and only the middle-aged and old women, children, and old men remain. As the author writes "The land was not giving out much. The Black man could work only the strip given him by the chief. The chief had no more to give out" (p. 12). The old man complained that most of their land had been taken away by the white man.

Eseki stayed in this dreary village with the stern grandmother for over seven years. When twelve however, he and his sister and brother rejoin their parents in the city of Pretoria. But it is not long, before, in an agonizing and brutal scene, we experience the break-up of the marriage of his father and mother. Eseki and his siblings are then transferred to the home of his maternal grandmother and Aunt Dora, two women who influence his life tremendously. While his mother does not live in the home, she remains linked to the family as she works in the suburb as a domestic. She contributes to its upkeep and support. The larger household on Second Avenue, headed by the grandmother includes Aunt Dora, Aunt Dora's husband, their three children, three uncles, and four other tenants who have leased rooms from the older woman, Eseki and his sister and brother. Although the grandfather is dead, his presence still prevails. The narrator states that he never knew this grandfather, but everyone talked endearingly of him and that he must have exercised rigid discipline in his house because grandmother liked to quote some of his maxims. The grandfather is described as having been a "self-taught shoe repairer." We see that before his death he had tried to provide both a physical and spiritual foundation for his family. Now that he is gone, it is left to the grandmother to keep the family together and progressing, in spite of all the obstacles.

Serving, in E. Franklin Frazier's terms, as "the guardian of the generations," these women are the acknowledged storytellers who pass on the family history and who know who is kin to whom. Characteristic of their African ancestors, they normally possess information on childbirth and lore on medicines and herbs for healing and curing various illnesses. In America, the white and the Black communities depended upon them to keep everyone healthy. Using what can only be described as their "female" talents—good cooking skills; keen insights into human relations; creative, spiritual, and artistic capabilities; proficiency in home and people management—many of these women developed into astute businesswomen. In this way, they were able to improve the lot of their families. They then transmitted this information, lore, and skill to their children and grandchildren, just as, in many cases, it had been passed on to them earlier.

Frederick Douglass writes that his grandmother was held in high esteem, far higher than was the lot of most colored persons in the region. He describes her as being a good nurse and "a capital hand at making nets used for catching shad and herring" and was withal somewhat famous as a fisherwoman. (pp. 35-36) The grandmothers in Angelou's autobiography also demonstrate business acumen. Grandmother Henderson of Stamps, Arkansas runs the family grocery store and manages the rental properties of the family that many of the poor whites of the community lived on. Speaking of her success as a businesswoman, the author writes: "Her crisp meat pies and cool lemonade, when joined to her miraculous ability to be in two places at the same time assured her business success" (p. 7). The Wm. Johnson General Merchandise Store began as a mobile lunch counter with the grandmother selling lunches to the workers at the lumberyard and cotton gin. Its growth to a stand and then to the store in the heart of the Black community, permitting it to become the lay center of activities in the town, is testimony of the grandmother's knowledge and insights into business matters. Grandmother Baxter in the city was no less skillful. She had been able to gain power and pull with all of the powerful elements in the city of St. Louis. People came to her to ask favors and in return she had her own needs fulfilled. While such roles certainly added to the other tasks these women already performed, they also earned many advantages and the grandchildren almost always benefitted from the goodwill and respect these grandmothers garnered from the larger community.

In the works of the African writers, the older women are no less resourceful, talented, wise, and knowledgeable. They too are eager to share their information and history with their children and grandchildren. Aidoo, in *No Sweetness Here* provides us with the character of Auntie Araba in the short story "Something to Talk About on the Way to the Funeral." The story points out that this African grandmother has been such a force in her community that her life story is now being narrated to the readers by two women who have come to pay their respects to her at her death. They recount Auntie Araba had come from one of those families which always have some members abroad, suggesting here again that the African family is no longer that tight knit community of people all in one village; yet it still functions as a large extended family. The story is told that as a young woman, Araba had been sent to these family members in the city to learn a skill. It was here that she had learned to be a baker, but she also had run into trouble. She became pregnant; but as the narrator informs us, her life was not ruined. For when she returned home to her mother, she was graciously received by her family. It was after her son's birth, however, that Auntie Araba grew to be an expert with the dough. Possessing similar business sense as Angelou's Grandmother Henderson, Auntie Araba soon discovered that her fancy city pastries were not profitable in the small village. Therefore, she turned to baking ordinary bread and achieved tremendous success.

As we pointed out earlier, one advantage in reading the works of Aidoo and especially the stories in *No Sweetness Here* is that the writer demonstrates "the repetition of old patterns" which occur in the lives of most Black people. She accomplishes this task by usually presenting at least two generations in her stories in order to compare and contrast the lives of her characters. Consequently, we are able to see immediately the impact, contributions, and influence of the grandmother. In the story, "Someting to Talk About on the Way to the Funeral," we hear that before too long Auntie Araba has become a grandmother. Significantly, it is her son who impregnates the young woman, Mansa. Unlike Auntie Araba's family, Mansa's family, is not as supportive. Her father wants nothing to do with her. it is Auntie Araba who takes the young woman in. The storyteller relates, "People did not even know how to describe the relationship between the two. Some people said they were like mother and daughter. Others that they were like sisters" (p. 149). Finally, the baby comes. Mansa and her son continue to live with Auntie Araba because her father is not interested in sending her back to school. In addition, it has been thought, that Ato, Auntie Araba's son, would finish his education, return and marry the young woman. But as his father before him, Ato could not marry Mansa because he had impregnated another young woman from a more prestigious family. Although disappointed, Mansa has begun to grow strong like Auntie Araba. In addition, she has learned to be an excellent baker, following the instructions of the older woman. Therefore, when Ato does not marry her, she moves to the city to stay with friends whom Auntie Araba has contacted and asked to take her in. Mansa is now able to find a job where as the narrator tells us; "They bake hundreds of loaves of bread an hour with machines" (p. 154). Mansa is referred to as a "good woman," like Auntie herself. "She has all of her character." The two women narrators conclude that she will get along fine. "A good person does not rot" (p. 154). The grandson is left with the maternal grandmother and as we have seen earlier, the story will probably be repeated.

In *Down Second Avenue* the grandmother is equally hard working and resourceful. She too serves as the storyteller who relates to her grandson the history of the immediate family and the axioms of the grandfather. Eseki recounts that his grandmother never tired of telling him about Paul Kruger's day; of the hard times under Boer rule; of the way they buried Africans alive who were suspected of fighting or spying for the British; of how Boer soldiers cut off Black women's breast; how she was great at answering all the catechism questions, and of how his grandfather Titus took his family from place to place looking for a better life and who didn't think Meneer Paul was better than he. This grandmother, like Frederick Douglass' grandmother, is intent on giving her children and grandchildren a sense of history, a feeling of family, that vital concept of self-worth, even if the society around them is intent on denying them their humanity. This grandmother is the link that unites the family to its past, but also she is its source of hope. As with the other grandmothers, this South African woman expands her resources and limitations. She takes the little house and stand that the grandfather had left and divides it up in such a way that her extended family has a home, and the family is also able to receive supplementary monies by leasing rooms to tenants. Like many of the grandmothers in the Black American stories, she washes clothes for the whites of the area, but she too increases her opportunities by creating another job. The only business that most people, and especially the women, were able to carve out for themselves is that of selling beer, which according to the South African officials was illegal. Yet, these women, Grandmother and Aunt Dora were intent on continuing their business. And in spite of police raids and the Blacks who served as the white officials' eyes, these women persevered. Using this income, grandmother sent most of her children to boarding school or elsewhere to be educated or to learn a trade.

Describing these grandmothers as women who were resourceful and full of wisdom because they were intent on insuring that their children would have a better life moves us to the final function that most of these grandmothers performed. They did not only will their children practical and business knowledge and encourage them to get an education. Most of these women were determined to endow their families with values and ideals which would enhance their lives and provide them with the essentials for survival, growth, and development. These sterling figures transmitted these gifts through both their words and their deeds. They themselves possessed strengths that often made them appear indomitable.

Most of them benefitted from a deep, abiding, and living religious faith. Grandmama Henderson in *I Know Why the Caged Bird Sings* is depicted as a devoutly religious woman who gathered her family in prayer each morning at 4:00 A.M. to begin the day. The autobiography opens with the scene of Marguerite, the granddaughter, in the Colored Methodist Episcopal Church where her grandmother has brought her in order to recite her Easter speech. While this occasion proves frightening and embarrassing for the painfully shy, young girl, it is significant that the work begins at the church; for it is at this institution that the children are introduced to the strengths of the community, but they also become equipped with the rituals, songs, and words which will later serve them as survival tools.

Angelou writes, "Momma," the name the children had given to their Grandmother shortly after their arrival, "intended to teach Bailey and me to use the paths in life that she and her generation and all the Negroes gone before had found and found to be safe ones" (p. 46). In *Down Second Avenue*, Ezekiel Mphahlele describes his pious grandmother as one who brought her family together at night in prayer and would awaken them each morning with prayer to begin the day. In both of the autobiographies, Ezekiel and Marguerite, as youths watching their grandmothers and being socialized by them, are not as convinced as their grandmothers that religion is a viable force for Blacks in a society where the concepts of Christianity are a mockery. But neither of the older women is disturbed too much by her grandchildren's doubts and lack of faith. They remain committed and firm.

These older women, though advanced in age, have accepted the younger children back into their homes, and they remain active participants in the daily survival and management of the family. Although the grandmothers are the storytellers and they love their grandchildren, they seldom spoil them; nor do they tell them stories merely to entertain. Their stories are designed to teach them the paths to survival and progress. While in these two works, the young narrators never confront their elders, in other works we have slight confrontations; but the older women are seldom upset by the criticism of their grandchildren. Accustomed to the struggles and great vicissitudes of life, they are not easily subdued by the smaller scrimmages. Most often, these women emerge victorious and with dignity. Whether their grandchildren wish to learn of their strength, great convictions, or not, they usually are always left impressed. Maya Angelou describes such an incident. On one occasion a group of the poor white girls of the town had come to the store to try to humiliate her grandmother. They did everything possible. One of the young girls even stood on her hands and revealed that she had on no underwear. As a young Black girl, the author relates that she was so angry as her grandmother stood, prayed, and sang through it all. But in closing the episode, Angelou writes of this magnificent woman:

> She stood another whole song through and then opened the screen door to look down on me crying in rage. She looked until I looked up. Her face was a brown moon that shone on me. She was beautiful. Something had happened out there which I couldn't completely understand but I could see that she was happy (p. 32).

The author states that then her grandmother bent down and touched her as the mothers of the church lay hands on the sick and afflicted, and she quieted. Already, the young girl is beginning to recognize the power, strength, and spirit of her grandmother and to appreciate her life and teachings.

Ama Ata Aidoo gives us an example from African literature where the older woman emerges as the strong, victorious, person in a struggle with the young. In the short story, "The Message," we have the young nurse's attempt to make the older woman appear ignorant, country, and small. When the old woman comes, anxious to find "her only pot", her granddaughter who has had the operation, the nurses make fun of her. At the end, the "Draba" (driver) calls the young nurse, Jessy Treeson, "a cassava stick" and thinks about kicking her; but rationalizes that he may break his toe, if he kicked her buttocks (p. 55). It is the grandmother who is triumphant and "big" in the story rather than the young nurse who would like to think her training has made her superior to the old woman.

Throughout the literature, we have evidence of the families growing together. Although in many situations the grandchildren may not always agree with their elders, they recognize that these women have provided them with some valuable gifts. In other works, especially in the poetry of the young Black American writers of the sixties, we have the grandmothers trying to understand their grandchildren better. For example, Haki Madhubuti (Don L. Lee) has a poem entitled "Bigmomma" which portrays the relationship of the grandson with the grandmother. In the poem, the young man has come to his grandmother's home for his "weekly visit and talking to." She is aware that her grandson has changed and is now involved in the "blackness" movement and that he is now planning to be a writer. All of these changes are confusing to the grandmother, but as the poet states, she is in a "seriously funny mood." She is also eager to relate to her grandson. Therefore she weaves her conversation around his new personality "u gonta be a writer, hunh/when u gon write me some writen."[9] Later, she exclaims "now *luther*, I knows you done changed a lots but if/you think back, we never did eat too much pork around here anyways . . . " After the two share a smile together, the young revolutionary leaves his grandmother's modest kitchen where the *"chicago tribune"* serves as the table cloth. But, the poet states, as the young man moves back to the streets, he reflects on Big Momma's words. "At sixty-eight/she moves freely, is often right. . ." (p. 32). In both sides there has been recognition and growth. The family remains harmonious.

Linda Brown Bragg in her poem "About Beauty, Blackness, and Poetry," confirms that these women, through the years have been determined to teach us that we must be beautiful, Black, and revolutionary.[10] Alice Walker in her essay, "In Search of our Mothers' Gardens," details how many of these women were thwarted in their efforts to be creative artists and to write about beauty.[11] Nevertheless, they have persisted in showing beauty. Ezekiel Mphahlele tells how valiantly his grandmother tried to grow flowers, but the best the family was ever able to do was "set up a grape-vine creeper which made pleasant shade for the family to do washing" (p. 25). Just as their talents and most often the flowers they planted were stifled and could not grow, the families of these women occasionally suffered setbacks. But these indomitable spirits struggled and were willing to make all kinds of sacrifices to preserve and perpetuate their families. Thus, they pass on an ancestral heritage which urges us all to be superior.

Fortunately, many of our writers have depicted these caring and resilient grandmothers, but unfortunately the depictions have almost been ignored. There are several reasons for this neglect; but the strongest one appears to be that, as critics and researchers, we have lingered too long under the influence of majority scholarship which has tended to recognize the heroes but ignore the "sheroes," to emphasize the weaknesses in Black life rather than its strengths, its sufferings rather than its triumphs, the destruction of the African family rather than its survival, growth, and development. Too often, we have overlooked female characters, perhaps in an effort to counter the accusations that to describe strong women would help to support the matriarchal theory which says that Black females castrate their men or the notion that Black males are dysfunctionally weak. But we, now, as critics, are being challenged to overcome such fears as many of our writers have done. Certainly, the African family has suffered tremendously under the burden of slavery and colonialism but it has also persevered. One of the major strengths in its survival has been the grandmother, and she deserves more of our attention and recognition. May I hasten to add that, as in real life, all Black grandmothers in literature have not been the loving, strong, devoted, selfless individuals. Maya Angelou, in her realistic depictions does not totally romanticize nor idealize her grandmother figures, nor does Ezekiel Mphahlele. Honest in her depiction, Ama Ata Aidoo in the title story of her volume, "No Sweetness Here," portrays a grandmother who is a vindictive and mean woman, determined to hurt her daughter-in-law (p.

84). Nevertheless, we need to look more keenly at all of these characters in fiction and above all begin to realize that these women represent heroic figures drawn from real life. By studying the works and concentrating on these female images, we can come to appreciate, affirm, celebrate as well as possibly emulate and be inspired by their many achievements and contributions.

NOTES

1. For more information on the Black family in the United States as a "destroyed" and pathological specimen of the white family, see E. Franklin Frazier's, *The Negro Family in the United States*, Chicago: The University of Chicago Press, 1939, reprinted 1968; and the Moynihan Report, offically entitled *The Negro Family: The Case for National Action*. U.S. Department of Labor, March, 1965, and reprinted in Lee Rainwater and William L. Yancy, eds., *The Moynihan Report and the Politics of the Controversy*, Cambridge, Mass. MIT Press, 1967.

2. For discussions on the Black Family in America as a continuant of the African extended family with many strengths, see Andrew Billingsley, *Black Families in White America*. Englewood Cliffs, N.J. Prentice Hall Inc. 1968; Robert Hill, *The Strength of Black Families*, New York: Emerson Hall publishers, Inc., 1972; Demitri B. Shimkin, Edithe M. Shimkin, Dennis A. Frate, editors. *The Extended Family in Black Societies*. The Hague, Paris: Mouton Publishers, 1978, and Herbert G. Gutman, *The Black Family in Slavery and Freedom, 1750-1925*, New York: Pantheon Books, 1976.

3. See the role of the grandmother in the following articles: "Marguerite Dupire, "The Position of Women in a Pastoral Society (The Fulani WoDaaBe Nomads of the Niger," in *Women of Tropical Africa*, edited by Denise Paulme, trans. by H. M. Wright (Berkeley University of California Press, 1963) 73-74; Ethel M. Albert, "Women of Burundi: A Study of Social Values," in *Women of Tropical Africa*, pp. 209-210; Elizabeth Fisher Brown, "Hehe Grandmothers"; *Journal of Royal Anthropology Institute*. XV, (1935) 83-96 quoted from "Introduction" *African Systems of Kinship and Marriage*, edited by A. R. Radcliffe-Brown and Daryl Ford (London: Oxford University Press, 1950) p. 26, 28; Hilda Kuper, "Kinship Among the Swazi," in *African Systems of Kinship and Marriage*, pp. 104-106; Meyer Fortes, "Kinship and Marriage Among the Ashanti" in *African System. . .*, pp. 263 and 276, Melville J. Herskovits. *Dahomey: An Ancient West African Kingdom* (Evanston: Northwestern University Press, 1976) p. 155.

4. As evidence of this possibility, refer to the strong and important role that Nyakinyua plays in Ngugi wa Thiong'o's last novel, *Petals of Blood*, London: Heinemann, 1977.

5. Frederick Douglass, *My Bondage and My Freedom*, (New York: Arno Press and the New York Times, 1968) p. 38. Additional references to this work will be cited in the body of the paper by page numbers.
6. Maya Angelou, *I Know Why the Caged Bird Sings* (New York: Random House, 1969) pp. 6-7. Additional references to this work will be cited in the body of the paper by page numbers.
7. Ama Ata Aidoo. *No Sweetness Here*. (London, Longman Drumbeat, 1970) p. 19. Future references to this edition will appear in the body of the paper with page numbers.
8. Ezekiel Mphahlele, *Down Second Avenue* (Garden City, New York. Anchor Books, 1971) p. 1. Future references to this work will appear in the body of the paper with page numbers.
9. Don L. Lee, "Bigmomma" in *We Walk the Way of the New World*," (Detroit: Broadside Press, 1970) p. 31. Future references will be cited by page numbers in the body of the paper.
10. Linda Brown Bragg, "Poem About Beauty, Blackness, Poetry (and how to be all three)" in *A Love Song to Black Men* (Detroit: Broadside Press, 1974) p.17.
11. Alice Walker, "In Search of Our Mothers' Gardens: The Creativity of Black Women in the South," *Ms*. (May 1974) pp. 64-70, 105.

Marriage, Tradition and Woman's Pursuit of Happiness in the Novels of Mariama Bâ

Edris Makward

Fatna Air Sabbah—a pseudonym for a well-known Algerian female writer—opens her recent stunning essay *La Femme Dans L'inconscient Musulman—Désir et Pouvoir*[1] with a vivid reminder of the famous and still highly respected XIth century Persian philosopher and theologian, Al Ghazzali's warning against what he considered as the most serious imperfection in a would-be-bride, that is, *vadaka* or talkativeness, a woman's legendary propensity to talk too much.

Fatna Ait Sabbah then exposes the premise of her essay in the form of a compelling series of questions:

> Pourquoi donc le silence et l'immobilité, c'est-à-dire les signes et la manifestation de l'inertie, sont-ils les critères de la beauté chez la femme musulmane? Qu'est-ce que la beauté a à voir avec le droit à l'expression? Pourquoi, selon les canons de la beauté en Islam, une femme qui ne s'exprime pas doit exciter le désir chez l'homme?. . . .[2]
>
> [Why is it that silence and immobility, that is, the signs and manifestations of inertia, are the criteria for the beauty of the Muslim

271

woman? What has beauty to do with the right to self-expression? Why is a woman who does not express herself, supposed to arouse desire in men, according to the Muslim canons of beauty?. . .]

These questions raised by Fatna Ait Sabbah indeed have relevance in the world of the late Mariama Bâ, the author of the celebrated *Une Si Longue Lettre*[3] [*So Long A Letter*]. For although the literary, cultural and theological corpus on which the Algerian author's study is based is, above all, Middle Eastern—Arab and Persian in particular—there is no denying that this corpus has had a very strong influence on many Islamized "Sub-Saharan" African societies over several centuries. And Sénégal is undoubtedly among these countries, considering its age-old contacts with North African and Middle Eastern Islam.[4]

Marima Bâ's discourse, however, while never questioning the fundamental precepts of Islam, stemmed deliberately and convincingly from a dynamic conception of society, a strong belief in social and political change and progress. At first glance, each of her two novels seems to center around one specific topic: the evils of polygamy in *Une Si Longue Lettre* and the failure of a racially mixed marriage in *Un Chant Ecarlate*[5] [*A Scarlet Song*], her second novel, published posthumously. However it is my contention that despite their apparently different foci, there is one underlying theme that runs through both novels, and that is the theme of personal happiness.

Une Si Longue Lettre is the story of two western-educated African women, Aïssatou and Ramatoulaye (Rama). They are both very actively involved in the process of social change that has been taking place in their country for two or three generations. The time framework is the effervescent and immediate era of independence and post-independence in Sénégal. Both women are happily married to dynamic conscientious, loving and understanding African husbands, and their marriages are indeed modern marriages in the sense that they originated from their own free choices and were not prearranged by their parents. Both women are confronted with the second marriages of their husbands as a *fait accompli*, but while Aïssatou rejects vehemently the polygamous situation and leaves her husband Mawdo, a doctor, for a successful professional career as an interpreter in New York, Ramatoulaye, the narrator, stays with her husband Modou with the hope that he will at least follow the traditional Islamic rule and practice of equal attention and sharing of the husband in a polygamous household. But in fact Ramatoulaye and her children will be deserted by Modou in favor of the new wife, Binetou. When Modou dies suddenly of a heart attack, Ramatoulaye will reject all the polygamous suitors who wish to take Modou's place. For, as she puts it in the closing paragraph of her "long letter" to her friend Aissatou:

Je t'avertis déjà, je ne renonce pas à refaire ma vie. Malgré tout—
déceptions et humiliations—l'espérance m'habite. C'est de l'humus
sale et nauséabond que jaillit la plante verte et je sens pointer en moi,
des bourgeons neufs.[6]
[I warn you already. I have not given up wanting to refashion my
life. Despite everything—disappointments and humiliations—hope
still lives on within me. It is from the dirty and nauseating humus that
the green plant sprouts into life, and I can feel new buds springing up in
me.]

Un Chant Ecarlate relates the story of an initially beautiful love affair
between two young students—the Sénégalese Ousmane and the French
Mireille—who end up marrying in France after completing separately their
studies, he, in Dakar, and she, in France where her intransigent father had
sent her by force when he found out about their relationship. Although
Ousmane does not neglect any of his duties towards his parents, his mother
Yaye Khady is not satisfied with her son's marriage with a foreigner, for
Mireille does not—and cannot possibly—fulfill towards her, all the
functions of a true daughter-in-law in accordance with traditional Wolof
expectations. Mireille has not been culturally prepared by her own
husband. Ousmane will then fall back on a childhood flame and former
neighbor Ouleymatou, in the name of "authenticity," and he will marry her
as a second wife. This "triangle," unlike the polygamous situation experienced
by Aïssatou and Ramatoulaye in Mariama Bâ's first novel, will end
tragically with Mireille, the French heroine, losing her mind and killing her
son—the symbol of her failed mixed marriage.

From these two summaries, one could be tempted to conclude that
Mariama Bâ's novels were nothing but pleas against polygamy. But that
would be definitely superficial. Mariama Bâ's central preoccupation in
these novels was more the pursuit of happiness than an outright attack on
polygamy. And when Rama praises her friend Aïssatou and calls her
"pionnière hardie d'une nouvelle vie" [daring pioneer of a new life], she was
indeed expressing her admiration for her friend's courage in continuing her
search for true happiness without any compromise with polygamy or any
other binding traditions. However, although she did not embark on an
outright diatribe against polygamy, Mariama Bâ was convinced that
happiness—and not just women's happiness, but men's as well, a whole
society's happiness—must be based on a monogamous marriage. And in
the modern context, for her, monogamous marriage meant a close
association between two equals, and the sharing of pains, joys, hopes,
disappointments and successes. The foundation stone of this happiness is
without doubt in the couple, a concept, an ideal that is clearly new in Africa.
Rama expresses this conviction in a revealing passage of her letter to her

friend Aïssatou who chose courageously to leave her husband Mawdo when he decided to "please his mother" by marrying a young cousin, a member of his caste:

> Je suis de celles qui ne peuvent se réaliser et s'épanouir que dans le couple. Je n'ai jamais conçu le bonheur hors du couple, tout en te comprenant, tout en respectant le choix des femmes libres.[7]
> [I am one of those who can realize themselves fully and bloom only when they form part of a couple. Even though I understand your stand, even though I respect the choice of liberated women, I have never conceived of happiness outside marriage.]

In rejecting her brother-in-law Tamsir's offer to replace his brother in accordance with Sénégalese Muslim traditions, Rama reasserts her desire to adhere to all the implications of the ideal of the couple:

> Tu oublies que j'ai un coeur, une raison, que je ne suis pas un objet que l'on se passe de main en main. Tu ignores ce que se marier signifie pour moi: c'est un acte de foi et d'amour, un don total de soi à l'être que l'on a choisi et qui vous a choisi. (J'insistais sur le mot choisi.)[8]
> [You forget that I have a heart, a mind, that I am not an object to be passed from hand to hand. You don't know what marriage means to me: it is an act of faith and love, the total surrender of oneself to the person one has chosen and who has chosen you. (I emphasized the word 'chosen'.)]

In emphasizing the idea of choice, Rama is clearly expressing her disapproval of the traditional "arranged" marriage where the parents or other relatives—the family—make the choice for the bride and groom.

Hence the clash with tradition is obvious, for marriage with its function for procreation is definitely a central institution in traditional African society. It is therefore not a matter under the primary responsibility of the individuals concerned, that is, the bride and groom, but for the community, the family, to decide.

Mariama Bâ did not attack tradition and custom blatantly, but she expressed her disapproval of certain glaring abuses of tradition which impede progress. While she demonstrated an unflinching faith in the freedom of choice and the personal nature of marriage and romantic love, she also expressed her belief in the gain that the community in the modern context—the nation—would reap from the success and the attainment of happiness by individual couples. For her, family success depended on the harmony of the founding couple, and in turn, it was the grouping of all these successful and happy families that would constitute the Nation. As in Rama's words:

C'est de l'harmonie du couple que naît la réussite familiale, comme l'accord de multiples instruments crée la symphonie agréable.

Ce sont toutes les familles, riches ou pauvres, unies ou déchirées, conscientes ou irréfléchies qui constituent la Nation. La réussite d'une nation passe donc irrémediablement par la famille.[9]

[The success of a family is born of a couple's harmony, as the harmony of multiple instruments creates a pleasant symphony.

The nation is made up of all the families, rich or poor, united or separated, aware or unaware. The success of a nation therefore depends on the family.]

One could argue that there was nothing new in this idea in the African context, for it was in the interest of the community in general that the family would initiate ties that would ultimately lead to the union in marriage of young men and women. What was new, however, was the notion that marriage was above all based on the choice and initial attraction of the two principal partners.

Mariama Bâ was not the first African writer to treat the subject. Two outstanding predecessors are the Tunisian Albert Memmi and the Sénégalese Ousmane Sembène. An even earlier precursor is René Maran with his *Un Homme Pareil Aux Autres*, published in 1947. Memmi shows in his 1955 novel, *Agar*, how enticing the western ideal of the couple can be for the young Tunisian medical student who falls in love with a blond Alsatian chemistry student. They marry and at the completion of his medical studies, travel to Tunisia where the protagonist has no doubt that they will settle and raise a family. Naturally, they are confronted with a number of cultural difficulties; the most devastating of all being the overwhelming weight of the family and the community on the young couple. Even the protagonist did not seem quite prepared for this clash of cultural world views on his "re-entry" among his own people:

Je constatais, une fois de plus, combien ils tenaient à moi et combien je leur appartenais. Pour mon père je n'étais pas seulement son fils mais un anneau de la grande chaîne. Je comprenais la responsabilité qui, d'après lui, m'incombait, et qu'il croyait me préserver d'une trahison.[10]

[Once more I was aware how much I meant to them, how closely I belonged. For my father I was not only his son, but a link in the great chain. I realized all the responsibility that he felt was mine, saw that his thought was to save me from betraying the family.]

This fear of betrayal is not just apparent in the father's mind; the son, our protagonist, is also aware of the danger and the temptation to "betray" his people and "let his French wife have her way". He is torn between two cultural worlds, and his dilemma lies in his wish to preserve both of these worlds: his adopted world, Marie's world on the one hand, and his people's world on the other. He had to admit that while he was often wary of his family's thoughtless invasion of his privacy and more often than not, tended to see their attachment to their age-old traditions and customs as offensive and backward, he could not at other times contain his genuine admiration for the profound meaning of some of his people's traditions. This paralyzing predicament is illustrated when he is choosing a name in anticipation of the birth of his first son. Tradition would want the grandson to bear his grandfather's name: Abraham, for the sake of continuity. Although the protagonist's impulsive answer to his parents is negative, he expresses later his understanding of this simple custom in compelling words:

> L'avouerai-je? Quelquefois je m'étonnais de L'espèce de grandeur de cet élan, de cette défaite du temps par la mémoire des hommes.[11]
> [And let me admit that sometimes I have wondered at the touch of greatness in this long linking, this triumph of men's memory over time.]

In spite of the somewhat apologetic tone, there is genuine admiration and profound understanding in these words. However, the conflict, the waverings persist and will eventually lead to Marie's decision to return to her native France. the significance of this failure should be seen as a sign of the deep alienation of the protagonist rather than "Memmi's unspoken conclusion that such an experiment in marriage is foredoomed to failure".[12]

It is the depth and pain of this alienation that Memmi expresses through the protagonist's thoughts in the closing chapters of the novel:

> La folie de Marie a été de croire que je serais entièrement à elle lorsqu'elle aurait tout arraché de moi, même l'odeur des pierres chaudes et du soleil. Cette femme que j'aime, qui fut le meilleur de moi-même, qui a voulu tout me donner, est devenu le symbole et la source de ma destruction. Je ne suis plus rien qu'un fantôme, mon propre ennemi et le sien. Je l'ai trahie et elle m'a détruit.
> Mais, en même temps, je ne peux plus vivre sans elle. Je n'ai plus ni pays, ni parents, ni amis; et la quitterais-je que je resterais ainsi double, en face de moi-même et juge des miens. Je supporte à peine de vivre avec elle, mais je ne supporte plus de vivre avec personne.[13]
> [It was Marie's folly to think that I would be entirely hers when she had drawn everything out of me, even the hot smell of the stones and the sun. This woman I had loved the best in myself, who wanted to give me all, had become the symbol and source of my destruction. And I was nothing now but a phantom, my own enemy and hers. I had been her betrayer, she my destroyer.

> Yet at the same time I could not live without her, I was without country, relatives or friends; and if I parted from her I should be as two men, one confronting myself and one criticising my people. Though life with her was almost unbearable, life with anyone was unbearable now.]

With this novel dedicated to his wife, who is French too, Albert Memmi was not making a decidedly negative statement about the outcome of mixed marriages. Even though the novel ends with a painful failure, Memmi seemed more involved here in describing the fascination of a young African—a Tunisian Jew—with the pursuit of happiness in marriage according to western norms and the harrowing contrasts between these norms and those prevalent in the traditional North African context. In my opinion, the failure of the union between Marie and the protagonist in Memmi's novel is meant to emphasize the difficulties inherent in such marriages and the painful dilemma of cultural alienation and should not be interpreted as an expression of Memmi's verdict regarding mixed marriages.

For his part, Ousmane Sembène portrayed also a mixed couple, Oumar Faye and Isabelle in his second novel, *O Pays, Mon Beau Peuple* (1957).[14] Oumar Faye who fought in World War II in Europe on the side of the French, returns home to his native Casamance, in southern Sénégal, with his French wife, Isabelle. Unlike Memmi's protagonist in *Agar*, Oumar Faye is a strong-willed young man who has set goals for himself and knows what to do to realize them. He wants to work with his people to end their economic exploitation by the white colonials who have taken advantage of their lack of organization and their inexperience. Oumar is a pragmatist for whom the choice of what should be retained from one's traditions and what should be borrowed from European culture and technology is very clear. He is not torn between two cultures, and his wife, Isabelle, seems well prepared to back him up and help him achieve his goals. Naturally, there is at first a clash between the young couple and Oumar's family, but these initial difficulties are easily overcome, for Oumar and Isabelle agree totally in pursuing an independent course without necessarily cutting themselves off from Oumar's family and the community at large.

Thus the major issue in Sembène's novel does not originate in Oumar's own alienation or in a clash of cultures, but in the bigotry and fear of the white colonials who feel threatened by Oumar, the harbinger of a new order. These colonials will eventually succeed in eliminating him, at least, physically. Oumar dies at the hands of his enemies, but the courage and spirit of resistance that he symbolized in the eyes of his people, remain vividly present in their hearts:

> Ce n'était pas la tombe qui était sa demeure, c'était le coeur de tous les hommes et de toutes les femmes. Il était présent le soir autour de feu

et le jour, dans les rizières; lorsqu'un enfant pleurait, sa mère lui racontait l'histoire de ce jeune homme qui parlait à la terre et, sous l'arbre à palabres, on honorait sa mémoire. Oumar n'était plus, mais son "Beau peuple" le chantait toujours.[15]

[It was not the graveyard that was his home, it was the heart of all the men and all the women. He was present at night around the fire and in the daytime, in the rice-fields; when a child cried, his mother would tell him the story of that young man who spoke to the earth and under the shady ancestral tree, his memory was honored. Oumar was no more, but his "Beautiful people" would sing his praises forever.]

While both Memmi and Sembène treated the couple as a central and exalting entity, Mariama Bâ was the first African writer to stress unequivocally the strong desire of the new generation of Africans to break away from the age-old marriage customs and adopt a decidedly more modern approach based on free mutual choice and the equality of the two partners.

In her two novels, she pointedly showed that the extended family's action could invariably make such relationships fizzle out in bitter failure. And while never indulging in an outright condemnation of the traditions of her society, she denounced the contemporary abuses of these traditions. Thus, while playing her role as a widow during the funeral of her husband Modou, Rama deplores the coarse attitude and the sheer materialism of her sisters-in-law who treat her and her late husband's young second wife equally:

Nos belles-soeurs traitent avec la même égalité trente et cinq ans de vie conjugale. Elles célèbrent, avec la même aisance et les mêmes mots, douze et trois maternités.[16]

[Our sisters-in-law give equal consideration to thirty years and five years of married life. With the same ease and the same words, they celebrate twelve maternities and three.]

In *Une Si Longue Lettre*, two initially successful marriages, between Mawdo and Aïssatou and Rama and Modou, ended in failure precipitated by the excesses of polygamy. But while the former couple's failure is partly due to Mawdo's mother's efforts to correct what she considered as her son's misalliance, his marriage with a member of a lower caste, the latter is simply caused by Modou's infatuation with a much younger woman who is, for her part, irresistibly attracted by the material comforts that Modou can provide for her and for her mother.

There is also the couple composed of Samba Diack and his wife Jacqueline from Ivory Coast. The failure of this couple is due partly to the refusal of Samba's family to accept an African from another African country. Jacqueline is Christian and Samba Diack is Muslim. But the major cause of this marriage's failure is Samba Diack's unfaithful and inconsiderate behavior.

Rama's two older daughters, Daba and Aïssatou, symbolize the future. Daba and her husband do indeed constitute the ideal couple and their attitudes and behavior reassure Rama in her faith in a better and more harmonious future:

> Je sens mûrir la tendresse de ce jeune couple qui est l'image du couple telle que je la rêvais. Ils s'identifient l'un à l'autre, discutent de tout pour trouver un compromis.[17]
>
> [I sense the tenderness growing between this young couple, an ideal couple, just as I have always imagined. They identify with each other, discuss everything so as to find a compromise.]

Likewise, young Aïssatou and her friend Iba seem to follow the same path with confidence and mutual esteem.

In *Un Chant Ecarlate* , the failure of the couple Ousmane/Mireille is due basically to Ousmane's nostalgic infatuation with an early flame of his adolescence, Ouleymatou. But the encouragement of his mother who benefits from Ouleymatou's triumph, is also a factor. In her description of the couple's initial happiness, Mariama Bâ uses a very convincing tone with no place for racial or even cultural considerations:

> Et le bonheur naît de rien, se nourrit de rien. On lui confère un prix énorme. Son acquisition paraît réclamer un prix fort. Et pourtant, le bonheur peut s'épanouir tout simplement dans un amphithéâtre d'Université.[18]
>
> [And happiness emerges from nothing, feeds on very little. One evaluates it at a high price. Its acquisition may appear to command a very substantial cost. And yet happiness can bloom very simply in a University lecture-room.]

Thus, while the cause for the subsequent disagreement between Ousmane and Mireille seems based only in part on racial and cultural differences, and above all, on Ousmane's own new sexual and romantic fantasies, another mixed couple's success in the novel, Pierrette and Lamine seems to indicate that these racial and cultural differences can indeed be overcome generally, but not without some amount of sacrifice and compromise from both sides.

Lamine who is said not to be "haunted by his négritude"[19] and showing "no internal anxiety" explains his position very clearly:

> On ne peut allier deux conceptions de vie différentes. Si l'on est honnête, il y a un choix à faire. Tu veux être heureux sans rien

sacrifier. Tu ne veux rien céder et tu exiges des concessions. La vie
conjugale est plutôt humaine approche et tolérance.[20]
[One cannot bring together two different conceptions of life. If one
is honest, one has to admit a choice. You want to be happy without
sacrifice. You do not want to give up anything and you demand
concessions. Married life implies above all humane approach and
tolerance.]

Albeit Mariama Bâ's second novel ends tragically with the French
heroine losing her senses and killing her child, it should not be read as an
outright condemnation of mixed marriages. For, like Memmi's *Agar*, it
exposes the question of cultural differences inherent in such marriages. But,
above all, it shows through the example of the successful and harmonious
couple, Lamine and Pierrette, that these differences can be overcome with
appropriate adjustments and compromise.

Thus Mariama Bâ upheld courageously throughout her life—in her
literary works as well as in her other involvements—her vision of an
African society where men and women would share equally in the duties as
well as in the joys and the rewards of a harmonious partnership between *one*
husband and *one* wife.

It is appropriate to conclude here with the words of another Muslim
woman who believes like Mariama Bâ that our societies are changing and
that these changes do involve both men and women in the pursuit of a
happier and a more harmonious life on this earth.

Je crois en l'être humain comme un être capable de faire et refaire son
histoire, et je crois donc qu'il est possible aux hommes et aux femmes
vivant dans les sociétés musulmanes de changer le cours de l'histoire,
de vivre mieux, d'aimer mieux. Les femmes ne sont pas condamnées
à vivre mutilées.[21]
[I believe in human beings as capable of making and remaking their
history, and I therefore, believe that it is possible for men and women
living in Muslim societies to change the course of history, *to live
better, to love better.* Women must not be condemned to live as
mutilated beings.]

NOTES

1. Editions le Sycomore, Paris, 1982, 205pp.
2. Op. cit., pp. 11-12. My translation.

3. Marima Bâ, *Une Si Longue Lettre.* Nouvelles Editions Africaines. Dakar, 1979. 131 pp. [English Trans. by Modupe Bode-Thomas, *So Long A Letter.* Heinemann.]

4. While the criteria of modesty and reserve for feminine behavior as described in the orthodox Islamic jurisprudential discourse examined by Fatna Ait Sabbah can be easily observed in most traditional African Muslim societies, I would contend that the graphic details of the Islamic erotic discourse that she quotes in her book would shock many ordinary—devout and not so devout—West African Muslims!

5. Mariama Bâ, *Un Chant Ecarlate.* Nouvelles Editions Africaines. Dakar, 1981, 251pp.

6. Op. cit., p. 131 [English trans. p. 89.]

7. Op. cit., p. 82. [English trans. p. 55-56.]

8. Op. cit., p. 85. [English trans. p. 58.]

9. Op. cit., p. 130. [English trans. p. 89.]

10. Albert Memmi, *Agar.* Corrêa, Paris, 1955, p. 119. [English trans. by Brian Rhys, *The Strangers.* Elek Books, London, 1958, p. 78]

11. Op. cit. p. 119. [English trans. p. 78.]

12. English trans., op. cit., title page.

13. Op. cit., pp. 224-225.

14. Ousmane Sembène, *O Pays, Mon Beau Peuple.* Amiot-Dumont, 243pp., 1957.

15. Op. cit., pp. 233-234. My translation.

16. Mariama Bâ, *Une Si Longue Lettre*, p. 11. [English trans. p. 4.]

17. Op. cit., p. 107. [English trans. pp. 73-74.]

18. Mariama Bâ, *Un Chant Ecarlate*, p. 28. My translation.

19. Op. cit., p. 150.

20. Op. cit., p. 151.

21. Fatna Ait Sabbah, *La Femme Dans L'inconscient Musulman.* Editions Le Sycomore, Paris, 1982, p. 15. My translation and my empahsis.

A Bibliography of
Criticism and Related Works

Carole Boyce Davies

Accad, Evelyne. "Interrelationship Between Arab Nationalism and Feminist Consciousness in the North African Novels Written by Women." *Ba Shiru* 8.2 (1977): 3-12.

_____. *Veil of Shame. The Role of Women in the Contemporary Fiction of North African and the Arab World.* Sherbrooke, Quebec. Naaman, 1978.

_____. "The Theme of Sexual Oppression in the North African Novel." Lois Beck and Nikki Keddie eds. *Women in the Muslim World.* Cambridge, Mass: Harvard University Press, 1978. 617-628.

Adam, Jeanne. "Le monde féminin de 'Grande Kabylie'." *Présence Francophone. Revue Littéraire* 22 (Spring, 1981): 5-19.

Adan, Amina H. "Women and Words." *Ufahamu* 10.3 (Spring, 1981): 115-142.

Aidoo, Ama Ata. "Unwelcome Pals and Decorative Slaves. The Woman as a Writer in Modern Africa." *AFA. Journal of Creative Writing* (Imo State, Nigeria) 1 November, 1982): 34-43.

_____. "To Be A Woman". *Sisterhood is Global.* Ed. Robin Morgan. New York: Doubleday, 1984: 258-265.

Akello, Grace. *Self Twice Removed.* London: Change, 1982. Rev. by Esther Ogunmodede, "Struggling Out of Traditional Strait-Jackets." *New African* (January, 1983): 48-49.

Akoua, Solange and Ibrahime Fofana. "La femme africaine dans 'Les Bouts de Bois de Dieu'." *Eburnea* 106 (1976): 17-19.

Amaizo, E. "La femme et les changements sociaux et culturels dans l'oeuvre romanesque de Chinua Achebe." *Annales de L'Université du Bénin, Togo.* Lettres 2.2 (1975): 101-108.

Asanga, Siga. "Firebrands: Women in the Drama of J. P. Clark." Unpublished African Literature Association (ALA) paper, 1984.

283

Babatunde, E. D. "Ketu Myths and the Status of Women. A Structural Interpretation of Some Yoruba Myths of Origin." *Journal of the Anthropological Society of Oxford* 14.3 (1983): 301-306.

Bazin, Nancy Topping. "Feminist Perspectives in African Fiction: Bessie Head and Buchi Emecheta." Unpublished ALA paper, 1984.

Beard, Linda Susan. "Bessie Head's *A Question of Power*: The Journey Through Disintegration to Wholeness." *Colby Library Journal* 15.4 (1979): 267-274.

Bede, J. "La donna e la terra natale in *'La Terra Promessa'* di Grace Ogot." *La Letteratura Della Nuova Africa*. Eds. Lina Angioletti and Armanda Guiducci. Rome: Lerici, 1979: 117-177.

Bell, Roseann P. "The Absence of the African Woman Writer." *CLA Journal* 21.4 (1978): 491-498.

Berrian, Brenda F. "African Women As Seen in the Works of Flora Nwapa and Ama Ata Aidoo." *CLA Journal* 25.3 (1982): 331-39.

Berrian, Brenda and Mildred Mortimer. *Critical Perspectives on African Women Writers*. Washington, D.C.: Three Continents Press, (forthcoming).

Brown, Lloyd. "Ama Ata Aidoo: The Art of the Short Story and Sexual Roles in Africa. *World Literature Written in English*. 13 (1974): 172-183.

_____. "The African Woman as Writer". *Canadian Journal of African Studies*. 9.3 (1975): 493-501.

_____. "Creating New Worlds in Southern Africa: Bessie Head and the Question of Power." *Umoja* 3.1 (1979): 43-53.

_____. *Women Writers in Black Africa*. Connecticut: Greenwood Press, 1981.

Bruner, Charlotte. "Been To or Has-Been: A Dilemma For Today's African Woman." *Ba Shiru* 8.2 (1977): 23-31.

_____. "Child Africa as Depicted by Bessie Head and Ama Ata Aidoo." *Studies in the Humanities* 7.2 (1979): 5-11.

_____. "Bessie Head: Restless in a Distant Land." *When the Drumbeat Changes*. Ed. Carolyn Parker and Stephen Arnold. Washington D.C.: Three Continents Press, 1980: 261-278.

_____. ed. *Unwinding Threads. Writing by Women in African* London: Heinemann, 1983.

_____. "A Decade for Women Writers." *African Literature Studies: The Present State L'état Présent*. Ed. by Stephen Arnold. Washington, D.C.: Three Continents Press, 1985: 217-227.

_____. "First Person Feminine: A Sequel to 'Talking Sticks'. Unpublished ALA paper, 1982.

Bryce, Jane. "Profile. Ngugi: 'My Novel of Blood Sweat and Tears.'" *New African* (August, 1982): 36.

Burness, Donald. "Womanhood in the Short Stories of Ama Ata Aidoo." *Studies in Black Literature*. 4.2 (1973): 21-24.

Case, F. I. Rev. *So Long A Letter* by Mariama Bâ. *World Literature Written in English*. 21.3 (1982): 538-539.

Cham, Mbye. "The Female Condition in Africa: A Literary Exploration by Mariama Bâ."*Current Bibliography on African Affairs*. 17:1 (1984/5): 29-52.

Chapman, Karen. "'Introduction' to Ama Ata Aidoo's 'Dilemma of a Ghost'." Rpt. in *Sturdy Black Bridges*. Ed. Bell, Parker and Guy-Sheftall. New York: Anchor Press/Doubleday, 1979: 25-38.

Chemain-Degrange, Arlette. "L'image de la femme noire dans la littérature négro africaine d'expression francaise." Diss. University of Grenoble, France, 1973.

_____. *Emancipation Féminine et Roman Africain*. Dakar: Les Nouvelles Editions Africaines, 1980.

Christian, Barbara. *Black Women Novelists. The Development of a Tradition*. Westport, Conn.: Greenwood Press, 1980.

_____. *Black Feminist Criticism. Perspectives on Black Women Writers*. New York: Pergamon Press, 1985.

Cochrane, Judith. "Women as the Guardians of the Tribe in Ngugi's Novels." *ACLALS-Bulletin* 4.5 (1977): 1-11.

_____. 'Some Images of Women in East African Fiction." *ACLALS-Bulletin* 5.1 (1978): 32-41.

_____. "The Theme of Sacrifice in the Novels of Nuruddin Farah." *World Literature Written in English*. 18.1 (April, 1979): 69-77.

Condé, Maryse. "Three Female Writers in Modern Africa: Flora Nwapa, Ama Ata Aidoo, Grace Ogot." *Presence Africaine* 82 (1972): 136-139.

_____. *Paroles des Femmes*. Paris, L'Harmattan, 1979.

Cosentino, Donald J. "The Onitsha Heroine." *Ba Shiru*. 7 (Fall, 1970/Spring, 1971: 52-62.

_____. "Jagua Nana: Culture Heroine." *Ba Shiru* 8 (1971): 11-17.

_____. Rev. of *The Royal Antelope and Spider* by Marion Kilson. *Research in African Literatures* 10 (1979): 296-307.

Cutrufelli, Maria Rosa. *Women of Africa. Roots of Oppression*. Trans. Nicolas Romano. London: Zed Press, 1983.

d'Almeida, Irene Assiba. "Prostitution in African Fiction and Beyond." Unpublished Monograph, Emory University, Institute of Liberal Arts, 1984.

Dathorne, O.R. *African Literature in the Twentieth Century*. Minneapolis: University of Minnesota Press, 1974.

Davies, Carole Boyce. "Maidens, Mistresses and Matrons: Feminine Images in Selected Soyinka Works." *Interdisciplinary Dimensions of African Literature*. Ed. Anyidoho, Porter, Racine, Spleth. Washington, D.C.: Three Continents Press, 1984: 89-99.

_____. "Completing the Story: Some Unexamined South African Women Writers". Unpublished manuscript of paper presented at the 1985 ALA Conference, Northwestern University, Illinois, March, 1985.

_____. "Wrapping Oneself In Mother's Akatado Cloths: Mother-Daughter Relationships in the Works of African Women Writers." Unpublished manuscript, 1985.

_____ and Elaine Savory Fido. "African Women Writers". *A History of African Literature in the Twentieth Century*. Ed. Oyekan Owomoyela. (University of Nebraska Press, forthcoming).

Emecheta, Buchi. "'It's Me Who's Changed.' An Interview with Buchi Emecheta." *Connexions* 4 (Spring, 1982): 4.

Emeka, Abanime. "La beauté feminine chez les romanciers négro-africains. Le probleme de l'idéal blanc." *Rev. de Lit. et D'Esthétique Négro-Africaines* 3 (1981): 7-14.

Emenyonu, Ernest N. "Who Does Flora Nwapa Write For?" *African Literature Today* 7. Ed. Eldred Durosimi Jones. London, Heinemann, 1975: 28-33.

Evans, Jennifer. "Mother Africa and the Heroic Whore: Female Images in *Petals of Blood*." *Contemporary African Literature*. Ed. Wylie, Julien and Linnemann. Washington D.C.: Three Continents Press, 1983: 57-65.

Fido, Elaine Savory. "'A Guest of Honour': A Feminine View of Masculinity." *World Literature Written in English* 17:1 (1978): 30-37.

————. "The Feminine Principle in the fiction of Elechi Amadi." Unpublished manuscript, University of the West Indies, Cave Hill, 1983.

————. "The Changing Role of Women in Relation to African Literary Studies." Unpublished ALA paper, 1985.

———— and Carole Boyce Davies. "African Women Writers." in *A History of African Literature in the Twentieth Century*. Ed. Oyekan Owomoyela (University of Nebraska Press, forthcoming).

Finnegan, Ruth. *Oral Literature in Africa*. Oxford: Clarendon Press, 1970.

Frank, Katherine. "The Death of A Slave Girl: African Womanhood in the Novels of Buchi Emecheta." *World Literature Written in English* 21:3 (1982): 476-496.

————. "Feminist Criticism and the African Novel." *African Literature Today*, 14. Ed. Eldred Durosimi Jones. London: Heinemann, 1984. 34-48.

Gachukia, Eddah. "The Role of Women in Ngugi's Novels." *Busara* 3.4 (1971): 30-33.

Gérard, Albert and Laurent, Jeanine. "Sembène's Progeny: A New Trend in the Senegalese Novel." *Studies in Twentieth Century Literature*. 4.2 (1980): 133-145.

Gunner, Elizabeth. "Songs of Innocence and Experience: Women as Composers and performers of *Izibongo*, Zulu Praise Poetry." *Research in African Literatures* 10:2 (1979): 239-267.

Hall, Susan. "African Women on Film." *Africa Report* 22.1 (January-February): 15-17.

Hammonds, Evelyn. "Toward a Black Feminist Aesthetic." *Sojourner*. October, 1980: 7.

Harrow, Kenneth. "Not Such a Long Way, Baby: The Situation of the Woman Today in the Maghreb and its Thematic Representation in Literature." *Current Bibliography of African Affairs*. 9.3 (1976-77): 228-249.

Herzberger-Fofana, Pierette. "Female Literature in Francophone Africa." Unpublished ALA paper, 1985.

Hill-Lubin, Mildred. "Ama Ata Aidoo: The Story Teller as professional Performer and Psychologist." Unpublished ALA paper, 1985.

Hubbard, Louise J. "Women in Mongo Beti's '*Perpétue*'." *Annales de L'Univ. de Bénin*, Togo. Serié Lettres 4.1 (1977): 63-73.

Ifeka, Caroline. "The World of Women. '*Efuru*'." *Nigeria Magazine* 89. June, 1966: 131.

Ifeka-Moller, Caroline. "Female Militancy and Colonial Revolt. The Women's War of 1929, Eastern Nigeria." *Perceiving Women*. Ed. Shirley Ardener. New York: John Wiley and Sons, 1975: 127-156.

Ikonne, Chidi. "The Society and Woman's Quest for Selfhood in Flora Nwapa's Early Novels." *Kunapipi* 6.1 (1984): 68-72.

_____. "Women in Igbo Folktales." Unpublished ALA paper, 1982.

Kane, Mohamadou. "Le féminisme dans le roman africain de langue francaise." *Univ. de Dakar Annales de Faculté des Lettres et Sciences*. 10 (1980): 14-20.

Kapumpa, Mumba. "Theatre: A New Challenge to Our Women." *Africa Woman* 23 (1979): 52-53.

Kilson, Marion. "Women and African Literature." *Journal of African Studies* 4:2 (1970): 161-166.

_____. *Royal Antelope and Spider: West African Mende Tales*. Cambridge, Mass: The Press of Langdon Associates, 1976.

Knipp, Thomas R. "Images of Women in West African Poetry." Unpublished ALA Paper, 1984.

Kunene, Daniel P. "La Guma's Women." Unpublished ALA paper, 1985.

Lee, Sonia. "L'image de la femme dans le roman francophone de l'Afrique occidentale." Diss. University of Massachusetts, 1974. Ann Arbor: UMI, 1974. 74-15028.

_____. "The Image of the Woman in the African Folktale from the Sub-saharan Francophone Area." *Yale French Studies*. 53 (1976): 19-28.

_____. "The Awakening of Self in the Heroines of Ousmane Sembene." Bell, Parker and Guy-Sheftall: 52-60.

_____. "Le theme du bonheur chez les romancieres africaines." Unpublished ALA paper, 1982.

Lindfors, Bernth. "Nigerian Chapbook Heroines." *Journal of Popular Culture.* Winter, 1968: 441-450.

Lippert, Anne. "Women Characters and African Literature." *Afriscope* 3:10 (1973): 45, 49.

_____. "The Changing Role of Women As Viewed in the Literature of English Speaking West Africa." Diss. Indiana University, 1972. Ann Arbor: UMI, 1972. 72-30425.

Little, Kenneth. "Mothers and Other Characters," *West Africa* 24 (September, 1979): 1759.

_____. *The Sociology of Urban Women's Image in African Literature*. London: Macmillan, 1980.

Lyonga, Pauline Nalova. "*Uhamiri*. A Feminist Approach to African Literature." Diss. University of Michigan, 1985.

Mack, Beverly B. "*Wakokin Mata*: Hausa Women's Oral Poetry." Diss. University of Wisconsin, 1981. Ann Arbor: UMI 82-05542.

_____. ' "*Waka Daya Ba Ta Kare Nika*'—One Song Will Not Finish the Grinding: Hausa Women's Oral Literature." *Contemporary African Literature*. Ed. Wylie, Julien and Linnemann. Washington, D.C.: Three Continents Press, 1983: 15-46.

_____. ed. *Alkalami: A Hannun Mata. A Pen in the Hand of Women*. Zaria: The Northern Nigeria Publishing Company, 1983.

_____. "Hausa Women Poets: Ghostwriters. Interviews with Hauwa Gwaram and Binta Katsina." *Ba Shiru* (forthcoming).

Mbughuni, L. A. Old and New Drama From East Africa. A Review of four Contemporary Dramatists: Rebecca Njau, Ebrahim Hussein, Peninah Muhando and Ngugi." *African Literature Today* 8 (London, Heinemann, 1976): 85-98.

McCaffrey, Kathleen M. "Images of Women in the Literature of Selected Developing Countries. Washington D.C.: Office of Women in Development, Agency for International Development, 1977.

_____. "Image of the Mother in the Stories of Ama Ata Aidoo." *Africa Woman* 23 (1979): 40-1.

_____. "Images of Women in West African Literature and Film: A Struggle Against Dual Colonization." *International Journal of Women's Studies* 3 (1980): 76-88.

McDowell, Deborah. "New Directions for Black Feminist Criticism." *Black American Literature Forum.* 14:4 (Winter, 1980): 153-159.

Melamu, M. "Prophets and Women in Nigerian Tragedy." *Pula* 1: 43-88.

Mikhail, Mona. "Senghor, Women and the African Tradition." *Rackham Literary Studies* (Ann Arbor, MI) 1 (1971): 63-70.

_____. *Images of Arab Women.* Washington D.C.: Three Continents Press, 1981.

Mojola, Ibiyema. "La femme dans l'oeuvre de Chinua Achebe." *Peuples Noirs, Peuples Africains* 16: 48-58.

Mokwenye, Cyril. "La polygamie et la revolte de la femme africaine moderne: Une Lecture d'*une si longue lettre* de Mariama Ba." *Peuples Noirs. Peuples Africains* 31: (Janvier-Fevrier, 1983): 91.

Moore, Gerald H. "Nomads and Feminists: The Novels of Nuruddin Farah." *The International Fiction Review.* 11.1 (Winter, 1984): 3-12.

Mortimer, Mildred. "The Feminine Image in the Algerian Novel of French Expression." *Ba Shiru* 8.2 (1977): 51-62.

_____. "The Evolution of Assia Djebar's Feminist Conscience." *Contemporary African Literature.* Ed. Wylie, Julien and Linnemann. Washington, D.C.: Three Continents Press, 1983: 7-14.

Mugo, Micere. Interview. "Dr. Micere Mugo, Kenya's Outspoken Intellectual and Academic Critic Talks to Nancy Owano." *Africa Woman* 6 (September-/October, 1976).

Mutiso, G-C. M. "Women in African Literature. *East Africa Journal* 3.3 (1971): 4-14. Rpt. in his *Socio-Political Thought in African Literature.* (London: Macmillan, 1974): 51-72.

Mvula, Enoch T. "Tumbuka Pounding Songs in the Management of Familial Conflicts." *Crossrhythms.* Ed. Daniel Avorgbedor and Kwesi Yankah. Indiana University, African Folklore Publications, 1983: 93-113.

Nandakumar, Prema. "An Image of African Womanhood: A Study of Flora Nwapa's *Efuru.*" *Africa Quarterly.* 2 (1967): 136-146.

_____. "Another Image of African Womanhood: An Appreciation of Elechi Amadi's '*The Concubine*'." *Africa Quarterly.* 13 (1973): 38-44.

Nasser, Merun. "Achebe and His Women: A Social Science Perspective." *Africa Today.* 27.3: 21-28.

Ngcobo, Lauretta. "Four Women Writers in Africa Today." *South Africa Outlook.* 114:1355 (May, 1984): 64-69.

Nkosi, Lewis. "Women in Literature." *Africa Woman* 6 (1976): 36-7.

Nwapa, Flora. "Meeting Flora Nwapa" An Interview with Allison Perry. *West Africa* 3487 (1984): 1262.

Ojo-Ade, Femi. "Female Writers, Male Critics." *African Literature Today* 13 (London: Heinemann, 1983): 158-179.

_____. "Bessie Head's Alienated Heroine: Victim or Villain?" *Ba Shiru* 8:2 (1977): 13-21.

_____. "Still a Victim? Mariama Ba's *Une si Longue Lettre*." *African Literature Today* 12. (London: Heinemann, 1982: 71-87.

Ogot, Grace. "Interview with Grace Ogot." With Bernth Lindfors. *World Written Literature in English* 18.1 (April, 1979): 57-68.

Ogundipe-Leslie, Omolara. "The Female Writer and Her Commitment." *Guardian* (Lagos) December 21, 1983: 11.

_____. "African Women, Culture and Another Development." *The Journal of African Marxists*. 5 (February, 1984): 77-92.

_____. "Not Spinning on the Axis of Maleness." *Sisterhood is Global*. Ed. Robin Morgan. New York: Anchor Press/Doubleday. 1984: 498-504.

Ogunyemi, Chikwenye Okonjo. "Buchi Emecheta: The Shaping of a Self." *Komparatistische Hefe*, Heft 8 (1983): 65-78.

Okonkwo, Juliet I. "Nuruddin Farah and the Changing Roles of Women." *World Literature Today* 58:2 (1984): 215-221.

_____. "Adam and Eve: Igbo Marriage in the Nigerian Novel." *The Conch* 3.2 (September, 1971): 137-151.

_____. "The Talented Woman in African Literature." *Africa Quarterly* 15 (1975): 35-47.

Okonkwo, Rina. "Adelaide Casely-Hayford; Cultural Nationalist and Feminist." *Journal of History and Society of Sierra Leone* 2.2 (1978): 10, 21.

Ola, V. U. "Aspects of Development in Chinua Achebe's Treatment of Women." *Journal of English* (Sena'a University) 7: 92-119.

_____. "The Feminine Principle and the Search for Wholeness in *The Healers*." Unpublished ALA paper, 1984.

Ortova, Jamila. "Les Femmes dans l'oeuvre littéraire d'Ousmane Sembène." *Présence Africaine* 71 (1959): 69-77.

Oyesakin, Adefioye. "The Image of Women in Ifa Literary Corpus." *Nigeria Magazine* 141 (1982): 16-23.

Palmer, Eustace. "Elechi Amadi and Flora Nwapa." *African Literature Today*. 1-4 (1968-1970): 56-58.

_____. "The Feminine Point of View: Buchi Emecheta's *The Joys of Motherhood*." *African Literature Today* 13. London: Heinemann, 1983. 38-55.

Parker, Carolyn. "How to Be/Treat A Lady in Swahili Culture: An Expression of Ideal." *Ba Shiru* 8.2 (1977): 37-45.

Pearse, Adetukunbo. "Symbolic Characterization Of Women in the Plays and Prose of Wole Soyinka." *Ba Shiru* 9.1 & 2 (1978): 39-46.

Pointer, Fritz. "Laye, Lamming and Wright: Mother and Son." *African Literature Today*, 14 (London: Heinemann, 1984): 19-33.

Porter, Abioseh. "Ideology and the Image of Women: Kenyan Women in Njau and Ngugi." *Ariel: A Review of International English Literature* 12.3 (July, 1981): 61-74.

Purisch, C. "Soyinka's Superwoman." Unpublished paper, University of Ibadan First Annual African Literature Conference, July 1976.

Reyes, Angelita. "'Dear God. . .': Impact of Confession in *Une si longue lettre* and *Juletane*." Unpublished ALA paper, 1985.

Rushing, Andrea Benton. "Images of Black Women in Modern African Poetry: An Overview." Bell, Parker, Guy-Sheftall: 18-24.

_____. "Comparative Study of the Idea of Mother in Contemporary African and African-American Poetry." *Colby Library Quarterly* 15.4 (1979): 275-288.

_____. "Family Resemblances: A Comparative Study of Women Protagonists in Contemporary African-American and Anglophone African Novels." Diss. University of Massachusetts, 1983. Ann Arbor: UMI, 1983. DEP 8310329.

Sacks, Karen. "Women and Class Struggle in Sembene's '*God's Bits of Wood*'." *Signs* 4: 363-70.

Scheub, Harold. "Two African Women". *Revue des Langues Vivantes* 37.5 (1971): 545-558, 664-681.

_____. *The Xhosa Ntsomi*. Oxford: Clarendon Press, 1979.

Schipper, Mineke. *Theatre and Society in Africa*. Johannesburg: Ravan Press, 1982.

_____. "'Who Am I?' Fact and Fiction in African First Person Narrative." *Research in African Literatures*. 16.1 (Spring, 1985): 53-79.

_____. "Women and Literature in Africa." *Unheard Words*. Ed. by Mineke Schipper. London: Allison & Busby, 1984: 22-58.

Schmidt, Nancy. "African Women Writers of Literature for Children." *World Literature Written in English* 17.1 (1978): 113-15.

Senkoro, F. E. M. K. *The Prostitute in African Literature*. Tanzania: Dar Es Salaam University Press, 1982.

Shoga, Yinka. "Women Writers and African Literature." *Afriscope* 3.10 (1973): 44-5.

Smith, Barbara. "Toward a Black Feminist Criticism." Trumansburg, New York: The Crossing Press, 1982.

Smith, Robert P. Jr. "Mongo Beti: The Novelist Looks at Independence and the Status of the African Woman." *CLA Journal* 19 (March, 1976): 301-311.

Smyley, Karen. "The African Woman: Interpretations of Senegalese Novelists Aboulaye Sadji and Ousmane Sembène." Diss. City University of New York, 1977. Ann Arbor, UMI, 1977.

_____. "Ousmane Sembène: Portraitist of the African Woman in the Novel." *The New England Journal of Black Studies*. (1981): 23-29.

Smyley-Wallace, Karen. "'*Les Bouts de Bois de Dieu*' and '*Xala*': A Comparative Analysis of Female Roles in Sembène's Novels." *Current Bibliography on African Affairs*. 17.2 (1984-5): 129-136.

Sonfo, Alphamoye. "La mère dans la littérature romanesque de la Guinée, du Mali et du Senegal." *West African Journal of Modern Languages*. 2 (1976): 95-107.

Staudt, Kathleen. "The Characterization of Women in Soyinka and Armah." *Ba Shiru* 8:2 (1977): 63-69.

_____. "The Feminine Image in the Algerian Novel of French Expression." *Ba Shiru* 8.2 (1977): 51-62.

Steady, Filomina Chioma. Ed. *The Black Woman Cross-Culturally*. Cambridge, Mass.: Schenkman Publishing Company, Inc., 1981: 1-41.

Stegman, Beatrice. "The Divorce Dilemma: The New Woman in Contemporary African Novels." *Critique* 15 (1974): 81-90.

Sweetman, David. *Women Leaders in Modern Africa*. London: Heinemann, 1984.

Taiwo, Oladele. *Female Novelists in Modern Africa*. London: Macmillan/New York: St. Martins, 1984.

Tate, Claudia. *Black Women Writers at Work*. New York: Continuum, 1983.

Thiam, Awa. *La Parole aux Négresses*. Paris: Denöel/Gonthier, 1978.

Thomas, Peter. "The Watermaid and the Dancer: Figures of the Nigerian Muse." *Literature East and West*. 12:1 (March, 1968): 85-93.

Umeh, Marie, Linton. "The African Heroine." Bell, Parker and Guy-Sheftall: 39-51.

_____. "African Women in Transition in the Novels of Buchi Emecheta." *Presence Africaine* 116 (1980): 190-201.

_____. "Interview with Buchi Emecheta." *Ba Shiru* 12:2 (1981).

_____. "The Joys of Motherhood: Myth or Reality." *Colby Library Quarterly* 18.1 (March, 1982): 39-46.

Wachtel, Eleanor. "The Mother and the Whore: Image and Stereotype of African Women." *UMOJA* 1.2 (1977): 31-48.

Walker, Alice. "A Writer Because of, Not In Spite of, Her Children." *In Search of Our Mothers' Gardens. Womanist Prose*. San Diego: Harcourt Brace, Jovanovich, 1983: 66-70.

_____. "Womanist" - (A Definition), Frontispiece to *In Search of Our Mothers' Gardens*. San Diego, Harcourt Brace, Jovanovich, 1983: xi-xii.

Washington, Mary Helen. Introduction to *Black Eyed Susans*. New York: Anchor Press/Doubleday, 1975.

Willentz, Gay. "The Playwright as Activist: Community Development in Efua Sutherland's '*Foriwa*'." Unpublished paper. University of Texas, Austin, 1984.

_____. "The Individual Voice in the Communal Chorus: The Search for Identity in Flora Nwapa's '*Efuru*'." Unpublished ALA paper, 1985.

Zimra, Clarisse. "Circular Structures of Linguistic Alienation in Assia Djebar's Early Novels." *Research in African Literatures*." (Summer, 1980): 206-223.

_____. "Women in Contemporary Arabic Fiction." *Bulletin of Southern Association of Africanists*. 7.2-3: 30-34.

_____. "Négritude in the Feminine Mode: the Case of Martinique and Guadeloupe." *The Journal of Ethnic Studies*. 12.1 (Spring, 1984): 53-77.

An Annotated Listing of Bibliographies

Berrian, Brenda. *Bibliography of African Women Writers and Journalists*. Washington, D.C.: Three Continents Press, 1985. The most comprehensive bibliography on African women writers to date. An important resource organized according to genres with extensive appendices for easy cross-reference. Recognized by the compiler as already in need of updating because of additional entries generated by its publication. Builds on her "Bibliographies of Nine Female African Writers. *Research in African Literatures* 12.2 (Summer, 1981): 215-238.

Bell, Roseann P., Bettye J. Parker and Beverly Guy-Sheftall, and Parker. *Sturdy Black Bridges. Visions of Black Women in Literature.* New York: Anchor Press/Doubleday, 1979: 379-417. This important first anthology of black women in literature organized into critical material, interviews and creative writing includes selected bibliographies of African, African-American and Caribbean women.

House, Amelia. "Black South African Women Writers in English: A Preliminary Checklist." Evanston, Illinois: Program on Women, Northwestern University, 1980. Provides the first listing of South African women writers, includes some biographical descriptions of each writer and an interview with Fatima Dike, South African playwright and a discussion on Women Writers by South African writer, Boitumelo.

Hull, D. M. "African Women In Development: An Untapped Resource." A Selected Bibliography. (Moorland-Spingarn Research Center, Howard University, 1983.) Currently being updated by the compiler, the librarian responsible for this field at Moorland. It contains about 200 entries on women in the social and economic life in Africa. Dr. Hull is also editor-in-chief of *A Current Bibliography on African Affairs* which has subject headings for literature and for women.

Hull, Gloria T., Patricia Bell Scott and Barbara Smith, eds. All the Women are White, All the Blacks are Men. *But Some of Us Are Brave.* Black Women's Studies. New York: The Feminist Press, 1982. This important collection contains a section on Bibliographies and Bibliographic Essays which contains some occasional listings on African women. Martha Brown's "A Listing of Non-Print Materials on Black Women" (pages 307-327) has a section on African women in films.

Morgan, Robin, Ed. *Sisterhood is Global. The International Women's Movement Anthology.* New York: Anchor Press/Doubleday, 1984. Contains a selected bibliography on women organized according to countries along with a general bibliography. Entries are taken from a variety of sources including newsletters, journals, magazines and books, government publications. Material is largely socio-political.

Rushing, Andrea Benton. "An Annotated Bibliography of Black Women in Black Literature." *CLA Journal* 25:2 (1981): 234-262. Contains entries on women in African, Caribbean, Latin-American and African-American literature. A nice selection of works with informative notes. A revised and updated version of the earlier "An Annotated Bibliography of Images of Black Women in Black Literature." *CLA Journal* 21:3 (1977-78): 435-442.

Scheub, Harold. *African Oral Narratives, Proverbs, Riddles, Poetry and Song.* Boston: G. K. Hall, 1977. An extensive listing of various forms of African oral literature. An important tool for anyone doing research in this field.

Steady, Filomina. "Select Bibliography on the Black Women Cross-Culturally." *The Black Woman Crossculturally.* Ed. Filomina Chioma Steady. Cambridge,

Mass. Schenckman Publishing Co., Inc., 1981: 615-635. Entries are organized according to Africa, the United States, the Caribbean and South America following the organizational pattern of the collection along with an additional section "Some Useful Bibliographies." The anthology itself contains sociological, historical, anthropological, economic, political and literary approaches to the study of the black woman internationally. Steady's introductory essay also contains a separate bibliography.

Zell, Hans, Carol Bundy and Virginia Coulon. *A New Readers Guide to African Literature*. New York: Africana Publishing Corp./London: Heinemann, 1983. An updated and more comprehensive version of the 1971 Zell and Silver *Readers Guide* by the same publisher.

Editors

Carole Boyce Davies is Assistant Professor of English and African and Afro-American Studies at the State University of New York at Binghamton and Director of Undergraduate Studies there. She received degrees from the University of Maryland, Howard University and the University of Ibadan, Nigeria. Her research and teaching interests include oral and written literature of the African peoples, Black women writers, feminist aesthetics and the criticism of African literatures, and children's literature. She has authored several essays on women in African literatures including a chapter "African Women Writers" for an authoritative volume on African literature in the Twentieth Century. She is currently working on a book on Caribbean women writers.

Anne Adams Graves is Assistant Professor in the Africana Studies and Research Center at Cornell University. She pursued her studies in European and Caribbean languages at Fisk University; the Free University of Berlin, West Germany; the University of Michigan; and Kent State University. Previous teaching positions have been at Morehouse College, Kent State University, and Université Marien Ngouabi in Brazzaville, Congo. She is co-editor, with E.W. Crosby and L. Davis, of a two-volume Black Studies introductory anthology, *The African Experience in Community Development* (1981) and has prepared a translation from French of a collection of short stories, *Tribaliques*, by Congolese author Henri Lopès, scheduled for publication by Editions Naaman. In addition, she has presented several papers from her research and teaching areas in African women's literature, Congolese national literature, and Black literature among German audiences.

Contributors

Naana Banyiwa-Horne is completing a Ph.D. in African literature at the University of Wisconsin, Madison. Born in Ghana, her Masters Thesis was on African women writers.

Brenda F. Berrian is Associate Professor of Black Studies (Humanities) at the University of Pittsburgh. She received her B.S. and M.A. from Hampton Institute and the doctorate from the University of Paris III. Prof. Berrian is the author of two monographs, and has published book reviews, bibliographies and articles in African literature. Her *Bibliography of African Women Writers and Journalists* (Washington, D.C.: Three Continents Press, 1985) is an important resource on the subject. She is co-editor of the forthcoming *Critical Perspectives on African Women Writers*.

Abena P. A. Busia is Assistant Professor of English at Rutgers, The State University, New Brunswick, N.J. She was born in Accra, Ghana and has worked as a research associate and visiting lecturer at Yale University. She is also a poet whose poems have been included in *Summer Fires: New Poetry From Africa* (Heinemann, 1983). She will publish *Africa in Anglo-American Fiction 1880-1980; An Annotated Bibliography* (New York, Garland Publications, 1985) and an essay "Manipulating Africa: The Bucaneer as 'Liberator' in Contemporary Fiction" in *The Black Presence in British Fiction* ed. by David Dabydeen (Manchester University Press, 1985).

Irene Assiba d'Almeida recently completed a Ph.D. on African critical theory in the Department of Comparative Literature, Emory University in Atlanta. A native of the Republic of Benin, she received an M.A. degree in English from the University of Ibadan, Nigeria and has taught at the University of Calabar, Nigeria and at the University of Kentucky, Lexington. She is the author of several articles in African literature and has a monograph on the prostitution theme in African literature. She maintains an on-going interest in the problems of translation and has translated Achebe's *Arrow of God* into French (Presence Africaine, 1978).

Elaine Savory Fido has taught African literature since 1975 at the University of the West Indies, Cave Hill, Barbados. She taught at the University of Ghana 1970-72 and was visiting lecturer at the University of Ibadan from 1982-83. Interested in women's writing in the continent, in the African-Caribbean and in African-America, she is an avid researcher in these areas. She has published articles on various aspects of African and Caribbean literature, particularly drama and women's writing or writing about women by men. She is authoring a novel and a book on women in the theatre in the Caribbean and Africa.

Mildred Hill-Lubin is Associate Professor, Department of English with a joint appointment in the Center for African Studies, at the University of Florida, Gainesville, where she has served as Dean of Graduate Studies. One of the editors of *Toward Defining the African Aesthetic* (Three Continents Press, 1982), she has also published articles on parallels in African and African-American literature, the Ghanaian author, Ama Ata Aidoo and the image of the Black grandmother, in *Southern Folklore Quarterly, CLA Journal, Presence Africaine, Okike,* and *Sojourner* and in Readings for the Florida Endowment for the Humanities. She has maintained a consistent stream of writing and research on women in African literature and on the oral tradition as it interacts with the written tradition and is readying a book-length manuscript on the Black grandmother for publication.

Tobe Levin is a lecturer with the European Division of the University of Maryland. She is active in the women's movement in Germany, contributing occasional articles and reports on third world women's struggles and Afro-American women's literature to the West German feminist magazine EMMA. She is a contributing editor to *Women's Studies Quarterly*. She is a member of feminist organizations Amnesty for Women and Terre des Femmes. Her degrees were received from Ithaca College, New York University in Paris, Cornell University with a dissertation on Feminist Ideology and Aesthetics in Neo-feminist German Fiction. She has participated in several conferences and workshops with African feminists.

Beverly B. Mack is Project Assistant for the Center for Women in Development of the South East Consortium for International Development. She also teaches African history at Georgetown University. Her M.A. and Ph.D. degrees, both from the University of Wisconsin, Madison, are in African Literature. Her dissertation on Hausa women's oral poetry is based on field research conducted in Kano, Nigeria, in 1979-80. Subsequent research conducted in the same area focuses on the changing socio-economic roles of Hausa Muslim women. She has published several articles on Hausa women's poetry and edited a volume of Hausa women's poetry published in Hausa by a northern Nigerian press in 1983.

Edris Makward is a well-known scholar/teacher of African literature. He has been professor of African Languages and Literature at the University of Wisconsin, Madison, since 1967. He has also taught at the University of Ibadan and more recently at the University of Calabar, Nigeria. He is the author of *Contemporary African Literature* and of numerous articles on African literature. He has been past president of the African Studies Association (1977-1978).

Rafika Merini was born in Fez, Morocco. She attended the University of Sanaa in Yeman, and the University of Utah (where she earned a B.A. in 1978 and an M.A. in 1981). She recently transferred to the State University of New York at Binghamton to complete her Ph.D. in Romance languages with an emphasis on Moroccan literature. Her masters thesis was done at the University of Washington on Driss Chraibi's *Succession Ouverte* a section of which is her contribution to this collection.

Charles Nama has an article on Ayi Kewi Armah forthcoming in *World Literature Written in English* and is currently translating *Le Deboussole* by Abdoul Doukoure, into English. His areas of interest are critical theory, translation and comparative literatures of the African world. He recently completed a Ph.D. in Comparative Litearture on Aesthetics and Ideology in African and Afro-American Fiction from the State University of New York, Binghamton, where he served as visiting lecturer in Afro-American and African Studies (1984-5). He recently returned to teach and do research in his native Cameroon.

Chimalum Nwankwo is a lecturer in the English and Dramatic Arts departments at the University of Nigeria, Nsukka. He received his Ph.D. from the University of Texas, Austin. His poetry and critical essays appear in journals such as *Obsidian, Umoja, Greenfield Review, Okike, Kunappipi, Ufahamu*, etc.

Esther Y. Smith is the French Language Coordinator with the Cameroon Project of the University of Florida, Gainesville, where she also serves as a professor of French language and literature. She has previously worked on a number of international/university projects and served as a language coordinator for the Peace Corps Training Center, Virgin Islands. She has published many articles and book reviews of African literature in major journals.

Karen Smyley-Wallace is Associate Professor of French and francophone African and Caribbean literature at Howard University. She received the M.A. Degree from the Middlebury Graduate School of French in Paris and the Ph.D. from the City University of New York. Her doctoral dissertation was entitled: "The African Woman: Interpretations of Novelists Aboulaye Sadji and Ousmane Sembene." Her current research and publications focus upon Black francophone female novelists. She has presented a number of papers and chaired panels on women in African literatures at national conferences.

Marie Linton Umeh is a lecturer in the Department of English Language and Literature, Anambra State College of Education, Awka, Nigeria. She has consistently maintained a research and publication reputation in the field of women in African literature. She completed her dissertation on Buchi Emecheta which she is revising and extending for publication. She has been an instructor of Third World Literature at the State University of New York, Brockport, in Oneonta. Her article, "The African Heroine" appeared in *Sturdy Black Bridges* ed. by Bell, Parker and Guy-Sheftall (New York, Anchor Books, 1979) and is one of the first major essays published on the subject.